Primate Research and Conservation in t

This book takes a new approach to understanding primate conservation research, adding a personal perspective to allow readers to learn what motivates those doing conservation work. When entering the field over a decade ago, many young primatologists were driven by evolutionary questions centred in behavioural ecology. However, given the current environment of cascading extinctions and increasing threats to primates, we now need to ensure that primates remain in viable populations in the wild before we can simply engage in research in the context of pure behavioural ecology. This has changed the primary research aims of many primatologists and shifted our focus to conservation priorities, such as understanding the impacts of human activity, habitat conversion or climate change on primates. This book presents personal narratives with empirical research results and discussions of strategies used to stem the tide of extinction. It is a must-have for anyone interested in conservation research.

Alison M. Behie is the Head of Biological Anthropology at the Australian National University and an Australian Research Council DECRA fellow. Her research interests focus on understanding the impact of severe habitat change on populations of both human and non-human primates.

Julie A. Teichroeb is Assistant Professor of Evolutionary Anthropology at the University of Toronto Scarborough. Her primary research interests are understanding the evolution of primate social organisation and individual and group decision-making processes.

Nicholas Malone is a Senior Lecturer in Biological Anthropology at the University of Auckland. His research interests are broad, looking into the social and ecological lives of primates, especially those of apes and humans.

Cambridge Studies in Biological and Evolutionary Anthropology

Consulting editors

C. G. Nicholas Mascie-Taylor, *University of Cambridge*

Robert A. Foley, *University of Cambridge*

Series editors

Agustín Fuentes, *University of Notre Dame*

Nina G. Jablonski, *Pennsylvania State University*

Clark Spencer Larsen, *The Ohio State University*

Michael P. Muehlenbein, *The University of Texas at San Antonio*

Dennis H. O'Rourke, *The University of Utah*

Karen B. Strier, *University of Wisconsin*

David P. Watts, *Yale University*

Also available in the series

53. *Technique and Application in Dental Anthropology* Joel D. Irish and Greg C. Nelson (eds.)
978 0 521 87061 0

54. *Western Diseases: An Evolutionary Perspective* Tessa M. Pollard 978 0 521 61737 6

55. *Spider Monkeys: The Biology, Behavior and Ecology of the Genus Ateles* Christina J. Campbell
978 0 521 86750 4

56. *Between Biology and Culture* Holger Schutkowski (ed.) 978 0 521 85936 3

57. *Primate Parasite Ecology: The Dynamics and Study of Host–Parasite Relationships*
Michael A. Huffman and Colin A. Chapman (eds.) 978 0 521 87246 1

58. *The Evolutionary Biology of Human Body Fatness: Thrift and Control* Jonathan C. K. Wells
978 0 521 88420 4

59. *Reproduction and Adaptation: Topics in Human Reproductive Ecology* C. G. Nicholas Mascie-
Taylor and Lyliane Rosetta (eds.) 978 0 521 50963 3

60. *Monkeys on the Edge: Ecology and Management of Long-Tailed Macaques and their Interface with
Humans* Michael D. Gumert, Agustín Fuentes and Lisa Jones-Engel (eds.) 978 0 521 76433 9

61. *The Monkeys of Stormy Mountain: 60 Years of Primatological Research on the Japanese
Macaques of Arashiyama* Jean-Baptiste Leca, Michael A. Huffman and Paul L. Vasey (eds.)
978 0 521 76185 7

62. *African Genesis: Perspectives on Hominin Evolution* Sally C. Reynolds and Andrew Gallagher
(eds.) 978 1 107 01995 9

63. *Consanguinity in Context* Alan H. Bittles 978 0 521 78186 2

64. *Evolving Human Nutrition: Implications for Public Health* Stanley Ulijaszek, Neil Mann and
Sarah Elton (eds.) 978 0 521 86916 4

65. *Evolutionary Biology and Conservation of Titis, Sakis and Uacaris* Liza M. Veiga,
Adrian A. Barnett, Stephen F. Ferrari and Marilyn A. Norconk (eds.) 978 0 521 88158 6

66. *Anthropological Perspectives on Tooth Morphology: Genetics, Evolution, Variation* G. Richard
Scott and Joel D. Irish (eds.) 978 1 107 01145 8

67. *Bioarchaeological and Forensic Perspectives on Violence: How Violent Death is Interpreted
from Skeletal Remains* Debra L. Martin and Cheryl P. Anderson (eds.) 978 1 107 04544 6

68. *The Foragers of Point Hope: The Biology and Archaeology of Humans on the Edge of the Alaskan Arctic* Charles E. Hilton, Benjamin M. Auerbach and Libby W. Cowgill (eds.) 978 1 107 02250 8

69. *Bioarchaeology: Interpreting Behavior from the Human Skeleton, 2nd Ed.* Clark Spencer Larsen 978 0 521 83869 6 & 978 0 521 54748 2

70. *Fossil Primates* Susan Cachel 978 1 107 00530 3

71. *Skeletal Biology of the Ancient Rapanui (Easter Islanders)* Vincent H. Stefan and George W. Gill (eds.) 978 1 107 02366 6

72. *Demography and Evolutionary Ecology of Hadza Hunter-Gatherers* Nicholas Blurton Jones 978 1 107 06982 4

73. *The Dwarf and Mouse Lemurs of Madagascar: Biology, Behavior and Conservation Biogeography of the Cheirogaleidae* Shawn M. Lehman, Ute Radespiel and Elke Zimmermann (eds.) 978 1 107 07559 7

74. *The Missing Lemur Link: An Ancestral Step in Human Evolution* Ivan Norscia and Elisabetta Palagi 978 1 107 01608 8

75. *Studies in Forensic Biohistory: Anthropological Perspectives* Christopher M. Stojanowski and William N. Duncan (eds.) 978 1 107 07354 8

76. *Ethnoprimatology: A Practical Guide to Research at the Human–Nonhuman Primate Interface* Kerry M. Dore, Erin P. Riley and Agustín Fuentes (eds.) 978 1 107 10996 4

77. *Building Bones: Bone Formation and Development in Anthropology* Christopher J. Percival and Joan T. Richtsmeier (eds.) 978 1 107 12278 9

78. *Models of Obesity: From Ecology to Complexity in Science and Policy* Stanley J. Ulijaszek 978 1 107 11751 8

79. *The Anthropology of Modern Human Teeth: Dental Morphology and Its Variation in Recent and Fossil Homo Sapiens, 2nd Ed.* G. Richard Scott, Christy G. Turner II, Grant C. Townsend and María Martinón-Torres 978 1 107 17441 2

80. *The Backbone of Europe: Health, Diet, Work, and Violence over Two Millennia* Richard H. Steckel, Clark Spencer Larsen, Charlotte A. Roberts and Joerg Baten (eds.) 978 1 108 42195 9

81. *Hunter-Gatherer Adaptation and Resilience: A Bioarchaeological Perspective* Daniel H. Temple and Christopher M. Stojanowski (eds.) 978 1 107 18735 1

Primate Research and Conservation in the Anthropocene

Edited by

ALISON M. BEHIE
The Australian National University

JULIE A. TEICHROEB
University of Toronto Scarborough

NICHOLAS MALONE
University of Auckland

CAMBRIDGE
UNIVERSITY PRESS

CAMBRIDGE
UNIVERSITY PRESS

University Printing House, Cambridge CB2 8BS, United Kingdom

One Liberty Plaza, 20th Floor, New York, NY 10006, USA

477 Williamstown Road, Port Melbourne, VIC 3207, Australia

314–321, 3rd Floor, Plot 3, Splendor Forum, Jasola District Centre, New Delhi – 110025, India

79 Anson Road, #06–04/06, Singapore 079906

Cambridge University Press is part of the University of Cambridge.

It furthers the University's mission by disseminating knowledge in the pursuit of education, learning, and research at the highest international levels of excellence.

www.cambridge.org
Information on this title: www.cambridge.org/9781107157484
DOI: 10.1017/9781316662021

© Cambridge University Press 2019

First published 2019

Printed in the United Kingdom by TJ International Ltd. Padstow Cornwall

A catalogue record for this publication is available from the British Library.

Library of Congress Cataloging-in-Publication Data
Names: Behie, Alison M., editor.
Title: Primate research and conservation in the anthropocene / edited by Alison M. Behie,
   The Australian National University, Julie A. Teichroeb, University of Toronto Scarborough,
   Nicholas Malone, University of Auckland.
Description: Cambridge, United Kingdom ; New York, NY : Cambridge University Press, 2019. |
   Series: Cambridge studies in biological and evolutionary anthropology | Includes bibliographical
   references and index.
Identifiers: LCCN 2018040320 | ISBN 9781107157484 (hardback : alk. paper) |
   ISBN 9781316610213 (paperback : alk. paper)
Subjects: LCSH: Primates–Conservation. | Primates–Research.
Classification: LCC QL737.P9 P735 2019 | DDC 599.8072–dc23
LC record available at https://lccn.loc.gov/2018040320

ISBN 978-1-107-15748-4 Hardback
ISBN 978-1-316-61021-3 Paperback

We dedicate this book to the late Emeritus
Professor Colin P. Groves, whose commitment to
primate research and conservation changed the discipline for the better.

Contents

List of Contributors   *page* xi
Foreword   *xiv*
Colin A. Chapman

1. **Changing Priorities for Primate Conservation and Research in the Anthropocene**   **1**
   Alison M. Behie, Julie A. Teichroeb and Nicholas Malone

Part I.   The Human–Non-human Primate Interface   15

2. **Struggling for Socioecological Resilience: A Long-Term Study of Silvery Gibbons (*Hylobates moloch*) in the Fragmented Sancang Forest Nature Reserve, West Java, Indonesia**   **17**
   Nicholas Malone and Made Wedana Adi Putra

3. **Monitoring the Sanje Mangabey Population in Tanzania while Engaging the Local Community**   **33**
   David Fernández, Carolyn Ehardt and Gráinne McCabe

4. **Uneasy Neighbours: Local Perceptions of the Cross River Gorilla and Nigeria–Cameroon Chimpanzee in Cameroon**   **52**
   Alison Wade, Nicholas Malone, Judith Littleton and Bruce Floyd

5. **Comanagement of Primate Hunting in Amazonian Indigenous Reserves: A Case Study from Guyana**   **74**
   Christopher A. Shaffer, Marissa S. Milstein, Phillip Suse, Elisha Marawanaru and Charakura Yukuma

Part II.   Habitat Alteration in the Anthropocene   99

6. **The Effects of Selective Logging on the Habitat Use of the Annamese Silvered Langur (*Trachypithecus margarita*) in Northeast Cambodia**   **101**
   Alvaro Gonzalez-Monge and Alison M. Behie

7. **The Immediate Impact of Selective logging on Rwenzori Angolan Colobus (*Colobus angolensis ruwenzorii*) at Lake Nabugabo, Uganda**   **120**
   Julie A. Teichroeb, Gregory R. Bridgett, Amélie Corriveau and Dennis Twinomugisha

8. **Threatened Hosts, Threatened Parasites? Parasite Diversity and Distribution in Red-Listed Primates**   141
Liesbeth Frias and Andrew J. J. MacIntosh

9. **Lemurs in Fragmented Forests: A Conservation and Research Collaboration**   165
Sheila M. Holmes, Edward E. Louis Jr and Steig E. Johnson

10. **Proboscis Monkey Conservation: Beyond the Science**   182
Stanislav Lhota, John C. M. Sha, Henry Bernard and Ikki Matsuda

Part III. Climate Change in the Anthropocene   197

11. **The Effect of Humans on the Primate Nutritional Landscape: A Review**   199
Jessica M. Rothman and Margaret A. H. Bryer

12. **Using Vegetation Phenology and Long-Term Demographic Data to Assess the Impact of Cyclone Fanele on a Lemur Population in Madagascar**   216
Rebecca Lewis and Anne Axel

13. **Alas the Storm Has Come Again! The Impact of Frequent Natural Disasters on Primate Conservation**   237
Alison M. Behie, Mary S. M. Pavelka, Kayla Hartwell, Jane Champion and Hugh Notman

14. **The Effect of Climate Change on the Distribution of the Genera _Colobus_ and _Cercopithecus_**   257
Amanda H. Korstjens

15. **Research(ers) and Conservation(ists) in the Anthropocene**   281
Nicholas Malone, Julie A. Teichroeb and Alison M. Behie

Index   285

Contributors

Anne Axel
Department of Biological Sciences, Marshall University, Huntington, USA

Alison M. Behie
School of Archaeology and Anthropology, The Australian National University, Canberra, Australia

Henry Bernard
Institute for Tropical Biology and Conservation, Universiti Malaysia Sabah, Sabah, Malaysia

Gregory R. Bridgett
Toronto Zoo, Education Branch, Toronto, Canada

Margaret A. H. Bryer
Department of Anthropology, Hunter College, New York, USA

Jane Champion
Department of Anthropology and Archaeology, University of Calgary, Alberta, Canada

Amélie Corriveau
Research Institute for the Environment and Livelihoods, Charles Darwin University, Nightcliff, Australia

Carolyn Ehardt
Department of Anthropology, University of Texas at San Antonio, USA

David Fernández
Department of Applied Sciences, University of the West of England, Bristol, United Kingdom

Bruce Floyd
Department of Anthropology, University of Auckland, Auckland, New Zealand

Liesbeth Frias
Kyoto University Primate Research Institute, Inuyama, Japan

Alvaro Gonzalez-Monge
School of Archaeology and Anthropology, Australian National University, Canberra, Australia

Kayla Hartwell
Department of Anthropology and Archaeology, University of Calgary, Alberta, Canada

Sheila M. Holmes
Department of Anthropology and Archaeology, University of Calgary, Alberta, Canada

Steig E. Johnson
Department of Anthropology and Archaeology, University of Calgary, Alberta, Canada

Amanda H. Korstjens
Bournemouth University, Poole, UK

Rebecca Lewis
Department of Anthropology, University of Texas at Austin, USA

Stanislav Lhota
Department of Animal Science and Food Processing, Faculty of Tropical Agrisciences, Czech University of Life Sciences, Prague, Czech Republic

Judith Littleton
Department of Anthropology, University of Auckland, Auckland, New Zealand

Edward E. Louis Jr
Grewcock Center for Conservation and Research, Omaha's Henry Doorly Zoo and Aquarium, Omaha, USA

Andrew J. J. MacIntosh
Kyoto University Primate Research Institute, Inuyama, Japan

Nicholas Malone
Department of Anthropology, University of Auckland, Auckland, New Zealand

Elisha Marawanaru
Konashen Indigenous District, Guyana

Ikki Matsuda
Chubu University Academy of Emerging Sciences, Kasugaishi, Japan
Wildlife Research Center, Kyoto University, Kyoto, Japan

Gráinne McCabe
Department of Field Conservation & Science, Bristol Zoological Society, UK

Marissa S. Milstein
College of Veterinary Medicine, University of Minnesota, Minnesota, USA

Hugh Notman
Department of Anthropology and Archaeology, University of Calgary, Alberta, Canada
Anthropology, Centre of Social Sciences, Athabasca University, Alberta, Canada

Mary S. M. Pavelka
Department of Anthropology and Archaeology, University of Calgary, Alberta, Canada

Jessica M. Rothman
Department of Anthropology, Hunter College, New York, USA

John C. M. Sha
School of Sociology and Anthropology, Sun Yat-sen University, Guangzhou, China

Christopher A. Shaffer
Department of Anthropology, Grand Valley State University, Michigan, United States

Phillip Suse
Konashen Indigenous District, Guyana

Julie A. Teichroeb
Department of Anthropology, University of Toronto Scarborough, Toronto, Canada

Dennis Twinomugisha
Makerere University Biological Field Station, Uganda

Alison Wade
Department of Anthropology, University of Auckland, Auckland, New Zealand

Made Wedana Adi Putra
The Aspinall Foundation Indonesia Programme, Bandung, West Java, Indonesia

Charakura Yukuma
Konashen Indigenous District, Guyana

Foreword

This edited volume by Alison Behie, Julie Teichroeb and Nicholas Malone, *Primate Research and Conservation in the Anthropocene*, is a very timely contribution because it is clear that the world is changing and, unfortunately for countless animals, including most primates, many of the changes are for the worst. The most straightforward measure of change is loss, and the pace of biodiversity loss is high and increasing, with current extinction rates approximately 1000 times higher than background rates (Pimm et al., 2014). Recent estimates suggest that surviving vertebrate species have declined in abundance by 25 per cent since 1970 (Dirzo et al., 2014). Overall, 60 per cent of all primate species are currently threatened with extinction (Estrada et al., 2017) and, while it remains to be confirmed, it seems almost a certainty that with the disappearance of Miss Waldron's red colobus (*Procolobus badius waldroni*) over a decade ago (McGraw, 2005), we have lost the first primate in the twenty-first century. Moreover, a recent analysis considering 22 of the 27 primate species in China suggests that 15 of the species have fewer than 3000 individuals – clearly indicating that more extinctions could come if more action is not taken (Chapman, 2018; Fan & Ma, in press). For our closest living relatives, the great apes, the situation is bleak. For example, chimpanzee (*Pan troglodytes*) population reduction over three generations is estimated to exceed 50 per cent (Walsh et al., 2003) and they have lost 10.3 per cent of their suitable habitat in ten years (i.e. an area approximately the size of the US state of Kansas or just larger than the country of Senegal) (Junker et al., 2012). The role that disease may be playing in causing declines in chimpanzee and gorilla numbers is a matter of great concern, as is the degree to which these diseases are transmitted from neighbouring human populations or tourists (Hoffmann et al., 2017; Kondgen et al., 2008). As I write this foreword there is the worry that a new respiratory epidemic may be occurring in Kibale National Park, where I have worked for the last almost 30 years. While the primate community had the delight to announce the discovery of a new orangutan species (*Pongo tapanuliensis*) this year, the species was immediately categorised as critically endangered and extremely rapid habitat loss is occurring throughout their range (Nater et al., 2017).

Humans are clearly responsible for the current decline of primate populations. Between 2000 and 2012, 2.3 million square kilometres of forest was lost globally and in the tropics forest loss increased each year (Hansen et al., 2013). To put this in perspective, this area is approximately the size of Mexico. Another action leading to the decline in primate numbers is bushmeat hunting. Global estimates of the extent of wildlife over-exploitation are very poor; however, in Africa, four million metric tonnes of bushmeat are thought to be extracted each year from the Congo basin alone (equivalent to approximately 4 500 000 cows, or 80 million small (5 kg) monkeys); of course, not all bushmeat is primate (Fa & Brown, 2009). Primates are also threatened by a changing climate that human actions have caused. Temperatures are predicted to increase by 1.5°C by the end of the twenty-first century (IPCC, 2014) and researchers have projected that by 2100 75 per cent of all tropical forests present in 2000 will experience temperatures that are higher than the temperatures presently supporting closed-canopy forests (Peres et al., 2016; Wright et al., 2009). Furthermore, the nutritional quality provided by the remaining trees is predicted to decline (Rothman et al., 2015; see also Rothman and Bryer in this volume). As forests change in this manner, primate populations of many species will decline precipitously.

This edited volume by Alison Behie, Julie Teichroeb and Nicholas Malone explores many of the challenges primate populations are facing. The different chapters take varying approaches, from the case study, to regional perspectives, to the examination of global patterns of change, to modelling, but all aim to provide insights into not just causes of declines, but ways forward for the protection and conservation of primate populations. The different approaches presented clearly illustrate the diversity of ways that advances can be made to conserve primate populations. Furthermore, as the co-editors point out in the concluding chapter, taken together the different approaches illustrate the value of collaboration among researchers with different skills and experiences. No one individual can have the breadth of knowledge to apply all the tools that could help conserve a particular primate species or a particular location.

A particularly innovative and motivating strategy that the book adopts is the use of narratives that start each chapter. These narratives are typically by the lead author and portray their personal stories of how they were drawn to the field of primate conservation and the value of the mentorship they received along the way, and they highlight some of their conservation achievements and frustrations. These narratives provide a number of very interesting observations on the field of primate conservation.

First, they provide more personal connections to the field sites and the motivations of the researchers and allow the reader to understand some of the challenges the authors faced to reach the stage of their careers where they could contribute to this edited volume. I believe that this will be particularly motivating for young researchers just thinking about entering this field of study or those designing PhD projects, as these narratives illustrate that a single individual, or hopefully a small group of individuals, can make a real difference and advance primate conservation. This contribution of the book will be interesting to evaluate in a decade's time.

Second, the narratives clearly demonstrate that the field of primate conservation is very young. As the introduction points out and as is echoed in a number of the narratives, when many of the authors of these chapters were entering academia over a decade ago, they were motivated to address interesting evolutionary questions, such as developing the socioecological model. Let me take a longer temporal perspective than is presented in the edited volume to illustrate the significance of this observation. In the first paragraph of the introduction, I was intrigued, and a bit surprised, by the fact that the authors compared current levels of endangerment to those that Carlos Peres and I reported in 2001 (Chapman & Peres, 2001) and reported a remarkably discouraging increase in the number of species on the IUCN Red List in just 15 years. This comparison set one of the lenses through which I read the book: how had primate conservation changed since I began my Masters studies in 1981? Sure, as most readers of the book will know or will find out by reading just a few chapters, the conservation situation has deteriorated for primates, but what else can we draw from such a comparison? The year I started my studies there were 34 papers that were shown to have been published, using Google Scholar with the search term 'Primate Conservation'; when I finished my PhD in 1987 there were 112 papers; when I got my first job in 1993 (after two great post-docs) the number had decreased slightly to 83. In 2001, when Carlos and I published our paper, 'Primate Conservation in the New Millennium: The Role of Scientists', 174 papers were found using this search term; and in 2016 there were 531 papers. This represents an exponential rise in effort and interest. This is very exciting as it illustrates a shift in priorities and with so many more people working in the field of primate conservation, surely we can start to see more positive change.

Third, many of the narratives highlight the importance of primate–host-country collaborations, and some of the chapters are co-authored with host-country researchers. This highlights the potential for further significant growth in the field. If the number of papers has increased so dramatically since I started three decades ago, and if host-country collaborators can be involved to a greater degree, as is indicated by this edited volume, we have the potential to reverse some of the depressing numbers on primate population declines. But, how do we facilitate such collaborations – it is clear there is a long way to go to improve the training of host-country primate conservation researchers. Take Africa as an example. Despite Africa's recent very positive economic growth, the GDP devoted per person to education is very low and spending per student has fallen in most countries (the average expenditure per student between 2011 and 2015 in 51 Africa countries was US$1489, while in large high-income countries it was US$13 466), and often the already low levels of research funding are syphoned off to cover the expenses associated with higher enrolment (Fashing et al., personal communication). To meet this increasing student demand, professors in Africa now have to teach more classes, to a greater number of students, leaving little time for research and mentoring (Fashing et al., personal communication). Collaborations that can help provide the students with the needed mentoring are greatly facilitated by long-term research sites. Thus, it is ironic and sad that at a time when long-term research sites are needed more than ever to promote meaningful, long-lasting collaborations and to understand the impact of phenomena like climate change (Chapman et al., 2018; Chapman et al., submitted), that funding for such sites and research in general is dwindling (Chapman et al., 2017). It is my strong belief that to see improved primate conservation we must see greater investment in host-country training capacity. However, we also need to change our own university system. Universities in high-income countries have largely failed to provide the atmosphere that would encourage their professors to invest their limited time, energy and resources in the training of host-country graduate students. In 2001, Carlos Peres and I suggested that our universities should change their reward system to meet the reality of a global society (Chapman & Peres, 2001). It is now well past the time we should change. Imagine how quickly things would improve if every paper published by a primate host-country graduate student supervised by a professor from a high-income country would count twice as much towards tenure and promotion compared to papers published by graduate students from the high-income country.

This volume tackles many of the most important issues that must be addressed if the actions and inaction of people are not to be responsible for the extinction of dozens of primate species before the turn of the century. The book provides a number of 'road maps' to a positive future for primate populations, but only if actions are dramatically increased. Most importantly, for the first time, this volume provides insights into how scholars became involved in primate conservation and thereby provides hope to the next generation that they too can make a difference. But we have a great deal to do. The need for action to conserve primate populations was illustrated by François Bourlière, who, in 1962, almost 60 years ago, wrote 'Unfortunately, at the very moment when we are becoming aware of the uniqueness of the Primates … we are also realizing how precarious is the future of the Primates and to what point competition with industrial man is threatening their survival … Can we remain unmoved at such annihilation?' (Bourlière, 1962).

Colin A. Chapman

Makerere University Biological Field Station, Fort Portal, Uganda,

Department of Anthropology, McGill University

Wildlife Conservation Society, Bronx, NY

School of Life Sciences, University of KwaZulu-Natal, Scottsville Pietermaritzburg

Shaanxi Key Laboratory for Animal Conservation, Northwest University, Xi'an

References

Bourlière, F. (1962). The need for a new conservation policy for wild primates. *Annals of the New York Academy of Sciences*, 102, 185–9.

Chapman, C. A. (2018). A road for a promising future for China's primates: the potential for restoration. *Zoological Research*, 39, 244–8.

Chapman, C. A. & Peres, C. A. (2001). Primate conservation in the new millennium: the role of scientists. *Evolutionary Anthropology*, 10, 16–33.

Chapman, C. A., Corriveau, A., Schoof, V. A. M., Twinomugisha, D. & Valenta, K. (2017). Long-term primate research and its significance for developing theory and conservation plans. *Journal of Mammalolgy*, 98, 652–60.

Chapman, C. A., Bortolamiol, S., Matsuda, I., et al. (2018). Primate population dynamics: variation over space and time. *Biodiversity and Conservation*. DOI: 10.1007/s10531-017-1489-3.

Chapman, C. A., Hou, R. & Kalbitzer, U. (submitted). What will climate change mean for primates? In *Primatology, Bio-cultural Diversity and Sustainable Development in Tropical Forests: A Global Perspective*. Mexico City: UNESCO.

Dirzo, R., Young, H. S., Galetti, M., et al. (2014). Defaunation in the Anthropocene. *Science*, 345, 401–6.

Estrada, A., Garber, P. A., Rylands, A. B., et al. (2017). Impending extinction crisis of the world's primates: why primates matter. *Science Advances*, 3, e600946.

Fa, J. E. & Brown, D. (2009). Impacts of hunting on mammals in African tropical moist forests: a review and synthesis. *Mammal Review*, **39**, 231–64.

Fan, P. & Ma, C. (in press). Primates and primatology in China. *Zoological Research*.

Hansen, M. C., Potapov, P. V., Moore, R., et al. (2013). High-resolution global maps of 21st-century forest cover change. *Science*, **342**, 850–3.

Hoffmann, C., Zimmermann, F., Biek, R., et al. (2017). Persistent anthrax as a major driver of wildlife mortality in a tropical rainforest. *Nature*, **548**, 82.

IPCC (2014). *Climate Change 2014: Synthesis Report. Contribution of Working Groups I, II and III to the Fifth Assessment Report of the Intergovernmental Panel on Climate Change.* Geneva: IPCC.

Junker, J., Blake, S., Boesch, C., et al. (2012). Recent decline in suitable environmental conditions for African great apes. *Diversity and Distributions*, **18**, 1077–91.

Kondgen, S., Kuhl, H., N'Goran, P. K., et al. (2008). Pandemic human viruses cause decline of endangered great apes. *Current Biology*, **18**, 260–4.

McGraw, W. S. (2005). Update on the search for Miss Waldron's red colobus monkey. *International Journal of Primatology*, **26**, 605–19.

Nater, A., Mattle-Greminger, M. P., Nurcahyo, A., et al. (2017). Morphometric, behavioral, and genomic evidence for a new Orangutan species. *Current Biology*, **27**, 3487–98.

Peres, C. A., Emilio, T., Schietti, J., Desmoulière, S. J. & Levi, T. (2016). Dispersal limitation induces long-term biomass collapse in overhunted Amazonian forests. *Proceedings of the National Academy of Sciences*, **113**, 892–7.

Pimm, S. L., Jenkins, C. N., Abell, R., et al. (2014). The biodiversity of species and their rates of extinction, distribution, and protection. *Science*, **344**, 1246752.

Rothman, J. M., Chapman, C. A., Struhsaker, T. T., et al. (2015). Cascading effects of global change: decline in nutritional quality of tropical leaves. *Ecology*, **96**, 873–8.

Walsh, P. D., Abernethy, K. A., Bermejo, M., et al. (2003). Catastrophic ape decline in western equatorial Africa. *Nature*, **422**, 611–14.

Wright, S. J., Muller-Landau, H. C. & Schipper, J. (2009). The future of tropical species on a warmer planet. *Conservation Biology*, **23**, 1418–26.

1 Changing Priorities for Primate Conservation and Research in the Anthropocene

Alison M. Behie, Julie A. Teichroeb and Nicholas Malone

There is no doubt that the majority of primate species are at a greater risk than ever of becoming extinct. Indeed, as we write this, a formative paper has recently been published outlining that 75 per cent of the world's primates are in steady decline and 60 per cent are threatened (Estrada et al., 2017). These numbers are staggering and confronting on their own, but perhaps are made even more so when comparing them to numbers presented in a pivotal 2001 paper by Chapman and Peres that reported that at the turn of the century only 50 per cent of species were threatened, indicating, regardless of taxonomy, a sharp increase in the number of species on the IUCN Red List in a mere 15 years. In addition, Estrada and colleagues (2017) report regional variation in primate decline, ranging from 36 per cent of primates in the Neotropics to 100 per cent in Madagascar. All of this explains why the IUCN lists Primates as being the order of mammals with the greatest number of species at a higher than average level of threat.

Even the discovery of new species, which used to be cause for celebration, is now also cause for alarm. Most recently, the discovery of the Tapanuli orangutan (*Pongo tapanuliensis*) created both great excitement and concern as it represents an additional species of great ape but was immediately listed as critically endangered due to low population size and extremely rapid habitat loss throughout their range (Nater et al., 2017). This was also the case in 2016 with the discovery of the Skywalker hoolock gibbon (*Hoolock tianxing*) (Fan et al., 2017) that was immediately listed as endangered, and in 2010 with the discovery of another gibbon, *Nomascus annamensis* (Van Ngoc Thinh et al., 2010). Although the latter species has not been formally evaluated by the IUCN it is expected to be listed as endangered as it is currently threatened by hunting and habitat loss throughout its range in Laos, Vietnam and Cambodia. Similar stories ring out on a regular basis from Madagascar, where new species of lemurs are discovered (i.e. *Microcebus ganzhorni* in 2016) just to be immediately placed on the endangered species list. It has thus become apparent that primatologists are being faced with extra challenges of not only learning about the behaviour and ecology of newly described species, but of ensuring these animals are alive long enough for us to be able to do so.

This widespread vulnerability of primates, which could lead to the imminent loss of our closest living relatives, is causing a shift in the way that we, as primatologists, do our jobs. Being driven by the real possibility that we may start witnessing species extinctions in our own lifetimes, we are shifting our research priorities and questions to those that are aimed to answer the question 'How we can slow or stop the loss of primates?' Our research has thus become focused on trying to understand how the major threats to primates, including habitat loss and hunting, are impacting existing populations to determine ways to mitigate the effects. Unlike past generations, we have also had to factor in the impact of climate change, which when acting on top of existing threats, is placing many populations and species in double jeopardy. In essence, such rapid changes to the viability of the majority of the world's primates have made us rethink our career goals.

When many young primatologists entered the field over a decade ago, including the editors of this book, we were driven by evolutionary questions centred in the field of behavioural ecology and, in fact, likely described ourselves as behavioural ecologists. Entering the field in the mid-1990s, many of us were first intrigued by the theory of sociobiology and the debates within the field about how much behaviour we could attribute to underlying strategies to maximise reproductive success. Indeed, the heated conversations around infanticide stimulated by the work of Sarah Hrdy (Hrdy et al., 1994) and the late Robert Sussman (Sussman et al., 1994) are some of our first memories of primatological theory. This was then followed by the emergence, and dominance, of the socioecological paradigm, following the publication of the pivotal 1997 paper 'The evolution of female social relationships in nonhuman primates' by Sterck and colleagues (1997) that incorporated the early work of Wrangham (1979; 1980). This theory not only posed interesting questions about how environmental factors, including the distribution and quality of food, influenced the way females and males behaved, but gave testable predictions derived from proposed hypotheses. This stimulated many of us to begin to answer questions such as, how do animals decide what to eat or who to interact with, or when and with whom to reproduce? However, it quickly became apparent that even these well borne out theories could not completely account for the range of intraspecific, population-level variability we were seeing in wild primate studies. Indeed, this may be because many of the ecological systems that we were initially intrigued by have been forever altered by anthropogenic impacts, highlighting the dynamic nature of these ecosystems and the importance of understanding the bigger picture of what this dynamism means for a given species and their ability to survive rapid environmental change.

These realisations have changed the primary research aims of many primatologists, requiring us to shift our priorities in an attempt to ensure that the species we are so fascinated by are not lost and are maintained for future generations to study, perhaps using the initial theories of behavioural ecology that drove us to the field some two decades ago. Not only that, but many of us have also shifted our methodological approaches and the ways we devise and seek answers to questions. In recognition of the dynamic nature of primate ecosystems and the entangled nature of the relationship between humans and our primate relatives, we are focusing on long-term, viable strategies that protect both human and animal welfare. Most recently, this has been personified in the proliferation of studies in the field of ethnoprimatology. Ethnoprimatology explicitly engages with the cultural and ecological lives of humans as important components of the broader social and ecological environment in which primates are studied (Dore et al., 2017; Fuentes, 2012; Fuentes & Wolfe,

2002; Malone et al., 2014). Theoretical and methodological developments now arm ethnoprimatologists in more holistic investigations of the human–non-human primate interface, and facilitate (or indeed oblige) the application of these insights into conservation practice (Fuentes et al., 2016; 2017). While, traditionally, primate studies were done under the assumption that primates are in 'pristine' settings where 'natural' behavioural phenomena are observed and interpreted through the lens of evolutionary models, we now acknowledge that primate social systems are subject to the influences of past and present anthropogenic alterations. Recent studies have thus documented the development of behavioural and ecological strategies in response to human activities. Rather than focusing just on the primate of interest, we are being forced to think outside the box about problems and solutions by working in multidisciplinary teams that take every part of the picture into consideration. This has been a ground-breaking development that has certainly shaped the way we think about our study subjects and the way we go about protecting them (see Chapters 3, 4 and 12 for case studies).

Such views have also changed the way many of us teach the next generation. In Australia, the first on-campus course dedicated to primate conservation began at the Australian National University in 2014, which followed on from the creation of a primate conservation field school in Cambodia in 2012. These courses trailed behind other primate conservation courses offered across the globe, including those in Canada at the University of Calgary, McGill University, and the University of Toronto. In the United States, courses with primate conservation in the title are offered at institutions such as the University of Notre Dame, Central Washington University, Columbia University, Duke University, Kent State University, the University of California at Davis, the University of Oregon, Barnard College and Colorado College. In addition, at least three universities in the United Kingdom have created entire Masters programmes devoted to the conservation of primates. The first such programme was started in 2000 at Oxford Brookes with the Master of Science in Primate Conservation. Since then, the University of Roehampton has created a Master in Primate Biology, Behaviour and Conservation and the University of Kent has begun a Master of Science in Conservation and Primate Behaviour. Researchers have thus also changed some of their education targets, recognising that the new generation of primatologists need to be exposed to conservation issues much earlier in their careers in order to provide them with the required tools to cope with the challenges facing them in the discipline. It is now the goal of many educators, the editors of this book included, to work with these budding conservation primatologists to come up with out-of-the-box, interdisciplinary solutions for the long-term threats facing our study subjects.

This sort of training has not remained exclusive to our home countries, with many primatologists also investing in education and infrastructure for people living around field research sites as a way to promote conservation and build capacity at a local level. For example, Chapter 3 of this volume outlines the successful engagement of local community members into the Sanje Mangabey Project as a way to increase local knowledge about the animals and the forest and to reduce tensions between local people and national park authorities. David Fernández and his colleagues have also established an education programme with local schools. For some of us, the capacity building of locals near our field sites happens at a smaller scale, with the training of a small number of research students. One editor of this volume (AB) has been involved in the co-supervision of Masters students working in Cambodia and Vietnam. Another (NM) has worked extensively with students and activists in Indonesia to facilitate ecological monitoring and conservation action. Volume contributor Jessica Rothman (Chapter 11) has also supervised Masters and doctoral students through her honorary appointment at Makerere University in Uganda. This engagement with local communities is proving very effective, which makes sense given that conservation will not work without involving those who live in the region (Muhumuza & Balkwill 2013). Research done by Riley and Zak (2015) on the impact of small primate conservation grants found that over 80 per cent of projects included listed capacity building at the individual or community level as one of their outputs, highlighting that this is becoming central to all our research questions. They also reported that grantees felt that one key to long-term conservation success is the successful collaboration with local governments and non-governmental organisations (NGOs).

The importance of collaboration with a variety of disciplines and organisations, as well as the need to engage national and international awareness through working with or establishing their own NGOs, is being recognised by many primatologists. As outlined in Chapter 9, Ed Louis established the Madagascar Biodiversity Partnership (MBP), which focuses on community-based education and research with a primary focus on the reforestation of land, including the development of nurseries to grow trees and a conservation credit rewards programme that encourages local people to participate in reforestation. While not all of us have formed our own NGOs, many of us work together with organisations such as Conservation International and Fauna & Flora International. These collaborations have proved critical for our own research, as science alone is not going to increase primate numbers and safeguard vulnerable habitats. Instead, we can use our scientific findings to inform the creation of species-specific conservation plans that are based in species biology and ecology.

A quick perusal of some of the recent scientific programmes of primatology conferences confirms this shift in the discipline. For example, when looking at the programme from the 2016 joint meeting of the American Society of Primatologists and the International Primatological Society in Chicago, Illinois, one is presented with multiple sessions in which conservation is the theme. In addition, organised symposia are becoming more often about conservation and the different challenges and approaches we face and use in the field. The editors of this book organised their own symposia around the theme of this book, which was in the esteemed company of specially organised conservation symposia including: regional conservation issues in Africa and China, issues surrounding the illegal pet trade, disease and health of non-human primates and reintroduction and translocation, as well as two that focused on working at the nexus of human and non-human primate interaction, focusing on health issues and cross-disciplinary approaches. While conservation sessions have been occurring for many years at these congresses, our feeling is that the number focused on how we can protect our primate research subjects is quickly growing as more and more people focus their efforts in that domain.

It is the goal of this edited volume to expand on these themes both by sharing some of the conservation-focused research that is taking hold of our discipline, and also by explaining this shift in research priority through the stories and experiences of early- to mid-career primatologists. By sharing their challenges and successes as primatologists in the Anthropocene, we hope to inspire and help unify others working in similar areas and to highlight that there is no one way or one path to becoming a conservation primatologist.

1.1   The Anthropocene

Given the intensity and scope of humankind's impact and influence on ecological processes (Crutzen & Stoermer, 2000; Ellis, 2015; Steffen et al., 2011), contemporary primate research and conservation activities take place amid, and in response to, the dynamic forces of the 'Anthropocene'. The Anthropocene is a proposed formal unit of geological time whereby humankind's 'signature' of alterations to basic biogeochemical processes is written into the earth's strata. Scholars in a variety of disciplines have been quick to promote the ascendency of the term. In contrast, the sanctioning body concerned with making the Anthropocene an official geological epoch, namely the Subcommission of Quaternary Stratigraphy operating within the overall structure of the International Commission on Stratigraphy, is content to move at 'geological speed' in an effort to identify suitable 'golden spikes', or Global Boundary Stratotype Sections and Points (J. McNeil, personal communication). Regardless of 'if and/or when' the demarcation between the Holocene and the Anthropocene is made official, and where the temporal boundary lies (i.e. prior to, at the onset of or more recently than the Industrial Revolution in Europe at c.1800 CE), the widespread adoption of the term by researchers in the biological and social sciences, as well as by philosophers and ethicists, speaks to the acceptance and analytical strength of the designation.

Conceptualising the relationships between humans and other ecosystem components, including the mutual shaping of evolutionary processes, is facilitated by embracing the Anthropocene. Humans are entangled within webs of both biotic and abiotic processes resulting in the construction of anthropogenic biomes, or *anthromes* (Fuentes & Baynes-Rock, 2017). Therefore, engaging in a primatological practice that perceives humans and other primates as co-resident in ecological and social landscapes is arguably a more efficacious approach to primate research and conservation than pretending that our study subjects are unaffected by current anthropological changes (Malone et al., 2014). For example, ethnoprimatological research, along with human–animal studies and multispecies ethnography, aims to equally emphasise ecological aspects of the focal species' space and cultural elements of these shared, multispecies places (Dore et al., 2017; Malone & Ovenden, 2017). Arguably, acknowledging humankind's near-ubiquitous impact on the environment may serve as a prerequisite for our active management of diverse, species-rich habitats (rather than attempts to protect unspoiled, 'natural' wilderness). However, others argue that the terminology of the Anthropocene presents both practical and ideological complications, as well as political implications (Caro et al., 2012; Sayre, 2012). For example, Caro and colleagues (2012) point to four potential negative consequences of thinking that *humans have altered everything*, including: (1) increasing our tolerance for highly manipulative rewilding campaigns; (2) deprioritising initiatives to protect nearly intact ecosystems; (3) an enhanced ability for governments to further land use projects if habitats are already viewed as degraded; and (4) risking the spread of public pessimism and loss of monetary support for conservation agendas if the whole of nature is perceived to be altered by humans.

As evidenced by our chosen title for this volume, we see the utility of placing our present research and conservation work within the conceptual and material framework of the Anthropocene. While we acknowledge the aforementioned debates, we are convinced that an approach that engages directly with the impact of humans on primate populations is essential, especially with respect to habitat alteration, climate change, and the complexity of human–non-human primate interactions and interdependency. Increasingly, behavioural and ecological studies of primates that fail to account for these dynamics risk scientific invalidity and conservation irrelevance. Indeed, all of the contributions in this volume highlight the convergence of research and conservation agendas brought about by the impending extinction crisis within the Order Primates (Estrada et al., 2017). We remain hopeful that today's primatologists, trained in behavioural ecology and conservation biology, and motivated by a passion for biodiversity, can meet the challenges of the coming decades.

1.2   Summary of the Book

We have organised the chapters in this book into three sections. The first, 'The Human–Nonhuman Primate Interface', highlights the complexity of research in the Anthropocene and the difficulty of monitoring and maintaining small populations. The second section contains chapters that address what has, for many years, been the most threatening issue facing primate populations, namely habitat alteration and fragmentation. The final section of the book addresses an emerging threat to primates that many researchers are still struggling to assess, the impact of climate change.

1.3   The Human–Non-human Primate Interface

Many research papers in primate conservation focus on the impact of single threats, or a synergistic set of threats, to primate populations. In contrast, the chapters in this section are unique in that they give historical information on the status of the study species, and holistic, detailed data on the current set of challenges that face these small populations, ending with a discussion of the conservation strategies that are being applied at these study sites. This section was initially going to focus on the threat of hunting to primates. Indeed, increases in hunting are a major issue for primate populations globally and are the result of an ever-increasing human population, driving the demand for primates to unsustainable levels. For instance, approximately 4.9 million tonnes of bushmeat is consumed annually in the Congo Basin, and demand continues to increase despite waning supplies (Fa et al., 2002). While some of this consumption is undoubtedly for subsistence of local people, the bushmeat industry has become largely commercialised in West and Central Africa (Fa & Brown, 2009). For large-bodied primates with slow life-history patterns, levels of hunting for bushmeat are beyond sustainability and are driving species to local extinction (Cronin et al., 2016; Linder & Oates, 2011). In other regions, like Asia, demand for traditional medicine or for the international pet trade is driving up hunting pressure (Nadler et al., 2007; Nekaris et al., 2010; Starr et al., 2010). Though hunting is one reason why the primate populations discussed in this section are small, the chapters detailed here show, rightly, how complicated and unique each situation is.

In Chapter 2, Nicholas Malone and Made Wedana Adi Putra show that hunting for the illegal pet trade is a serious issue leading to the decline of silvery gibbon populations in West Java, Indonesia, and that small remaining populations struggle for viability and coexistence with the ever-growing human population. Their field site, Cagar Alam Leuweung Sancang (CALS), is an important spiritual site for Sundanese pilgrims, which leads to high human presence in the forest and increasing forms of disturbance. Yet, despite the spiritual importance of the forest, both large-scale and small-scale timber extraction have already led to the loss of half of the forest within the reserve. In Chapter 3, David Fernández, Gráinne McCabe and Carolyn Ehardt examine the current conservation situation for the Sanje mangabey in Tanzania, showing that the remaining individuals of this species are distributed in two isolated subpopulations. The authors focus on the importance of understanding female reproductive biology and dispersal patterns in assessing the long-term viability of the population. They also highlight the ways that primatologists can work with local communities, improving the lives of those living near threatened primates, to show the importance of the animals as a long-term economic resource. In Chapter 4, Alison Wade, Nicholas Malone, Judith Littleton and Bruce Floyd document range use and nest site selection of two ape species, the Cross River gorillas and Nigeria–Cameroon chimpanzees, in an unprotected forest matrix. They also interview local people to try to understand local attitudes towards these apes and barriers to successful conservation. People in this area used to hunt both ape species but as they are now protected by the Wildlife Conservation Society (WCS), hunting pressure has decreased. This has also caused local people to believe that they can no longer legally defend themselves if they are attacked by an ape. Wade and colleagues show that the gorillas and chimpanzees occupy different areas of the forest, with gorillas being more tolerant of human disturbance than chimpanzees. This is problematic because people especially fear encounters with gorillas because they are so large, usually do not flee, and range near farm boundaries. One disconcerting fact that came out of interviews with people was the almost universal idea that the forest is an endless resource.

The final chapter of this section focuses more on hunting than the other chapters, but demonstrates that primate hunting can be sustainable in certain situations.

In Chapter 5, Chris Shaffer, Marissa Milstein, Phillip Suse, Elisha Marawanaru and Charakura Yukuma review the extent, drivers and effects of primate hunting in South America and examine how Amazonian indigenous reserves vary in management of resources. At their study site in Guyana, primates are an important source of food for the Waiwai and the authors use models of hunting depletion that include estimates of human population growth and predicted changes in hunting methods to determine how sustainable current and future hunting will be. The case study that Shaffer and colleagues present is informative as it shows how partnerships between indigenous groups, conservation organisations and international researchers can lead to successful ecosystem-monitoring projects that ensure the long-term health of ecosystems.

1.4   Habitat Alteration in the Anthropocene

Habitat degradation and loss are clearly recognised as leading threats to primates. According to Estrada and colleagues (2017), 76 per cent of primates are threatened with habitat loss due to agriculture, 60 per cent face habitat loss due to logging and 31 per cent are losing habitat for ranching and animal husbandry. This suggests that for many species, more than one form of habitat alteration is currently impacting their geographical range. According to the UN FAO (2015) report, there was a loss of 18 561 000 ha of forest cover from 1990 to 2015. In addition, from 2010 to 2015 the top ten countries with the greatest rates of forest loss are all primate-habitat countries (Brazil, Indonesia, Myanmar, Nigeria, United Republic of Tanzania, Paraguay, Zimbabwe, Democratic Republic of Congo, Argentina and Bolivia) that collectively lost 4 530 000 ha of forest cover. It is thus not surprising that investigating the impact of habitat alteration on primates has become a major focus of many primatologists. The chapters in this volume show the complex ways that primates react to habitat degradation and how certain species can adapt and tolerate some disturbance in the short term but may still be affected detrimentally in the long term through loss of recruitment or increased disease risk. The persistence of primate populations in fragmented and degraded landscapes requires tested conservation strategies and some of the authors in this section frankly discuss what has worked for them at their field sites.

In Chapter 6, Alvaro Gonzalez-Monge and Alison M. Behie focus on the impact of selective logging while it is in progress on the range use of Annamese silvered langurs in northeast Cambodia. At the time of their study, a decreased budget for law enforcement led to an increase in illegal logging within Veun Sai-Siem Pang National Park, which was rectified the following year, allowing for a comparison of langur behaviour in times of high and low levels of selective logging. Not surprisingly, langurs were found to use areas with higher levels of logging less, and to spend more time in the high canopy when logging was nearby or chainsaws were running for long time periods. This study demonstrates the important impact of law enforcement activities on decreasing illegal activities. In Chapter 7, Julie Teichroeb, Greg Bridgett, Amélie Corriveau and Dennis Twinomugisha focus on a site where selective logging was brief and stopped by the local community, examining the responses of Rwenzori Angolan colobus immediately after the loggers left the forest. While the monkeys fled active logging areas, they did return to their former range after logging ceased. However, the study population showed all of the hypothesised changes in behaviour post-logging compared to pre-logging data. Despite the relatively small amount of damage that was done, post-logging the colobus spent less time feeding, more time resting and in social behaviours, with less frugivory and more folivory, suggesting that there could be longer-term changes in their population as a result of logging.

When animal communities are impacted by human activities and disturbance, habitats become fragmented, and biodiversity declines. This can usher in many changes that impact the abilities of the remaining animals to persist in altered habitats. Liesbeth Frias and Andrew MacIntosh, in Chapter 8, examine the relationship between host threat status and parasite prevalence and species richness, updating the classic study on these patterns by Altizer et al. (2007). The threat of infectious disease on endangered animals could either increase, as potential hosts are lost from ecosystems and pathogens are left with only the remaining animals to infect, or decrease as fewer hosts lead to the extinction of parasite species, especially host-specific parasites. Previous research supported the latter conclusion (Altizer et al., 2007) and Frias and MacIntosh used an additional ten years of data and an expanded dataset to show that though the results of Altizer et al. (2007) still hold true, the picture is complicated. Specialist parasites were found to be declining in threatened hosts but generalist parasites were actually more prevalent, perhaps finding more opportunities for niches not occupied by lost specialist species.

In Chapter 9, Sheila Holmes, Ed Louis and Steig Johnson provide valuable information on the lessons that they have learned while setting up a conservation NGO and research station in a highly fragmented area of Madagascar. They show that success in conservation practice requires effective communication between researchers and conservation managers and that the interests of multiple parties need to be considered in any conservation action. It thus pays to consult with local communities, NGOs and other stakeholders before conservation projects begin and to continue to work with them in the long term to allow success. Holmes and colleagues lay out several strategies that they have used to encourage reforestation, including participatory conservation and mixed-species planting, that take into account the needs of both people and wildlife. The authors also provide a comprehensive discussion of some of the challenges that they have faced in setting up a conservation programme, hoping to help others avoid making the same mistakes and duplicating useless efforts. In the final chapter in this section (Chapter 10), Stanislav Lhota, John Sha, Henry Bernard and Ikki Matsuda discuss the current conservation status of proboscis monkeys throughout their range. The remaining populations of this species are in scattered, fragmented areas and are often genetically isolated from one another. The authors use their years of experience in the area to lay out the most effective conservation strategies that could be used to stop declines in proboscis monkey populations and enhance connectedness between some areas.

1.5   Climate Change in the Anthropocene

Climate change is an important emerging threat to primates. While recent studies have shown some impacts of climate change on primate habitats and populations, this concept is more difficult to quantify as impacts are less tangible than those seen from habitat loss and hunting, and examining the effects of climate change often requires long-term datasets. Researchers are, however, finding more and more ways to measure the impact of climate change on their study populations. For instance, Rothman and colleagues (2015) were able to reanalyse the nutritional chemistry of ten plant species from Kibale National Park, Uganda after three decades (original data collected 1976–82 and 1994–6, and follow up in 2007–10), which showed declines in protein values and increases in fibre values, and thus concrete evidence of how climate change may threaten primate survival through the degradation of the food supply. Given the importance of the overall protein–fibre ratio of available leaves for maintaining colobine biomass, colobine populations may be expected to decrease by up to 31 per cent as a result of the changes in their food sources (Rothman et al., 2015). There has also been an increase in recent years of the numbers of studies that investigate the impacts of natural disasters on primate populations, and the increase in both the frequency and intensity of storms is at least partly due to changing climates. Our volume touches on several climate change phenomena, including changes in the resource base for primates, and the impact of natural disasters.

In Chapter 11, Jessica Rothman and Margaret Bryer review research showing that climate change can affect the distribution, availability and nutritional composition of food trees, with largely unknown impacts on primate populations. Rothman and Bryer also demonstrate how anthropogenic changes to primate habitats can affect the nutritional landscape, with loss of food due to fragmentation, the introduction of exotic species, the use of pesticides and toxins, as well as the use of crops as food. Chapters 12 and 13 focus on how the changing frequency and intensity of natural disasters are impacting primate populations. In Chapter 12, Rebecca Lewis and Anne Axel examine the effects of a damaging category-3 cyclone on the Verreaux's sifaka population at Kirindy Mitea National Park, on the western edge of Madagascar. Though no difference in sifaka body mass and reproduction was detected several months after the storm (Lewis & Rakotondranaivo, 2011), Lewis and Axel show with long-term demographic data and monitoring of food availability that the resources available in the year prior to conception had a strong impact on female ability to produce an offspring and on infant survival. Thus, the negative effects of the cyclone on infant recruitment in the sifakas was not seen until three years after the storm, highlighting the importance of long-term data in determining primate resilience, or not, to frequent natural disasters. In Chapter 13, Alison M. Behie, Mary Pavelka, Kayla Hartwell, Jane Champion and Hugh Notman compare the responses of two primate species in Belize – black howler monkeys and Yucatan spider monkeys – to hurricanes. After Hurricane Iris, a category-4 storm, hit Monkey River, black howler monkeys suffered high mortality and low infant recruitment for several years. However, spider monkeys impacted by the category-2 Hurricane Richard at Runaway

Creek Nature Reserve did not show mortality as a result of the storm, or lowered infant recruitment. Both primates reduced the time spent feeding and increased resting after the storms, and also showed a shift from frugivory to greater folivory. The authors suggest that the greater effect of Hurricane Iris on howler monkeys compared to Hurricane Richard on spider monkeys could be due to the fact that the storm, and resulting damage, was more severe at Monkey River, but could also be partly due to the flexibility of spider monkey fission–fusion behaviour, which may have mitigated food competition after the storm. In the final data chapter of the book (Chapter 14), Mandy Korstjens takes a proactive approach, working to model the effects that climate change is likely to have on the suitability of habitat and potential spread of species within the genera of *Cercopithecus* and *Colobus*. She develops species distribution models based on high-resolution climate data and estimates for future climatic changes. These models show that most sites in Africa that have suitable habitat for these genera are predicted to remain suitable in the future (2050 and 2070) and most unsuitable sites remain that way, however *Colobus* is predicted to lose suitable habitat overall in the future to a greater degree than *Cercopithecus*. These models show how two genera that are similar in their habitat requirements may respond differently to climate change and the dangers of assuming a single response from primate species.

1.6   Conclusion

Our goal was to produce a volume that will prove useful for a variety of readers, from the most experienced researcher in search of cutting-edge data, to the student wishing to position themselves for a career in primate research and conservation. Our contributors were able to draw connections between their own personal narratives and their recent research findings, demonstrating that while there is no replacement for solid disciplinary training (be it biology, anthropology or ecology), this should be enhanced by both experience and collaboration. The challenges we face in confronting the primate extinction crisis are by no means easy, but they may not be insurmountable either. With the continued dedication of primatologists the world over, in conjunction with an expanding agenda of research-informed conservation theory and praxis, a viable path forward can be forged. We personally thank the contributors to this volume for their efforts and patience as we finalised the project, and extend our gratitude to the scores of reviewers, colleagues, family and friends for their generosity, expertise and support. We are also especially grateful to Dr Rebecca Hendershott for all her assistance in the final stages of manuscript preparation.

References

Altizer, S., Nunn, C. L. & Lindenfors, P. (2007). Do threatened hosts have fewer parasites? A comparative study in primates. *Journal of Animal Ecology*, **76**(2), 304–14.

Caro, T., Darwin, J., Forrester, T., Ledoux-Bloom, C. & Wells, C. (2012). Conservation in the Anthropocene. *Conservation Biology*, **26**(1), 185–8.

Chapman, C. A. & Peres, C. A. (2001). Primate conservation in the new millennium: the role of scientists. *Evolutionary Anthropology*, **10**(1), 16–33.

Cronin, D. T., Riaco, C., Linder, J. M., et al. (2016). Impact of gun-hunting on monkey species and implications for primate conservation on Bioko Island, Equatorial Guinea. *Biological Conservation*, **197**, 180–9.

Crutzen, P. J. & Stoermer, E. F. (2000). The Anthropocene. *Global Change Newsletter*, **41**, 17–18.

Dore, K. M., Riley, E. P. & Fuentes, A. (eds) (2017). *Ethnoprimatology: A Practical Guide to Research at the Human–Nonhuman Primate Interface*. Cambridge: Cambridge University Press.

Ellis, E. C. (2015). Ecology in an anthropogenic biosphere. *Ecological Monographs*, **85**(3), 287–331.

Estrada, A., Garber, P. A., Rylands, A. B., et al. (2017). Impending extinction crisis of the world's primates: why primates matter. *Science Advances*, **3**, e600946.

Fa, J. E. & Brown, D. (2009). Impacts of hunting on mammals in African tropical moist forests: a review and synthesis. *Mammal Review*, **39**(4), 231–64.

Fa, J. E., Peres, C. A. & Meeuwig, J. (2002). Bushmeat exploitation in tropical forests: an intercontinental comparison. *Conservation Biology*, **16**, 232–7.

Fan, P. F., He, K., Chen, X., et al. (2017). Description of a new species of Hoolock gibbon (Primates: Hylobatidae) based on integrative taxonomy. *American Journal of Primatology*, **79**(5), e22631.

FAO. (2015). *Global Forest Resource Assessment 2015: How are the World's Forests Changing?* 2nd edition. Rome: FAO. Available at www.fao.org/3/a-i4793e.pdf.

Fuentes, A. (2012). Ethnoprimatology and the anthropology of the human–primate interface. *Annual Review of Anthropology*, **41**, 101–17.

Fuentes, A. & Baynes-Rock, M. (2017). Anthropogenic landscapes, human action and the process of co-construction with other species: making Anthromes in the Anthropocene. *Land*, **6**(1), 15.

Fuentes, A. & Wolfe, L. D. (2002). *Primates Face to Face: the Conservation Implications of Human–Nonhuman Primate Interconnections*. Cambridge: Cambridge University Press.

Fuentes, A., Cortez, A. D. & Peterson, J. V. (2016). Ethnoprimatology and conservation: applying insights and developing practice. In Waller, M. (ed.) *Ethnoprimatology. Developments in Primatology: Progress and Prospects*. New York: Springer, pp. 1–19.

Fuentes, A., Riley, E. P. & Dore, K. M. (2017). Ethnoprimatology matters: integration, innovation and intellectual generosity. In Dore, K. M., Riley, E. P. & Fuentes, A. (eds) *Ethnoprimatology: A Practical Guide to Research at the Human–Nonhuman Primate Interface*. Cambridge: Cambridge University Press, pp. 297–301.

Hrdy, S. B., Janson, C. & van Schaik, C. P. (1994). Infanticide: let's not throw out the baby with the bath water. *Evolutionary Anthropology*, **3**(5), 151–4.

Lewis, R. J. & Rakotondranaivo, F. (2011). The impact of Cyclone Fanele on sifaka body condition and reproduction in the tropical dry forest of western Madagascar. *Journal of Tropical Ecology*, **27**(4), 429–32.

Linder, J. M. & Oates, J. F. (2011). Differential impact of bushmeat hunting on monkey species and implications for primate conservation in Korup National Park, Cameroon. *Biological Conservation*, **144**(2), 738–45.

Malone, N. & Ovenden, K. (2017). NatureCulture. In Bezanson, M., MacKinnon, K. C., Riley, E., et al. (eds) *The International Encyclopedia of Primatology*. New York: Wiley-Blackwell.

Malone, N., Wade, A. H., Fuentes, A., et al. (2014). Ethnoprimatology: critical interdisciplinarity and multispecies approaches in anthropology. *Critique of Anthropology*, **38**, 8–29.

Muhumuza, M. & Balkwill, K. (2013). Factors affecting the success of conserving biodiversity in national parks: a review of case studies from Africa. *International Journal of Biodiversity*, **2013**, 798101.

Nadler, T., Thanh, V. N. & Streicher, U. (2007). Conservation status of Vietnamese primates. *Vietnamese Journal of Primatology*, **1**(1), 7–26.

Nater, A., Mattle-Greminger, M. P., Nurcahyo, A., et al. (2017). Morphometric, behavioral, and genomic evidence for a new orangutan species. *Current Biology*, **27**(22), 3487–98.

Nekaris, K. A. I., Shepherd, C. R., Starr, C. R. & Nijman, V. (2010). Exploring cultural drivers for wildlife trade via an ethnoprimatological approach: a case study of slender and slow lorises (*Loris* and *Nycticebus*) in South and Southeast Asia. *American Journal of Primatology*, **72**(10), 877–86.

Riley, E. P. & Zak, A. A. (2015). The conservation impact of the American Society of Primatologists' Conservation Small Grant Program. *Primate Conservation*, **29**, 1–7.

Rothman, J. M., Chapman, C. A., Struhsaker, T. T., et al. (2015). Long-term declines in nutritional quality of tropical leaves. *Ecology*, **96**, 873–8.

Sayre, N. F. (2012). The politics of the Anthropogenic. *Annual Review of Anthropology*, **41**, 57–70.

Starr, C., Nekaris, K. A. I., Streicher, U. & Leung, L. (2010). Traditional use of slow lorises *Nycticebus bengalensis* and *N. pygmaeus* in Cambodia: an impediment to their conservation. *Endangered Species Research*, **12**(1), 17–23.

Steffen, W., Grinevald, J., Crutzen, P. & McNeill, J. (2011). The Anthropocene: conceptual and historical perspectives. *Philosophical Transactions of the Royal Society of London A: Mathematical, Physical and Engineering Sciences*, **369**(1938), 842–67.

Sterck, E. H., Watts, D. P. & van Schaik, C. P. (1997). The evolution of female social relationships in nonhuman primates. *Behavioral Ecology and Sociobiology*, **41**(5), 291–309.

Sussman, R. W., Cheverud, J. M. & Bartlett, T. Q. (1994). Infant killing as an evolutionary strategy: reality or myth? *Evolutionary Anthropology*, **3**(5), 149–51.

Van Ngoc Thinh, Mootnick, A. R., VuNgoc Thanh, Nadler, T. & Roos, C. (2010). A new species of crested gibbon, from the central Annamite Mountain Range. *Vietnamese Journal of Primatology*, **1**(4), 1–12.

Wrangham, R. W. (1979). On the evolution of ape social systems. *Social Science Information*, **18**(3), 336–68.

Wrangham, R. W. (1980). An ecological model of female-bonded primate groups. *Behaviour*, **75**(3), 262–300.

Part I

The Human–Non-human Primate Interface

2 Struggling for Socioecological Resilience

*A Long-Term Study of Silvery Gibbons (*Hylobates moloch*) in the Fragmented Sancang Forest Nature Reserve, West Java, Indonesia*

Nicholas Malone and Made Wedana Adi Putra

2.1 Personal Narrative

A scholar's research trajectory is influenced beyond measure by academic mentors. Personally, my (NM) training in primatology began with exposure to the basics of socioecological models from Michelle Sauther (University of Colorado), with her insightful lessons on the ecological underpinnings of social and mating systems. Subsequently, my early postgraduate years were heavily influenced by Agustín Fuentes (then at Central Washington University) and his critical perspectives on overarching models and their requisite assumptions, as well as a reflexive approach to the interpretation of salient data. From both of these mentors, the intellectual history of *their* supervisors is readily apparent, namely Robert Sussman and Phyllis Dolhinow, respectively. Later, while studying for my PhD at the University of Oregon (and as a post-doc in the Democratic Republic of Congo), I received rigorous training from Joanna Lambert and Frances White in both conservation (theory and praxis) and behavioural ecology. All of my aforementioned mentors provided formative contributions to my academic development, and these influences are clearly detectable in my past and present research engagements. Specifically, I endeavour to understand how the observed patterns of variability within and between hominoid taxa are simultaneously shaped by, and act as shaping factors of, evolutionary processes. Through careful research, apes have revealed their ability to adjust behaviourally to minor shifts in ecological and demographic conditions via social innovation and learning. However, these same species are also slow-reproducing and therefore vulnerable to rapid environmental alterations, such as those brought about by humans. What are the limits of resilience in the face of human activities? How can we use that knowledge to inform conservation theory and practice?

In the year 2000, under the supervision of Agustín Fuentes, I travelled to Java, Indonesia and began a research relationship and friendship with I Made Wedana Adi Putra. Our collaborations have now spanned over 15 years, as our contribution to the present volume attests. Arguably, a foreign researcher's most valuable asset is a network of trusted local counterparts and skilled research assistants. Beginning with an initial assessment of the non-human primate trade in animal markets across Java and Bali, and culminating with the long-term investigation of gibbon population dynamics, my research in Indonesia has involved (and indeed depended upon) myriad dedicated Indonesian researchers and conservationists. During my various projects, simultaneous attention to both socioecological data and ethnographic insights continue to reveal the complex ecology and nuanced perceptions of primate life in Java. Understanding these interwoven layers, and working productively towards sustainable outcomes for both human and non-human primates is the promise of an informed, anthropological primatology. While previously compartmentalised, the objectives of obtaining socioecological data and contributing to conservation measures have become integrated and mutually reinforcing over time, and are now bound by theoretical ties that attend to the entanglement of human and other species' lives in the Anthropocene. In hindsight, the training I received from all of my academic mentors prepared me to absorb and process the experiences I accumulated as a foreign researcher working in primate range countries. Lessons learned, both in the classroom and in the field, have prepared me to embrace the ubiquitous presence and impact of humans as an opportunity to understand primate behavioural flexibility within ecological systems.

2.2   Introduction

Traditionally, the application of socioecological models guides primatologists to investigate and identify social and behavioural phenomena that are sensitive to an array of ecological variables (Clutton-Brock, 1974; Sterck et al., 1997; van Schaik & van Hooff, 1983; Wrangham, 1979; 1980). However, it is now increasingly understood that in addition to the distribution of risks, resources and the competitive regimes of conspecifics, primate social systems are subject to the influences of past and present anthropogenic alterations (Campbell-Smith et al., 2011; Hockings et al., 2015). Anthropogenic patterns of ecological disturbance, including habitat degradation and hunting pressure, drive ecological, and subsequently social, systems into states of disequilibrium, sometimes leading to higher densities and larger group sizes, and sometimes leading to declines in density and group sizes (Struhsaker, 1997; 1999). Actively perceiving that humans and other primates co-reside in ecological and social landscapes is now recognised as both a necessary and efficacious approach in primatology. Studies across a variety of taxa have successfully documented the development of primate behavioural and ecological strategies in response to habitat alterations by humans (e.g. Hockings & McLennan, 2012; Strum, 2010; see also Chapters 6–10 in this volume). Data from these studies are achieving salience in both evolutionary analyses and management/conservation contexts. A consequence of disturbance is the indirect manipulation of ecological and demographic variables that may favour phenotypic flexibility. Indeed, there is an emerging recognition in evolutionary theory that continuous and reversible transformations in behaviour, physiology and morphology in response to rapid environmental fluctuations are important for many organisms (Malone et al., 2012a; Piersma & Drent, 2003). The interplay of human and non-human primate ecologies creates a complex dynamic that can be characterised as a form of co-participatory niche construction (Laland et al., 2001; Odling-Smee, 2007; Riley & Fuentes, 2010).

As there are few, if any, ecosystems on the planet where humans have no impact, studying primates in minimally impacted 'natural' settings is both unlikely and misrepresentative of most primate populations (Dore et al., 2017; Fuentes, 2012; Malone et al., 2014b). If human-impacted localities typify primatology's new 'sites of relevance', then arguably no other location is more relevant than Java. Java's distinctiveness emerges from its unique combination of biotic richness, physical geography and complex human history. An estimated 135 million human inhabitants exert enormous pressure on the remaining area of forested land, which is estimated at less than 10 per cent of its original expanse (Whitten et al., 1996). Losses of lowland forests (from sea level to 500 metres asl) have been disproportionately large, and approximately only 2 per cent of lowland forests remain intact (Nijman, 2004; Smiet, 1990). The remaining fragments of primary forest are set among a mosaic of government-controlled protection and production forests, and an ever-growing local population seeking to maintain subsistence livelihoods from agricultural crops (Malone et al., 2014a; Meijerink, 1977; USAID, 2004). The extant community of non-human primates includes: the silvery gibbon (*Hylobates moloch*); the grizzled leaf monkey or Javan surili (*Presbytis comata*); the Javan lutung (*Trachypithecus auratus*); the Javan slow loris (*Nycticebus javanicus*); and the long-tailed macaque (*Macaca fascicularis*). With the exception of the macaque, each of these species has a very limited geographic distribution with a current IUCN Red List status of either endangered or vulnerable (IUCN, 2017).

The prevalence and persistence of threatened primates in the pet trade reflects a serious impediment to the viability of free-living populations (Eudey, 2008; Maldonado & Peck, 2013). In Java, non-human primates continue to be removed from protected populations at an alarming rate (Malone et al., 2004; Nijman, 2005a; 2005b; 2010). In Indonesia, various laws prohibit the killing, capturing, possession of or trading in protected wildlife. However, for both formal and informal reasons, enforcement of the laws and/or enactment of the associated penalties are rare (Malone et al., 2017; Nijman, 2005b). Furthermore, the management of the displaced population (e.g. confiscation and rehabilitation activities) consumes significant resources and creates additional challenges for habitat country conservationists (Wedana Adi Putra & Jeffery, 2016). While the remainder of this case study focuses on the silvery gibbon, many of the dynamics apply to some or all of the other species on Java as well (Malone et al., 2014b; Wedana Adi Putra, unpublished data).

Within this context, the endangered silvery gibbon is confined to roughly 30 heterogeneous fragments of variably disturbed lowland and lower montane rainforest with total population estimates ranging from an optimistic 3000 to a more conservative 1500 individuals remaining (Nijman, 2004; Supriatna, 2006; Supriatna et al., 2010; Wedana Adi Putra et al., 2010). Knowledge of silvery gibbon behaviour, ranging and ecology is now informed from studies in both lowland and submontane sites across West and Central Java (Kappeler, 1981; 1984a; 1984b; Kim et al., 2011; Malone, 2007). Home-range sizes and daily path lengths (comparative indicators of energy expenditure or foraging effort in various ecological contexts) vary among sites, attributable primarily to altitudinal influences on resource availability (Kim et al., 2011). Intra- and inter-site differences related to the degree of anthropogenic changes are only now becoming fully appreciated (Reisland, 2013; Reisland & Lambert, 2016). Ultimately, these data are critical to a more complete understanding of silvery gibbon socioecology.

Finally, the accurate estimation of the total number of individuals (in a given taxon) that remain living in both protected and unprotected areas is equally pressing with regard to the development of species-specific conservation strategies. Repetitive surveys, while time- and resource-intensive, are critical to assessing population viability, as well as documenting the complexity of inter- and intragroup social relationships. Here, we present a detailed examination of silvery gibbon groups in and around Cagar Alam Leuweung Sancang (CALS), West Java to document changes to group compositions over time, and place these changes within the context of human activities and habitat alterations. We then consider how anthropogenically impacted populations like this can inform the development of a new synthetic socioecological model (Sterck et al., 1997; Thierry, 2008; van Schaik, 1989).

2.3   Methods

2.3.1   Research Site

Our primary research locality comprises the 2157 ha CALS and its immediate surroundings. Located on the south coast of West Java (S 07°43′30″, E 107°52′30″), CALS was established in 1978 (Decree 370/KPTS/UM/6/1978) to protect the lowland dipterocarp (Family Dipterocarpaceae) and mangrove (Family Rhizophoraceae) forests, as well as a unique assemblage of endemic fauna (Figure 2.1). The site has now been the subject of multiple investigations primarily focused on the behaviour, ecology and conservation of the small population of silvery gibbons contained therein (Malone, 2007; Malone et al., 2012b; 2014a; Reisland, 2013; Reisland & Lambert, 2016). Within CALS are fragments of unequal sizes and gibbon group densities. A fragment of approximately 200 ha and a second fragment of 400 ha are inhabited by six and two gibbon groups, respectively (Malone, 2007; Malone & Oktavinalis, 2006; Reisland, 2013). This inverse relationship between fragment size and the number of gibbon groups can only be understood historically in the context of forest loss, territorial size and group compositions, as well as intergroup relationships.

The lead author (NM), with extensive logistical support from the co-author and others, has studied the gibbon population at CALS during multiple fieldwork seasons between 2005 and 2016. In this research, a combination of ethological observations (>300 hours of scan sampling and fixed-point counts of gibbon vocalisations), ecological monitoring (longitudinal assessments of habitat alterations over an 11-year period) and ethnographic methods (participant observation, cultural mapping and semi-structured interviews with more than 40 participants) has been utilised. In some cases, the duration of research visits to the site was rather short (less than one month) and therefore certain information remains at a lower resolution (e.g. the specific timing of births). However, consistently returning to an anthropological field site permits a chronological account of salient changes, in addition to strengthening an array of important interpersonal relationships (Ramos, 1990).

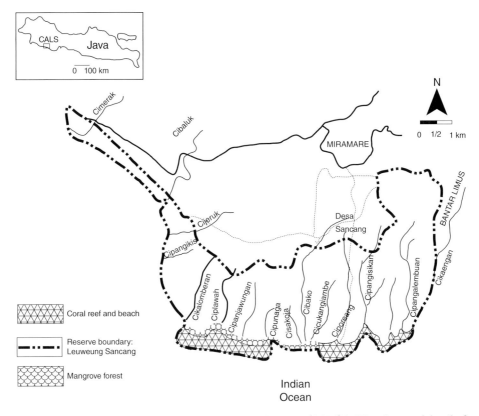

Figure 2.1 The location of the Cagar Alam Leuweung Sancang (CALS) in West Java and detail of the major geographical features within the reserve boundary.

2.3.2 Group Counts and Density Estimates

Initially, we employed range-mapping methodology (National Research Council, 1981) of all known gibbon groups to estimate the true density of silvery gibbons in CALS between late 2005 and early 2007. Determining the number of groups present in the reserve, and subsequent recording of individual group sizes and compositions, was completed in several stages. First, fixed-point counts of gibbon morning song-bouts were conducted from listening locations throughout the reserve. The distribution of fixed points allowed for the general mapping of gibbon groups using GPS, compass, protractor and detailed topographic maps. Male and female vocalisations are readily distinguishable as males produce song-bouts less frequently than females and their songs consist of short phrases uttered in a non-stereotypic order (Geissmann & Nijman, 2006). These fundamentals permit a conservative calculation of the minimum number of individuals present and basic compositions of silvery gibbon groups. Areas of forest where gibbons were detected were then surveyed by walking existing trails at a pace of approximately 1 km/h. We recorded the location, age/sex class and perpendicular distance from the trail of all visible individuals. Further, four of the major north–south flowing rivers were surveyed in a similar manner by walking the banks. Surveying rivers in this way not only provides access to a variety of habitat types, but also provides access to the remaining areas of (generally) undisturbed forest. We are confident that given the combination of detection methods used, combined with the fragmentation, accessibility and geographical features of the reserve, all groups within the reserve have been identified and their ranges mapped to a reasonable degree of accuracy (±0.5 ha) (Table 2.1).

Research conducted between 2009 and 2011 confirmed the presence, location and composition of this same subset of groups, and therefore contributes to the chronological account of group changes we present here (Reisland, 2013). Additionally, we conducted subsequent population assessments for a subset of focal groups (Groups A–C) in 2012, 2013 and 2016. Even though gibbons alter certain behavioural patterns in response to anthropogenic disturbance (Reisland & Lambert, 2016), we have reliably recorded the age/sex class of all individuals and recorded the location and characteristics of intergroup interactions for this subset of groups for just over a decade. Finally, this long-term engagement has facilitated the development of trusted relationships with a variety of local stakeholders, host families, village and conservation officials, as well as a team of local assistants. In addition to providing robust research support, this network of people has provided systematically collected ethnographic insights and reliable information regarding the general timing of gibbon births and disappearances, as well as an accounting of illegal activities within the protected reserve (Malone et al., 2014a; 2017).

Table 2.1 Minimum size and composition of gibbon groups within CALS during the study period (2005–7) when the most comprehensive survey work was completed

Group ID	Minimum size	Composition[a]	Complete count?[b]	Home-range size (ha)
A	5	2 AM, 1AF, 1 JF, 1 I	Yes	6.25
B	3	1 AM, 1 AF, 1 I	Yes	13.50
C	2	1 AM, 1 AF	Yes	15.00
D	1	1 AF	No	18.00 (estimate)
E	3	1 AM, 1 AF, 1 SAF	Yes	16.375
F	2	1 AM, 1 AF	No	16.50 (estimate)
G	1	1 AF	No	14.50 (estimate)
H	2	1 AM, 1 AF	No	18.75 (estimate)
Total	19	7 AM, 8 AF, 1 SAF, 1 JF, 2 I	No	AVG. 14.86 (estimate)

a. Minimum verifiable group composition based on multiple encounters (either audio, visual or both). Minimum composition for Groups G and H are based on repeated audio observation of female song-bouts from various listening posts and spatial relationship to the simultaneous vocalisation of known groups. Age/sex class: AM = adult male; AF = adult female; SAF = subadult female; JF = adolescent female; I = infant.
b. Counts are considered complete when frequent contacts produced reliable individual identifications by two or more observers.

2.4   Results and Interpretation

2.4.1   Changes to Group Compositions Over Time

The respective group compositions of focal groups (A, B and C) have changed in distinctly different ways from 2005 to 2016 (Figure 2.2). The once numerous Group A was largely decimated by a reported hunting/capture event in 2008 (multiple informants, personal communications). The remaining individual, a subadult female, persisted within a diminishing range until the last reported sighting of this individual in 2013. It is possible, but not confirmed, that this female completed a successful emigration from her natal range. In Group B, we have documented a history of births ($n = 4$) and infant/juvenile disappearances ($n = 2$). The successive disappearances in 2008 and 2012 are either directly the result of human capture (Wedana Adi Putra, unpublished data) or indirectly related to the increase in invasive human activities within this group's range (see Section 2.4.2). As both of the disappearances occurred during the time of transition to locomotor independence (ages 1.5–3.0 years), these losses may be indirectly attributable to human activity if the adult female fled in response to a perceived threat resulting in the temporary abandonment of her offspring (Malone, 2007; Reisland, 2013). A subsequent canopy fall could account for the disappearances. Gibbon behaviour is heavily influenced by their habitual (and often ricochetal) brachiation. For example, ventral carrying of infants, the development of perceptual motor skills and learned canopy pathways factor into the timing of the onset of independent travel. Independent movement *within* a canopy precedes independent movement *between* canopies, with the onset of the latter occurring in the second year of life. Gaps in the canopy have been shown to constrain gibbon travel patterns with a demonstrated maximum crossing ability of 12 metres (Cheyne, 2011; Cheyne et al., 2013).

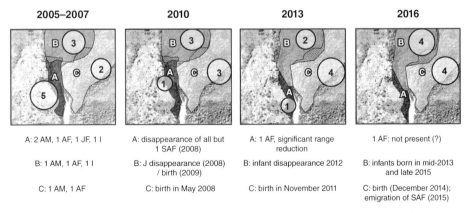

2005–2007	2010	2013	2016
A: 2 AM, 1 AF, 1 JF, 1 I	A: disappearance of all but 1 SAF (2008)	A: 1 AF, significant range reduction	1 AF: not present (?)
B: 1 AM, 1 AF, 1 I	B: J disappearance (2008) / birth (2009)	B: infant disappearance 2012	B: infants born in mid-2013 and late 2015
C: 1 AM, 1 AF	C: birth in May 2008	C: birth in November 2011	C: birth (December 2014); emigration of SAF (2015)

Figure 2.2 Chronology of changes to the home ranges and compositions of Groups A, B and C at select times over the duration of the study period (2005–16). Numbers are indicative of group sizes only; composition details are below the images. Home-range sizes are approximate, with one grid square equal to 1 ha. Hatch-marked areas between ranges represent zones of non-exclusive use.

Table 2.2 Comparison of the census (N) population size and effective population size (N_e) for a subset of focal groups (A–C) in CALS, where $N_e = 4N_mN_f / N_m+N_f$

Year	Number of breeding males	Number of breeding females	N	N_e
2007	4	3	10	6.85
2010	2	3	7	4.8
2013	2	3	7	4.8
2016	2	3	8	4.8

In a compelling and complementary study, Reisland and Lambert (2016) observed Groups B and C in CALS over a period of ten months and found Group B to be more sensitive to the presence of humans than Group C, occupying their range in non-random patterns to avoid humans which they may perceive as risky. In contrast, Group C's behaviour did not support the hypothesis that humans were a risk to be avoided, and this group was just as likely to be observed within areas of intensifying human presence as in areas without humans (Reisland & Lambert, 2016). Interestingly, it is Group C that has demonstrated a more stable succession of individuals due to births, maturation and dispersal. Given the aforementioned patterning of deaths and disappearances (either directly or indirectly attributable to human activity), it is clear that the individual losses to Groups A and B offset the addition of individuals to the population associated with survival and maturation of subadult offspring in Group C. This is evident in a comparison of census population (N) and effective population sizes (N_e) over time for this subset of groups within CALS (Table 2.2). Different and opposing experiences with humans are possible for these groups because in some parts of the reserve humans represent both a real and a perceived risk to gibbons, whereas elsewhere the presence of spiritual sites and practices seems to limit detrimental human activities to the potential advantage of gibbon population health.

2.4.2   Habitat Alterations Over Time

Elsewhere, we have described the cultural and spiritual importance of the Sancang forest (Malone, 2007; Malone et al., 2014a). To briefly summarise, the Sancang forest is believed to be the location where the former ruler of the Sundanese (West Javan) Kingdom of Pajajaran escaped in order to avoid a confrontation with his close kin regarding conversion from Hindu to Islamic hegemony. As the site of Prabu Sili-wangi's transformation into the spiritually powerful form of a tiger, the Sancang forest becomes a physico-symbolic border between nature and society, as well as between historical eras (Wessing, 1993; 2006). Generations of Sundanese pilgrims have visited the Sancang forest to engage in ritualistic practices that combine mysticism and Islam. These pilgrims seek to attain the promise of prosperity in difficult times. Spiritual visits vary in length from several hours to several months or longer, and have traditionally been supervised by local spiritual mediators or *kuncen* (Malone, 2007; Malone et al., 2014a; Reisland, 2013).

Over the past decade, in correlation with a general trend of economic instability, there has been an increase in the number of pilgrim visits to the reserve (although the volume is considered low from a historical perspective) (Malone et al., 2014a). Traditionally, simple wooden or cement platforms have been constructed both to enhance the cavernous features of the sacred sites (*keramat*) and to facilitate the aforementioned ritual ceremonies. Throughout the study period, however, the structures have proliferated and now include cement-walled structures to facilitate private bathing and a small mosque (*musholla*) for more formalised prayer. These structures incorporate more durable building materials, thus making the presence of humans more conspicuous within the gibbon ranges. The use of corrugated metal roofing material, for example, amplifies the sound of falling rain and human voices. At the end of the study period (2015–16) we observed, for the first time, humans entering the canopy within gibbon home ranges to partake in the harvesting of forest honey (*madu lebah hutan* or *madu odeng* in Sundanese) for commercial trade. These activities have the potential to change the long-established dynamic within the shared, human–gibbon spaces (Figure 2.3).

Despite both the official protections and the cultural significance, the forest has been dramatically altered by logging, forest conversion and other human alterations that greatly facilitate increased access and exploitation (e.g. motorbike paths, semi-permanent shelters, etc.) (Malone, 2007; Reisland, 2013). To date, approximately half

Figure 2.3 A sample of photos documenting human activities within CALS, including: (a) more traditional structures facilitating ritualistic practices at sacred sites (*keramat*); (b) more recent structures constructed with more durable building materials; (c) discarded evidence (a fashioned smoke repellent) of honey extraction activities; and (d) a hive of *Apis dorsata* on the branch of dipterocarp within the core area of gibbon Group B.

Table 2.3 Estimate of deforestation within CALS (1995–2015)

Year	Forested area (ha)	Logged area (ha)	Percentage deforestation of total area (2157 ha)
1995[a]	1995.0	162.0	7.51
1998[b]	1769.0	388.0	17.98
2000[b]	1459.0	698.0	32.36
2002[b]	1221.0	936.0	43.39
2005[c]	1215.5	941.5	43.65
2015[d]	1107.0	1050.0	48.68

a. Megantara 1995.
b. Data for 1998, 2000 and 2002 from analysis of Landsat 7 image maps; Pakpahan 2003.
c. Data for 2005 from ground-check methodologies and the analysis of an aerial photo-composite map at a scale of 1:10 000.
d. Estimate of logged areas for the decade 2005–2015 is based on the observed expansion of agricultural plots and the widening of access trails, but excludes the presence of maturing cultivar species within the reserve boundary.

of the forest within the reserve boundary has been lost (Table 2.3). The majority of these losses occurred between 1999 and 2001, and are attributable to a period of large-scale timber extraction. The newly felled forest/village border provided residents the opportunity to expand agricultural fields, and establish access trails that have been subsequently widened over time. Additionally, there is ongoing evidence that small-scale, illegal extraction of valuable trees continues within the reserve boundary.

2.5   Discussion

Given the potential lag-time of small-population processes (e.g. downward spirals resulting from edge effects and inbreeding depression), the increase in extractive activities within CALS raises deep concerns about the long-term viability of this population (Cowlishaw & Dunbar, 2000; Malone, 2007; Malone & Oktavinalis, 2006; Malone et al., 2012b; Marsh, 2003). Within the reserve, the ecological parameters of the forest, absent of human alterations, fail to predict patterns of gibbon spatial distribution and ranging behaviour. The density and distribution of gibbon groups in CALS, in relation to habitat quality and availability, can only be understood historically, in the context of deforestation and subsequent anthropogenic alterations.

This type of primate population, one that is affected so intensely by human habitat alteration, hunting and capture, is ideal to aid in the development of a synthetic socioecological model (Sterck et al., 1997; Thierry, 2008; van Schaik, 1989). For the gibbons at CALS, both modifications to the social and ecological niche by the non-human primates (e.g. range occupancy and territorial defence), as well as anthropogenic influences, are integral to understanding the animals' current ranging and behaviour. A new synthetic socioecological model would need to incorporate anthropogenic pressures and make predictions about how animals will respond. Hypothetically, if habitat degradation alters group density and/or the amount of territorial overlap, the resulting crowding may lead to an increase in time allocated to the defence of resources. Similarly, hunting of females (and capture of dependent offspring) for the live pet trade could exacerbate the decline of small populations, shift patterns of resource utilisation and eventually impact social and mating systems.

At CALS, we see an active and emergent relationship between individuals, groups, populations and their environments. This perspective is compatible with an increasing acknowledgement in evolutionary biology that a mutually interactive relationship exists between organisms and their environment through niche construction (Kendal et al., 2011; Laland et al., 2001; Odling-Smee et al., 2003). Niche construction conceptualises evolution of *both* populations of organisms and their environments through a dynamic, mutually mutable process that shapes the behaviour of organisms and the patterning of selective pressures in ecosystems (Odling-Smee, 2007). The ability for organisms to not only impact their environment, but also, in part, shape the selective forces that they face, may result in more plastic or variable behavioural profiles (Malone et al., 2012a; West-Eberhardt, 2003). In the case of gibbons, the construction of territories and territorial relationships among contiguous groups creates a social and ecological niche relationship via genetic and ecological inheritance systems. At CALS, these processes are further influenced by the activities of humans, including (though not limited to): (1) cultural beliefs about the sacredness of the forest; (2) the consistent human presence that variably impacts the range use of gibbon groups (Malone, 2007; Reisland & Lambert, 2016); and (3) acute, intermittent human activities that directly impact the demography of the gibbon population. A model for population-level change over generational time that includes all of these factors will result in a comprehensive understanding of feedback pathways within the system (Figure 2.4).

The illegal trade in silvery gibbons is ongoing and poses a serious risk to the remaining population of silvery gibbons. Nijman (2005a) calculated a potential loss of up to 6.86 per cent from the wild population per year as a direct result of the illegal

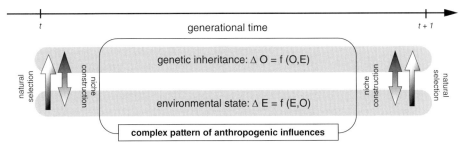

Figure 2.4 A model for socioecological change through time that combines the effects of natural selection, niche construction and the locally specific, salient patterns of anthropogenic influences.
Source: adapted from Odling-Smee, 2007.

trade. Displaced silvery gibbons are found in all stages of the illegal trade network, including private homes, animal markets and wildlife rescue centres. At the Javan Primates Rehabilitation Centre (JPRC), between 2011 and 2016 more than 30 silvery gibbons have been rescued from private ownership (Wedana Adi Putra & Jeffery 2016; Wedana Adi Putra, unpublished data). Of the confiscated silvery gibbons, it is likely, based on an assessment of the age, sex, physical appearance and details related to the timing and location of possession, that at least one or two of the missing gibbons from CALS have been recovered from the illegal trade (Wedana Adi Putra, unpublished data). Understanding the dynamics of the illegal procurement and trade of wild silvery gibbons remains the greatest challenge towards facilitating a survival strategy for this endangered species.

What we know about gibbons (with respect to social systems and behavioural flexibility) has changed substantially in the past decade. Specifically, we now recognise that individual gibbons are connected reproductively and behaviourally to a broader community beyond the immediate social group (Lappan & Whittaker, 2009; Malone et al., 2012a; Reichard et al., 2012). Has our conservation toolkit kept pace? Adger and colleagues (2005: 1036) define conservation resilience as 'the capacity of linked social-ecological systems to absorb recurrent disturbances … so as to retain essential structures, processes, and feedbacks'. Given the complexity of issues surrounding the CALS protected area, we argue that shifting from a targeted 'species conservation' paradigm to a 'resilience' framework establishes a realistic lens through which to envision a future for the forest and its denizens. Going forward, facilitation of the gibbon–human interface ultimately requires the establishment of strong relationships with people who are dependent on forest resources for their livelihoods and subsistence needs (e.g. food, medicine and materials for housing construction). It is unlikely, and potentially counterproductive, to seek a ban on all human activities within the gibbon habitat at CALS. Instead, striving to understand the benefits inherent to this complex gibbon–human interface may inform the management, and facilitate the resiliency, of this linked human–gibbon socioecological system.

2.6   Future Directions/Conclusions

To summarise and conclude, CALS harbours a small population of an endangered and endemic ape species. Sacred sites nestled within the CALS forest have consistently attracted spiritual guests from throughout West Java. Such mysticism gives this forest a particular allure. Despite the official protections and cultural significance, the forest has been dramatically impacted by human actions that facilitate access and permit exploitation. Concomitantly, the small population of silvery gibbons continues to persist, but illegal hunting and habitat degradation may ultimately lead to the demise of this population. While the present research has emphasised the ecological and demographic aspects of the focal species' space, ongoing research at the site explores the spiritual elements of this shared, interspecies place. In these investigations we endeavour to more fully understand local socioeconomic structures and belief systems. Cultural beliefs and livelihood practices are shaping factors of landscapes in ways that have vital implications for the resilience of ecological and social systems. In short, these landscapes are as much socially constructed as they are physical (Fuentes & Baynes-Rock, 2017; Malone, 2007; Malone et al., 2014a; 2014b). Here we have demonstrated sensitivity to human activities in a population of endangered apes. As such, the deployment of effective conservation strategies for silvery gibbons will depend upon a continued understanding of behavioural responses to human-modified habitats. These insights, in conjunction with more traditional primatological assessments, will assist in the facilitation of a viable gibbon–human interface.

Acknowledgements

We gratefully acknowledge: Universitas Padjadjaran and especially Dr Teguh Husodo (research counterpart); Ajat Surtaja (research assistant); Haes Family in Desa Sancang (local host); Faculty of Arts Research Development Fund at the University of Auckland (funding); Melissa Reisland, Alison Wade, Kathryn Ovenden and Meg Selby (contributions to data collection); permission from RISTEK (238/SIP/FRP/SM/VIII/2015) and BKSDA (SI.1860/BBKSDA JABAR-2/2015); Briar Sefton, illustrator, Anthropology, School of Social Sciences, University of Auckland; and University of Auckland's Human Participants Ethics Committee.

References

Adger, W. N., Hughes, T. P., Folke, C., Carpenter, S. R. & Rockström, J. (2005). Social-ecological resilience to coastal disasters. *Science*, **309**(5737), 1036–9.

Campbell-Smith, G., Campbell-Smith, M., Singleton, I. & Linkie, M. (2011). Apes in space: saving an imperilled orangutan population in Sumatra. *PLoS ONE*, **6**(2), e17210.

Cheyne, S. M. (2011). Gibbon locomotion research in the field: problems, possibilities, and benefits for conservation. In D'Août, K. & Vereecke, E. E. (eds) *Primate Locomotion*. New York: Springer, pp. 201–13.

Cheyne, S. M., Thompson, C. J. & Chivers, D. J. (2013). Travel adaptations of Bornean agile gibbons *Hylobates albibarbis* (Primates: Hylobatidae) in a degraded secondary forest, Indonesia. *Journal of Threatened Taxa*, **5**(5), 3963–8.

Clutton-Brock, T. H. (1974). Primate social organization and ecology. *Nature*, **250**, 539–42.

Cowlishaw, G. & Dunbar, R. (2000). *Primate Conservation Biology*. Chicago, IL: University of Chicago Press.

Dore, K. M., Riley, E. P. & Fuentes, A. (eds) (2017). *Ethnoprimatology: A Practical Guide to Research at the Human–Nonhuman Primate Interface*. Cambridge: Cambridge University Press.

Eudey, A. A. (2008). The crab-eating macaque (*Macaca fascicularis*): widespread and rapidly declining. *Primate Conservation*, **23**, 129–32.

Fuentes, A. (2012). Ethnoprimatology and the anthropology of the human–primate interface. *Annual Review of Anthropology*, **41**, 101–17.

Fuentes, A. & Baynes-Rock, M. (2017). Anthropogenic landscapes, human action and the process of co-construction with other species: making anthromes in the Anthropocene. *Land*, **6**(1), 15.

Geissmann, T. & Nijman, V. (2006). Calling in wild silvery gibbons (*Hylobates moloch*) in Java (Indonesia): behaviour, phylogeny, and conservation. *American Journal of Primatology*, **68**, 1–19.

Hockings, K. J. & McLennan, M. R. (2012). From forest to farm: systematic review of cultivar feeding by chimpanzees – management implications for wildlife in anthropogenic landscapes. *PLoS ONE*, **7**(4), e33391.

Hockings, K. J., McLennan, M. R., Carvalho, S., et al. (2015). Apes in the Anthropocene: flexibility and survival. *Trends in Ecology & Evolution*, **30**(4), 215–22.

IUCN. (2017). *The IUCN Red List of Threatened Species*. Version 2017.1. Available at: www.iucnredlist.org.

Kappeler, M. (1981). The Javan silvery gibbon (*Hylobates lar moloch*). PhD Thesis, Universitat Basel.

Kappeler, M. (1984a). The gibbon in Java. In Prueschoft, H., Chivers, D., Brockelman, W. Y. & Creel, N. (eds) *The Lesser Apes: Evolution, Behaviour, and Biology*. Edinburgh: Edinburgh University Press, pp. 19–31.

Kappeler, M. (1984b). Vocal bouts and territorial maintenance in the Moloch gibbon. In Prueschoft, H. D., Chivers, D. J., Brockelman, W. Y. & Creel, N. (eds) *The Lesser Apes: Evolution, Behaviour, and Biology*. Edinburgh: Edinburgh University Press, pp. 376–89.

Kendal, J., Tehrani, J. J. & Odling-Smee, J. (2011). Human niche construction in interdisciplinary focus. *Philosophical Transactions of the Royal Society B*, **366**, 785–92.

Kim, S., Lappan, S. & Choe, J. C. (2011). Diet and ranging behaviour of the endangered Javan gibbon (*Hylobates moloch*) in a submontane tropical rainforest. *American Journal of Primatology*, **73**, 270–80.

Laland, K. N., Odling-Smee, J. & Feldman, M. W. (2001). Niche construction, ecological inheritance, and cycles of contingency in evolution. In Oyama, S., Griffiths, P. E. & Gray, R. D. (eds) *Cycles of Contingency: Developmental Systems and Evolution*. Cambridge, MA: MIT Press, pp. 117–26.

Lappan, S. & Whittaker, D. (eds) (2009). *The Gibbons: New Perspectives on Small Ape Socioecology and Population Biology*. New York: Springer Science & Business Media.

Maldonado, A. & Peck, M. (2013). The role of primate conservation to fight the illegal trade in primates: the case of the owl monkeys in the Colombian–Peruvian Amazon. *Folia Primatologica*, **84**, 299–300.

Malone, N. (2007). The socioecology of the Critically Endangered Javan gibbon (*Hylobates moloch*): assessing the impact of anthropogenic disturbance on primate social systems. PhD Thesis, University of Oregon.

Malone, N. & Oktavinalis, H. (2006). The socioecology of the silvery gibbon (*Hylobates moloch*) in the Cagar Alam Leuweung Sancang (CALS), West Java, Indonesia. *American Journal of Physical Anthropology*, **129**(S42), 124.

Malone, N., Fuentes, A., Purnama, A. R. & Wedana Adi Putra, I. M. (2004). Displaced Hylobatids: biological, cultural, and economic aspects of the primate trade in Java and Bali, Indonesia. *Tropical Biodiversity*, **40**, 41–9.

Malone, N., Fuentes, A. & White, F. J. (2012a). Variation in the social systems of extant hominoids: comparative insight into the social behaviour of early hominins. *International Journal of Primatology*, **33**(6), 1251–77.

Malone, N., Wade, A., Wedana Adi Putra, I. M., Reisland, M. & Selby, M. (2012b). Calibrating a conservation strategy for silvery gibbons (*Hylobates moloch*). *American Journal of Physical Anthropology*, **147**(S54), 202.

Malone, N., Selby, M. & Longo, S. B. (2014a). Political and ecological dimensions of silvery gibbon conservation efforts: an endangered ape in (and on) the verge. *International Journal of Sociology*, **44**(1), 34–53.

Malone, N., Wade, A. H., Fuentes, A., et al. (2014b). Ethnoprimatology: critical interdisciplinarity and multispecies approaches in anthropology. *Critique of Anthropology*, **38**, 8–29.

Malone, N., Palmer, A. & Wade, A. H. (2017). Incorporating the ethnographic perspective: the value, process and responsibility of working with human participants. In Dore, K. M., Riley, E. P. & Fuentes, A. (eds) *Ethnoprimatology: A Practical Guide to Research on the Human–Nonhuman Primate Interface*. Cambridge: Cambridge University Press, pp. 176–89.

Marsh, L. K. (2003). The nature of fragmentation. In Marsh, L. K. (ed.) *Primates in Fragments: Ecology and Conservation*. New York: Kluwer Academic/Plenum Publishers, pp. 1–10.

Megantara, E. N. (1995). *Distribusi, habitat dan populasi Owa (Hylobates moloch: Cabrera 1930) di Cagar Alam Leuweung Sancang, Jawa Barat*. Bandung: Universitas Padjadjaran.

Meijerink, A. M. J. (1977). A hydrological reconnaissance survey of the Serayn river basin, Central Java. *I. T. C. Journal*, **4**, 646–73.

National Research Council (1981). *Techniques for the Study of Primate Population Ecology*. Washington, DC: National Academy Press.

Nijman, V. (2004). Conservation of the Javan gibbon (*Hylobates moloch*): population estimates, local extinctions, and conservation priorities. *The Raffles Bulletin of Zoology*, **52**(1), 271–80.

Nijman, V. (2005a). *In Full Swing: An Assessment of the Trade in Gibbons and Orang-utans on Java and Bali, Indonesia*. Petaling Jaya: TRAFFIC South-east Asia.

Nijman, V. (2005b). *Hanging in the Balance: An Assessment of Trade in Orang-utans and Gibbons in Kalimantan, Indonesia*. Petaling Jaya: TRAFFIC South-east Asia.

Nijman, V. (2010). An overview of international wildlife trade from Southeast Asia. *Biodiversity and Conservation*, **19**, 1101–14.

Odling-Smee, J. (2007). Niche inheritance: a possible basis for classifying multiple inheritance systems in evolution. *Biological Theory*, **2**(3), 276–89.

Odling-Smee, J., Laland, K. N. & Feldman, M. W. (2003). *Niche Construction: The Neglected Process in Evolution*. Princeton, NJ: Princeton University Press.

Pakpahan, H. (2003). Owa Jawa (*Hylobates moloch*: Cabrera 1930) menghilang dari Cagar Alam Leuweung Sancang. *Habitat*, **3**(1), 2–4.

Piersma, T. & Drent, J. (2003). Phenotypic flexibility and the evolution of organismal design. *Trends in Ecology and Evolution*, **18**, 228–33.

Ramos, A. R. (1990). Ethnology Brazilian style. *Cultural Anthropology*, **5**(4), 452–72.

Reichard, U. H., Ganpanakngan, M. & Barelli, C. (2012). White-handed gibbons of Khao Yai: social flexibility, complex reproductive strategies, and a slow life history. In Kappeler, P. & Watts, D. (eds) *Long-Term Field Studies of Primates*. Berlin: Springer, pp. 237–58.

Reisland, M. A. (2013). Conservation in a sacred forest: an integrated approach to assessing the management of a community-based conservation site. PhD Thesis, University of Wisconsin–Madison.

Reisland, M. A. & Lambert, J. E. (2016). Sympatric apes in sacred forests: shared space and habitat use by humans and endangered Javan gibbons (*Hylobates moloch*). *PLoS ONE*, **11**(1), e0146891.

Riley, E. P. & Fuentes, A. (2010). Conserving social-ecological systems in Indonesia: human–nonhuman primate interconnections in Bali and Sulawesi. *American Journal of Primatology*, **73**(1), 62–74.

Smiet, A. C. (1990). Forest ecology on Java: conversion and usage in a historical perspective. *Journal of Tropical Forest Science*, **2**, 286–302.

Sterck, E. H. M., Watts, D. P. & van Schaik, C. P. (1997). The evolution of female social relationships in nonhuman primates. *Behavioural Ecology and Sociobiology*, **41**, 291–309.

Struhsaker, T. T. (1997). *Ecology of an African Rainforest: Logging in Kibale and the Conflict Between Conservation and Exploitation*. Gainesville, FL: University of Florida Press.

Struhsaker, T. T. (1999). Primate communities in Africa: the consequences of long-term evolution or the artifact of recent hunting? In Fleagle, J. G., Janson, C. & Reed, K. E. (eds) *Primate Communities*. Cambridge: Cambridge University Press, pp. 289–94.

Strum, S. C. (2010). The development of primate raiding: implications for management and conservation. *International Journal of Primatology*, **31**, 133–56.

Supriatna, J. (2006). Conservation programs for the endangered Javan gibbon (*Hylobates moloch*). *Primate Conservation*, **21**, 155–62.

Supriatna, J., Mootnick, A. & Andayani, N. (2010). Javan gibbon (*Hylobates moloch*): population and conservation. In Gursky-Doyen, S. & Supriatna, J. (eds) *Indonesian Primates*. New York: Springer, pp. 57–72.

Thierry, B. (2008). Primate socioecology, the lost dream of ecological determinism. *Evolutionary Anthropology*, **17**, 93–6.

USAID (2004) *USAID Strategic Plan for Indonesia 2004–2008: Strengthening a Moderate, Stable, and Productive Indonesia.* Washington DC: USAID.

van Schaik, C. P. (1989). The ecology of social relationships amongst female primates. In Standen, V. & Foley, R. A. (eds) *Comparative Socioecology.* Oxford: Blackwell Scientific Publications, pp. 195–218.

van Schaik, C. P. & van Hooff, J. A. R. A. M. (1983). On the ultimate causes of primate social systems. *Behaviour*, 85, 91–117.

Wedana Adi Putra, I. M. & Jeffery, S. (2016). Reinforcing the Javan silvery gibbon population in the Mount Tilu Nature Reserve, West Java, Indonesia. Presentation poster at the XXVIth Congress of the International Primatological Society Chicago, IL, USA, August 21–27, 2016.

Wedana Adi Putra, I. M., Atmoko, S. S., Oktavinalis, H. & Setiawan, A. (2010). Survey on the abundance and distribution of Javan silvery gibbons and endemic langur species outside of national park areas in West Java and Central Java. The Aspinall Foundation Indonesia Program.

Wessing, R. (1993). A change in the forest: myth and history in West Java. *Journal of Southeast Asian Studies*, 24(1), 1–17.

Wessing, R. (2006). Symbolic animals in the land between the waters: markers of place and transition. *Asian Folklore Studies*, 65(2), 205–39.

West-Eberhardt, M. J. (2003). *Developmental Plasticity.* Oxford: Oxford University Press.

Whitten, T., Soeriaatmaddja, R. E. & Afiff, S. A. (1996). *The Ecology of Java and Bali.* North Clarendon, VT: Periplus Editions.

Wrangham, R. W. (1979). On the evolution of ape social systems. *Social Science Information*, 18, 335–69.

Wrangham, R. W. (1980). An ecological model of female-bonded primate groups. *Behaviour*, 75, 262–300.

3   Monitoring the Sanje Mangabey Population in Tanzania While Engaging the Local Community

David Fernández, Carolyn Ehardt and Gráinne McCabe

3.1   Personal Narrative

I (DF) have always liked animals. As a child, who doesn't? For a time, growing up, I almost exclusively read natural history books. I learned about animal diversity, evolution and behaviour. As the years passed, it became clear that what may have been a temporary phase for other children was much more than that for me. After finishing my primary education, I enrolled in Alcalá University (Spain), majoring in zoology. This was followed by the unique opportunity to participate in an expedition organised by the Bioko Biodiversity Protection Programme (BBPP) to survey primates in Bioko Island, Equatorial Guinea. After that, I continued my work with BBPP, leading various projects aimed at understanding and reducing the bushmeat trade in Bioko. Despite witnessing what is today one of the main drivers behind the decline in primate populations, what ultimately drove me into primatology was not the conservation of these animals, but the complexity of their social behaviour. As such, I enrolled in Stony Brook University's graduate programme in biological anthropology, where I set out to study female reproductive strategies.

I was looking for a species in which to conduct my research when I first heard about the Sanje mangabey. This species' highly female-biased sex ratio, conspicuous sexual swellings and mating calls perfectly suited my research interests. I immediately contacted Carolyn Ehardt, who, as discussed later in this chapter, had been working towards the conservation of the Sanje mangabey since 1994. Carolyn kindly invited me to join the Sanje Mangebey Project and study the habituated group of mangabeys she monitored (the Mizimu group). As it happens, at that time one of Carolyn's graduate students, Gráinne McCabe, was also about to start her PhD research. Just like me, Gráinne's interest in this species was not related to their conservation status but to their feeding ecology: Sanje mangabeys' complex and varied diet would be the perfect comparison to the capuchin monkeys she had previously studied in Costa Rica. So, in the autumn of 2008, Gráinne and I started collecting data for our doctoral research. These data included sexual and social behaviour, sexual swelling size, ovarian hormone levels, diet and feeding behaviour, energy balance and parasite infection levels. The longer we lived in the region, however, the more concerned we became about the future of this little-known species.

First, we learned about the conflict that existed between villagers and national park authorities. Since the Udzungwa Mountains National Park (UMNP) was established in 1992, local women (not men) had been allowed to enter the park once per week to collect firewood. This practice was to be stopped in 2011, when many villagers were already feeling animosity towards the national park because they saw the forest as rich in resources they needed but could no longer access. This resulted in protests and fires being set in the park in retaliation. In addition, conflicts between farmers and wildlife, particularly elephants and baboons, were on the rise due to crop raiding (Scheijen, 2014).

We also realised that, in addition to the existing gap in our own knowledge about this species, there was also a gap in the knowledge of people living alongside these animals in the communities surrounding the park, particularly school children. Soon after Gráinne and I started working in Tanzania, we became involved in a local environmental education programme run by the Udzungwa Ecological Monitoring Centre, a research station run by the Science Museum in Trento, Italy. As part of this involvement, we delivered talks about the Sanje mangabey to primary and secondary schools surrounding the UMNP. We quickly learned how little students knew about the animals living within the park. Many of them did not even know about the existence of the endemic Sanje mangabey. They had never seen one.

After a few months of fieldwork it became clear to us that if we wanted to ensure the long-term survival of this primate, we had to broaden our focus. It may have been theoretical questions and not conservation *per se* that drove us to this species, but we could not ignore the dire situation of the Sanje mangabey. We realised we had the responsibility to contribute to the conservation of this rare species, and that as scientists we were in a unique position to do so. Understanding the function of sexual swellings, or how energy balance affects reproduction, was not enough. We also needed data that would allow us – or other researchers in the future – to better understand the viability of the remaining population and how to address the growing breadth of threats facing this species.

In addition, we realised we had to ensure the continuous involvement of the local community in our efforts. This involvement would not only raise awareness of the mangabeys among villagers, it would also provide direct benefits, such as employment. Having a steady income from conservation and research in a region with an estimated 3.4 per cent annual population growth rate (Harrison, 2006), where most people rely on small-scale subsistence agriculture, but where available land is a scarce commodity (Harrison 2006; Kikula et al., 2003), could create a positive perception of the UMNP. It could also improve relationships with the UMNP author-ities, and transform the local viewpoint of the park into an opportunity to improve, rather than an impediment to, the villagers' livelihoods.

Thus, in addition to collecting those data we needed for our doctoral research, we started collecting data on the mangabey's reproductive biology and life-history. We also aimed to establish a long-term monitoring protocol for the Mizimu group. This monitoring would be conducted by a team of local assistants, who would be respon-sible for acquiring valuable information on group dynamics and demography, which can also affect population viability. Today, almost ten years since we started our PhD fieldwork, our long-term monitoring, combined with Carolyn's previous work, have yielded critical information – which will be discussed further in this chapter – that will enable the development of evidence-based conservation strategies for this species and other *Cercocebus* mangabeys. Equally important, our long-term work has allowed us to build a strong relationship with the local community.

3.2   Introduction

Contemporary conservation scientists are increasingly making use of mathematical modelling to forecast the efficacy of different management strategies, reintroduction programmes, and/or changes in ongoing conservation efforts (Beissinger, 2002; Sjögren-Gulve & Ebenhard, 2000). Such models rely on factors such as a species' life-history and reproductive biology, as well as individual dispersal patterns (Brook et al., 1999; Lacy, 1993). As such, gathering information on these parameters is a priority for species under threat of extinction (Brook et al., 2000).

Life-history is defined as the timing of the major phases of development and reproduction during the life of an organism, and includes variables such as age at maturation, gestation length, inter-birth interval, and longevity (Sadleir, 1969). Consistent monitoring of these factors allows researchers and conservation scientists to better understand a species' life-history evolution, to study and predict long-term population patterns, and to inform conservation and management strategies (Gilmore & Cook, 1981). For example, an analysis of the demographics of the critically endangered muriqui (*Brachyteles arachnoides*) in Minas Gerais, Brazil, revealed that in a 28-year period, the population experienced a five-fold increase, from 60 to almost 300 individuals (Strier & Ives, 2012). This change was due to a reduction in the muriquis' inter-birth interval, which translated into a steady increase in the females' fertility rate (Strier & Ives, 2012). Similarly, a comparison of population dynamics between mountain gorillas at Bwindi Impenetrable Forest and Virunga National Park found that the former had an inter-birth interval that was 17 per cent longer than the latter. Thus, Bwindi gorillas had lower female fertility and a slower population growth rate than gorillas at Virunga (Robbins et al., 2009). Conservation actions, therefore, must integrate knowledge of a species' habitat, life-history and reproductive biology in order to ensure population growth and prevent local population crashes or extinctions (Gilmore & Cook, 1981).

In primates, most data available on life-history have been collected on captive or provisioned populations (Martin, 2007) and thus may not reflect appropriate values for wild groups of the same species. These populations are nutritionally enhanced compared to wild ones, and nutrition is one of the most important variables affecting life-history traits in mammals (Ellison, 2003; Pusey et al., 1997). For example, Borries et al. (2001) compared two wild populations of the Hanuman langur (*Semnopithecus entellus*) with diets of differing nutritional quality – one provisioned and one non-provisioned. The provisioned population at Jodhpur matured earlier and had shorter gestation lengths, lactational periods and inter-birth intervals compared to the non-provisioned population at Ramnagar. Such observations emphasise the necessity of collecting data on reproductive and life-history characteristics from wild, non-provisioned populations whenever possible, to fully understand the viability of species in their natural habitats (Gilmore & Cook, 1981).

Collecting life-history data from wild populations is not an easy task. Such work requires long-term projects, with data collected on the basis of individual recognition, and consistent, systematic, year-round monitoring. Thus, there remain limited data on life-history parameters from wild, non-provisioned populations of many primate taxa. For *Cercocebus* mangabeys, this information is scarce. Currently, out of the seven extant species of *Cercocebus*, life-history information is only available for three: the Tana River mangabey (*C. galeritus*), mainly from the work of Karen Homewood in the 1970s and Margaret Kinnaird in the 1990s (Homewood, 1975; Kinnaird, 1990; Kinnaird & O'Brien, 1991), the sooty mangabey (*C. atys*) (Range et al., 2007) and recent work by our team on the Sanje mangabey (Fernández et al., 2014).

Aspects of dispersal, such as the ability to disperse among groups and populations, sex-biased dispersal and the percentage of individuals that disperse, may also affect the long-term survival of a species (Lacy, 1993). Dispersal enables regular gene flow between groups and across a population, increasing heterozygosity and maintaining a level of genetic variance that allows the species to respond to changes in the environment (Lacy, 1997). Accordingly, animals' inability to move between populations, such as in fragmented habitats and human-dominated landscapes, can decrease genetic variability (Charpentier et al., 2007). For example, a study on a population of spider monkeys (*Ateles geoffroyi*) in Nicaragua found that the reduction in gene flow caused by deforestation resulted in a significantly lower than expected level of heterozygosity, a reduction in genetic diversity, and an increase in the risk of inbreeding (Hagell et al., 2013). This, in turn, may increase neonatal and infant mortality, and ultimately lower recruitment and population growth (Charpentier et al., 2007).

Sex-biased dispersal can also have an effect on the risk of extirpation for a population. Frequent male dispersal, for example, translates into higher genetic variation within groups and lower variation between groups (Pope, 1992; Whitlock & McCauley, 1990), reducing the risk of inbreeding. Accordingly, low levels of male dispersal caused by fragmentation could lead to higher levels of inbreeding in the population. Female dispersal, however, does not always contribute to the long-term survival of a species. On the one hand, female dispersal is beneficial because it can homogenise a population's genetic structure and reduce the risk of inbreeding depression, while female philopatry leads to low within-group variation and high genetic isolation by distance (Melnick & Kidd, 1983; Whitlock & McCauley, 1990; Wright, 1943). On the other hand, an increase in female dispersal due to ecological factors, such as limiting resources (Dittus, 1988), can negatively affect population growth due to dispersal costs (Alberts & Altmann, 1995; Isbell & Van Vuren, 1996). For example, in chimpanzees (*Pan troglodytes schweinfurthii*) and Thomas langurs (*Presbytis thomasi*), females that dispersed gave birth to their first infant later in life than did females that remained in their natal group (Pusey et al., 1997; Sterck 1997). The costs of dispersal for females may be particularly acute in species in which females rely on kin for support (Perry et al., 2008).

Prior to our work, the Sanje mangabey (*Cercocebus sanjei*), an endangered primate endemic to the Udzungwa Mountains of Tanzania, typified the common problem faced by primate researchers trying to assess a species' viability: a lack of information on behaviour and reproductive parameters. Despite having been first described in 1979 (Homewood & Rodgers, 1981), when Carolyn Ehardt set off in 1994 to start the first systematic study on this species, even baseline information such as distribution and relative abundance was lacking for this mangabey (Ehardt 2001; Ehardt et al., 2005). With the help of fellow primatologists and a botanist – Tom Butynski, Tom Struhsaker and Quentin Luke – Carolyn conducted multi-year field surveys throughout the fragmented forests of the Udzungwa Mountains to determine the distribution of this species (Ehardt et al., 1999; 2001). That work, combined with that of Danish researchers working in the area (Dinesen et al., 2001), revealed that the Sanje mangabey population (estimated to be *c.*1350–1500 animals; Dinesen et al., 2001; Ehardt et al., 2005) was divided into two isolated subpopulations separated by over 60 km of fire-maintained grassland. The largest population (60 per cent) was in Mwanihana Forest, within the relatively well-protected UMNP. The other subpopulation was confirmed to reside within what was then known as the Udzungwa Scarp Forest Reserve, characterised by virtually no active protection on the ground (Rovero et al., 2010), and with illegal logging and hunters with dogs encountered regularly during surveys (Ehardt et al., 1999; 2005). This area has recently been elevated to a nature reserve, although it remains without active protection.

Efforts to locate the subpopulation once believed to reside in the West Kilombero Scarp forests outside of the UMNP were never successful. Continued work by Carolyn and her team eventually 'discovered' a completely new species of primate, the kipunji (*Rungwecebus kipunji*) in Ndundulu Forest in this area (contemporaneously 'discovered' in the Southern Highlands of Tanzania by T. Davenport and his associates), which may have been erroneously identified as Sanje mangabeys by ornithologists working in this area during the 1990s (Ehardt & Butynski, 2006a; Jones et al., 2005). As such, it became known that the entire population of the Sanje mangabey was small and restricted to only two subpopulations with no gene flow presumed to be occurring.

The concerns raised by these initial surveys led to the assessment of the Sanje mangabey as endangered on the IUCN Red List (Ehardt et al., 2008), and its inclusion in the *World's 25 Most Endangered Primates* list from the publication's inception in 2000 through 2006 (Ehardt & Butynski, 2006b). Also, in acknowledgement of the mounting conservation concern for this primate, and recognising that sound and comprehensive scientific data are requisite to the conservation of threatened species, Carolyn habituated a study group of Sanje mangabeys in 2004 (Ehardt et al., 2005). This group, known as the Mizimu Group, was located within the Mwanihana Forest in the UMNP. In the ensuing years, data were collected on their basic ecology, including diet and ranging patterns (Ehardt et al., 2005), followed by more systematic studies of their behaviour, reproductive biology, physiology, ecology and demography (Fernández 2017; Fernández et al., 2014; 2017; McCabe & Emery Thompson,

2013; McCabe et al., 2013), laying the foundation for subsequent, more focused research and providing further support for Tanzania's conservation efforts (Ehardt et al., 2005).

Given the critical importance of reproduction and dispersal to assessing the viability of a threatened species such as the Sanje mangabey, we herein report updated life-history, reproductive and demographic data from our ongoing research with this species. To augment our previously reported reproductive parameters (Fernández et al., 2014), we update the species' postpartum amenorrhoea and inter-birth intervals using additional data and new analytical procedures. We also report on the patterns of male group membership and dispersal, as well as the occurrence of temporary female transfer. We conclude by identifying how our results can guide our long-term research and inform conservation efforts for this endangered primate.

3.3   Methods

3.3.1   Study Site and Subjects

This study was conducted on a habituated group of Sanje mangabeys inhabiting the UMNP, Tanzania. The UMNP consists of a mosaic habitat of tropical sub-montane evergreen and deciduous primary and secondary forest, interspersed with open areas maintained by elephant activity (Ehardt et al., 2005; Lovett, 1993). Rainfall averages 1750 mm/year (Lovett, 1993), peaking at 1650 mm between November and May (McCabe & Emery Thompson, 2013). Sanje mangabeys give birth throughout the year, although they show a peak between July and September (McCabe & Emery Thompson, 2013; McCabe et al., 2013). Cycling females develop an exaggerated sexual swelling that becomes shinier in appearance immediately before deflation (Fernández et al., 2017). It is during this shiny phase when ovulation is most likely to occur (Fernández et al., 2014). The Mizumu Group was habituated in 2004 – when it was composed of c.36 individuals – and has been followed regularly ever since (Ehardt et al., 2005; Fernández et al., 2017; McCabe & Emery Thompson, 2013). This group varied in size from 63 to over 70 individuals during data collection for this chapter, and included 6–10 adult males, 18–20 adult females, as well as adolescents, juveniles and infants. All adult individuals were identifiable using scars and/or facial colouration.

3.3.2   Data Collection

Data were collected by DF, GMM and our team of local Tanzanian field assistants. Some of these assistants have worked with the Mizimu Group since it was first habituated, thus know the study subjects very well, and over the years have become highly proficient in data collection methodology. From September 2008 through November 2011, the group was followed on a monthly basis, between 4 and 31 days per month (mean: 19.5 ± 8.4, range: 4–31 days). After November 2011, the group was followed for between four and nine days per month. Unfortunately, due to gaps in funding, group follows were suspended intermittently, from December 2011 through August 2012, from August 2013 through November 2014, and from June 2015 through June 2016. In this chapter we include data collected through full-day group follows from September 2008 through December 2014 ($N = 819$ follow days collected over 51 months). Not all data were included for every analysis.

Each day we followed the group, we conducted a census of all adult individuals and nursing infants, recording any new immigrants, the presence of new-born infants and disappearances of individuals. We also recorded sexual swelling size for all adult females and *ad libitum* sexual behaviour of all adults. Sexual swelling size was recorded using a nine-point visual scale (Fernández et al., 2017). We used this information to calculate the length of postpartum amenorrhoea and inter-birth intervals, as well as to examine group dynamics and dispersal patterns.

3.3.3   Reproductive Parameters

We defined postpartum amenorrhoea as the number of days from the date of birth to the last day before the onset of the next sexual swelling (Altmann et al., 1977; Fernández et al., 2014). We only included females that resumed cycling when their previous infant was still alive. In cases when females resumed cycling during a non-observational day ($n = 3$), we estimated the onset of the sexual swelling as the middle day between the last observation day and the first day the female was observed with a swelling.

We defined inter-birth interval as the number of days between two consecutive parturitions, and these were calculated for surviving and non-surviving infants separately. As with postpartum amenorrhoea, the date of birth of infants born during non-observation days ($n = 3$) was estimated as the middle day between the last day the female was observed without the infant and the first day the infant was observed. The date of birth for infants present at the beginning of the monitoring project ($n = 6$) was estimated based on the infant's degree of independence from the mother and their motor skills (Fernández et al., 2014).

3.3.4   Data Treatment and Analyses

We used Kaplan–Meier survival analysis to investigate the duration of inter-birth intervals and male group tenure. Survival analysis permits the inclusion of cases for which we did not know the complete duration of an event, such as the time between two consecutive births, because the female had not given birth yet by the end of the study period. Such cases in which an event has not occurred to complete an interval by the end of the study are termed 'censored', compared to complete cases, also known as 'uncensored'. Results of the survival analysis are presented as survival curves, indicating the proportion of completed cases at each time interval. Patterns of male group arrival were analysed using circular statistics. We examined whether males were more likely to enter the group at certain times of the year using Rao's Spacing Test of Uniformity (Rao, 1972). Values were transformed into months by dividing them by 30.4 (1 month = 30.4 days). All statistical analyses were conducted in R version 3.3.2 for Windows (R Core Team, 2017) using the Survival (Therneau, 2015) and Circular (Agostinelli & Lund, 2013) packages. Tests were two-tailed and evaluated with an alpha level of 0.05.

3.4   Results/Interpretation

3.4.1   Postpartum Amenorrhoea

To calculate postpartum amenorrhoea, we include data from the start of the study (September 2008) up to 26 August 2011 (n = 39 months), which yielded five additional complete cases beyond those previously analysed (Fernández et al., 2014). On average, females resumed developing sexual swellings 6.5 ± 2.0 months after giving birth (range = 3.8–13.3 months; n = 20 cases).

3.4.2   Inter-Birth Interval

From September 2008 through December 2014, we recorded a total of 54 births: 24 females, 18 males and 12 sex unknown. We were able to calculate inter-birth intervals for all infants born between September 2008 and November 2011 (n = 41 infants). Of these 41 infants, 24 survived and 17 died. For females with surviving infants, we had complete (uncensored) inter-birth interval durations for 13 cases, and 11 (censored) cases in which the female had not given birth by the end of the study period. The Kaplan–Meier estimator yielded a median inter-birth interval of 24.1 months (95 per cent confidence interval of 17.8–44.3 months, n = 24 infants; Figure 3.1).

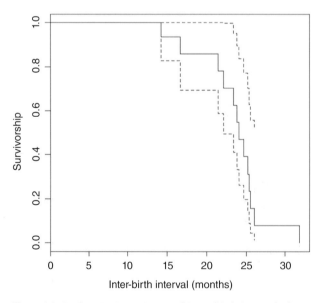

Figure 3.1. Kaplan–Meier estimate of inter-birth intervals for surviving infants.

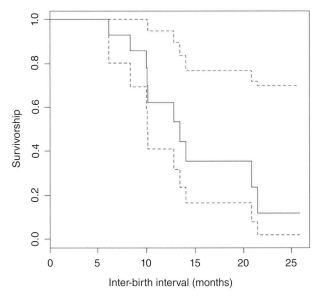

Figure 3.2. Kaplan–Meier estimate of inter-birth intervals for non-surviving infants.

Of the 17 cases in which the previous infant had not survived, we had ten complete (uncensored) and seven incomplete (censored) cases. The Kaplan–Meier estimator of inter-birth intervals for non-surviving infants yielded a median duration of 13.5 months (95 per cent confidence interval: 10.3–24.7 months; $n = 17$ infants; Figure 3.2).

3.4.3   Male Membership and Male Tenure

Over the course of the study period, 23 adult males were members of the group. Six males were present at the start of the study (September 2008), while at least 17 arrived (and some subsequently left) over the following six years (last documented arrivals with known date occurred on 1 April 2013). Of those 17 males, the exact arrival date was known for 13. The timing of arrivals was uniformly distributed throughout the year (Rao's Spacing Test of Uniformity = 139.4, level 0.05, critical value = 167.9; $n = 13$ males) (Figure 3.3), although no males joined in June, July or August (Figure 3.3).

We were able to calculate the length of group membership for seven males that arrived during the study. We used the Kaplan–Meier estimator to calculate the median length of group tenure, using seven complete (uncensored) and five incomplete (censored) records. Adult males remained in the group a median of 41.8 months (3.5 years) (range: 0.6–57.5 months, 95 per cent confidence interval: 33.1–80.1 months; $n = 12$ males) (Figure 3.4).

3.4.4   Female Transfer

During the study, we observed three confirmed temporary female transfers: one by a resident female, and two by non-resident females. The resident female disappeared

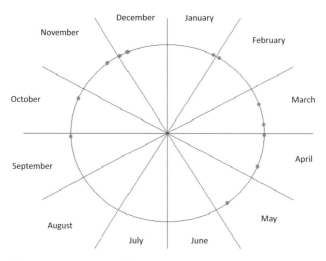

Figure 3.3. Distribution of adult male arrivals, marked as a grey dot, in the study group. All dots indicate the arrival of one adult male, except for the arrival in November, in which two males joined the group simultaneously. Dates of arrivals were not significantly different from an even distribution.

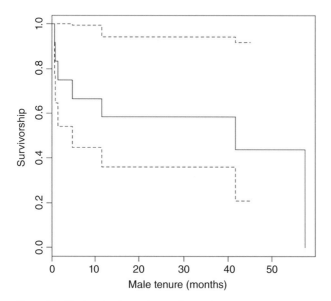

Figure 3.4. Kaplan–Meier estimate for male group tenure.

on 20 October 2009 while she was displaying a sexual swelling in maximum tumescence. She was not seen for 31 days, until she re-entered the group on 20 November 2009. Immediately preceding her return, we heard a neighbouring group in the vicinity. When she re-entered the group, she also was displaying a swelling in maximum tumescence in the shiny phase, which is when females of this species are most likely to ovulate. She maintained the sexual swelling at maximum tumescence for 22 consecutive days, during which time she eventually conceived. Back-counting from the day of birth to the likely day of conception using the average gestation length for this species indicated that this female conceived after her return.

The two non-resident females that joined the group did so only for short periods of time. On 20 April 2010 an unknown adult female with a swelling in maximum tumescence was seen within the study group. She remained with the group for 25 consecutive days. She was last seen on 4 May 2010. During that time, the female was not observed mating. She was observed menstruating eight days after her arrival, and she disappeared when her swelling again was increasing in size, indicating that it was very unlikely that she conceived during her time in the study group. The second non-resident female was observed within the group for only one day on 13 January 2010. She also displayed a swelling with maximum tumescence when she was first seen; it is therefore possible that she was ovulating. It is not known if she mated during her time with the group.

3.5   Discussion

Understanding the basic life-history and reproductive biology of a species is vital to their long-term conservation. In this chapter, we updated the postpartum amenorrhoea and inter-birth interval for the Sanje mangabey to better inform conservation efforts of this endangered primate. Our updated value for the period of postpartum amenorrhoea for Sanje mangabeys (6.5 ± 2.0 months) is similar to our previous estimate of 6.7 months (Fernández et al., 2014). As this value is relatively short compared to other mangabeys in captivity, and to related cercopithecine primates (reviewed by Fernández et al., 2014), we previously argued that it may have been influenced by a male takeover that occurred during our study (Fernández, 2017; Fernández et al., 2014). In particular, females may have developed deceptive swellings by which they advertised sexual receptivity and ovulation at a time when conception was highly unlikely – such as when females have a dependent offspring – in order to minimise the risk of infanticide (e.g. Colmenares & Gomendio, 1988; Zinner & Deschner, 2000). One consequence of such a strategy is the shortening of females' postpartum amenorrhoea. During our current study, there was another takeover in June 2011 by a male that first appeared in March of that year. Three of the new females incorporated in the dataset for this chapter started swelling in March 2011, at approximately the same time the male, who would later become the alpha, joined the group. This finding would support our deceptive swelling hypothesis. The other two females included in the dataset used here, however, started developing their swellings in January and February 2011, before the arrival of the future alpha male. Thus, although the results presented here provide further evidence that at least some females may use deceptive swellings as a reproductive strategy, we still need a better understanding of the relationship between male arrival, male takeovers and female reproductive characteristics to confirm whether females are indeed developing deceptive swellings, as well as the effectiveness of this strategy on female fitness.

We found a median inter-birth interval considerably longer than our previous calculation of 20.0 months (Fernández et al., 2014). The updated value, however, is similar to the average inter-birth interval reported for other wild *Cercocebus* (24 months), and longer than values from captive individuals (20.3 ± 2.2 months, reviewed by Fernández et al., 2014). This updated result suggests that the Sanje mangabey population in the UMNP may not be growing as fast as the previously reported inter-birth interval of 20 months would suggest, but that it is doing so at a rate that we would expect in a wild setting.

Currently, it is not possible to extrapolate this value to the subpopulation of Sanje mangabeys inhabiting the Udzungwa Scarp Nature Reserve (USNR). The forests of USNR shows significant levels of human disturbance compared to the Mwanihana Forest (Rovero et al., 2012), where the study group resides, and research shows that habitat quality can affect the viability of primate populations (Skorupa, 1986; Struhsaker, 1999). A study on the closely related Tana River mangabey (*C. galeritus*) found that increasing forest disturbance was related to the decline in that species' numbers (Medley, 1993), and there is evidence that the subpopulation of Sanje mangabeys in the USNR has declined over the last decade (Rovero et al., 2012). A comparison of inter-birth intervals and other life-history parameters for Sanje mangabeys inhabiting the USNR with values from the study population would help elucidate whether both subpopulations have the same potential for growth, and whether additional conservation measures are needed in the USNR.

Our long-term study has also allowed us to confirm that Sanje mangabeys follow the characteristic cercopithecine pattern of male-biased dispersal (Campbell et al., 2011). Male Sanje mangabeys regularly transfer between groups upon reaching maturity. What remains unclear, however, is whether any dispersal is possible between the two subpopulations of the species. Given that the subpopulation living within the UMNP is relatively well protected and there is no evidence of targeted hunting of Sanje mangabeys (Fernández and McCabe, personal observation), we expect that males are able to transfer among groups in the national park. The subpopulation in the USNR, on the other hand, is threatened by human encroachment, habitat destruction and possibly hunting (Ehardt et al., 1999; 2005; Rovero et al., 2010; 2012). All of these anthropogenic factors have led to a significant decline, to near-extinction levels, for the populations of two colobines in the USNR (Rovero et al., 2015), as well as a drop in the population of Sanje mangabeys and Syke's monkeys (Rovero et al., 2012). In addition, these factors may also interfere with males' dispersal abilities, and hence increase their risk of inbreeding (Hagell et al., 2013). More importantly, given that the subpopulations are separated by over 60 km of agricultural land, it is very unlikely that individuals could freely transfer between subpopulations. No, or little, gene flow between the subpopulations could produce low levels of heterozygosity that could impact the adaptability of the subpopulations to future changes in their environment (Lacy, 1997); a factor we are currently examining. Furthermore, confirmation that the subpopulations are effectively isolated would highlight the need to take legislative actions to manage the land between UMNP and USNR to increase connectivity between them, and to increase the level of protection of the USNR to halt the existing threats.

We have also confirmed at least three cases of temporary female transfer in this species, which adds to the body of evidence suggesting that primate dispersal patterns may be more complex than previously thought (e.g. Jack & Isbell, 2009). Our observations also suggest that adult females may occasionally transfer between groups permanently, rather than just temporarily as we report here. In all three cases of temporary transfer that we documented, females transferred during the period of maximum tumescence, when ovulation occurs (Fernández et al., 2014). It is possible that females are using their swellings as 'passports' during group transfer, potentially minimising aggression and increasing acceptance by males in the new group (Deschner & Boesch, 2007; Pusey, 1979). It is unclear why some females may decide to leave their natal group, given that group transfers impose costs to individuals, including an increased risk of predation, loss of allies, aggression in the new group and unfamiliarity with a new home range (Alberts & Altmann, 1995; Isbell & Van Vuren, 1996). Female Sanje mangabeys display linear dominance hierarchies (McCabe & Emery Thompson, 2013); thus, it is possible that low-ranking females are more likely to disperse to try to reduce the costs associated with being subordinate in their natal group, which could include aggression, lack of access to quality resources and/or little preferential mate choice (Crockett, 1984; Moore, 1984; Watts, 1990). In the case of Sanje mangabeys, the shortest inter-birth interval was displayed by the alpha female, suggesting that rank in this species may be correlated with reproductive success. Furthermore, the resident female that left the group for over 30 days was one of the lowest-ranking females (Fernández and McCabe, unpublished data); thus, it is possible that her low position in the dominance hierarchy was the driving factor behind her transfer attempt. Alternatively, rather than true transfer attempts, females may be 'visiting' other groups to try to mate with neighbouring males. As we have shown in this chapter, male transfer is relative common in this species; thus, it is likely that these neighbouring males may eventually join the females' group. Temporarily leaving the resident group and mating with neighbouring males, therefore, may not be an attempt to transfer between groups, but an infanticide-avoidance strategy (Palombit, 2015).

If occasional female dispersal occurs in Sanje mangabeys, this could potentially affect the conservation of this species. First, dispersing females are exposed to higher predation risk (Alberts & Altmann, 1995), and there is evidence that Sanje mangabeys are occasionally predated upon (Jones et al., 2006; Fernández and McCabe, unpublished). Alternatively, female dispersal could homogenise the population genetic structure, decreasing the pronounced between-group genetic variation that characterises female philopatric species (Melnick & Hoelzer, 1996; Whitlock & McCauley, 1990). For example, a recent study on the Tana River mangabey, a species characterised by female philopatry and male dispersal, found that this species had higher between-group genetic variation than expected, which could have negative consequences for the survival of this species (Mbora & McPeek, 2015). Currently, however, there is no evidence that female Tana River mangabeys disperse (Wieczkowski & Butynski, 2013). Female dispersal in Sanje mangabeys, albeit rare, may therefore reduce between-group genetic variation and the risk of inbreeding depression. Further investigation would be required, however, to establish whether females entering new groups actually rise in rank relative to their position in their former group, whether this transfer negatively affects females' reproductive success, and the consequences this behaviour may have on the conservation of this species.

3.6   Future Directions/Conclusion

Since the Sanje Mangabey Project was established, we have made great strides in improving our knowledge of the behaviour, ecology and conservation status of this species. We are now able to compare key life-history and reproductive parameters, such as gestation length, postpartum amenorrhoea, inter-birth interval and infant survival, with related species (Fernández et al., 2014; McCabe & Fernández, in press). Such comparisons can significantly contribute to estimations of potential reproductive rates for this species until more specific measures become available. Central to our future research will be data on life expectancy, age at first reproduction and number of surviving infants produced per female, permitting more informed estimations of population viability for this endangered primate.

Since the very inception of the project, we have engaged with Tanzanian colleagues to foster capacity transfer, support educational opportunities (in one case, supporting completion of a Master's degree), and provide continuous employment opportunities for a small (currently three, but we employed up to nine Tanzanians during David's and Gráinne's PhD field research) but extremely dedicated team of local assistants. Their work has not only made our research possible, it has also contributed to raising awareness about this species and the importance of the UMNP among the local community. They now share stories about their monthly trips into the park, and the animals they study, with their families and friends in the village. Moreover, the research, observational and professional skills that they have attained through their work with the project have presented opportunities for additional employment by other researchers working in the area when not working on our project, including research led by the Udzungwa Ecological Monitoring Centre (UEMC), three other PhD projects and various MSc projects. One of them was even recruited by Tanzanian National Parks to become a park ranger.

Our strategic plan for the project is to continue the long-term monitoring of the Mizimu Group, particularly in regards to the demography and life-history data for this species. We aim to use this information to conduct a population viability analysis. In June 2017, we started a population-wide survey of the Sanje mangabey, as the previous and only census attempt was based on surveys conducted more than 15 years ago (Ehardt et al., 1999; 2005). During the new survey, we also intend to collect samples to assess the genetic structure of the population to examine heterozygosity, gene flow between the two subpopulations and the risk of inbreeding depression. These molecular data, in conjunction with the updated census and our continued accumulation of reproductive and demographic data, will sustain the ongoing efforts to generate evidence-driven conservation action plans for this species, in collaboration with Tanzanian government authorities and policy makers.

Finally, we aim to continue raising awareness of the biodiversity of the Udzungwas among the local community, particularly school children. Since 2009, we have been working with Msalise Primary School. In 2008, Msalise was the school that performed the poorest in environmental education evaluations undertaken by the UEMC. The school also lacked basic resources, such as running water and electricity. It has a very low teacher to student ratio: six teachers for 600 students, a situation that is further exacerbated given that during the rainy season the road to the school floods and some teachers are not able or willing to go to work. When we began our engagement with this school, we met Mwalimu Ahmed Churi, who is exceptionally invested in education as a means of fostering a brighter future for local children. Recognising the importance of education for the future of children, Mwalimu Churi approached us to ask for help to improve the library, which at the time was in poor condition and had hardly any books. He produced a detailed budget of what was needed and with great help from our friends and families, we were able to raise the funds needed to improve the structure of the library, stock it with books and install solar panels on the school. Now Msalise School is the only source of electricity in the area, and consequently is able to hold evening study sessions and even provide a space for the town council to hold official meetings. The school also organised a phone-charging business; for a small fee, villagers have a place to charge their phones, and the money raised is used to maintain the library and buy supplies for the students. The funds also provided a computer, printer and projector, which they use to show videos and documentaries to the students. As part of future engagements with the school, we plan to assist in the building of a residential house for the teachers on site to minimise teacher absenteeism during the rainy season, and to provide support to expand the school's farm so that teachers can provide one daily porridge meal to students. Such a practice is common in Tanzania, and Msalise's teachers have reported that many students are hungry during classes, compromising their ability to fully focus during the lessons.

More than 20 years ago, when Carolyn set out to study one of the least known primates at the time, she did so with the conviction that effective conservation rests on thorough, scientific research, and that scientists studying threatened primates have an obligation to use our work to foster their long-term conservation. Though the work of David and Gráinne was initially driven by theoretical concepts in reproductive biology and ecology, we quickly adopted Carolyn's principles. We realised that our approach had to be quite different if we wanted to have a real impact on the long-term survival of Sanje mangabeys. This included a more conservation-focused approach to our research, as well as a commitment to work alongside the local community such that they can see the tangible benefits of the national park and the presence of researchers. Ultimately, this work has influenced our identities as researchers and we now self-identify as conservation biologists rather than simply biologists.

Acknowledgements

The Sanje Mangabey Project was initially established and sustained by funding support to CE and her collaborators from (in alphabetical order): British Airways; Conservation, Food and Health Foundation; Conservation International; Critical

Ecosystem Partnership Fund; Margot Marsh Biodiversity Foundation; National Science Foundation; Primate Action Fund; Primate Conservation, Inc.; Primate Society of Great Britain; University of Georgia Research Foundation and Office of the Dean of the Franklin College; Wildlife Conservation Society; WWF-Tanzania; and Zoo Atlanta. Additional support to DF and GM was provided by Primate Conservation Inc., Mohammed bin Zayed Species Conservation Fund, National Science Foundation-DDIG, the Leakey Foundation, Margot Marsh Biodiversity Foundation, Sigma Xi, Ideal Wild, and Wildlife Direct. Logistical support has been provided over the years by the park wardens and staff of UMNP, Francesco Rovero, Arafat Mtui, and other staff members of the Udzungwa Ecological Monitoring Centre, the Conservation Resource Centre, Guillaume Pages, Emily Lloyd and Mr Hilary Biduga. Data collection would not have been possible without the extraordinary support of the numerous assistants who have collaborated in the project over the years, particularly Yahaya Sama, Bakari Ponda and Loy 'Babu' Loishoki for the data central to this chapter. Other assistants who have contributed to data collection are Aniceth Alchard, Saidi Amili, Alli Chitita, Aloyce Kisoma, Richard Laizzer, Amos Lumage, Francis Masinde, the late Amani Mahundu, Athumani Mndeme, Clever Ngatwika, Salimini Saidi and Baraka Sehaba.

References

Agostinelli, C. & Lund, U. (2013). R package 'circular': circular statistics. Available at: https://r-forge.r-project.org/projects/circular.

Alberts, S. C. & Altmann, J. (1995). Balancing costs and opportunities: dispersal in male baboons. *The American Naturalist*, 145, 279–306.

Altmann, J., Altmann, S. A., Hausfater, G. & McCuskey, S. (1977). Life history of yellow baboons: physical development, reproductive parameters, and infant mortality. *Primates*, 18, 315–30.

Beissinger, S. R. (2002). Population viability analysis. In Beissinger, S. R. & McCullough, D. R. (eds) *Population Viability Analysis: Past, Present, Future*. Chicago, IL: University of Chicago Press, pp. 5–17.

Borries, C., Koenig, A. & Winkler, P. (2001). Variation of life history traits and mating patterns in female langur monkeys (*Semnopithecus entellus*). *Behavioral Ecology and Sociobiology*, 50, 391–402.

Brook, B. W., Cannon, J. R., Lacy, R. C., Mirande, C. & Frankham, R. (1999). Comparison of the population viability analysis packages GAPPS, INMAT, RAMAS and VORTEX for the whooping crane (*Grus americana*). *Animal Conservation*, 2, 23–31.

Brook, B. W., O'Grady, J. J., Chapman, A. P., et al. (2000). Predictive accuracy of population viability analysis in conservation biology. *Nature*, 404, 385–7.

Campbell, C. J., Fuentes, A., Mackinnon, K. C., Bearder, S. K. & Stumpf, R. M. (2011). *Primates in Perspective*, 2nd edn. New York: Oxford University Press.

Charpentier, M. J. E., Widdig, A. & Alberts, S. C. (2007). Inbreeding depression in non-human primates: a historical review of methods used and empirical data. *American Journal of Primatology*, 69, 1370–86.

Colmenares, F. & Gomendio, M. (1988). Changes in female reproductive condition following male takeovers in a colony of hamadryas and hybrid baboons. *Folia Primatologica*, 50, 157–74.

Crockett, C. M. (1984). Emigration by female red howler monkeys and the case for female competition. In Small, M. F. (ed.) *Female Primates: Studies by Women Primatologists*. New York: Alan R. Liss., Inc., pp. 159–73.

Deschner, T. & Boesch, C. (2007). Can the patterns of sexual swelling cycles in female Taï chimpanzees be explained by the cost-of-sexual-attraction hypothesis? *International Journal of Primatology*, **28**, 389–406.

Dinesen, L., Lehmberg, T., Rahner, M. C. & Fjeldsa, J. (2001). Conservation priorities for the forests of the Udzungwa Mountains, Tanzania, based on primates, duikers and birds. *Biological Conservation*, **99**, 223–36.

Dittus, W. P. J. (1988). Group fission among wild toque macaques as a consequence of female resource competition and environmental stress. *Animal Behaviour*, **36**, 1626–45.

Ehardt, C. L. (2001). The endemic primates of the Udzungwa Mountains, Tanzania. *African Primates*, **4**, 15–26.

Ehardt, C. L. & Butynski, T. M. (2006a). The recently described highland mangabey *Lophocebus kipunji* (Cercopithecoidea, Cercopithicinae): current knowledge and conservation assessment. *Primate Conservation*, **21**, 81–88.

Ehardt, C. L. & Butynski, T. M. (2006b). Sanje mangabey, *Cercocebus sanjei* (Mittermeier, 1986). In Mittermeier, R. A., Valladares-Padua, C., Rylands, A. B., et al. (eds) *Primates in Peril: The World's 25 Most Endangered Primates 2004–2006*. Washington, DC: IUCN Species Survival Commission.

Ehardt, C. L., Struhsaker, T. T. & Butynski, T. M. (1999). Conservation of the endangered primates of the Udzungwa Mountains, Tanzania: surveys, habitat assessment, and long-term monitoring. Unpublished report to Margot Marsh Biodiversity Foundation, Conservation International.

Ehardt, C. L., Butynski, T. M. & Struhsaker, T. T. (2001). Conservation of the endangered endemic primates of the Udzungwa Mountains, Tanzania, phase II: population survey and census, demography, and socioecology. Unpublished report to Margot Marsh Biodiversity Foundation, Conservation International.

Ehardt, C. L., Jones, T. P. & Butynski, T. M. (2005). Protective status, ecology and strategies for improving conservation of *Cercocebus sanjei* in the Udzungwa Mountains, Tanzania. *International Journal of Primatology*, **26**, 557–83.

Ehardt, C. L., Butynski, T. M. & Struhsaker, T. T. (2008). *Cercocebus sanjei*. IUCN 2008. IUCN Red List of Threatened Species. Version 2012.2. Available at: www.iucnredlist.org (accessed 27 January 2013).

Ellison, P. T. (2003). Energetics and reproductive effort. *American Journal of Human Biology*, **15**, 342–51.

Fernández, D. (2017). Consequences of a male takeover on mating skew in wild Sanje mangabeys. *American Journal of Primatology*, **79**, e22532.

Fernández, D., Doran-Sheehy, D., Borries, C. & Brown, J. L. (2014). Reproductive characteristics of wild Sanje mangabeys (*Cercocebus sanjei*). *American Journal of Primatology*, **76**, 1163–74.

Fernández, D., Doran-Sheehy, D., Borries, C. & Ehardt, C. L. (2017). Exaggerated sexual swellings and the probability of conception in wild Sanje mangabeys (*Cercocebus sanjei*). *International Journal of Primatology*, **38**, 513–32.

Gilmore, D. & Cook, B. (1981). *Environmental Factors in Mammal Reproduction*. London: Palgrave Macmillan.

Hagell, S., Whipple, A. V. & Chambers, C. L. (2013). Population genetic patterns among social groups of the endangered Central American spider monkey (*Ateles geoffroyi*) in a human-dominated landscape. *Ecology and Evolution*, **3**, 1388–99.

Harrison, P. (2006). *Socio-Economic Study of Forest-Adjacent Communities from Nyanganje Forest to Udzungwa Scarp: A Potential Wildlife Corridor*. Dar es Salaam: World Wide Fund for Nature. Available at: www.cepf.net/Documents/wwf_5fudzungwas.pdf (accessed 2 September 2017).

Homewood, K. (1975). Monkey on a riverbank. *Natural History*, **84**, 68–73.

Homewood, K. & Rodgers, W. A. (1981). A previously undescribed mangabey from Southern Tanzania. *International Journal of Primatology*, **2**, 47–55.

Isbell, L. A. & Van Vuren, D. (1996). Differential costs of locational and social dispersal and their consequences for female group-living primates. *Behaviour*, **133**, 1–36.

Jack, K. & Isbell, L. (2009). Dispersal in primates: advancing an individualized approach. *Behaviour,* **146,** 429–36.

Jones, T., Ehardt, C. L., Butynski, T. M., et al. (2005). The highland mangabey *Lophocebus kipunji*: a new species of African monkey. *Science,* **308,** 1161–4.

Jones, T., Mselewa, L. S. & Mtui, A. (2006). Sanje mangabey *Cercocebus sanjei* kills an African crowned eagle *Stephanoaetus coronatus*. *Folia Primatologica,* **77,** 359–63.

Kikula, I. S., Mnzava, E. Z. & Mung'ong'o, C. G. (2003). *Shortcomings of Linkages Between Environmental Conservation Initiatives and Poverty Alleviation in Tanzania*. Dar es Salaam: Research on Poverty Alleviation. Available at: www.repoa.or.tz/documents/03.2_-_Kikula_Mnzava_Mungongo_.pdf (accessed 2 September 2017).

Kinnaird, M. F. (1990). Pregnancy, gestation and parturition in free-ranging Tana River crested mangabeys (*Cercocebus galeritus galeritus*). *American Journal of Primatology,* **22,** 285–9.

Kinnaird, M. F. & O'Brien, T. G. (1991). Viable populations for an endangered forest primate, the Tana River crested mangabey (*Cercocebus galeritus galeritus*). *Conservation Biology,* **5,** 203–13.

Lacy, R. C. (1993). VORTEX: a computer simulation model for population viability analysis. *Wildlife Research,* **20,** 45–65.

Lacy, R. C. (1997). Importance of genetic variation to the viability of mammalian populations. *Journal of Mammalogy,* **78,** 320–35.

Lovett, J. C. (1993). Eastern Arc moist forest flora. In Lovett, J. C. & Wasser, S. K. (eds) *Biogeography and Ecology of the Rain Forest of Eastern Africa*. New York: Cambridge University Press, pp. 33–55.

Martin, R. D. (2007). The evolution of human reproduction: a primatological perspective. *Yearbook of Physical Anthropology,* **134,** 59–84.

Mbora, D. N. M. & McPeek, M. A. (2015). How monkeys see a forest: genetic variation and population genetic structure of two forest primates. *Conservation Genetics,* **16,** 559–69.

McCabe, G. M. & Emery Thompson, M. (2013). Reproductive seasonality in wild Sanje mangabeys (*Cercocebus sanjei*), Tanzania: relationship between the capital breeding strategy and infant survival. *Behaviour,* **150,** 1399–429.

McCabe, G. M. & Fernández, D. (in press). Seasonal patterns of infant mortality in wild sanje mangabeys, *Cercocebus sanjei*. In Kalbitzer, U. & Jack. K. M. (eds) *Primate Life Histories, Sex Roles, and Adaptability: Essays in Honour of Linda M. Fedigan*. New York: Springer.

McCabe, G., Fernández, D. & Ehardt, C. (2013). Ecology of reproduction in Sanje mangabeys (*Cercocebus sanjei*): dietary strategies and energy balance during the high fruit period. *American Journal of Primatology,* **75,** 1196–208.

Medley, K. E. (1993). Primate conservation along the Tana River, Kenya: an examination of the forest habitat. *Conservation Biology,* **7,** 109–21.

Melnick, D. J. & Hoelzer, G. A. (1996). The population genetic consequences of macaque social organization and behaviour. In Fa, J. E. & Lindburg, D. G. (eds) *Evolution and Ecology of Macaque Societies*. Cambridge: Cambridge University Press, pp. 413–43.

Melnick, D. J. & Kidd, K. K. (1983). The genetic consequences of social group fission in a wild population of rhesus monkeys (*Macaca mulatta*). *Behavioural Ecology and Sociobiology,* **3,** 229–36.

Moore, J. (1984). Female transfer in primates. *International Journal of Primatology,* **5,** 537–89.

Palombit, R. A. (2015). Infanticide as sexual conflict: coevolution of male strategies and female counterstrategies. *Cold Spring Harbor Perspectives in Biology,* **7,** a017640.

Perry, S. E., Manson, J. H., Muniz, L., Gros-Louis, J. & Vigilant, L. (2008). Kin-biased social behaviour in wild adult female white-faced capuchins, *Cebus capucinus. Animal Behaviour,* **76,** 187–99.

Pope, T. R. (1992). The influence of dispersal patterns and mating systems on genetic differentiation within and between populations of red howler monkeys (*Alouatta seniculus*). *Evolution,* **46,** 1112–28.

Pusey, A. E. (1979). Intercommunity transfer of chimpanzees in Gombe National Park. In Hamburg, D. A. & McCown, E. R. (eds) *The Great Apes*. Menlo Park, CA: Benjamin/Cummings, pp. 465–579.

Pusey, A., Williams, J. & Goodall, J. (1997). The influence of dominance rank on the reproductive success of female chimpanzees. *Science*, **277**, 828–31.

R Core Team (2017). *R: A Language and Environment for Statistical Computing*. Vienna: R Foundation for Statistical Computing.

Range, F., Foerderer, T., Storrer-Meystre, Y., Benetton, C. & Fruteau, C. (2007). The structure of social relationships among sooty mangabeys in Taï. In McGraw, W. S., Zuberbuehler, W. S. & Noe, R. (eds) *Monkeys of the Taï Forest: An African Primate Community*. New York: Cambridge University Press, pp. 109–30.

Rao, J. S. (1972). Some variants of chi-square for testing uniformity on the circle. *Zeitschrift fr Wahrscheinlichkeitstheorie und Verwandte Gebiete*, **22**, 33–44.

Robbins, M. M., Gray, M., Kagoda, E. & Robbins, A. M. (2009). Population dynamics of the Bwindi mountain gorillas. *Biological Conservation*, **142**, 2886–95.

Rovero, F., Mtui, A., Kitegile, A., Nielsen, M. & Jones, T. (2010). Udzungwa Scarp Forest Reserve in crisis. Available at: www.cepf.net/Documents/UdzungwaSFR_Report_FINAL_High_Res.pdf (accessed 2 September 2017).

Rovero, F., Mtui, A. S., Kitegile, A. S. & Nielsen, M. R. (2012). Hunting or habitat degradation? Decline of primate populations in Udzungwa Mountains, Tanzania: an analysis of threats. *Biological Conservation*, **146**, 89–96.

Rovero, F., Mtui, A., Kitegile, A., et al. (2015). Primates decline rapidly in unprotected forests: evidence from a monitoring program with data constraints. *PLoS ONE*, **10**, e0118330.

Sadlier, R. M. F. S. (1969). *The Ecology of Reproduction in Wild and Domestic Animals*. London: Methuen.

Scheijen, C. (2014). Human–elephant conflict along the eastern boundary of the Udzungwa Mountains National Park, Tanzania. Available at: www.samhao.nl/webopac/MetaDataEditDownload .csp?file=2:141504:1 (accessed 2 September 2017).

Sjögren-Gulve, P. & Ebenhard, T. (2000). *The Use of Population Viability Analyses in Conservation Planning*. Copenhagen: Munksgaard International Publishers.

Skorupa, J. P. (1986). Responses of rainforest primates to selective logging in Kibale Forest, Uganda. In Benirschke, K. (ed.) *Primates: The Road to Self-Sustaining Populations*. New York: Springer Verlag, pp. 57–70.

Sterck, E. H. M. (1997). Determinants of female dispersal in Thomas langurs. *American Journal of Primatology*, **42**, 179–98.

Strier, K. B. & Ives, A. R. (2012). Demography in the recovery of an endangered primate population. *PLoS ONE*, **7**, e44407.

Struhsaker, T. T. (1999). Primate communities in Africa: the consequence of longterm evolution or the artifact of recent hunting? In Fleagle, J. G., Janson, C. & Reed, K. E. (eds) *Primate Communities*. Cambridge: Cambridge University Press, pp. 289–94.

Therneau, T. (2015). A package for survival analysis in S. Available at: https://cran.r-project.org/ web/packages/survival/index.html.

Watts, D. P. (1990). Ecology of gorillas and its relation to female transfer in mountain gorillas. *International Journal of Primatology*, **11**, 21–45.

Whitlock, M. C. & McCauley, D. E. (1990). Some population genetic consequences of colony formation and extinction: genetic correlations within founding groups. *Evolution*, **7**, 1717–24.

Wieczkowski, J. & Butynski, T. M. (2013). *Cercocebus galeritus*. In Kingdon, J., Happold, D. & Butynski, T. M. (eds) *The Mammals of Africa. Primates, Vol. II*. London: Bloomsbury Publishing, pp. 167–70.

Wright, S. (1943). Isolation by distance. *Genetics*, **28**, 114–38.

Zinner, D. & Deschner, T. (2000). Sexual swellings in female hamadryas baboons after male take-overs: 'deceptive' swellings as a possible female counter-strategy against infanticide. *American Journal of Primatology*, **52**, 157–68.

4   Uneasy Neighbours

Local Perceptions of the Cross River Gorilla and Nigeria–Cameroon Chimpanzee in Cameroon

Alison Wade, Nicholas Malone, Judith Littleton and Bruce Floyd

4.1   Personal Narrative

I (AW) have been fascinated with primates since I was young. Specifically, my passion for gorillas grew from family holidays to Australia, where I was captivated by the behaviour of zoo-housed animals. My undergraduate career at the University of Auckland, New Zealand began with studying law and history. I fell into anthropology when I discovered that I could learn more about primate behaviour and ecology in this field. I was fortunate to have Judith Littleton and Bruce Floyd as lecturers who indulged my curiosities and allowed me to focus my studies towards primates even in the absence of a primatologist on staff or specific courses in primatology being on offer. I also continued to study law with a focus on international, environmental and animal law. This opened my eyes to the many ways that humans impact both animals and the environment.

This interplay between people, animals and the environment was reinforced when I took a break from study before enrolling in my Master's programme, also at the University of Auckland. In 2010, I volunteered for a research position with a local NGO in Cameroon that focuses on conserving the Cross River gorilla (*Gorilla gorilla diehli*). Through this programme, I began to see, first-hand, the interplay between local people and NGOs, and the effects this can have on the conservation of a relatively unknown gorilla taxon. While I was in Cameroon, I also became enchanted by the country and its people. On my way back to New Zealand, I visited the mountain gorillas (*G. beringei beringei*) in Uganda. This allowed me to see the differences between these two gorilla species, which have experienced different levels of protection over time. After this trip, I knew that I wanted to continue my studies with a focus on conserving the Cross River gorilla in Cameroon.

When I returned to the University of Auckland to begin my Master's in 2011, I was fortunate to find that the newly hired primatologist, Nicholas Malone, and I share an interest in human–primate interconnections. I had to put my plans for Cameroon on hold, but I was given the opportunity to travel with Nicholas to Java, Indonesia for my Master's research. Here, I was able to apply an ethnoprimatological framework to investigate the suitability of a site for the release of rehabilitated Javan gibbons (*Hylobates moloch*). This research allowed me to put into practice a combination of ethnographic and ecological methods.

I began my doctoral studies in 2013 under the supervision of Nicholas Malone and Judith Littleton at the University of Auckland. With the Cross River gorilla population consisting of only 250–300 individuals across a tenuously connected landscape, I wanted to explore how the local communities interacted with the gorillas in unprotected areas in order to understand the conservation implications of these interconnections. My research soon expanded to include the Nigeria–Cameroon chimpanzees (*Pan troglodytes ellioti*) that occupy the same forest landscape and of which we have comparatively limited ecological knowledge. What I am learning, as others also have, is that human and primate interconnections extend past the local level to encompass relationships at a larger scale. These interconnections are also subject to temporal fluctuations. For example, the increase in the price of cocoa during the late 1990s enticed many farmers to clear large sections of lowland forest for cocoa farms. If we are to understand the threats facing primates with a goal of conservation within a particular area, we need to consider the wider social, political and economic drivers acting in the region. In seeking to achieve this overarching objective, my research has now become inextricably linked to the political and economic realities of the area and the feasibility of conservation initiatives.

4.2   Introduction

Primates are known for their behavioural flexibility and ability to adapt (Fuentes, 2007). Despite this, almost 60 per cent of primate species are threatened with extinction as a result of increasing anthropogenic pressures on primates and their habitats (Estrada et al., 2017). The aim of primate conservation is preserving the 'diversity of species and subspecies whose futures are endangered and preventing those taxa that are still relatively secure from becoming endangered themselves' (Strier, 2011: 664). However, how to go about conserving primates in the face of global change is an issue facing many primatologists (Setchell, 2013). While it is evident that primate conservation requires an understanding of the major threats to primates and how these relate to each taxon's degree of behavioural and ecological specialisation, threats to primate species survival are mostly anthropogenic. In order to understand conservation problems, we need to gather information on both human and non-human primate responses to conservation policies and threats, respectively (Ceballos et al., 2015; Setchell et al., 2016).

While there has been a history of separating humans from the 'natural' world in many disciplines, both social and biological anthropologists have expanded conceptual and theoretical approaches to break down dichotomies of human and animal and of culture and nature (e.g. Fuentes, 2012; Fuentes & Wolfe, 2002). Ethnoprimatology arose within this conceptual shift, abandoning the view that primates in contact with humans represent an 'unnatural' situation; rather, these interspecies interactions, while varied, represent the typical rather than the exceptional (Fuentes & Wolfe, 2002; Sponsel, 1997). The approach also affirms that humans are primates and that human and non-human primates are co-participants in shaping shared ecological and social worlds (Fuentes, 2012). Ethnoprimatology provides a robust methodology for understanding the conservation problems and complex interactions between humans and non-human primates by drawing from ecological, biological, ethnographic, political, economic and historical approaches (Dore et al., 2017).

Our research employs an ethnoprimatological approach to investigate the interrelationships between free-ranging Cross River gorillas (*Gorilla gorilla diehli*), Nigeria–Cameroon chimpanzees (*Pan troglodytes ellioti*) and local human communities within the unprotected Mone-Oku Forest, Cameroon. The Cross River gorilla is currently classified as critically endangered due to its low population estimates of approximately 250–300 mature individuals, combined with threats of habitat loss (Bergl et al., 2016). The Nigeria–Cameroon chimpanzee generally occupies the same environment as the Cross River gorilla and is classified as an endangered species, with an estimated population of 3500–9000 individuals, facing high levels of exploitation and habitat loss (Oates et al., 2016). A significant proportion of both the gorilla and chimpanzee populations are found in Cameroon, and many range in areas which have no formal protection (Dunn et al., 2014; Morgan et al., 2011).

Our increasing understanding of these apes' distribution across the landscape is highlighting the need to design new approaches for conservation in areas that have no formal legal protection. This requires the establishment of strong relationships with the local communities who are often highly dependent on forest resources for their livelihoods and subsistence needs (e.g. food, medicine and materials for housing construction). Conservation action plans for these apes acknowledge the need to maintain local customs and traditions that facilitate wildlife conservation. They also emphasise the need to improve education outreach programmes in an effort to foster greater local responsibility for forest and wildlife conservation (Dunn et al., 2014; Morgan et al., 2011). This is based on the assumption that education will increase the rate of change in societal attitudes towards wildlife, and that positive attitudes will persist in the long term (Jacobson, 2010). However, there is limited knowledge surrounding how local communities perceive the apes or the forests within Cameroon. Our research thus uses a combination of ecological and ethnographic methods to see how human activities within the Mone-Oku Forest may be affecting the nesting behaviours of the apes, and to gain an insight into the local perceptions of the forest and the apes. If conservation efforts are focused on changing societal attitudes, we need to identify the driving attitudes and actions behind the main threats to the apes, so they can be incorporated in the wider conservation scheme.

4.3   Methods

4.3.1   Study Site

This research was conducted in a 50 km^2 area of the Mone-Oku Forest complex, Manyu Division, Southwest Cameroon (Figure 4.1). Specifically, the area is an unclassified forest corridor located between Mone Forest Reserve and the Mbulu Forest, and provides tenuous links in the north to Takamanda National Park and the Kagwene Gorilla Sanctuary. The forest is topographically diverse as elevations range between 130 m and 1000 m, and vegetation falls into the Guinea Congolian type (White, 1983). It is a mosaic landscape of villages, farmland and secondary and primary forest. The climate is tropical, with a long wet season from April to October

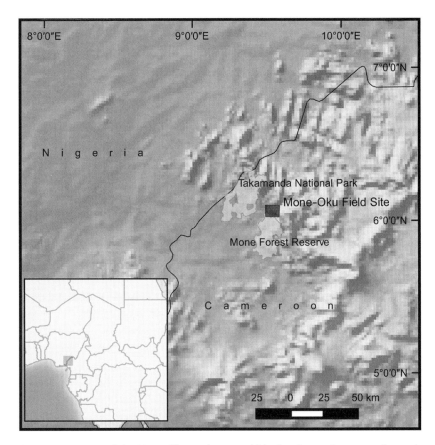

Figure 4.1 Location of the Mone-Oku study area within Southwest Cameroon. Insert: location of the region within Central-West Africa.

and a shorter dry season from November to March (Mboh & Warren, 2007). Within the forest complex it is estimated there is a population of 6–15 Cross River gorillas (Dunn et al., 2014) and 50–200 Nigerian–Cameroon chimpanzees (Warren & Ekinde, 2007), neither of which are habituated to researcher presence.

There are seven villages within the area that access the forest and its resources, with Eshobi and Nga claiming traditional ownership over the study area. The people of Eshobi are predominately Anyang, whose spoken language is Denya, while the people of Nga are predominately Manta, 'hill people', and speak the Manta language. The area is fertile and most individuals gain an income through small landholdings producing cocoa, oil palm, coconut, maize, vegetables and fruits. However, the area suffers from limited vehicle transportation links to the nearest towns (Mamfe and Bamenda) and the roads are only passable via motorbike during the rainy season. The Wildlife Conservation Society (WCS) has been consistently monitoring both ape species in the region since 2009, with the initiation of the Gorilla Guardian programme (GGP). The GGP promotes the conservation of both ape species in villages outside of protected areas and provides individuals nominated within each village with tracking and ecological training (Jameson, 2012).

AW conducted this research between May 2014 and March 2015. As there is no habituated population of either ape, night nests were used to gain insights into the apes' behaviour and how behaviour is shaped by ecological interactions. All great ape taxa are known to construct new nests each night, with the decision of where to nest and what type of nest to construct variable both between and within taxa (e.g. Fruth & Hohmann, 1996). Many factors have been shown to influence the selection of nesting sites, including vegetation types, human disturbance and predator avoidance (Furuichi & Hashimoto, 2004).

4.3.2   Surveying

Reconnaissance surveys were used to record human presence within the forest and to locate gorilla and chimpanzee nest sites as the difficult nature of the terrain made transects impractical (Kühl et al., 2008). Surveys were conducted during daylight hours, with the direction of travel usually determined by the location of the randomly selected botanical plot coordinates. Nest sites were additionally located from hunter observations and reports as part of the GGP or after opportunistic sightings of the apes. Along each reconnaissance route, AW recorded all human signs as GPS waypoints, including spent bullet cartridges, snares, traps, bush huts, hunter camps, forest clearings and farms. Surveys covered 272 km within the study area (Figure 4.2). GPS waypoints were also

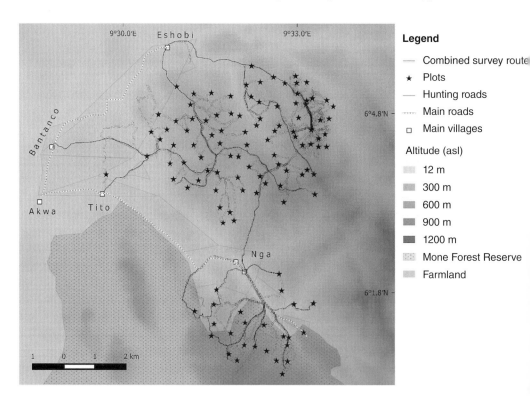

Figure 4.2 Map illustrating the areas surveyed throughout the study period and the locations of botanical plots.

taken at the centre of each nest site and the centre of each botanical plot. All GPS tracklogs and waypoints were imported into QGIS for analysis (QGIS, 2014). Within QGIS, the measurement tool was used to calculate distances between nest sites and hunting roads, along with calculations of the total survey distances. The heatmap tool was used for both nesting sites and human signs to allow for a visualisation of waypoint clusters as a means to identify high concentrations of activity (both human and ape). To determine whether human activity varied throughout the study area, four forest zones were created: the gorilla range, the chimpanzee range, lowland forest (<500 m) and upland forest (>500 m). Encounter rates (ERs) for each zone were calculated by dividing the number of human signs observed for each zone by the total distance surveyed in that zone.

4.3.3 Botanical Sampling

Stratified random sampling was used to sample the forest vegetation. The study area was divided into 500 × 500 m quadrants and coordinates for each plot were randomly selected with 121 plots sampled (Brownlow et al., 2001). Plots were 20 × 50 m (1000 m^2) and all tree species with a diameter at breast height (DBH) greater than 10 cm were identified with the aid of a locally trained botanist. For each tree, DBH was recorded to the nearest 0.1 cm using a diameter tape and the height was measured with a clinometer. Within the centre of each plot, a 4 × 4 m subplot was established to record the understorey vegetation. Vegetation was then classified according to the presence of key indicator plants and the area was defined as old secondary forest, lowland forest, lowland ridge forest, mid-elevation forest or montane forest (Table 4.1). Habitat

Table 4.1 Descriptions of vegetation classes and key indicator plant species as defined by Sunderland et al. (2003)

Vegetation class	Description	Indicator plants
Old secondary forest	Forest recovering from disturbance; trees are smaller and canopy height is lower than in primary forest, either from human modification or natural disturbances	*Elaeis guineensis, Musanga ceropiodes, Piptadenianstrum africanum, Tabernaemontana crassa, Pycnanthous angolensis*
Lowland forest <500 m	Mature forest with tall and large trees; a high canopy and a distinctive middle storey	*Afrostyrax kameroensis, Desbordesia* spp.*, Carapa procera, Parkia bicolor, Strombosia grandifolia*
Lowland ridge forest 300–500 m	Mature forest growing on the sides of finger-like ridges; at some places the forest is interspersed with rocky cliffs	*Allenblackia floribunda, Tapura africana, Chrysophyllum* spp.*, Lophira alata, Pseudospondias microcarpa*
Mid-elevation forest 500–800 m	Mature forest with a lower canopy and denser understorey; a reduction in diversity but also contains elements of both lowland and montane forests	*Homalium* spp.*, Syzygium* ssp.*, Xylopia staudtii, Carpolobia lutea, Rinorea dentata, Dichapetalum* spp.
Montane forest 800–1500 m	Mature forest with a further reduction in canopy height which is often disjunct; a decrease in species richness	*Dactyladeina staudii, Dracenea arborea, Eugenia* spp.

Table 4.2 Descriptions of categories relating to the density of understorey vegetation, slope and canopy cover as defined by De Vere et al. (2011: 256)

Category	Description	
Density of understorey	Very dense	(Stems <50 cm apart)
	Dense	(Stems <1 m apart)
	Sparse	(Stems >1 m apart)
Slope	Precipitous	(Over 50%, >26.6°)
	Steep	(10–50%, 5.7–26.6°)
	Gentle	(0–10%, 0–5.7°)
	Flat	
Canopy cover	Very closed	(>75%)
	Closed	(51–75%)
	Open	(26–50%)
	Very open	(0–25%)

Table 4.3 Operational definitions for estimating the age of nests following Koops et al. (2012) and Tutin et al. (1995)

Age category	Approximate age	Definition
New	Less than two days	Nest has green unwilted leaves. Presence of dung and urine in or around the nest.
Recent	Less than one week	Nest has wilted green leaves.
Old and intact	Between one week and one month	Nest remains intact but leaves have turned brown.
Decomposing	More than one month	Nest consists of interwoven stems and branches that lack leaves.

characteristics were also recorded at each plot. These included elevation, understorey density, degree of slope and the amount of canopy cover (Table 4.2).

4.3.4   Nest Sites

When a nest or a group of nests was observed, the area within an approximate radius of 100 m was carefully searched to locate other nests. As both chimpanzees and gorillas are known to nest in trees or on the ground, the presence of lobed versus scattered dung, odours and hairs was used to distinguish a gorilla nest from a chimpanzee nest where the sites were fresh (White & Edwards, 2000). We also measured the distance between nests, as the spacing between individual nests has also been found to be a reliable indicator for species identification (White & Edwards, 2000). Where we were unsure as to which species constructed the nest site, the site was recorded as an ape nest site. Nest sites were assigned approximate ages based on the visual appearance of the vegetation and the presence of dung, odours and other signs of ape activity. The categories for the age of a site were 'new', 'recent', 'old and intact' and 'decomposing' (Table 4.3)

(Koops et al., 2012; Tutin et al., 1995). Nest sites were classified as arboreal, ground or mixed sites (De Vere et al., 2011). For each arboreal nest, we recorded the height of the nest and the nesting tree, the DBH of the nesting tree, and the tree species. For ground nests, the number of plant genera used within the nest and the number of plant genera within a 2 m radius of the nest were counted (Rothman et al., 2006). Habitat characteristics were also recorded at the centre of each nest site using the same definitions as for the botanical plots (Table 4.2).

4.3.5   Ecological Analysis

To determine whether the apes showed preference for particular habitat types within the study area, chi-square tests were initially run in SPSS 20 (SPSS, 2011). The observed values were taken from nest sites for each species and compared to expected frequencies taken from the botanical plot data. As the results were statistically significant with the exception of understorey density, a multinomial logistic regression was then run in SYSTAT 13 (SYSTAT, 2009). The dependent variables were chimpanzee sites, gorilla sites and botanical sites, which represented the total forest. This was to determine which of the examined habitat characteristics – vegetation class, elevation, degree of slope or the amount of canopy cover – had a greater influence on the selection of nest sites.

Manly's alpha was used to identify whether there were preferences for arboreal nesting tree species. This index measures resource preference based on a selection ratio comparing the proportion of a nesting species used to the proportion of available trees of that species (Brownlow et al., 2001). The resulting value is then compared to a ratio of neutral preference based on the number of all species available. To determine the statistical significance of these nesting preferences, a binomial test of the difference between observed and expected numbers of trees used for nesting was then run in SPSS.

To determine plant preferences in ground nest construction, the proportion of each genus used within the nest and the proportion of that genus within a 2 m radius were calculated. A one-sample Wilcoxon signed rank test was then run for each plant genus to determine whether the medians differed (Rothman et al., 2006). The significance level was set at 0.05.

4.3.6   Ethnographic Data Collection

AW carried out 50 semi-structured interviews (Table 4.4) encompassing a range of topics, including forest use, farming practices, economic pathways, and village history. Interviews were conducted within either the village hall or the participant's home at a time of their choosing. The majority of interviews were conducted in a mixture of English and Pidgin. Where participants were unable to understand or express ideas in Pidgin, a research assistant translated into the local dialects. Interview data were supplemented with participant observation focusing on farming and forest use, providing further insight into which resources people use and how

Table 4.4 Demographic profile of participants involved in semi-structured interviews

Question	Demographic group	Number of participants	Percentage (%)
Village	Nga	28	56
	Eshobi	22	44
Sex	Male	31	62
	Female	19	38
Age	20–29	11	22
	30–44	25	50
	45+	14	28
Encounters with the apes	Never	26	52
	Chimpanzees only	5	10
	Gorillas only	6	12
	Both	13	26

they use them (Malone et al., 2017; Riley & Ellwanger, 2013). Interviews and field notes were transcribed and thematically coded, supported by discussions with key informants which clarified meanings and interpretations and allowed an expansion of ideas.

This research was approved by the University of Auckland Human Participants Ethics Committee (Reference 011245), and the Cameroonian Ministry of Scientific Research and Innovation (MINRESI) in collaboration with the Wildlife Conservation Society (Research Permit #65, 2014). While the University of Auckland Animal Ethics Committee did not consider that observational field research required ethical approval, this research adhered to the ethical principles of the International Primatological Society (Fedigan, 2010).

4.4   Results

4.4.1   Ape Nesting Preferences

We found that chimpanzees and gorillas had distinct nesting ranges within the Mone-Oku Forest. The chimpanzees were found to nest within an area of 3.3 km^2 southeast of Eshobi, with the gorillas nesting over an area of 4.5 km^2 south of Nga (Figure 4.3). Participants stated that the chimpanzees and gorillas had not altered their ranges during the participants' lifetime. One older hunter from Nga believed that the chimpanzees and gorillas do not cross sides of the forest – they each have their own place (Interview 15).

The chimpanzees were found to nest in an area of forest with low human activity (ER = 0.98 signs/km), 4 km from Eshobi village (Figure 4.4). Many participants said it was an area they did not often visit as it was too far away and too steep; hunters thus had to be 'strong' to travel to that area of the forest. However, we know hunting of the chimpanzees has occurred within the last five years, with one Eshobi informant discussing the consequences when authorities discovered bones of the chimpanzees he had recently hunted. While the average distance between a chimpanzee nest site

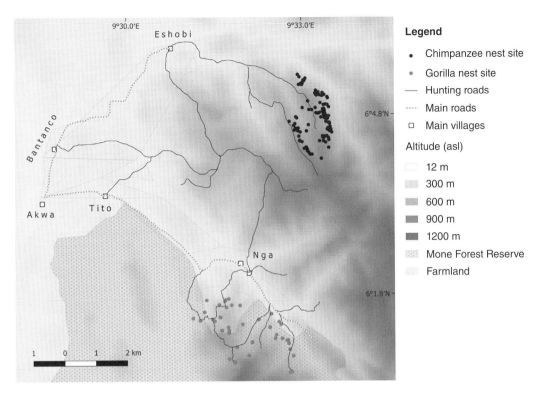

Figure 4.3 Map illustrating the location of chimpanzee and gorilla nest sites within the study area.

($n = 95$) and a hunting road was 310 ± 130 m, the topography and selection of preferred habitat characteristics allowed for effective concealment of nests. The chimpanzees preferentially located nests in areas of mid-elevation (500–700 m asl), under a closed forest canopy and on steep to precipitous slopes (above $5.7°$). The results of multinomial logistic regression show that these three variables are all statistically significant predictors of chimpanzee nest sites, with a model success rate of 66 per cent (Table 4.5). The chimpanzees were also found to have tree species they preferred for nest construction. Differences between the observed and the expected numbers of trees used for nesting showed statistically significant results for 11 of the 13 most commonly used tree species (Table 4.6). However, the chimpanzees also used a wide range of nesting tree species, with nests constructed in 48 per cent of tree species recorded throughout their nesting range ($n = 180$ tree species).

The gorillas nested in close proximity to the nearest village, Nga, with some nest sites located within 150 m of farm–forest boundaries (Figure 4.3). This close proximity to the village is reflected in the higher levels of human activity throughout the nesting range (ER = 2 signs/km), and in reports by Nga participants that the gorillas occasionally enter their farms and destroy their banana or plantain plants as they consume the piths. The gorillas showed preference for locating nest sites in areas of

Table 4.5 Results of multinomial logistic regression testing habitat characteristics of chimpanzee nest sites

Parameter	Estimate	Standard error	Z-score	*p*-value	95% confidence interval	
					Lower	Upper
Canopy cover	1.316	0.232	5.673	<0.001	0.861	1.770
Elevation	0.428	0.144	2.971	0.003	0.146	0.710
Degree of slope	0.287	0.287	5.267	<0.001	0.949	2.073

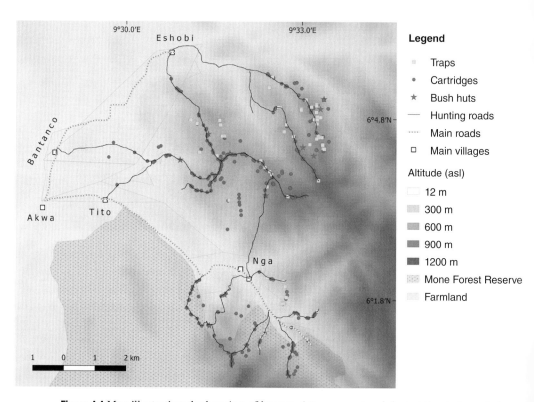

Figure 4.4 Map illustrating the location of human signs encountered during the study period. Note that traps are likely to be underrepresented due to the seasonal nature of trapping. The majority of human signs occur in close proximity to a main hunting trail.

old secondary and lowland forest (300–450 m asl) and on steep slopes (*n* = 30). The hunters from Nga advised AW that many of the nest sites are in areas of farmland that were abandoned when the village split into two areas (Nga and Tito) over the last 30 years. These hunters were also aware of the gorillas' nesting preferences and would purposefully seek out areas of dense vegetation in open canopy to help locate nest sites. While we found areas of open canopy to be a useful indicator for locating

Table 4.6 Chimpanzee arboreal nesting tree species preferences for the 15 most commonly used nesting tree species

Tree species	Observed number of trees used for nesting (1)	Cumulative percentage	Proportion of (1) to all trees used for nesting	Number of trees sampled in botanical plots (2)	Proportion of (2) to all trees sampled	Expected number of trees used for nesting	Manley's α	Category by significant preference	Sig. (p)
Treculia obovoidea	34	6	0.061	38	0.023	13.0	0.015	Preferred	<0.001
Strombosia grandifolia	33	12	0.059	44	0.027	15.1	0.013	Preferred	<0.001
Plagiostyles africana	30	17	0.054	27	0.017	9.3	0.019	Preferred	<0.001
Santiria trimeria	25	22	0.045	18	0.011	6.2	0.023	Preferred	<0.001
Coelocaryon preussii	24	26	0.043	16	0.010	5.5	0.025	Preferred	<0.001
Microdesmis sp.	24	31	0.043	38	0.023	13.0	0.011	Preferred	0.003
Chrysophyllum sp.	23	35	0.041	42	0.026	14.5	0.009	Preferred	0.021
Tapura africana	22	39	0.040	3	0.002	1.1	0.124	Preferred	<0.001
Chytranthus talbotii	18	42	0.032	42	0.026	14.5	0.007	Preferred	NS
Anthonotha sp.	16	45	0.029	22	0.014	7.6	0.012	Preferred	0.006
Pycnanthus angolensis	15	48	0.027	27	0.017	9.3	0.009	Preferred	NS
Anonidium mannii	13	50	0.023	12	0.007	4.1	0.018	Preferred	<0.001
Zenkerella sp.	13	52	0.023	10	0.006	3.4	0.022	Preferred	<0.001
Drypetes sp.	12	54	0.022	17	0.010	5.8	0.012	Preferred	0.011
Hymenostegia afzelii	10	56	0.018	39	0.024	13.4	0.004	Less Preferred	NS

Note: value for neutral preference for Manly's α was 0.005.

Table 4.7 Results of multinomial logistic regression testing habitat characteristics of gorilla nest sites

Parameter	Estimate	Standard error	Z-score	p-value	95% confidence interval	
					Lower	Upper
Canopy cover	−0.357	0.253	−1.412	0.158	−0.853	0.139
Elevation	−0.679	0.189	−3.589	<0.001	−1.049	−0.308
Degree of slope	1.029	0.387	2.660	0.008	0.271	1.788

nest sites, the results of the multinomial logistic regression found only elevation and degree of slope to be statistically significant predictors (Table 4.7). This may be a reflection of the smaller sample size and the low prediction success rate of 30 per cent. The gorillas did show preferences for some plants in the construction of their arboreal ($n = 58$) and ground nests ($n = 82$). Arboreal nests were constructed in 17 per cent of the available species throughout their range, with five of the eight most preferred nesting species used significantly more than would be expected based on availability (Table 4.8). Ground nests were generally constructed using immediately available materials. However, three plant genera were incorporated into ground nests in significantly higher proportions than their availability predicted. These were *Aframomum* ($Z = 157$, $p = 0.016$), *Protomegabaria* ($Z = 2$, $p = 0.025$), and a vine from the Tiliaceae family ($Z = 6$, $p = 0.028$).

4.4.2   Local Perceptions of the Apes

Interviewees expressed conflicted feelings towards the apes, which varied depending on context. For example, many people feared the apes, but they also enjoyed the economic benefits the apes brought to their villages through the GGP and the occasional researcher. The level of fear attributed to either the gorillas or chimpanzees differed based on the varied behaviour of the apes in an encounter and people's perceptions of the apes. For example, many men stated that gorillas are less likely to run away from them, especially when they encountered the gorillas bedding down at their evening nest sites. They also emphasised the large size of gorillas, with the gorilla frequently described as 'overbig'. Some of this fear of gorillas appeared to stem from a recent attack on a ranger during a GGP training session at the Kagwene Gorilla Sanctuary. However, other than unbelievable stories of gorillas capturing hunting dogs and removing their canines, there were no reports of Mone-Oku gorillas attacking people within recent memory. Despite this, the fear was present even among those who did not frequent the forest. A farmer from Nga stated: '[g]orillas are wild and dangerous, people shouldn't go closer to them, if you go closer it can kill you' (Interview 9). AW witnessed this fear during a brief encounter with two gorillas in the forest. While AW encouraged the team to stand quietly and observe the elusive gorillas climb the trees about 30 m away, the local hunters were panicking as they believed the gorillas would trap and harm us, and expressed their wish that we return to the village as quickly as possible.

Table 4.8 Gorilla arboreal nesting tree species preference in the 13 most commonly used nesting tree species

Tree species	Observed number of trees used for nesting (1)	Cumulative percentage	Proportion of (1) to all trees used for nesting	Number of trees sampled in botanical plots (2)	Proportion of (2) to all trees sampled	Expected number of trees used for nesting	Manley's α	Category by significant preference	Sig. (p)
Sorindeia spp.	10	17	0.172	63	0.033	1.9	0.019	Preferred	<0.001
Pycnanthus angolensis	6	28	0.103	49	0.026	1.5	0.015	Preferred	0.004
Microdesmis sp.	3	33	0.052	24	0.013	0.7	0.015	Preferred	0.04
Angylocalyx pynaertii	2	36	0.034	44	0.023	1.3	0.005	Neutral	NS
Chrysophyllum sp.	2	40	0.034	12	0.006	0.4	0.020	Preferred	0.048
Cola lateritia	2	43	0.034	8	0.004	0.2	0.030	Preferred	0.023
Maesobotrya sp.	2	47	0.034	18	0.009	0.5	0.013	Preferred	NS
Napoleonaea vogelii	2	50	0.034	24	0.013	0.7	0.010	Preferred	NS
Protomegabaria sp.	2	53	0.034	18	0.009	0.5	0.013	Preferred	NS
Pseudospondias sp.	2	57	0.034	29	0.015	0.9	0.008	Preferred	NS
Tabernaemontana crassa	2	60	0.034	49	0.026	1.5	0.005	Neutral	NS
Trema sp.	2	64	0.034	1	0.001	0.0	0.240	Preferred	0.002
Trichilia rubescens	2	67	0.034	46	0.024	1.4	0.005	Neutral	NS

Note: value for neutral preference for Manley's α was 0.005.

The level of fear expressed was lower when people described their encounters with chimpanzees. As chimpanzees like to 'halla and shout', people were less likely to encounter chimpanzees within the forest unaware. While some participants acknowledged they were just as afraid of chimpanzees as they were of gorillas, others noted that the chimpanzees were more afraid of people and would run away, so there was no need to fear them. AW also witnessed the different reactions towards chimpanzees when the team encountered them on several occasions within the forest. We would hear the chimpanzees approaching and stand quietly together, with one of the hunters also offering to get closer to the chimpanzees to take photographs.

The GGP staff (locally named 'wildlife') are viewed by villagers as government representatives, who have the power to tell them how they can use their forest and detain them if they break the law. The fear expressed by the participants also arose from the perceived power imbalance between the participants and 'wildlife' officials. When discussing the GGP, a hunter from Eshobi agreed that the programme has changed the way people use the forest. It is only through the programme that many people have stopped killing animals like gorillas because they fear the consequences if they are caught (Interview 36). Participants explained that, in the past, people were not afraid and would kill now-protected animals to feed their families. The hunting of big animals, including gorillas and chimpanzees, also gained the hunter prestige among other villagers. Today, people are afraid of these big animals because they believe they cannot legally defend themselves if they encounter either ape and are attacked. However, the ideals and effectiveness of the GGP may be limited. One hunter was very open when they acknowledged that, if a protected animal was killed by accident, such as in a trap, then the whole village would come together to share the meat of that animal rather than report the death and have the trapper get in trouble with the authorities or have the meat rot in the bush (Interview 11). However, there was a general absence of a discussion relating to the bushmeat trade. This notable absence is likely related to the perception that AW was 'wildlife' and the possibility that such discussion may be reported to the government.

Although many participants voiced their fear of government reprisal, they were also honoured to have the chimpanzees and gorillas in their forest due to the economic benefits they bring. These ideas were summarised by an Nga farmer who stated that they liked the GGP as it provides money to the village; however, it is not the same as before, as the GGP is government (Interview 2). While many respondents stated that the GGP has helped to stop the hunting of the apes or hunting within the ape's ranges, observations from forest surveys differed. As illustrated above, hunting signs were frequently located within the nesting range of the gorillas, and to a lesser degree within the nesting range of the chimpanzees. A hunter from Eshobi admitted their concern about what may happen to them, legally, as they believed chimpanzees had been caught in their traps but managed to free themselves on several occasions.

These results highlight that people's actions are often different from what they report. While the gorillas and chimpanzees may not be the direct targets of hunting efforts, both hunting and trapping occur within their range, increasing the apes' likelihood of harm. The fear of the apes exists as people acknowledge their strength, and this fear is intensified as they believe they are unable to defend themselves if attacked, without being arrested by government officials.

4.4.3   The Forest as an Unlimited Economic Resource

The Mone-Oku Forest is perceived and used by participants as an economic resource, either through hunting or the collection of non-timber forest products (NTFPs). Participants' descriptions of a 'fine' or good forest included: many NTFPs, animals that could be eaten as opposed to those that damage crops, and that the forest's land was fertile upon clearing. A 'bad' forest was generally one that lacked these resources. When participants were asked about the changes to the forest they had seen during their lifetimes, the majority stated that the forest itself had not changed but the animals had reduced. Older participants noted the local extinction of many animals, including the forest elephant. Only a few participants acknowledged that the lowland forest is 'shrinking' as it is cleared for farmland. Despite this, these participants believe there will always be enough forest, no matter how much is cleared for farmland.

There was a strong desire by nearly all the participants to expand their farmland as a means to increase their income to provide education and healthcare for their children. The exceptions were the elderly and ill, who recognised the limits of their strength. For villagers, the only provision regarding farmland is that you do not intrude upon neighbouring farms. As one woman from Nga explained, there are 'no rules just extend as far as your strength takes you. The forest is too wide so can make the farm as big as you can. You expand to get more yields and more money' (Interview 5). Farms can be created anywhere within the forest. A person can have multiple farms and they can be of any size. A large farm was stated to be around 5–7 ha. Both villages held some of these large farms, but the majority of farms were only 2–3 ha. Having a large farm brings additional benefits as it is a reflection of the individual's strength, earning prestige and some power within village politics.

While at first glance it may appear that the clearance of forest is random, there are limits, with the technology currently available, to the areas that are suitable for expanding villages and farmland. Villages must be in close proximity to a large water body for drinking and washing, have land that is relatively level, the ground should not have too many stones and there must be adequate space for everyone to construct a house. People also look for a variety of qualities when selecting new areas of forest to clear for farmland, including proximity to the village, level or gently sloping land, and the ability of the land to produce many crops. The forest may also be cleared to solidify borders with neighbouring villages. This has been the case with both Eshobi and lower Nga (Tito), ensuring the people from Bantaco and Akwa do not claim land they believe is within their traditional boundaries. These requirements do leave areas of the forest, such as the chimpanzee nesting range, relatively safe from immediate forest clearance; however, they also have the potential to isolate chimpanzee communities as the undulating landscape favours the clearance of lowland forest for village locations and the expansion of farmland.

4.5   Discussion

Human hunting activity within the Mone-Oku Forest appears to influence the nesting behaviour of the Nigeria–Cameroon chimpanzee and to some degree the Cross River gorilla. Primates may show a range of behavioural adjustments in response to anthropogenic pressures (McLennan et al., 2017). These include habitat shifts whereby primates increasingly spend more time in areas of reduced resources than more disturbed areas of high resource abundance (Frid & Dill, 2002). The Mone-Oku chimpanzees nested in a wide range of tree species in areas of mid-elevation, with a dense canopy cover and on steep to precipitous slopes, effectively concealing nest sites from main hunting roads. This suggests the chimpanzees are favouring a particular nesting area over preferred tree species that are likely to produce a more suitable or comfortable nest. Previous studies of Nigeria–Cameroon chimpanzees at Gashaka Gumti National Park and Ngel Nyaki Forest Reserve in Nigeria also found a strong preference for nest sites located on steep to precipitous slopes, with Dutton (2012) suggesting these preferences may be a reflection of the landscape configuration. As around half of the Mone-Oku landscape can be described as being of gentle slope, the preference of these chimpanzees for steeper slopes cannot solely be attributed to the landscape. The Mone-Oku chimpanzees have been hunted by humans in this forest until fairly recently, and hunting of other animals still occurs. The results presented here suggest that the Mone-Oku chimpanzees avoid areas of high human hunting activity as a type of disturbance risk. However, future research also needs to take into consideration the feeding ecology of these chimpanzees and its influence on nesting behaviour (Furuichi & Hashimoto, 2004).

The Mone-Oku gorillas also avoided nesting in areas of high human activity, preferring to locate nest sites on steep slopes in lowland and secondary forest. However, they do nest in close proximity to hunting trails, increasing the likelihood of encountering hunters. The Mone-Oku gorillas used a narrow range of tree species when constructing arboreal nests, and nest sites were more likely to be constructed in areas that appear to hold both preferred nesting and food resources (Sawyer, 2012). Since the time of Sawyer's (2012) research, the gorillas are now nesting in closer proximity to Nga village, in areas of abandoned farmland. To understand this movement, better long-term data on the gorillas' ranging patterns is required. In contrast to chimpanzees, gorillas are not territorial and have overlapping home ranges (Ganas & Robbins, 2005; Remis, 1997; Tutin, 1996). Western lowland gorillas are known to revisit feeding areas, and their accumulated monthly ranges usually reach the size of their annual range over a few months (Doran-Sheehy et al., 2004). Based on research at Afi Mountain, Nigeria, and Kagwene Gorilla Sanctuary, the Cross River gorilla appears to have a relatively large home range of 10–30 km^2 (McFarland, 2007; Sunderland-Groves et al., 2009). The recorded nesting range of 4.5 km^2 for the Mone-Oku gorillas is therefore likely to represent only a fraction of their entire home range. However, it is also an area that is most at risk of lowland forest clearance, which has the potential to reduce preferred nesting and food resources, and increase encounters between gorillas and humans, depending on the gorillas' ranging movements.

The tolerance of the Mone-Oku gorilla population to nesting in lowland forests and in close proximity to higher human activity is not something that has been previously reported. Historically, it is believed the Cross River gorilla had a widespread distribution in lowland forests and underwent a marked decline 100 years ago (Mansfield, 1908, cited in Bergl et al., 2012; Thalmann et al., 2011). Recent analysis at the landscape level suggests that the distribution of Cross River gorillas is influenced by human activities and village locations, with the gorillas most likely to range in areas of more complex topography (Bergl et al., 2012; Imong et al., 2014). Other Cross River gorilla groups have been found to avoid areas of high anthropogenic pressure irrespective of resource richness (Etiendem et al., 2013; McFarland, 2007). Further investigation into the interactions between the gorillas' resource use, local perceptions and local use of the forest at other sites may help to understand the degree and type of human activities gorillas will tolerate within their range in unprotected areas.

There were clear differences in the participants' perceptions regarding the apes' behaviour towards people, despite the observed physical similarities of the two species. Chimpanzees were generally not seen to be as dangerous as gorillas and hunters were less intimidated when they encountered a chimpanzee group. Oishi (2013) found Baka hunters in Southeastern Cameroon also emphasised the danger of gorillas (*G. g. gorilla*), differentiating them from chimpanzees (*P. t. troglodytes*), as the gorillas are not afraid of encounters with humans. The Baka believe the gorillas try to keep people out of their range and will sometimes ambush them unexpectedly. This behaviour of the gorillas ensured that the Baka were cautious when hunting, to make sure they avoided the gorillas (Oishi, 2013). This cautious human behaviour was also observed among the Nga hunters. That the hunters flee from a gorilla encounter may reduce the threat they posed to the gorillas, allowing the gorillas to range in closer proximity to the village.

While the direct hunting of the apes appears to be a diminishing threat, the near-universal view that the Mone-Oku Forest is an unlimited economic resource for the people of Nga and Eshobi is a major concern for the conservation of both taxa. Agricultural intensification often places a large amount of pressure on environments. The clearing of forests can result in forest fragments, frequently producing new ecological edges that alter microclimates and can cause shifts in the biodiversity of the area (Struhsaker, 1997). Forest fragmentation has been shown to reduce gene flow and isolate populations of chimpanzees (*P. t. schweinfurthii*) and gorillas (*G. g. gorilla*) when forest corridors that promote connectivity are lost (e.g. Gagneux et al., 2001; Tutin et al., 1997). At this stage, the chimpanzees' nesting habitat is not at risk from agricultural expansion. However, as the lowland forest is cleared there is the potential for the chimpanzee community to become isolated. The gorillas' nesting habitat is at risk; during the study period, areas where gorilla nests had been recorded were cleared for farmland. There appears to be a delicate interplay between agricultural cycles and the gorillas' preferences for nesting materials that are more frequently found in regenerating secondary forest. These types of forest could become less prevalent as farmers move towards establishing permanent crops of cocoa and farmland is less likely to be abandoned. A change to cocoa production also has the potential to increase the likelihood of the gorillas ranging within farms. Currently these events appear to be isolated and are generally tolerated by the people of Nga. However, as farms encroach on the gorillas' range, these events could become more frequent and have the potential to harm farmers' income and cause conflict, especially if the gorillas begin feeding on cocoa fruit, as they have been observed to do around Nki National Park, East Cameroon (Oishi, 2013).

4.6   Conclusions and Future Directions

This research illustrates the ways in which an ethnoprimatological approach can enhance our understanding of the interrelationships that exist between primates and people and how the outcomes of such research may help to inform conservation initiatives. The methods and insights gained from an ethnoprimatological approach highlight the complexity and heterogeneity that exist among human communities (Ellwanger et al., 2017). How local communities interact with the apes can change depending on the context at that particular point in time. We found that participants from Nga and Eshobi villages held contradictory ideas and context-dependent perceptions of the apes. However, the most important issue discovered was the near-universal perception of the Mone-Oku Forest as an unlimited economic resource. While the Cross River gorillas and Nigeria–Cameroon chimpanzees are primates of special significance to researchers and conservationists, for the villagers of Nga and Eshobi the significance lies in the forest itself rather than particular animals within it.

Conservation initiatives need to acknowledge that the ways local communities interact with their environments are continually changing, and understand that a one-size-fits-all model focusing on the Cross River gorilla as a flagship species may not protect the Nigeria–Cameroon chimpanzee or other intended species (Radhakrishna, 2017). While both of our study taxa are threatened by habitat alteration, they are threatened in different ways. The Mone-Oku chimpanzee nesting range is not directly threatened, but there is the potential for the loss of forest connectivity and isolation of the chimpanzee community. In contrast, parts of the Mone-Oku gorilla nesting range is directly threatened by habitat loss, especially favoured areas of lowland and secondary forest. There is also the possibility of future conflict between the gorillas and villages as farms encroach into the gorillas' range. Conservation initiatives need to work with the local communities to address these potential threats. Together, it is possible that land use management practices could be agreed upon that allow forest corridors to remain intact in certain areas, to prevent the isolation of chimpanzee communities and to limit the expansion of farms into gorilla ranges.

Our future research will seek to investigate the drivers behind agricultural intensification in the Mone-Oku Forest by considering the socioeconomic and political situation in the region. We will also assess the economic reliance on the forest. People are actors within ecosystems and the links between ecology, policy and economy are multidimensional and dialectical (Gezon, 2006). In the long term, AW's future research goals include a study of the feeding ecology of both ape taxa. Expanding research to include feeding ecology will help to improve our knowledge of the multiple factors influencing each ape's distribution, ranging patterns and core habitat requirements. This will provide a greater understanding of the human–ape interconnections and may require conservation initiatives to place greater emphasis on farming practices and land use in unprotected areas.

References

Bergl, R. A., Warren, Y., Nicholas, A., et al. (2012). Remote sensing analysis reveals habitat, dispersal corridors and expanded distribution for the Critically Endangered Cross River gorilla *Gorilla gorilla diehli*. *Oryx*, **46**(2), 278–289.

Bergl, R. A., Dunn, A., Fowler, A., et al. (2016). *Gorilla gorilla* spp. *diehli*. *The IUCN Red List of Threatened Species 2016*. Available at: www.iucnredlist.org/details/39998/0 (accessed 28 December 2016).

Brownlow, A. R., Plumptre, A. J., Reynolds, V. & Ward, R. (2001). Sources of variation in the nesting behavior of chimpanzees (*Pan troglodytes schweinfurthii*) in the Budongo Forest, Uganda. *American Journal of Primatology*, **55**, 49–55.

Ceballos, G., Ehrlich, P. R., Barnosky, A. D., et al. (2015). Accelerated modern human-induced species losses: entering the sixth mass extinction. *Scientific Advances*, **1**, 1–5.

De Vere, R. A., Warren, Y., Nicholas, A., MacKenzie, M. E. & Higham, J. P. (2011). Nest site ecology of the Cross River gorilla at the Kagwene Gorilla Sanctuary, Cameroon, with special reference to anthropogenic influence. *American Journal of Primatology*, **73**, 253–61.

Doran-Sheehy, D. M., Greer, D., Mongo, P. & Schwindt, D. (2004). Impact of ecological and social factors on ranging in western gorillas. *American Journal of Primatology*, **58**, 91–116.

Dore, K. M., Riley, E. P. & Fuentes, A. (eds) (2017). *Ethnoprimatology: A Practical Guide to Research at the Human–Nonhuman Primate Interface*. Cambridge: Cambridge University Press.

Dunn, A., Bergl, R., Byler, D., et al. (2014). *Revised Regional Action Plan for the Conservation of the Cross River Gorilla (*Gorilla gorilla diehli*): 2014–2019*. New York: IUCN/SSC Primate Specialist Group and Wildlife Conservation Society.

Dutton, P. E. (2012). *Chimpanzee (*Pan troglodytes ellioti*) ecology in a Nigerian montane forest*. PhD Dissertation, University of Canterbury.

Ellwanger, A. L., Riley, E. P., Niu, K. & Tan, C. L. (2017). Using a mixed-methods approach to elucidate the conservation implications of the human–primate interface in Fanjingshan National Nature Reserve, China. In Dore, K. M., Riley, E. P. & Fuentes, A. (eds) *Ethnoprimatology: A Practical Guide to Research at the Human–Nonhuman Primate Interface*. Cambridge: Cambridge University Press, pp. 257–70.

Estrada, A., Garber, P. A., Rylands, A. B., et al. (2017). Impending extinction crisis of the world's primates: why primates matter. *Science Advances*, **3**, 1–16.

Etiendem, D. N., Funwi-Gabga, N., Tagg, N., Hens, L. & Indah, E. K. (2013). The Cross River gorillas (*Gorilla gorilla diehli*) at Mawambi Hills, south-west Cameroon: habitat suitability and vulnerability to anthropogenic disturbance. *Folia Primatologica*, **84**, 18–31.

Fedigan, L. M. (2010). Ethical issues faced by field primatologists: asking the relevant questions. *American Journal of Primatology*, **72**, 754–71.

Frid, A. & Dill, L. (2002). Human-caused disturbance stimuli as a form of predation risk. *Conservation Ecology*, **6**, 11–26.

Fruth, B. & Hohmann, G. (1996). Nest building behavior in the great apes: the great leap forward? In McGrew, W. C., Merchant, L. F. & Nishida, T. (eds) *Great Ape Societies*. Cambridge: Cambridge University Press, pp. 225–40.

Fuentes, A. (2007). Monkey and human interconnections: the wild, the captive, and the in-between. In Cassidy, R. & Mullin, M. (eds) *Where the Wild Things Are Now: Domestication Reconsidered*. Oxford: Berg, pp. 123–45.

Fuentes, A. (2012). Ethnoprimatology and the anthropology of the human–primate interface. *Annual Review of Anthropology*, **41**, 101–17.

Fuentes, A. & Wolfe, L. D. (2002). *Primates Face to Face: The Conservation Implications of Human–Nonhuman Primate Interconnections*. Cambridge: Cambridge University Press.

Furuichi, T. & Hashimoto, C. (2004). Botanical and topographical factors influencing nesting-site selection by chimpanzees in Kalinzu Forest, Uganda. *International Journal of Primatology*, **25**, 755–65.

Gagneux, P., Gonder, M. K., Goldberg, T. A. & Morin, P. A. (2001). Gene flow in wild chimpanzees: what genetic data tell us about chimpanzee movements over space and time. *Philosophical Transactions of the Royal Society B*, **356**, 889–97.

Ganas, J. & Robbins, M. M. (2005). Ranging behaviour of the mountain gorillas (*Gorilla beringei beringei*) in Bwindi Impenetrable National Park, Uganda: a test of the ecological constraints model. *Behavioral Ecology and Sociobiology*, **58**, 277–88.

Gezon, L. L. (2006). *Global Visions, Local Landscapes: A Political Ecology of Conservation, Conflict, and Control in Northern Madagascar*. Lanham, MD: Altamira Press.

Imong, I., Robbins, M. M., Mundry, R., Bergl, R. & Kühl, H. S. (2014). Distinguishing ecological constraints from human activity in species range fragmentation: the case of Cross River gorillas. *Animal Conservation*, **17**, 323–31.

Jacobson, S. K. (2010). Effective primate conservation education: gaps and opportunities. *American Journal of Primatology*, **72**, 414–19.

Jameson, C. (2012). Gorilla Guardian update: expansion of the community-based monitoring network. *Gorilla Journal*, **45**, 13–15.

Koops, K., McGrew, W. C., de Vries, H. & Matsuzawa, T. (2012). Nest-building by chimpanzees (*Pan troglodytes verus*) at Seringbara, Nimba Mountains: antipredation, thermoregulation, and antivector hypotheses. *International Journal of Primatology*, **33**, 356–80.

Kühl, H., Maisels, F., Ancrenaz, M. & Williamson, E. A. (2008). *Best Practice Guidelines for Surveys and Monitoring of Great Ape Populations*. Gland: IUCN SSC Primate Specialist Group.

Malone, N., Palmer, A. & Wade, A. H. (2017). Incorporating the ethnographic perspective: the value, process, and responsibility of working with human participants. In Dore, K. M., Riley, E. P. & Fuentes, A. (eds) *Ethnoprimatology: A Practical Guide to Research at the Human–Nonhuman Primate Interface*. Cambridge: Cambridge University Press, pp. 176–89.

Mboh, H. & Warren, Y. (2007). Large mammal survey of the proposed Takamanda National Park. Unpublished report. Wildlife Conservation Society.

McFarland, K. L. (2007). Ecology of Cross River gorillas (*Gorilla gorilla diehli*) on Afi Mountain, Cross River State, Nigeria. PhD Dissertation, City University of New York.

McLennan, M. R., Spagnoletti, N. & Hockings, K. J. (2017). The implications of primate behavioral flexibility for sustainable human–primate coexistence in anthropogenic habitats. *International Journal of Primatology*, **38**, 105–21.

Morgan, B., Adeleke, A., Bassey, T., et al. (2011). *Regional Action Plan for the Conservation of the Nigeria-Cameroon Chimpanzee (*Pan troglodytes ellioti*)*. San Diego, CA: IUCN/SSC Primate Specialist Group and Sociological Society of San Diego.

Oates, J. F., Doumbe, O., Dunn, A., et al. (2016). *Pan troglodytes* ssp. *ellioti*. The IUCN Red List of Threatened Species 2016. Available at: www.iucnredlist.org/details/40014/0 (accessed 28 December 2016).

Oishi, T. (2013). Human–gorilla and gorilla–human: dynamics of human–animal boundaries and interethnic relationships in the central African rainforest. *Revue de Primatology*, **5**, 1–23.

QGIS. (2014). QGIS 2.12.3: a free and open source geographic information system. Available at: www.qgis.org/en/site.

Radhakrishna, S. (2017). Culture, conflict, and conservation: living with nonhuman primates in Northeastern India. In Dore, K. M., Riley, E. P. & Fuentes, A. (eds) *Ethnoprimatology: A Practical Guide to Research at the Human–Nonhuman Primate Interface*. Cambridge: Cambridge University Press, pp. 271–83.

Remis, M. J. (1997). Ranging and grouping patterns of a western lowland gorilla group at Bai Hokou, Central African Republic. *American Journal of Primatology*, **43**, 111–33.

Riley, E. P. & Ellwanger, A. L. (2013). Methods in ethnoprimatology: exploring the human–nonhuman primate interface. In Sterling, E., Bynum, N. & Blair, M. (eds) *Primate Ecology and Conservation: A Handbook of Techniques*. Oxford: Oxford University Press, pp. 128–50.

Rothman, J. M., Pell, A. N., Dierenfeld, E. S. & McCann, C. M. (2006). Plant choice in the construction of night nests by gorillas in the Bwindi Impenetrable National Park, Uganda. *American Journal of Primatology*, **68**, 361–8.

Sawyer, S. C. (2012). The ecology and conservation of the Critically Endangered Cross River gorilla in Cameroon. PhD Dissertation, University of California.

Setchell, J. M. (2013). Editorial: the top 10 questions in primatology. *International Journal of Primatology*, **34**, 647–61.

Setchell, J. M., Fairet, E., Shutt, K., Waters, S. & Bell, S. (2016). Biosocial conservation: integrating biological and ethnographic methods to study human–primate interactions. *International Journal of Primatology*, **38**, 1–26.

Sponsel, L. E. (1997). The human niche in Amazonia: explorations in ethnoprimatology. In Kinzey, W. G. (ed.) *New World Primates*. New York: Aldine de Gruyter, pp. 143–65.

SPSS (2011). SPSS Statistics Version 20.0.0. IBM Corporation. Available at: www.ibm.com/support/knowledgecenter/en/SSLVMB_20.0.0/com.ibm.spss.statistics_20.kc.doc/pv_welcome.html.

Strier, K. B. (2011). Conservation. In Campbell, C. J., Fuentes, A., MacKinnon, K. C., Bearder, S. K. & Stumpf, R. M. (eds) *Primates in Perspective*. New York: Oxford University Press, pp. 664–75.

Struhsaker, T. T. (1997). *Ecology of an African Rain Forest: Logging in Kibale and the Conflict Between Conservation and Exploitation*. Gainesville, FL: University of Florida Press.

Sunderland, T. C. H., Comiskey, J. A., Besong, S., et al. (2003). Vegetation assessment of Takamanda Forest Reserve, Cameroon. In Comiskey, J. A., Sunderland, T. C. H. & Sunderland-Groves, J. L. (eds) *Takamanda: The Biodiversity of an African Rainforest*. Washington, DC: Smithsonian Institution, pp. 19–54.

Sunderland-Groves, J. L., Ekinde, A. & Mboh, H. (2009). Cross River gorilla (*Gorilla gorilla diehli)* nesting behaviour at Kagwene Mountain, Cameroon: implications for assessing group size, age structure and density at other Cross River gorilla localities. *International Journal of Primatology*, **30**, 253–66.

SYSTAT (2009). SYSTAT Version 13. SYSTAT Software. Available at: www.systatsoftware.com.

Thalmann, O., Wegmann, D., Spitzner, M., et al. (2011). Historical sampling reveals dramatic demographic changes in western gorilla populations. *BMC Evolutionary Biology*, **11**, 85–95.

Tutin, C. E. G. (1996). Ranging and social structure of lowland gorillas in the Lope Reserve, Gabon. In McGrew, W. C., Marchant, L. F. & Nishida, T. (eds) *Great Ape Societies*. Cambridge: Cambridge University Press, pp. 58–70.

Tutin, C. E. G., Parnell, R. J., White, L. J. T. & Fernandez, M. (1995). Nest building by lowland gorillas in the Lopé Reserve, Gabon: environmental influences and implications for censusing. *International Journal of Primatology*, **16**, 53–76.

Tutin, C. E. G., White, L. J. T. & Mackanga-Missandzouo, A. (1997). The use by rain forest mammals of natural forest fragments in an equatorial African savanna. *Conservation Biology*, **11**, 1190–203.

Warren, Y. & Ekinde, A. (2007). Large mammal recce survey of the Mone Forest Reserve. Unpublished report. Wildlife Conservation Society.

White, F. (1983). *The Vegetation of Africa, a Descriptive Memoir to Accompany the UNESCO/AETFAT/UNSO Vegetation Map of Africa (3 plates, Northwestern African, Northeastern Africa, and Southern Africa, 1:5,000,000)*. Paris: UNESCO.

White, L. & Edwards, A. (2000). Methods for assessing the status of animal populations. In White, L. & Edwards, A. (eds) *Conservation Research in the African Rain Forests: A Technical Handbook*. New York: Wildlife Conservation Society, pp. 191–201.

5 Comanagement of Primate Hunting in Amazonian Indigenous Reserves

A Case Study from Guyana

Christopher A. Shaffer, Marissa S. Milstein, Phillip Suse, Elisha Marawanaru and Charakura Yukuma

5.1 Personal Narrative

When I (CAS) was young, I was fascinated by nature. I spent as much time as I could hiking in the forest, and I read insatiably about plants and animals. I was particularly enthralled when I read about the tropical rainforest and the diversity of life within it. In the summer of my freshman year of high school, I had the incredible opportunity to travel to Peru and experience the Amazon rainforest in person. Seeing the extraordinary variety of flora and fauna in this beautifully complex environment, especially the primates, made me realise that primate ecology was what I wanted to study. However, I was also interested in learning about how humans subsisted in this productive but challenging ecosystem. Because it involves the study of both non-human and human primates, I decided to study anthropology.

I went on to pursue a Bachelor of Science in biological anthropology at Emory University, focusing on primate behavioural ecology. After conducting fieldwork studying howler monkeys in Nicaragua, I became increasingly interested in primate feeding and ranging behaviour. I was especially interested in the ranging and grouping strategies that primates have evolved to minimise the costs associated with finding food. After graduating from Emory, I entered a PhD programme at Washington University in St. Louis, working with Bob Sussman. It was during my third year at Washington University that I first travelled to the remarkable country of Guyana. Bob had conducted preliminary surveys of the primates in Guyana ten years earlier and regaled me with stories about this amazing country that still retained over 80 per cent of its original forest. My lifelong love for nature and passion for conserving wildlife made me eager to work in a place that offered a great deal of promise for promoting rainforest conservation. I knew that I wanted to combine my research interests in primate behavioural ecology with applied conservation work and I thought that studying the rainforest ecosystem through primatology would help demonstrate the value of these habitats and the need to conserve them.

During my first trip to Guyana, I spent two months travelling around the country looking for a suitable field site where I could study bearded sakis (*Chiropotes sagulatus*). Little was known about the behavioural ecology of these seed predators and I was eager to understand why they lived in such large groups and travelled over enormous ranges. Strongly influenced by the dominant natural/anthropogenic dichotomy paradigm of the time, I sought a field site where there was as little human disturbance as possible and I could study the 'natural' behaviour of these animals. I chose an extremely remote area in the southern part of the country (in a protected area leased by Conservation International (CI) called the Upper Essequibo Conservation Concession) located more than 80 km from the nearest human settlement (a village of 200 indigenous people). This area was as 'pristine' as any rainforest environment in the world and walking through the forest gave the impression that no human had been there before.

Almost immediately, however, I realised that my ideas of 'natural' and 'pristine' did not correspond to reality. As my field assistants and I prepared our camp – clearing brush and digging our latrines – we started to pull up large amounts of pottery and stone axeheads. When we started conducting botanical transect surveys, we noticed that many areas of the forest exhibited tell-tale botanical signs of past human settlement, including high concentrations of cultivated plant species (like the turu palm *Oenocarpus bacaba*). It became apparent that this environment had once been occupied by a relatively sizeable human population and that these humans had modified the environment considerably. Thus the 'natural' behavioural ecology of bearded sakis that I was studying was, to a certain extent, a product of past human activity. This experience challenged me to realise that humans and non-human primates had lived sympatrically in Amazonia for thousands of years and to rethink the idea that human influence on Amazonian primates was always negative. I became increasingly interested in studying these relationships and, particularly, how this understanding could be used to promote animal conservation.

At the same that I was thinking about these questions, I was approached, through CI, by representatives from an indigenous group in the far south of Guyana, called the Waiwai. The Waiwai had recently been given title to their land and had signed a memorandum with the government of Guyana and CI that stated their enormous territory, the Konashen Community Owned Conservation Area, would be managed for sustainable use. The Waiwai were interested in collaborating with researchers to help them sustainably manage their resources. Officials from CI suggested to the Waiwai that I might be interested in conducting surveys of the abundance of primates and other mammals that they hunted for food. I jumped at the opportunity, as I was extremely excited to be able to combine my increasing interest in studying human–non-human primate ecological and social relationships with applied, community-based conservation work.

This began a long-term partnership with the Waiwai that I hope will continue for the rest of my career. Although it was at first extremely difficult to watch primates being hunted and eaten, I began to realise that primate conservationists and the indigenous Amazonians that live with and consume primates are shared stakeholders in the long-term viability of primate populations. As an anthropologist, I also understood that conservation is just as much about working closely with people as it is studying animals. My work studying bearded sakis and living and working with the Waiwai has challenged my ideas about what is 'natural' in the Anthropocene and has shown me the importance of indigenous people as potential conservation allies. I now believe that developing mutually beneficial partnerships with indigenous groups, including those that continue to hunt primates, is essential for successful conservation of primates in South America.

5.2   Introduction

Non-human primates (hereafter primates) and humans have lived sympatrically in Amazonia for at least 10 000 years (Balée, 2015; Heckenberger, 1998; Oliver, 2001). During this period, primate hunting has likely formed a significant part of the subsistence strategies, symbolism and cosmology of indigenous societies (Cormier, 2003, 2006; de Thoisy et al., 2009). Unfortunately, increasing population densities, changing hunting technology, and the synergistic effects of hunting and anthropogenic habitat disturbance have led to the broad-scale extirpation of primate populations throughout Amazonia (de Thoisy et al., 2009; Fa et al., 2002; Peres, 2000; Peres et al., 2016). At the same time, indigenous reserves have become increasingly common in South America, and now make up over 50 per cent of protected areas and over 20 per cent of the total land area of the Amazon Basin (RAISG, 2016). These areas are designed to protect biodiversity while simultaneously allowing indigenous groups to continue practising traditional subsistence strategies, often including the hunting of primates and other wildlife (Peres, 1994; Schwartzman & Zimmerman, 2005). As eliminating primate hunting may not be feasible in these areas, primate conservationists must work collaboratively with indigenous groups to promote long-term sustainable hunting. This requires understanding the economic and social importance of primates to indigenous societies and using this knowledge to collectively develop and implement methods for hunting comanagement that meet the goals of both conservationists and indigenous groups (Constantino et al., 2008; Schwartzman & Zimmerman, 2005; Shaffer et al., 2017a; Shepard et al., 2012).

In this chapter, we review the extent, drivers and effects of primate hunting in South America, focusing particularly on hunting by indigenous groups. We also provide an overview of Amazonian indigenous reserves, including goals, management and conservation challenges. We then use a case study of the primate hunting of indigenous Waiwai in Guyana to show the importance of primates to indigenous food security and culture and provide a model for effective comanagement of primate hunting. Finally, we reflect on the role of indigenous reserves for the future viability of primate populations in Amazonia.

5.2.1   Primate Hunting in South America

Primates have been hunted by indigenous Amazonians since the region was first colonised over 10 000 years ago (Balée, 2015; Cartelle & Hartwig, 1996) and accounts from early European explorers frequently mention primate hunting as an important subsistence activity of the indigenous peoples they encountered (Edmundson, 1922; Schomburgk, 1836; Wallace, 1835; Waterton, 1825). Hunting by prehistoric populations appears to have played a role in the extinction of several platyrrhine taxa

(Balée, 2015; Cartelle & Hartwig, 1996; de Thoisy et al., 2009) and has likely shaped the biogeography of primate populations in several areas of Amazonia (Shepard et al., 2012). Primates continue to be among the most important prey species for Amazonian peoples, particularly indigenous groups (de Thoisy et al., 2009; Jerozolimski & Peres, 2003; Stafford et al., 2017). Non-indigenous Amazonians, including 'colonist' populations like caboclos in Brazil and Ribereños in Peru (populations that have moved to Amazonia for rubber extraction and fishing within the past two centuries) and 'Maroons' or 'Bushnegroes' (populations descended from escaped slaves), generally prefer species that resemble domestic livestock, like ungulates and large rodents (Barnett et al., 2002; de Thoisy et al., 2009; Mittermeier, 1991; Richard-Hansen et al., 2004). Primates generally make up less than 10 per cent of prey for these non-indigenous groups, and primates are frequently avoided altogether because of their physical similarities to humans (de Thoisy et al., 2009; Jerozolimski & Peres, 2003; Mittermeier, 1991). While commercial bushmeat harvesting, including for urban consumers, is becoming increasingly common in Amazonia, the general avoidance of primate meat by non-indigenous populations means that the demand for primate meat in commercial markets remains low (Nasi et al., 2011).

In contrast, for indigenous Amazonians, primates are often the most numerically dominant order of prey mammals and generally make up a considerable portion of their harvested biomass (de Souza-Mazurek et al., 2000; de Thoisy et al., 2009; Franzen, 2006; Ohl-Schacherer et al., 2007; Peres & Nascimento, 2006; Stafford et al., 2017; Townsend, 2000; Zapata-Ríos et al., 2009). The most frequently targeted species are the large-bodied Atelines, particularly spider monkeys (*Ateles* spp.) and woolly monkeys (*Lagothrix* spp.). For example, among the Waorani in Ecuador, *Ateles belzebuth* was the most numerically important and second-ranked prey species by weight of over 51 species hunted over a five-month period (Franzen, 2006). *Logothrix lagotricha* was the second most important prey species both numerically and by weight among Shuar hunters in Ecuador (Zapata-Ríos et al., 2009). The Matsigenka in Peru harvested *Ateles chamek* at a rate more than twice that of any other primate species and it was the third most important species in terms of weight (after two peccary species) (Shepard, 2002; Ohl-Schacherer et al., 2007). Medium-sized species are also frequently targeted, and can be more important than large-bodied species in some areas, particularly central Amazonia and the Guiana Shield (Cormier, 2006; de Souza-Mazurek et al., 2000; de Thoisy et al., 2005; Peres & Nascimento, 2006). For the Kayapó of A'Ukre, Brazil, brown capuchins (*Sapajus apella*) and bearded sakis (*Chiropotes utahicki*) were among the top five most numerically important prey among 42 different species (Peres & Nascmiento, 2006). Similarly, brown capuchins and bearded sakis were the two most commonly hunted primates among the Waimiri-Atorai of Central Brazil (de Souza-Mazurek et al., 2000) and brown capuchins were one of the most important of all prey species for the Ka'apor in northern Brazil (Balée, 2015).

One of the primary reasons primates are such an important resource for Amazonian people is that they make up a considerable portion of the mammalian biomass in South American forests (Endo et al., 2010; Peres, 2000; Peres et al., 2016). In a survey of 56 northern Neotropical sites under varying degrees of hunting pressure, Peres (2000) found that primates made up a mean of 42 per cent of the biomass of large-bodied taxa across all sites and over 55 per cent of the biomass in lightly hunted or non-hunted sites. Further, because of their conspicuous foraging habits, large group sizes and high encounter rates with hunters, primates provide a relatively predictable food source for indigenous hunters, particularly compared to the larger bodied but more difficult to find ungulates (e.g. tapirs, peccaries and deer) (Shaffer et al., 2018).

In addition to their dietary importance, primates and primate hunting also play an important role in the symbolism, mythology and group identity of many indigenous groups (Cormier, 2006; Parathian & Maldonado, 2010; Shepard, 2002). Cultural beliefs and practices can strongly influence hunting behaviour and modulate harvesting decisions. Primate parts, including teeth, tails and bones, are frequently used for utilitarian and ritual objects (Cormier, 2003; Mittermeier, 1991; Shaffer et al., 2017b; Yde, 1965). For example, tamarins (*Saguinus* spp.) and titi monkeys (*Callicebus* spp.) are preferentially targeted by the Matis of Brazil, as their teeth are used in necklaces that indicate hunting prowess (Erikson, 2001). In addition, among some indigenous groups, the consumption of primates is thought to imbue the consumer with positive traits like speed and strength (Crocker, 1985; Shaffer et al., 2018) and primate hunting is often an important arena in which a man acquires masculine prestige (Shaffer et al., 2018; Shepard, 2002). Infant primates are among the most commonly kept pets by indigenous Amazonians, and hunters have been reported to target mothers with young specifically to obtain pets (Cormier, 2003, 2006; Lizarralde, 2002; Shepard, 2002). Many indigenous groups also have specific taboos on the consumption of certain primate species that directly relate to symbolism and cosmology (Cormier, 2003). Howler monkeys (*Alouatta* spp.) are avoided by several Amazonian societies, often because their perceived laziness and low intelligence are thought to be transferred to hunters if they are consumed (Holmberg, 1969; Kensinger et al., 1975; Lizarralde, 2002; Shepard, 2002). In contrast, howlers are the most preferred prey species among the Guaja of Brazil due to their privileged status as human-like 'persons' (Cormier, 2003).

Primate hunting is, therefore, an integral part of the subsistence strategies and social lives of Amazonian indigenous societies. Unfortunately, hunting is also one of the greatest threats to primate populations throughout the Amazon (Peres et al., 2016). Because of their low reproductive rates, long inter-birth intervals and small litter sizes, primates, particularly the Atelines, are among the most vulnerable Neotropical animals to overhunting (de Thoisy et al., 2009; Peres, 2000; Redford & Robinson, 1991). At most sites where hunting occurs, densities of large- and medium-bodied taxa are greatly reduced (de Thoisy et al., 2005; Freese et al., 1982; Peres, 1990; 2000) and hunting has directly led to local primate extinctions in several areas (Peres, 1990; 2000; Peres & Palacios, 2007). Such depletion is particularly troubling given the critical importance of large-bodied primates as seed dispersers (Nuñez-Iturri & Howe, 2007; Peres & Palacios, 2007; Peres et al., 2016).

While the sustainability of indigenous subsistence hunting in South America has been studied intensively for three decades, researchers disagree on the specific conditions under which hunting can be sustainable and the best methods for assessing sustainability (Bodmer et al., 1997; Levi et al., 2011; Milner-Gulland & Akcakaya, 2001; Novaro et al., 2000; Peres, 2000; Robinson & Bennett, 2004; Robinson & Redford, 1991; Van Vliet et al., 2015; Weinbaum et al., 2013). Prior to quantitative studies of bushmeat harvesting that began in the 1990s, conclusions about the sustainability of indigenous hunting were strongly influenced by the idea of what Redford and Robinson (1991) termed 'the ecologically noble savage' (Alvard et al., 1997; Hamas, 2007; Redford & Robinson, 1991). Researchers promoting the ecologically noble savage view of Amazonians, many influenced by the cultural ecology paradigm, suggested that indigenous societies existed in relative harmony with sympatric animal species and had a negligible effect on prey populations (Chagnon, 1968; Gross, 1975; Meggars, 1971). This assumption was based partially on observations that indigenous groups had long practised subsistence hunting and prey populations still persisted in most areas. Therefore, hunting must be, to a certain extent, sustainable. Further, indigenous groups were argued to have developed cultural mechanisms for actively managing prey animal populations and preventing overharvesting, including taboos, rotational hunting systems and regular settlement movements (Balée, 2015; Carneiro, 1978; Ross, 1978).

However, as researchers began to collect quantitative data on the actual harvesting patterns of indigenous Amazonians (Alvard et al., 1997; Bodmer, 1994; Hamas, 1991; Robinson & Redford, 1991) and conduct censuses of prey animals in areas affected by hunting pressure (Peres, 1990; 2000), the narrative of the ecologically noble savage was quickly replaced with one of invariable overhunting. The development of relatively simple sustainability indices like the production model (Robinson & Redford, 1991), harvest model (Bodmer, 1994) and stock–recruitment model (Bodmer & Robinson, 2004) allowed researchers to quantitatively determine sustainability with data on human harvesting and prey animal densities. These indices compare a maximum sustainable yield (calculated from the carrying capacity and population growth rate of the target species) with the observed offtake for a particular catchment area to produce a dichotomous sustainable/nonsustainable output (Bodmer & Robinson, 2004; Robinson & Redford, 1991). A litany of studies have been published using these methods, with a vast majority concluding that indigenous groups are not hunting sustainably (Alvard et al., 1997; Bodmer, 1994; de Souza-Mazurek et al., 2000; Franzen, 2006; Mena et al., 2000; Nasi et al., 2008; Zapata-Ríos et al., 2009). Changes in hunting technology, increased incorporation into the cash economy and, especially, increases in population size were thought to have led to unsustainable hunting in areas where it may once have been sustainable. In an overview of subsistence hunting in South America, de Thoisy and colleagues (2009: 406) summarised contemporary scientific understanding of sustainability thusly: 'All Amazonian studies show that most primates are simply unable to coexist with unregulated hunting, even for the most benign subsistence purposes, as soon as human population densities increase.'

More recently, however, several researchers have argued that indigenous hunting can, in fact, be sustainable, and that poor research methods may be leading to inaccurate conclusions about sustainability (Levi et al., 2009; 2011; Novaro et al., 2000; Ohl-Schacher et al., 2007; Shaffer et al., 2017b; Shepard et al., 2012; Sirén et al., 2004). Pointing to the lack of depletion in some primate populations that had been 'unsustainably' hunted for decades, these researchers argued that more robust methods for assessing sustainability, particularly ones that incorporated spatial heterogeneity and source–sink dynamics, were necessary to accurately measure prey animal depletion. Researchers using models that incorporate spatial dynamics are increasingly demonstrating that subsistence hunting, including of primates, can be sustainable under some circumstances (Iwamura et al., 2014; Levi et al., 2009; 2011; Novaro et al., 2000; Ohl-Schacher et al., 2007; Salas & Kim, 2002; Shaffer et al., 2017c; Shepard et al., 2012; Sirén & Parvinen, 2015; Sirén et al., 2004). For example, Levi and colleagues (2009; 2011) found that hunting by the Matsigenka in Manu National Park, Peru was likely to be sustainable over the next 50 years even if the population tripled. They also found that technology (bow and arrow versus shotgun) and the spatial spread of settlements were much more important factors in determining sustainability than overall population size. The work of others suggests that the most important factors promoting sustainable primate hunting by indigenous groups are relatively low population densities (although the effect of population density on prey depletion appears to be less than previously assumed), large 'source' areas that are unhunted, the concentration of human populations into one or a few settlements, and use of traditional technology (Levi et al., 2011; Ohl-Schacher et al., 2007; Shepard et al., 2012; Sirén et al., 2004). Fortunately, many of these conditions are present in the hundreds of millions of hectares of Amazonia protected by indigenous reserves (Peres, 1994; RAISG, 2012).

5.2.2   Amazonian Indigenous Reserves

As indigenous groups have been increasingly successful in securing their land rights throughout South America, indigenous reserves have become the largest category of protected areas in Amazonia (Peres, 1994; RAISG, 2012). Indigenous reserves consist of areas that have been legally designated by national governments for exclusive use by indigenous groups, although the lands themselves usually remain the property of the government and mineral and water rights are often under government control (Schwartzman & Zimmerman, 2005). Land rights are provided based on the areas the groups have traditionally occupied and the justification for these reserves is well summarised by this excerpt from the Brazilian constitution: 'indigenous lands are those permanently inhabited by them, those used for their productive activities, those indispensable to the environmental resources necessary to their well-being, and those necessary to their physical and cultural reproduction, according to their uses, customs and traditions' (Constituicao da Republica Federativa do Brasil, Art. 231, §1). Indigenous reserves vary considerably in their management policies, governance and degree of conservation enforcement, but are generally managed with the goal of maintaining traditional subsistence strategies and cultural autonomy while simultaneously engaging in sustainable development (Peres, 1994; Peres & Nascimento, 2006; Zimmerman et al., 2001).

Over 55 per cent of the area under government protection and about 28 per cent of the total area of Amazonia occurs within indigenous reserves (Figure 5.1). This includes over two million square kilometres of land and over 50 per cent of the land area of several South American countries (e.g. Venezuela, Colombia, Ecuador) (RAISG, 2012). In addition, many indigenous reserves are extremely large, with a mean size of

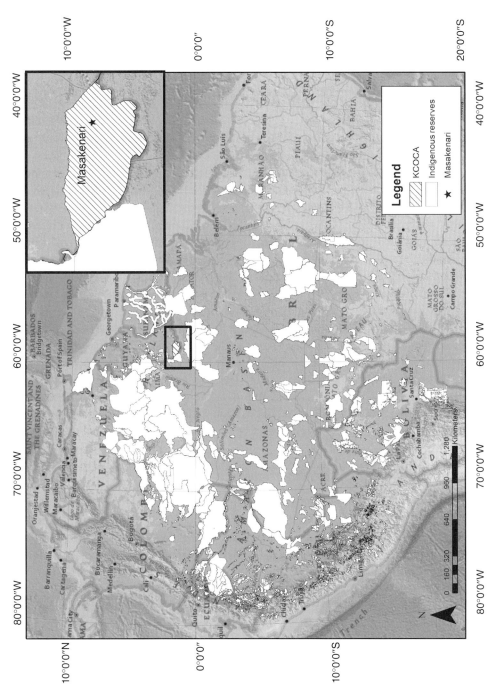

Figure 5.1 Map of indigenous reserves across Amazonia. The inset map shows the location of the Konashen Community Owned Conservation Area, Guyana.

over 500 000 ha. The number of indigenous reserves larger than one million hectares exceeds that of all other types of reserves in Amazonia combined (Peres, 1994). They thus represent a broader geographic representation and protect more undisturbed forest than any other type of protected area, and often have low population densities (fewer than 0.5 people/km^2). Further, a vast majority of these areas are closed to outsiders without permission from their landowners and many are actively patrolled and defended by indigenous groups (RAISG, 2012; Schwartzman & Zimmerman, 2005; Zimmerman et al., 2001). Several researchers have shown that indigenous reserves can be as effective as strictly protected parks for preventing deforestation, as they prevent large-scale conversion of forests to cattle pastures and logging concessions and the traditional swidden agriculture of indigenous populations has little negative impact on forest structure (Nepstad et al., 2006; Ohl et al., 2008; Sirén et al., 2004). Therefore, indigenous reserves offer tremendous opportunities for biodiversity conservation in Amazonia. Unfortunately, the need for economic opportunities and money in increasingly market-integrated societies has led some indigenous groups to engage in large-scale commercial mining and logging in their territories (Verissimo et al., 1995; Zimmerman et al., 2001). In addition, increasing population densities and population spread, changing subsistence strategies and the virtually ubiquitous use of firearms in some indigenous reserves may quickly lead to extirpation of vulnerable prey species, particularly primates, in places where hunting is currently sustainable (Peres et al., 2016; Shepard et al., 2012). Given the prevalence of indigenous reserves in Amazonia, the future success of primate conservation in this region will be largely determined by the ability of conservationists and indigenous groups to work together towards collaborative resource management. Fortunately, successful partnerships between researchers and indigenous groups for comanagement are now occurring at several sites across Amazonia (Bodmer & Puertas, 2000; Schwartzman & Zimmerman, 2005; Shaffer et al., 2017a; Shepard et al., 2012; Zimmerman et al., 2001).

5.2.3   A Case Study of Waiwai Primate Hunting

In this chapter, we use ethnographic methods to understand the importance of primate hunting to the food security and cultural identity of indigenous Waiwai in the Konashen Community Owned Conservation Area (KCOCA) in Guyana. We also employ spatially explicit biodemographic modelling to assess hunting sustainability and discuss the Konshen Ecosystem Health Project, a comanagement programme focused on promoting long-term sustainable hunting in the KCOCA.

5.3   Methods

5.3.1   Study Site: The KCOCA

The KCOCA is a 625 000 ha indigenous reserve in Southern Guyana that was granted to the Waiwai by the government of Guyana in 2004 (Figure 5.1). The memorandum that provided the Waiwai with their land rights, signed by the Waiwai village council, the Guyanese government and the conservation organisation CI, stipulated that the reserve was to be managed for sustainable use. More recently, the KCOCA was officially incorporated into the protected areas system of Guyana, making it the first protected area in the country to be under indigenous control. The KCOCA is located in the far South of Guyana, adjacent to the Brazilian border. The reserve consists primarily of undisturbed lowland rainforest and seasonally flooded riparian forest, and protects the headwaters of the Essequibo River, the largest river in Guyana. As with most areas of Guyana, the KCOCA experiences high seasonality in rainfall, with a long wet season lasting from May through August and a short wet season lasting from mid-December to mid-January. The area harbours eight species of sympatric primates, comprising two Atelids (*Alouatta macconnelli* and *Ateles paniscus*), three Cebids (*Saimiri scieurus*, *Cebus olivaceus* and *Sapajus apella*), two Pitheciids (*Chiropotes sagulatus* and *Pithecia pithecia*) and one Callitrichid (*Saguinus midas*).

The KCOCA is populated by approximately 225 Waiwai, concentrated in the village of Masekenari. Masekanari is the only permanent settlement in the reserve, although multiple settlements were occupied in the relatively recent past (Mentore, 2005). The people that currently identify as 'Waiwai' are a conglomeration of various ethnic groups, including Mowayenna, Hixkaryana, Shereo and Taruma (Mentore, 2005). Therefore, many Waiwai simultaneously hold other ethnic identities. While the Waiwai have had extensive contact with outsiders, particularly missionaries, for more than 50 years, they retain many traditional cultural elements and continue to practise the longstanding Amazonian subsistence strategy of swidden cassava horticulture supplemented with hunted meat and fish (Meggars, 1971; Mentore, 2005; Yde, 1965). Hunting is solely for subsistence and no meat is exchanged outside of the KCOCA, with the exception of trips to visit relatives in neighbouring communities.

5.3.2   Konshen Ecosystem Health Project

In concert with the memorandum that led to the establishment of the KCOCA, the Waiwai and CI sought to collaborate with international researchers for sustainable management of their resources. In 2012, C. A. Shaffer was approached by CI and representatives from the Waiwai village council to begin working towards comanagement of subsistence hunting in the KCOCA. Shaffer began initial fieldwork in 2013 to identify comanagement goals that were shared by all stakeholders (CI, the Waiwai, the government of Guyana and the research team). After extensive discussions with the community and detailed ethnographic research (see below), several shared goals were identified, including documenting the extent of Waiwai harvesting, assessing the long-term sustainability of subsistence hunting and establishing the training and capacity building necessary for long-term management. This led to the development of the Konshen Ecosystem Health Project, a long-term partnership with the Waiwai focused on comanagement of hunting and promotion of shared human–wildlife health. This project involves the employment of several methodologies, including ethnography, hunter self-monitoring, line-transect surveys and spatially explicit sustainability modelling.

5.3.3   Ethnographic Research

To assess the economic and cultural importance of primates to Waiwai society, provide context on Waiwai subsistence behaviour and determine the suitability of conservation interventions, we have conducted extensive ethnographic research with the Waiwai over several years (Shaffer et al., 2017b; 2018). Our ethnographic methods consisted of a combination of semi-structured interviews, unstructured interviews and participant observation. We conducted semi-structured interviews with 30 of the 44 hunters in Masakenari during two 2.5-month study periods from June to August 2013 and June to August 2015. We initially recruited participants for semi-structured interviews through snowball sampling. The village council suggested five hunters who might be interested in being interviewed, and these hunters provided the names of five more hunters. Interview questions addressed hunting frequency, techniques and practices, food consumption and non-economic uses for prey species.

We also conducted in-depth unstructured interviews with four key informants (two male and two female) to understand the relationship of primates to Waiwai identity and belief systems (Levy & Hollan, 2014). In addition, we regularly conducted unstructured interviews with hunters participating in the self-monitoring programme by discussing the self-monitoring forms that they filled out after a hunt. Hunters were generally eager to describe all aspects of the hunt, particularly when a primate or a large animal had been shot. These interviews often lasted many hours, as informants recounted the hunts in intricate detail. We found these interviews to be extremely valuable for understanding why hunters choose particular hunting locations, why hunts were perceived to be successful and what economic and sociocultural variables were influencing prey choice. Interviews were conducted in either Waiwai, English or a combination of both. About half of the Waiwai speak fluent English and a Waiwai field assistant fluent in English translated when necessary.

We used participant observation conducted from June to August 2013, 2015 and 2016 to contextualise our interviews, assess the reliability of our other data collection methods, and further our understanding of Waiwai subsistence behaviour (Fricke, 2005). We conducted participant observation during regular Waiwai activities, including hunting, farming, arrow making, food preparation and food consumption.

5.3.4   Hunter Self-Monitoring

After consultation with Waiwai hunters and the Waiwai village council, we began a participatory hunter self-monitoring programme in July 2014 (Shaffer et al., 2017a). As we initially had a limited amount of data collection equipment (GPS units, springscales, monitoring forms), we decided to recruit a random sample of 20 hunters for participation in the programme. Two of the recruited individuals subsequently left the village and three individuals declined participation. Therefore, our sample included 15 hunters. To estimate harvesting totals for all 44 hunters in Masakenari, we multiplied our sample by three (Shaffer et al., 2017b; 2018).

Each hunter was provided with two types of self-monitoring forms that they filled out after each hunt, and a spring scale for weighing prey. These forms were adapted from Ohl-Schacherer and colleagues (2007) to be appropriate for use with the Waiwai. One form provided detailed data on the total number of animals harvested, prey choice, hunting technology and hunt location, and variation in these variables across months. Locations were recorded by hunters using their Waiwai names and subsequently georeferenced by the researchers during interviews. The other form provided data on hunting preferences and kill rates (number of individuals of a species killed per group encountered), how these varied across months, and type of technology (bow and arrow versus shotgun). Sample forms can be found in Shaffer et al. (2017a). We also provided each of the participating hunters with GPS units, allowing hunters to collect data on the locations of each animal killed and the specific paths that they used during hunts. In this chapter, we present harvesting totals from 1 August 2014 to 1 August 2015.

5.3.5   Biodemographic Modelling

To assess the sustainability of Waiwai primate hunting, determine how variables like human population density, population spread and changing technology influence sustainability, and to design conservation strategies, we incorporated our ethnographic and harvesting data into spatially explicit biodemographic models. Initially developed by Levi and colleagues (2009), the biodemographic approach uses characteristics of hunter behaviour, prey animal densities and reproductive outputs, and the population growth for one or more human settlements to produce a continuous spatial surface of prey animal densities (Levi et al., 2009; Shaffer et al., 2017a). This method has been described in detail elsewhere (Levi et al., 2009; 2011; Shaffer et al., 2017a; 2017c) and the specific equations and a Python script for ArcGIS are available in Levi et al. (2009; 2011). Biodemographic models provide a number of advantages over traditionally used sustainability indices, including their incorporation of source–sink dynamics, the capacity to model densities into the future based on current or changing hunting pressure and their ability to assess the effect of hunting pressure on the density of prey across space rather than treating sustainability as a simple yes/no binary (Levi et al., 2009; Shaffer et al., 2017a). In addition, model outputs can be easily validated using hunter-collected data (Shaffer et al., 2017a).

In this chapter, we predicted the densities of the most important and most vulnerable Waiwai primate prey species, the black spider monkey (*Ateles paniscus*), 20 years into the future (Table 5.1). We used two different demographic scenarios: a 'doubling' scenario, where the village of Masakenari is projected to grow from 225 individuals to 500 during the 20-year period (with the same percentage of hunters); and an 'expansion' scenario where the total Waiwai population was projected to increase to 500 people and three additional settlements were established in areas that are currently household farms. Each of these settlements was projected to grow to a population of 33 individuals over the 20-year period, while Masakenari was projected to grow to 400 people. We modelled three types of technology use (only bow and arrow; a combination of 80 per cent shotgun and 20 per cent bow and arrow as currently practised by the

Table 5.1 Parameters for biodemographic models

Parameter	Definition	Value *A. pansicus*	Data source
K	Carrying capacity	8.07	Shaffer et al., 2017c
r	Maximum intrinsic growth rate	0.07	Robinson & Redford, 1991
d	Kill rate: individuals killed per group encounter	0.2, 0.9, 1.5[a]	Self-monitoring forms
hphy	Hunts per person per year	24	Self-monitoring forms
σ	Mean distance from settlement centre during hunts	6	Self-monitoring forms, interviews
D	Diffusivity of species or ¼ annual mean-square displacement	0.1	Levi et al., 2009

[a] Each kill rate reflects a different hunting technology scenario; bow and arrow only; 80 per cent shotgun and 20 per cent bow; and shotgun only. Values were empirically derived from hunter self-monitoring forms.

Waiwai; and only shotgun hunting) for each demographic scenario, providing six total scenarios. For each prey species, we calculated the extinction envelope around Masakenari and the percentage of the KCOCA where the species was predicted to be extirpated (densities $\leq$10 per cent of carrying capacity). We obtained values for r, the maximum intrinsic growth rate, from the literature and obtained estimates for carrying capacity (K) from line-transect surveys (Shaffer et al., 2017b) (Table 5.1). We estimated d, σ and *hphy* from hunter self-monitoring forms and interview data. The models assume that hunters are central-place foragers, an assumption that is consistent with the hunting behaviour of the Waiwai (Shaffer et al., 2017a; 2017b). However, because the Waiwai hunt opportunistically along the Essequibo and Kassikaityu Rivers during long-distance travel, we also modelled a hunting pressure of ten hunts per year at 2 km intervals along commonly travelled portions of these rivers within 16 km of Masakenari, and five hunts per year at 2 km intervals >16 km from Masakenari.

5.4   Results

5.4.1   Waiwai Primate Hunting

As is the case for most indigenous Amazonians, primates are among the most frequently harvested prey by Waiwai hunters. Based on our sample of 15 hunters, we estimated that the 44 Waiwai hunters in Masakenari harvested 288 individual primates from eight species, with a combined weight of over 1600 kg over the one-year period in our analysis (Table 5.2). This represents 27 per cent of all individual animals and 12.6 per cent of all biomass harvested. Spider monkeys were the most important primate species, ranking among the top five most important prey species both numerically and by weight. Bearded sakis were also highly preferred, with 54 individuals estimated to have been harvested during the year. Despite their large

Table 5.2 Number of primate individuals harvested by Waiwai hunters from 1 August 2014 to 1 August 2015 in the Konashen Community Owned Conservation Area (KCOCA)

Species	Number harvested for village[a]	Rank for number harvested[b]	Percentage of all prey harvested	Total weight for village (kg)[c]	Rank for weight harvested[d]	Percentage of total weight
Black spider monkey (*Ateles paniscus*)	117	3	10.9	1064.7	4	8.2
Bearded saki (*Chiropotes sagulatus*)	54	5	5.0	167.4	8	1.3
Brown capuchin (*Sapajus apella*)	39	9	3.6	128.7	12	1.0
Howler monkey (*Alouatta macconelli*)	21	13	2.0	157.5	9	1.2
Squirrel monkey (*Saimiri sciureus*)	21	14	2.0	16.8	26	0.1
White-faced saki (*Pithecia pithecia*)	18	15	1.7	52.2	19	0.4
Wedge-capped capuchin (*Cebus olivaceus*)	15	16	1.4	46.5	18	0.4
Golden-handed tamarin (*Saguinus midas*)	3	30	0.3	1.5	32	0.0
total	288		26.8	1635.3		12.6

[a] Estimated number of individuals harvested by all 44 hunters in Masakenari; obtained by multiplying the self-reported sample of 15 hunters by 3.
[b] Out of 33 species.
[c] Estimated total weight of prey harvested by all 44 hunters in Masakenari; obtained by multiplying the self-reported sample of 15 hunters by 3.
[d] Out of 33 species.

body size, howler monkeys were relatively infrequently targeted, with only 21 individuals estimated to have been harvested during the study period, the same number as the small-bodied squirrel monkey (*Saimiri sciureus*).

Traditionally, the Waiwai hunted primates using eight-foot long bows with similarly long, poison-tipped arrows (Figure 5.2). However, almost all Waiwai now own shotguns and 80 per cent of primate individuals were harvested using shotguns during the study period. Nevertheless, all Waiwai men still make and use bows and arrows. Shotguns are obtained through trade with Waiwai living in Brazil, as obtaining a firearm licence is extremely difficult in Guyana. Cartridges are similarly difficult to obtain and lack of ammunition was cited by hunters as the main reason for using bow and arrow. In addition, because cartridges are very expensive, shotguns are generally only used for preferred prey (like spider monkeys and bearded sakis). Small-bodied species like squirrel monkeys and tamarins are almost always shot with bow and arrow.

Waiwai primate hunting is highly seasonal, with a majority of individual primates (203 of 288) harvested during the long wet season (Figure 5.3). The Waiwai reported that primates, particularly the highly preferred spider monkeys and bearded sakis, are much fatter during this period and taste 'sweet'. The large quantity of subcutaneous fat from both species is often rendered for cooking oil, and spider monkeys will occasionally be targeted specifically to obtain oil. During the rest of the year, primates were generally avoided and were only hunted if other game were abnormally scarce. Hunters said that the taste of primates is poor outside of the wet season and many Waiwai suggested that hunting during these periods is taboo. The wet season in the KCOCA is a time when rising river levels make fish more dispersed and relatively difficult to catch. In addition, many non-primate prey species are difficult

Figure 5.2 Waiwai hunter showing the spider monkey that he shot with bow and poisoned arrows.

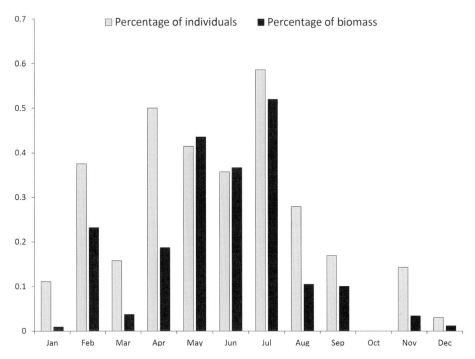

Figure 5.3 Seasonal variation in Waiwai hunting from 1 August 2014 to 1 August 2015. The light bars show primates as a percentage of all individuals harvested and the dark bars show primates as a percentage of total biomass harvested.

to hunt during this period. Due to their relatively high densities, loud foraging habits, and large group sizes, primates are more predictably encountered and easier to hunt than most other Waiwai prey species. Therefore, primates become an extremely important source of protein and fat during the wet season months.

In addition to its importance for food security, primate hunting is also an important social and symbolic practice for the Waiwai, and primate parts are used for a variety of utilitarian and ritual objects. The long, bushy tails of bearded sakis and white-faced sakis are mounted on sticks and used as dusters for both utilitarian and spiritual cleaning of houses. The fur of either howler or squirrel monkeys is used to create a brush for applying the arrow poison to arrowpoints and spider monkey radii are used to create ornate combs. The enlarged hyoid bones of howler monkeys are used as cups, and drinking from them is thought to cure colds and other sicknesses. A variety of primate bones are kept in the houses of hunters, usually stuck in the roof or lying on wood platforms above the fire. These bones are kept as raw materials for arrowpoints and combs and also serve as hunting souvenirs that indicate a hunter's prowess.

Our ethnographic research has also shown that primate hunting plays an important role in the construction of Waiwai cultural identity. The Waiwai are viewed derisively by many of Guyana's other indigenous groups for the perceived willingness to 'eat anything', especially primates, which are rarely hunted by most other groups (Henfrey, 2002). In contrast, the Waiwai proudly hunt primates and frequently express their desire to 'eat lots of monkey meat' during the wet season months. Waiwai informants repeatedly mention that they are the only 'true' forest people in Guyana, with forest people implicitly synonymous with hunting skill, best demonstrated during primate hunts. Most Waiwai exhibit a cultural aversion to meat from domesticated animals, the consumption of which they associate with the neighbouring Wapishana. Primate hunting also plays an important role in Waiwai masculinity, as hunting prowess confers a high degree of prestige on individuals. Spider monkey hunting, particularly with bow and arrow, is an especially important realm for a man to demonstrate hunting skill and acquire prestige.

5.4.2   Sustainability Modelling

The results of our biodemographic models suggest that the Waiwai will cause relatively modest levels of depletion in the KCOCA spider monkey population, even if the Waiwai population doubles over the next 20 years (Figure 5.4). If hunters

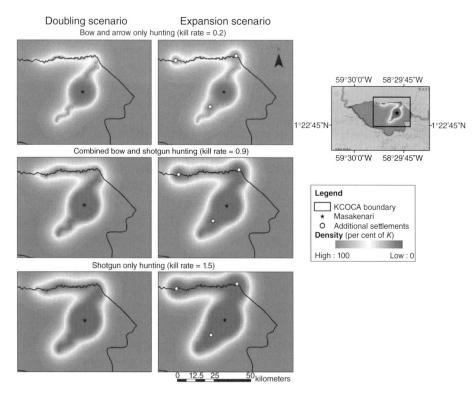

Figure 5.4 Projected densities from biodemographic models for black spider monkeys (*A. paniscus*) in 20 years. Masakenari is predicted to grow from 225 to 500 individuals in the scenarios on the right (the 'doubling' scenario), while images on the left depict the 'expansion' scenario, in which the total population of the KCOCA grows to 500 people but additional settlements are formed in areas that are currently household farms. The top row shows a bow-only technology scenario, the middle row shows a combination of bow and shotgun hunting, and the last row shows a shift to shotgun-only hunting.

continue to use bow and arrow for 20 per cent of kills, spider monkeys are predicted to exhibit a radius of extinction of 7.6 km and be extirpated from only about 7 per cent of the KCOCA. A switch to all-shotgun hunting would considerably increase the radius of extinction (9.1 km), although broad-scale extirpation would still be relatively limited (9.2 per cent). The spreading scenario with bow and arrow hunting actually decreases depletion compared to having the population concentrated in Masakenari (4.5 per cent depletion and a radius of extinction of 5.1 km for the expansion scenario compared to 5.7 per cent depletion and 5.7 km radius of extinction for the stationary scenario). This results from the increased perimeter of hunting zones and corresponding increase in primate immigration from source populations. However, this effect is not observed for combined shotgun and bow or shotgun-only hunting, where the establishment of the additional settlements scenario results in considerably larger areas of depletion than the sedentary population scenarios. As even small numbers of shotgun hunters can considerably deplete primate populations, the hunting zones in the spread scenario become contiguous and there is a corresponding decrease in the perimeter available for monkey immigration. Therefore, if the Waiwai population spread into additional settlements, particularly if this was accompanied by a shift to all-shotgun hunting, spider monkeys would be extirpated over a considerable area of the KCOCA (15 per cent).

Our models also show that hunting technology has the largest impact on hunting sustainability, a result consistent with those of other researchers who have used biodemographic modelling. Because bow and arrow hunting is highly inefficient (with kill rates of 0.1 to 0.2 individuals harvested per group encounter), even large bow-hunting populations do not cause broad-scale depletion. In contrast, human population size has a relatively modest effect on depletion, particularly if hunters are concentrated into a single settlement. Hunters in larger populations pseudo-interfere with one another, limiting their ability to deplete populations beyond a certain distance from the settlement centre.

5.4.3   Comanagement in the KCOCA

While our biodemographic results indicate that Waiwai hunting of spider monkeys is likely to be sustainable under a realistic population growth and technology scenario (see Shaffer et al., 2018 for results for other primate species), a shift to all-shotgun hunting, the establishment of additional settlements in the KCOCA, and/or broad-scale habitat disturbance would vastly increase depletion of spider monkey populations, jeopardising Waiwai food security and forest regeneration. Therefore, long-term monitoring and active management will be necessary for primate conservation in the KCOCA. Our comanagement programme involves Waiwai hunters continually collecting harvesting data, which we use to update model parameters every year. Each year, we share the outputs from the updated models with the community and discuss whether community-based interventions are necessary. Informed by our extensive ethnographic research, we discuss maps of predicted depletion overlaid on hunting trails over several weeks, both individually with hunters and with the community as a whole. Patterns of depletion and potential interventions are framed within a Waiwai hunting ontology that explains prey harvesting as a generalised reciprocity between human and animal persons (Shaffer et al., 2018).

This approach allows us to assess, in real time, what the effects will be if kill rates increase (as would be the case with an increase in shotgun hunting), hunters increase the number of hunts per year, or hunters expand their hunting catchment area. If model outputs indicate a level of depletion that will threaten food security and biodiversity conservation, no-harvest zones and/or quotas can be established based on quantitative data. The biodemographic approach allows for an assessment of the predicted effects of these interventions. We have also trained Waiwai parabiologists in line-transect survey methodology and these data, as well as hunter-collected catch-per-unit-effort (CPUE), are used to validate predicted patterns of depletion (Shaffer et al., 2017a). Model projections are compared to empirically derived density and CPUE estimates biennially, allowing us to consistently validate the predictive power of model scenarios.

5.5   Discussion

The primate hunting of the Waiwai is consistent with what has been reported for most indigenous groups in Amazonia. Primates are a critical component of the Waiwai diet, particularly during the wet season months, when other sources of protein and fat are scarce. In addition, primate hunting is an important social and symbolic activity that transcends its economic importance. Primate parts are used for a variety of ritual purposes and primate hunting is important for the construction of masculine identity. Further, the hunting and consumption of primates appears to be an important marker of collective Waiwai identity, uniting the multiple ethnic groups that constitute the people that today call themselves 'Waiwai' and distinguishing them from their indigenous neighbours. The high economic and cultural value that primate hunting has to the societies of indigenous Amazonians indicates that it is unlikely to stop in the near future. As indigenous reserves now make up a majority of the protected areas in Amazonia, primatologists must recognise that working collaboratively with indigenous groups towards sustainable management of primate hunting, rather than eliminating it entirely, is absolutely essential for successful conservation.

Fortunately, researchers are increasingly demonstrating that the subsistence hunting of primates may be sustainable under certain circumstances (Levi et al., 2009; Peres & Nascimento, 2006; Shaffer et al., 2017a; Shepard et al., 2012; Sirén et al., 2004). Despite dire predictions from previous studies, large-bodied primates persist in several indigenous reserves with relatively little depletion, even after decades of 'unsustainable' hunting (Hill et al., 2003; Koster, 2008; Levi et al., 2009; Ohl-Schacher et al., 2007; Peres & Nascimento, 2006; Shepard et al., 2012). For the Waiwai, the primary factors promoting sustainable hunting are the low population density in the KCOCA, the concentration of hunters in one settlement, the large areas of unhunted forest that operate as 'sources' for primate dispersal, and the continued use of bow and arrow for 20 per cent of hunting. These factors are also present in many other indigenous reserves throughout Amazonia (Constantino et al., 2008; Iwamura et al., 2014; Peres & Nascimento, 2006; Shepard et al., 2012; Zimmerman et al., 2001), providing optimism for the future success of comanagement efforts.

It is important to note that we are not suggesting that indigenous hunting of primates will always or even usually be sustainable. As our models show, the complete replacement of traditional hunting technology with shotguns, as is almost certain to occur across Amazonia, can quickly lead to broad-scale depletion, especially when accompanied by a spreading population. Further, conservation in indigenous reserves is wrought with challenges. In some cases, the goals of indigenous groups are not compatible with those of conservationists. For example, the desire for development has led some indigenous groups to engage in large-scale liquidation of natural resources, including unselective logging, extensive mining, cattle ranching and commercial agriculture (Peres, 1994; Redford & Robinson, 1991; Schwartzman & Zimmerman, 2005). Even when conservationists and indigenous groups share management goals, these may conflict with those of national governments (Shepard et al., 2010). In addition, comanagement with indigenous groups often requires the commingling of divergent ontologies, and monitoring large areas of forest against outside incursions poses an additional set of problems (Constantino et al., 2008; Parathian & Maldonado, 2010; Peres, 1994; Shepard et al., 2010; Zimmerman et al., 2001). Instead, we argue that indigenous hunting *can* be sustainable, and, more generally, that comanagement *must* be a critical component of Amazonian conservation moving forward.

5.6   Conclusions and Future Directions

Effective conservation in the Anthropocene requires recognition of the fact that setting aside 'pristine' areas where primates are unaffected by human influence is increasingly unrealistic. Nowhere is this more clear than in Amazonia, where a majority of protected areas have humans and primates living in sympatry. However, most of these areas haven't been 'pristine' for millennia, with humans and primates long influencing each other's ecology. While changing technology, increasing population densities, and incorporation into the market economy have altered these ecological relationships, indigenous reserves still provide tremendous opportunities for primate conservation. Researchers, policy makers and governments have increasingly recognised this, and successful comanagement programmes are protecting thousands of hectares of rainforest habitat in indigenous reserves throughout the Amazon (Bodmer & Puertas, 2000; Constantino et al., 2008; Schwartzman & Zimmerman, 2005; Shepard et al., 2012; Zimmerman et al., 2001). The long-term goal of the Konashen Ecosystem Health Project is to provide the training and capacity building necessary for the Waiwai to sustainably manage their own resource use. In addition to training Waiwai hunters to collect harvesting data and parabiologists to conduct line-transect surveys, we are developing a simple spatial modelling platform that will allow the community to continually monitor predicted patterns of prey depletion. Community members will be able to update model parameters each year based on hunter-collected data and use model results to determine whether no-harvest zones or quotas should be implemented. We hope that this project will serve as a model for comanagement of hunting in indigenous reserves throughout Amazonia.

Acknowledgements

We thank the Environmental Protection Agency of Guyana and the Ministry of Amerindian Affairs for granting permission for us to conduct this research and we are grateful for the logistic support provided by Major General Joe Singh, E. Alexander, D. Defreites, and K. Defreites. We also thank two reviewers whose comments helped improve the manuscript. Funding was provided by the National Geographic Society, the Veterinary Pioneers in Public Health Research Fund of the University of Minnesota's Center for Animal Health and Food Safety, the American Association of Physical Anthropologists, the Primate Action Fund of Conservation International, the International Primatological Society, Grand Valley State University and the University of Minnesota College of Veterinary Medicine. We are particularly grateful to the Waiwai of Masakenari Village for permitting us to conduct this study and welcoming us into their lives.

References

Alvard, M. S., Robinson, J. G., Redford, K. H. & Kaplan, H. (1997). The sustainability of subsistence hunting in the Neotropics. *Conservation Biology*, 11, 977–82.
Balée, W. (2015). *Cultural Forests of the Amazon: A Historical Ecology of People and Their Landscapes*. Tuscaloosa, AL: University of Alabama Press.
Barnett, A. A., Borges, S. H., de Castilho, C. V., Neri, F. M. & Shapley, R. L. (2002). Primates of the Jaúnational park, Amazonas, Brazil. *Neotropical Primates* 10, 65–70.
Bodmer, R. E. (1994). Managing wildlife with local communities: the case of the Reserva Comunal Tamshiyacu-Tahuayo. In Western, D., Wright, M. & Strum, S. (eds) *Natural Connections*. Washington, DC: Island Press, pp. 113–34.
Bodmer, R. & Puertas, P. E. (2000). Community-based comanagment of wildlife in the Peruvian Amazon. In Robinson, J. G. and Bennet, E. L. (eds) *Hunting for Sustainability in Tropical Forests*. New York: Columbia University Press, pp. 395–409.
Bodmer, R. & Robinson, J. (2004). Evaluating the sustainability of hunting in the neotropics. In Silvius, K., Bodmer, R. & Fragoso, J. (eds) *People in Nature: Wildlife Conservation in South and Central America*. New York: Columbia University Press, pp. 299–323.
Bodmer, R. E., Eisenberg, J. F. & Redford, K. H. (1997). Hunting and the likelihood of extinction of Amazonian mammals. *Conservation Biology*, 11, 460–6.
Carneiro, R. L. (1970). Hunting and hunting magic among the Amahuaca of the Peruvian Montana. *Ethnology*, 9, 331–41.
Cartelle, C. & Hartwig, W. C. (1996). A new extinct primate among the Pleistocene megafauna of Bahia, Brazil. *Proceedings of the National Academy of Sciences*, 93, 6405–9.
Chagnon, N. A. (1968). *Yanomamo: The Fierce People*. New York: Holt, Rinehart and Winston.
Constantino, P. A. L., Fortini, L. B., Kaxinawa, F. R. S., et al. (2008). Indigenous collaborative research for wildlife management in Amazonia: the case of the Kaxinawa, Acre, Brazil. *Biological Conservation*, 141, 2718–2729.

Cormier, L. A. (2003). *Kinship with Monkeys: The Guajá Foragers of Eastern Amazonia*. New York: Columbia University Press.

Cormier, L. A. (2006). A preliminary review of neotropical primates in the subsistence and symbolism of indigenous lowland South American people. *Ecological and Environmental Anthropology*, **2**, 14–32.

Crocker, J. C. (1985). *Vital Souls, Bororo Cosmology, Natural Symbolism, and Shamanism*. Tucson, AZ: University of Tucson Press.

de Souza-Mazurek, D., Roselis, R., Pedrinho, T., et al. (2000). Subsistence hunting among the Waimiri Atroari Indians in Central Amzonia, Brazil. *Biodiversity and Conservation*, **9**, 579–96.

de Thoisy, B., Renoux, F. & Julliot, C. (2005). Hunting in northern French Guiana and its impacts on primate communities. *Oryx*, **39**, 149–57.

de Thoisy, B., Richard-Hansen, C. & Peres, C. A. (2009). Impacts of subsistence game hunting on Amazonian primates. In Garber, P. A., Estrada, A., Bicca-Marques, J. C., Heymann, E. W. & Strier, K. B. (eds) *South American Primates: Comparative Perspectives in the Study of Behavior*. New York: Springer, pp. 389–412.

Edmundson, R. G. (1922). *Journal of the Travels of Father Samuel Fritz in the River of the Amazonas between 1686 and 1723*. London: Hakluyt Society.

Endo, W., Peres, C. A., Salas, E., et al. (2010). Game vertebrate densities in hunted and nonhunted forest sites in Manu National Park, Peru. *Biotropica*, **42**, 251–61.

Erikson, P. (2001). Myth and material culture: Matis blowguns, palm trees, and ancestor spirits. In Rival, L. and Whitehead, N. (eds) *Beyond the Visible and the Material: The Amerindianization of Society in the Work of Peter Rivière*. Oxford: Oxford University Press, pp. 101–121

Fa, J. E., Peres, C. A. & Meeuwig, J. (2002). Bushmeat exploitation in tropical forests: an international comparison. *Conservation Biology*, **16**, 232–37.

Franzen, M. (2006). Evaluating the sustainability of hunting: a comparison of harvest profiles across three Huaorani communities. *Environmental Conservation*, **33**, 36–45.

Freese, C. H., Heltne, P. G., Castro, N. & Whitesides, G. (1982). Patterns and determinants of monkey densities in Peru and Bolivia, with notes on distribution. *International Journal of Primatology* **3**, 53–90.

Fricke, T. (2005). Taking culture seriously: making the social survey ethnographic. In Weisner, T. S. (ed.) *Discovering Successful Pathways in Children's Development: Mixed Methods in the Study of Childhood and Family Life*. Chicago, IL: University of Chicago Press, pp. 185–218.

Gross, D. R. (1975). Protein capture and cultural development in the Amazon Basin. *American Anthropologist*, **77**, 526–49.

Hamas, R. (1991). Wildlife conservation in tribal societies. In Oldfield, M. & Alcorn, J. (eds) *Biodiversity: Culture, Conservation, and Ecodevelopment*. Denver, CO: Westview, pp. 172–99.

Hamas, R. (2007). The ecologically noble savage debate. *Annual Review of Anthropology*, **36**, 177–190.

Heckenberger, M. J. (1998). Manioc agriculture and sedentism in Amazonia: the Upper Xingu example. *Antiquity*, **72**, 633–48.

Henfrey, T. B. (2002). Ethnoecology, resource use, conservation, and development in a Wapishana community in South Rupununi, Guyana. PhD Thesis, University of Kent at Canterbury.

Hill, K., McMillan, G. & Farina, R. (2003). Hunting-related changes in game encounter rates from 1994 to 2001 in the Mbaracayu Reserve, Paraguay. *Conservation Biology*, **17**, 1312–23.

Holmberg, A. R. (1969). *Nomads of the Long Bow: The Siriono of Eastern Bolivia*. Prospect Heights, NY: Waveland Press.

Iwamura, T., Lambin, E. F., Silvius, K. M., Luzar, J. B. & Fragoso, J. M. V. (2014). Agent-based modeling of hunting and subsistence agriculture on indigenous lands: understanding interactions between social and ecological systems. *Environmental Modelling and Software*, **58**, 109–27.

Jerozolimski, A. & Peres, C. A. (2003). Bringing home the biggest bacon: a cross-site analysis of the structure of hunter-kill profiles in Neotropical forests. *Biological Conservation*, **111**, 415–425.

Kensinger, K. M., Rabineau, P., Tanner, H., Ferguson, S. G. & Dawson, A. (1975). The Cashinahua of Eastern Peru. In Dwyer, J. P. (ed.) *Studies in Anthropology and Material Culture, Volume 1.* Providence, RI: The Haffenferrer Museum of Anthropology, Brown University.

Koster, J. (2008). The impact of hunting with dogs on wildlife harvests in the Bosawas Reserve, Nicaragua. *Environmental Conservation*, **35**, 211–20.

Levi, T., Shepard Jr, G. H., Ohl-Schacherer, J., Peres, C. A. & Yu, D. W. (2009). Modeling the long-term sustainability of indigenous hunting in Manu National Park, Peru: landscape-scale management implications for Amazonia. *Journal of Applied Ecology*, **46**, 804–14.

Levi, T., Shepard, G. H., Ohl-Schacherer, J., et al. (2011). Spatial tools for modeling the sustainability of subsistence hunting in tropical forests. *Ecological Applications*, **21**, 1802–1818.

Levy, R. I. & Hollan, D. W. (2014). Person-centered interviewing and observation. In Bernard, R. H. & Gravlee, C. C. (eds) *Handbook of Methods in Cultural Anthropology*. London: Rowman & Littlefield, pp. 313–342.

Lizarralde, M. (2002). Ethnoecology of monkeys among the Bari of Venezuela: perception, use, and conservation. In Fuentes, A. & Wolfe, L. D. (eds) *Primates Face to Face: The Conservation Implications of Human and Nonhuman Primate Interconnections*. Cambridge: Cambridge University Press, pp. 85–100.

Meggars, B. J. (1971). *Amazonia: Man and Culture in a Counterfeit Paradise*. Chicago, IL: Aldine, Atherton, Inc.

Mena, V. P., Stallings, J. R., Regalado, J. B. & Cueva, R. L. (2000). The sustainability of current hunting practices by the Huaorani. In Robinson, J. G. & Bennett, E. L. (eds) *Hunting for Sustainability in Tropical Forests*. New York: Columbia University Press, pp. 57–78.

Mentore, G. P. (2005). *Of Passionate Curves and Desirable Cadences: Themes on Waiwai Social Being*. London: University of Nebraska Press.

Milner-Gulland, E. J. & Akcakaya, H. R. (2001). Sustainability indices for exploited populations. *Trends in Ecology and Evolution*, **18**, 351–7.

Mittermeier, R. A. (1991). Hunting and its effects on wild primate populations in Suriname. In Robinson, J. G. & Redford, K. H. (eds) *Neotropical Wildlife Use and Conservation*. Chicago, IL: University of Chicago Press, pp. 93–106.

Nasi, R., Brown, D., Wilkie, D., et al. (2008). *Conservation and Use of Wildlife-Based Resources: The Bushmeat Crisis*. Bogor: Secretariat of the Convention on Biological Diversity and Center for International Forestry Research (CIFOR).

Nasi, R., Taber, A. & Van Vliet, N. (2011). Empty forests, empty stomachs? Bushmeat and livelihoods in the Congo and Amazon basins. *International Forestry Review*, **13**, 355–68.

Nepstad, D., Schwartzman, S., Bamberger, B., et al. (2006). Inhibition of Amazon deforestation and fire by parks and indigenous lands. *Conservation Biology*, **20**, 65–73.

Novaro, A. J., Redford, K. H. & Bodmer, R. E. (2000). Effect of hunting in source–sink systems in the Neotropics. *Conservation Biology*, **14**, 713–21.

Nuñez-Iturri, G. & Howe, H. F. (2007). Bushmeat and the fate of trees with seeds dispersed by large primates in a lowland rainforest in western Amazonia. *Biotropica*, **39**, 348–54.

Ohl, J., Wezel, A., Shepard, G. H., Yu, D. W. (2008). Swidden agriculture in a protected area: the Matsigenka native communities of Manu National Park, Peru. *Environmental Development and Sustainability*, **10**, 827–43.

Ohl-Schacherer, J., Shepard Jr, G. H., Kaplan, H., et al. (2007). The sustainability of subsistence hunting by Matsigenka native communities in Manu National Park, Peru. *Conservation Biology*, **21**, 1174–85.

Oliver, J. R. (2001). The archaeology of forest foraging and agricultural production in Amazonia. In McEwan, C., Neves, E. G. & Barreto, C. (eds) *The Unknown Amazon: Culture in Nature in Ancient Brazil*. London: British Museum Press, pp. 50–85.

Parathian, H. E. & Maldonado, A. M. (2010). Human–nonhuman primate interactions amongst Tikuna people: perceptions and local initiatives for resource management in Amacayacu in the Colombian Amazon. *American Journal of Primatology*, **72**, 855–65.

Peres, C. A. (1990). Effects of hunting on western Amazonian primate communities. *Biological Conservation*, **54**, 47–59.

Peres, C. A. (1994). Indigenous reserves and nature conservation in Amazonian forests. *Conservation Biology*, **8**, 586–88.

Peres, C. A. (2000). Effects of subsistence hunting on vertebrate community structure in Amazonian forests. *Conservation Biology*, **17**, 240–53.

Peres, C. A. & Nascimento, H. S. (2006). Impact of game hunting by the Kayapó of southeastern Amazonia: implications for wildlife conservation in Amazonian indigenous reserves. *Biodiversity and Conservation*, **15**, 2627–53.

Peres, C. A. & Palacios, E. (2007). Basin-wide effects of game harvest on vertebrate population densities in Amazonian forests: implications for animal-mediated seed dispersal. *Biotropica*, **39**, 304–15.

Peres, C. A., Emilio, T., Schietti, J., Desmoulière, S. J. M. & Levi, T. (2016). Dispersal limitation induces long-term biomass collapse in overhunted Amazonian forests. *Proceedings of the National Academy of Sciences*, **113**, 892–7.

RAISG (2012). Amazonía bajo presión. Available at: www.raisg.socioambiental.org.

Redford, K. (1991). The ecologically noble savage. *Orion* **9**, 24–9.

Redford, K. H. & Robinson, J. G. (1991). Subsistence and commercial uses of wildlife in Latin America. In Robinson, J. G. & Redford, K. H. (eds) *Neotropical Wildlife Use and Conservation*. Chicago, IL: University of Chicago Press, pp. 6–23.

Richard-Hansen, C. & Hansen, E. (2004). Hunting and wildlife management in French Guiana: current aspects and future prospects. In Silvius, K., Bodmer, R. & Fragoso, J. (eds) *People in Nature: Wildlife Conservation in South and Central America*. New York: Columbia University Press, pp. 400–410.

Robinson, J. G. & Bennett, E. L. (2004). Having your wildlife and eating it too: an analysis of hunting sustainability across tropical ecosystems. *Animal Conservation*, **7**, 397–408.

Robinson, J. G. & Redford, K. H. (1991). Sustainable harvest of Neotropical wildlife. In Robinson, J. G. & Redford, K. H. (eds) *Neotropical Wildlife Use and Conservation*. Chicago, IL: University of Chicago Press, pp. 415–29.

Robinson, J. G. & Redford, K. H. (1994). Measuring the sustainability of hunting in tropical forests. *Oryx*, **28**, 249–56.

Ross, E. B. (1978). Food taboos, diet, and hunting strategy: the adaptation to animals in Amazon cultural ecology. *Current Anthropology*, **19**, 1–36.

Salas, L. A. & Kim, J. B. (2002). Spatial factors and stochasticity in the evaluation of sustainable hunting of tapirs. *Conservation Biology*, **16**, 86–96.

Schomburgk, R. (1836). Report of an expedition into the interior of British Guiana in 1835–1836. *Journal of the Royal Geographical Society*, **4**, 224–84.

Schwartzman, S. & Zimmerman, B. (2005). Conservation alliances with indigenous peoples of the Amazon. *Conservation Biology*, **19**, 721–7.

Shaffer, C. A., Milstein, M. S., Yukuma, C., Marawanaru, E. & Suse, P. (2017a). Sustainability and comanagement of subsistence hunting in an indigenous reserve in Guyana. *Conservation Biology*, **31**, 119–31.

Shaffer, C. A., Marawanaru, E. & Yukuma, C. (2017b). An ethnoprimatological approach to assessing the sustainability of primate subsistence hunting of indigenous Waiwai in the Konashen Community Owned Conservation Concession, Guyana. In Dore, K. M., Riley, E. P. & Fuentes, A. (eds) *Ethnoprimatology: A Practical Guide to Research on the Human–Nonhuman Primate Interface*. Cambridge: Cambridge University Press, pp. 219–31.

Shaffer, C. A., Yukuma, C., Marawanaru, E. & Suse, P. (2017c). Assessing the sustainability of Waiwai subsistence hunting in Guyana by comparison of static indices and spatially explicit, biodemographic models. *Animal Conservation*. DOI: 10.1111/acv.12366.

Shaffer, C. A., Milstein, M. S., Yukuma, C., et al. (2018). Integrating ethnography and hunting sustainability modeling for primate conservation in an indigenous reserve in Guyana. *International Journal of Primatology*. In review.

Shepard, G. H. (2002). Primates in Matsigenka: subsistence and world view. In Fuentes, A. & Wolfe, L. D. (eds) *Primates Face to Face: The Conservation Implications of Human and Nonhuman Primate Interconnections*. Cambridge: Cambridge University Press, pp. 101–36.

Shepard, G. H., Rummenhoeller, K., Ohl, J. & Yu, D. W. (2010). Trouble in paradise: indigenous populations, anthropological policies, and biodiversity conservation in Manu National Park, Peru. *Journal of Sustainable Forestry*, 29, 252–301.

Shepard, G. H., Levi, T., Neves, E. G., Peres, C. A. & Yu, D. W. (2012). Hunting in ancient and modern Amazonia: rethinking sustainability. *American Anthropologist*, 114, 652–67.

Sirén, A. & Parvinen, K. (2015). A spatial bioeconomic model of the harvest of wild plants and animals. *Ecological Economics*, 116, 201–10.

Sirén, A., Hambäck, P. & Machoa, J. (2004). Including spatial heterogeneity and animal dispersal when evaluating hunting: a model analysis and an empirical assessment in an Amazonian community. *Conservation Biology*, 18, 1315–29.

Stafford, C. A., Preziosi, R. F. & Sellers, W. I. (2017). A pan-neotropical analysis of hunting preferences. *Biodiversity and Conservation*, 26, 1877–97.

Townsend, W. R. (2000). The sustainability of subsistence hunting by the Sirionó Indians of Bolivia. In Robinson, J. G. & Bennett, E. L. (eds) *Hunting for Sustainability in Tropical Forests*. New York: Columbia University Press, pp. 267–82.

Van Vliet, N., Fa, J. & Nasi, R. (2015). Managing hunting under uncertainty: from one-off ecological indicators to resilience approaches in assessing the sustainability of bushmeat hunting. *Ecology and Society*, 20. DOI: 10.5751/ES-07669-200307.

Verissimo, A., Barreto, P., Tarifa, R. & Uhl, C. (1995). Extraction of a high-value natural resource from Amazonia: the case of mahogany. *Forest Ecology and Management*, 72, 39–60.

Wallace, A. R. (1835). *A Narrative of Travels on the Amazon and Rio Negro*. London: Reeve and Co.

Waterton, C. (1825). *Wanderings in South America, the North-West of the United States, and the Antilles*. London: Cassell and Company.

Weinbaum, K. Z., Brashares, J. S., Golden, C. D. & Getz, W. M. (2013). Searching for sustainability: are assessments of wildlife harvests behind the times? *Ecology Letters*, 16, 99–111.

Yde, J. (1965). *Material culture of the Waiwai*. Copenhagen: National Museum of Denmark.

Zapata-Ríos, G., Urgilés, C. & Suárez, E. (2009). Mammal hunting by the Shuar of the Ecuadorian Amazon: is it sustainable? *Oryx*, 43, 375–85.

Zimmerman, B., Peres, C. A., Malcolm, J. & Turner, T. (2001). Conservation and development alliances with the Kayapo of south-eastern Amazonia, a tropical forest indigenous peoples. *Environmental Conservation*, 28, 10–22.

Part II

Habitat Alteration in the Anthropocene

6 The Effects of Selective Logging on the Habitat Use of the Annamese Silvered Langur (*Trachypithecus margarita*) in Northeast Cambodia

Alvaro Gonzalez-Monge and Alison M. Behie

6.1 Personal Narrative

I (AG-M) grew up in Salamanca (Spain) where, despite existing conservation challenges, wildlife demand is minimal and most national parks are well established and protected institutions. In this context, casual observers are typically unaware of clashes between conservation and development. Thus, it was not until I did my Bachelor of Science studies in Biology in Salamanca that I first got acquainted with some of the issues that affect nature conservation. It was later on, during my studies at the University of Iceland, doing research on the glacial eelpout (*Lycodes frigidus*), that I realised the profound effects that different human activities, such as pollution or fishing, have on a species, even one that lives at depths below 1500 metres. This knowledge was further solidified when I worked as a field assistant in the Atlas Mountains of Morocco, and saw that even good intentions can cause problems, where unregulated numbers of visitors not only created a highly noisy and stressful environment for local groups of Barbary macaques (*Macaca sylvanus*), but also endangered their overall health and viability through the sharing of food, including soda and chocolate.

After these experiences I was driven to conduct a PhD with non-human primates to investigate the effects of human activity on their ecology. After being accepted into the PhD programme at the Australian National University, I became acutely aware of the current challenges facing biodiversity in Southeast Asia, which I was confronted with when I began my research at Veun Sai-Siem Pang Conservation Area in Cambodia (now Veun Sai-Siem Pang National Park). This was the first time I had lived in the midst of these impacts as they were happening on a daily basis.

For several reasons, Cambodia has retained most of its wildlife and habitats until recent years, but these are now disappearing at an alarming rate. While wildlife demand used to be quite low, economic development of local Khmer and Chinese villages, coupled with a higher influx of Vietnamese people, have changed the trend and wildlife populations are under increasing human pressure. As a result of these changes, selective logging has become widespread in northeast Cambodia, and the lack of enforcement makes it easy for a casual visitor to see logs being transported not only in all sorts of trucks, but also on passenger vans and even buses from legitimate companies. It is thus important to know how human disturbances impact local wildlife and what can be done to protect it. At the same time, it is important to balance human needs in a way that ensures humans and wildlife can coexist, making it crucial that we do research that helps to come up with solutions that will allow improvements to the well-being of local human populations as well as the conservation of the incredible natural heritage of Southeast Asia.

6.2   Introduction

Southeast Asia contains some of the highest biodiversity in the world and is part of the Indo-Burma Biodiversity Hotspot. Sadly, it is also one of the regions where human activities most threaten wildlife. Due to rapid development in recent decades, the populations of many species have declined (Critical Ecosystem Partnership Fund, 2012). Generally, this is exacerbated by attitudes and behaviour that encourage the illicit trade in wildlife, fuelling a biodiversity crisis that has recently reached a global scale. Cambodia, in contrast, has retained a large portion of its natural habitats and wildlife populations. This is possibly due to a combination of low human population density coupled with Khmer traditional views on wildlife, which are less utilitarian than in neighbouring countries that present a higher demand for wildlife products (TRAFFIC, 2008). Additionally, an extended period of civil conflict that lasted into the current century prevented Cambodian economic development and resulted in most remote regions in the country remaining inaccessible, particularly those with large forest tracts in the north, northeast and southwest. Thus, while Cambodia does not hold more biodiversity or levels of endemism than neighbouring countries (Bain & Hurley, 2011; Rawson, 2010), this history has left relatively high populations of many key endangered species within the country.

This, however, is quickly changing. Although Cambodia banned wood exports from national sources, there has been a failure to enforce this legislation through law enforcement (Critical Ecosystem Partnership Fund, 2012; Global Witness, 2015; Peter & Pheap, 2015; Titthara, 2014; Wolf, 1996). Logs illegally sourced out of protected areas are exported by sea or road to neighbouring countries, where they or derived products are exported to other countries (de Lopez, 2002; Global Witness, 2015; Pye, 2013; 2015a; 2015b; Pye & Titthara, 2014; 2015; Titthara, 2014; Wolf, 1996). This has resulted in Cambodia now suffering one of the highest deforestation rates in the region (Global Witness, 2007; 2015; Hansen et al., 2008; 2013; Petersen et al., 2015).

Human activities are the main threat to primates globally (de Almeida-Rocha et al., 2017; Estrada et al., 2017), and different primate species react differently to human disturbance, depending on their ecological plasticity and the severity and effects that these anthropogenic activities have on the environment (Heiduck, 2002). Small-scale disturbances may benefit some primate species as they may increase their population numbers by exploiting favourable new conditions (Chivers, 1977; Grieser-Johns & Grieser-Johns, 1995; Johns, 1983; Plumptre & Reynolds, 1994; Skorupa, 1985) or by modifying their behaviour to adapt to smaller forest patches (Onderdonk & Chapman, 2000; Riley, 2008; Singh et al., 2001; Umapathy et al., 2011). This is often related to differences in diet, as folivorous species cope better post-disturbance than frugivorous species, given their ability to rely on leaves of pioneer species. Depending on such intrinsic factors, different species in the same area can react differently to anthropic pressure (Borgerson, 2015). This discrepancy, however, may be due to the use of different methods and timescales among studies, resulting in an incomplete picture of the overall effect of anthropic and environmental influences (Chapman et al., 2006; Johns, 1992).

Nevertheless, logging often is a threat to primates, and several studies have investigated the effects of logging on the population density of primates, including orangutans (Felton et al., 2003; Knop et al., 2004; Marshall et al., 2006), chimpanzees (Potts, 2011) and several African Old World and New World monkeys (Anderson et al., 2007; Chapman et al., 2000; 2007; Estrada & Coates-Estrada, 1996; Plumptre & Reynolds, 1994; Remis & Jost Robinson, 2012; Waltert et al., 2002; Zunino et al., 2007). The impact of logging on the ranging behaviour of primates, however, has been less studied, although the few available studies tend to show that logging does impact primate ranging. Masked titi monkeys (*Callicebus personatus*), for example, spend less time in logged areas of their home range (Heiduck, 2002), while lion-tailed macaques (*Macaca silenus*) significantly increase the time they spend in the lower canopy and on the ground after selective logging (Singh et al., 2001). Conversely, Chapman et al. (2006) found no significant differences in daily path lengths of black-and-white colobus (*Colobus guereza*) and Ugandan red colobus (*Piliocolobus tephrosceles*) in logged versus unlogged fragments, again suggesting that the impact of logging will vary depending on the intrinsic factors of the species.

In Asia, some species of colobines (*Presbytis femoralis, Rhinopithecus roxellana, Semnopithecus johnii, Trachypithecus obscurus*) tend to abandon logged portions of their home range and reduce home-range size (Grieser-Johns & Grieser-Johns, 1995; Guo et al., 2008; Li, 2004; Poirier, 1968). Conversely, other species like Hose's langur (*Presbytis hosei*) living in forests under logging pressure occupy much larger home ranges than those that live in undisturbed forests (Nijman, 2010). In addition, langurs in Peninsular Malaysian rainforests (*P. femoralis*) are also more likely to move to lower canopy levels after logging as tall, canopy-forming trees became scarcer (Johns, 1986). Increased infant mortality and slow population recovery numbers in colobines have also been reported as consequences of logging (Grieser-Johns & Grieser-Johns, 1995).

While the above studies have explored the impacts of logging on primates after it was carried out, there is a dearth of studies that focus on changes in primate behaviour that occur while logging is actually in progress. However, we were able to observe such changes in the behaviour of the Annamese silvered langurs (*Trachypithecus margarita*) in Veun Sai-Siem Pang National Park (VSSPNP) during our 2013–14 field season. This was the same time that a budgetary issue led to a reduction in law enforcement in the area, which resulted in an increase in selective logging. As a silvered langur group was periodically observed in a particular section of the national park close to the field station, where logging was occurring frequently in 2013, it was decided that we would commence a study on how selective logging affected the ecology of this silvered langur group.

In this chapter, we report the results regarding the short-term impact of logging activity on the home-range use of this Annamese silvered langur group at VSSPNP in northeast Cambodia. Specifically, we investigate how the number of chainsaws, the mean daily length of logging bouts and the distance from logging to the study group impacted their ranging and canopy use. We predicted that logging would create disturbances in the canopy that would influence the group's movements and ranging patterns. In particular, we expected them to avoid areas of their home range where logging was occurring. We also expected that they would move higher up in the canopy when logging was occurring. Finally, we expected that the more chainsaws that were in use and the closer the disturbance was to the group location, the more significant the effect on the group would be.

6.3   Methods

6.3.1   Study Site and Study Group

This study was carried out in VSSPNP, Ratanakiri Province, Cambodia, from May 2013 to May 2014. VSSPNP (14°01′N, 106°44′E) comprises 55 000 ha of evergreen and semi-evergreen forest bordering the larger 320 000 ha Virachey National Park. It has high levels of species diversity, with camera trap studies revealing it to be home to 60 species of mammals, 133 species of birds and 60 species of reptiles and amphibians (King et al., 2016). Of those species, 34 are listed as vulnerable, endangered or critically endangered on the International Union for the Conservation of Nature (IUCN) Red List. At the time of the study, the site was managed in collaboration between the Cambodian Forestry Administration and Conservation International. Despite there being no logging concessions in VSSPNP and regular patrols, illegal logging still occurs.

This study was conducted on an unhabituated group of Annamese silvered langurs (*Trachypithecus margarita*), a species for which very little is known about their ecology and behaviour due to a lack of prior long-term studies. This multi-male, multi-female group was found in a forest patch close to the field station that is isolated from other forest tracts in the park. The northern section borders on savannah habitat, the eastern section borders on treeless farmland, while the southern section borders on thick, low scrub habitat that buffers the forest from further farmland; all of these are unsuitable for langurs. This group had a maximum recorded number of 62 individuals but an average of 16 (out of 49 days where langurs were found), which might be due to the fact that it was hard to observe more than a few individuals at any given time due to their reluctance to come out around human observers. While it is possible that this group could represent several unhabituated langur groups, due to the isolation of the forest patch and the low encounter rates (the group was found on 49 out of 198 study days), coupled with information from local guides who have been monitoring primates in the park, we think it is highly unlikely another group was living in the region and thus treat this as one large group.

Logging activity was compared between datasets recorded in 2013 and 2014 due to a change in law enforcement between these two periods. Due to a lack of budget, law enforcement personnel and patrols decreased in 2013 which led to an increase in logging. As funding became available in 2014, law enforcement activities increased through additional patrols and more personnel. There was a noticeable decrease in logging activity with these changes. These conditions thus presented an interesting opportunity to compare logging and langur behaviour between the two enforcement conditions.

6.3.2   Logging Information

Whenever a logged tree was encountered within the home range of the langur group, its position was recorded using a Garmin 62s GPS unit, and its species identified with help of local guides. The date of felling was also noted (with an error of up to two days), also with the assistance of local guides who could accurately pinpoint where chainsaws had been active in the forest in previous days. Freshly cut trees could also be distinguished by the presence of fresh resin, bright colours on cut surfaces, partially processed blocks of wood and small quantities of sawdust along the forest path. These data were collected as soon as logging in the given area had ceased and loggers were not present anymore. In the early days of the study, contact with loggers was tense and resulted in the lead author and the field assistants being asked quite forcibly to leave the forest. Thus, for safety reasons, logging could not be assessed at the moment that it was occurring.

During behavioural observations, any chainsaw activity was noted along with the general location relative to the GPS location of the group. Once logging had ceased, this was used to determine the actual location of the logged tree, which was then compared to the GPS location of the study group at that time using Google Earth Pro version 7.1.2.2041. Distances obtained were pooled in six categories separated by 500 metres to account for degrees of immediate impact, with 0 acting as absence of logging; 1 (1–500 m); 2 (501–1000 m); 3 (1001–1500 m); 4 (1501–2000 m); and 5 (2001+ m). In addition, on days when logging was occurring, the number of chainsaws heard was recorded along with the length of each logging bout. This was measured in hours by noting the exact time when logging started and when it finished.

6.3.3   Langur Ranging Behavioural Data

On each day scheduled for behavioural observation, the lead author would leave the field station at 5:30 a.m. and track the langur group using established trails in the home range with the help of local guides and research assistants. When located, the location and group composition were noted. The group would then be followed from that initial time until the end of the day or until 90 minutes passed without any signs of the group being present (indicating the animals had been lost). When with the group, its location would be noted every 30 minutes in UTM coordinates using a Garmin 62s GPS unit.

Every time an animal was observed, its age (adult, juvenile, infant) and sex class was noted, as well as the canopy level in which it was found. Canopy levels were measured using a Haglöf clinometer and categorised as low (0–9.99 m), medium (10–20.99 m) and high (21+ m). The forest type where the animal was found was also noted (mixed evergreen forest, mixed deciduous forest, dry deciduous forest), following the criteria noted by Gonzalez-Monge (2016).

6.3.4   Data Analysis

The UTM coordinates of all felled trees were plotted on a map using Google Earth Pro version 7.1.2.2041. Ranging locations were then overlaid on this map and the home range divided into a grid of 100×100 m to investigate the use of different parts of the range (Di Fiore, 2003; Fan & Jiang, 2008; Wallace, 2006; White et al., 2010; Zhang et al., 2014). To investigate the relationship between home-range use and logging during the study period, a linear regression was done to look at the impact of the number of logged trees on the number of the study group's use of each home-range cell.

To establish any influence of logging on canopy use by the study group, a generalised linear multinomial (GLM) model with a cumulative negative log–log link function was run with canopy level as the response variable and daily number of chainsaws, daily length of logging bouts and the distance to the closest logging event as the predictor variables. All statistical analyses were performed using IBM SPSS Statistics version 23 with the significance value set at $p < 0.05$.

6.4   Results

6.4.1   Logging Activity

Logging activity was recorded on 257 days during this study, which amounted to 70 per cent of total study days. Of these, 152 occurred during 2013 (when law enforcement was weak) and 105 during 2014 (when law enforcement had increased). This equated to a total of 147.25 hours of logging overall: 105.25 hours (71 per cent) in 2013 and 42 hours during 2014 (29 per cent). Within the home range of the study group we identified 89 logged trees, of which 79 were logged during 2013 and 10 were logged during 2014. Four species were targeted during 2013, while five were targeted during the first five months of 2014.

Table 6.1 Plant families and species targeted by illegal loggers in VSSPNP during the study

Family	Genus	Species	Logged trees in 2013	Logged trees in 2014
Fabaceae			76	1
	Pterocarpus	macrocarpus	71	0
	Dalbergia	oliveri	5	0
	Sindora	cochinchinensis	0	1
Dipterocarpaceae			3	2
	Hopea		2	2
	Dipterocarpus	alatus	1	0
Lythraceae	Lagerstroemia	calyculata	0	4
Sapindaceae	Nephelium	mutabile	0	2
Euphorbiaceae	Baccaurea	ramiflora	0	1

Pterocarpus macrocarpus was the most commonly logged species overall, with 71 individual trees (84 per cent of all logged stems) being felled. This was followed by *Dalbergia oliveri* with five felled trees and *Hopea* sp. with four. The most sought-after tree during 2013 was *P. macrocarpus*: all 71 felled trees of this species were cut down during that year. The most commonly logged tree in 2014 was *Lagerstroemia calyculata*, at four (Table 6.1).

6.4.2   Logging Impacts on Ranging and Canopy Use

Using the regression equation of $Y = -55.6 + 0.7X$ we found that the number of logged trees in a part of the group's home range had a significantly negative influence on the group's use of that area ($r^2 = 0.08$, df = 119, $p < 0.01$). In addition, we found the majority of logging ($n = 45$ trees) was done in the northernmost portion of the langur home range. While this area was commonly visited by the study group in 2013, it was not visited at all in 2014. Areas in the southern and eastern portions of the home range that were less intensely logged, however, were visited by the group during the whole length of the study (Figure 6.1).

We also found a significant relationship between the distance from logging locations and the study group's location and canopy use (likelihood ratio $\chi^2 = 436.86$, df = 70, $p < 0.01$; AIC = 258.82), with medium canopy being more commonly used by group members when there was no logging or when it occurred more than 2000 m away from the group. When logging was closer to the study group, animals spent more time in the high canopy layers (Figure 6.2). High canopy use also significantly increased when there were more daily chainsaws in the vicinity of the group (Figure 6.3; likelihood ratio $\chi^2 = 58.96$, df = 3, $p < 0.01$; AIC = 70.76) and when the mean daily length of logging bouts was more than two hours (Figure 6.4; likelihood ratio $\chi^2 = 153.61$, df = 14, $p < 0.01$; AIC = 137.90).

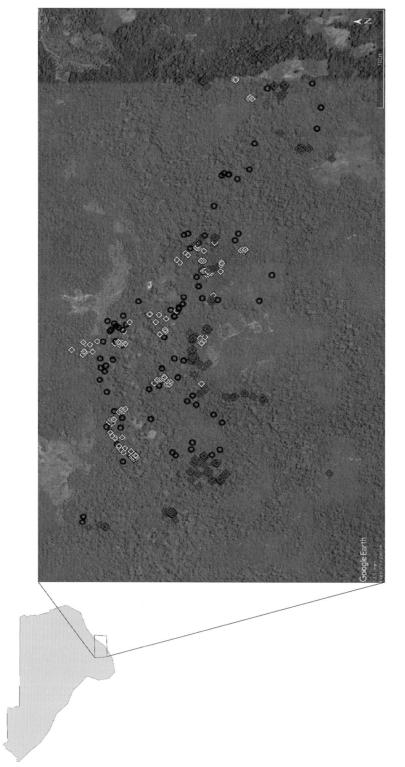

Figure 6.1 Geographical distribution of langur ranging points (white squares are 2013 locations and grey are 2014 locations) and logging hotspots (black rings) in the home range of the study group of *Trachypithecus margarita* in Veun Sai-Siem Pang National Park, Cambodia.

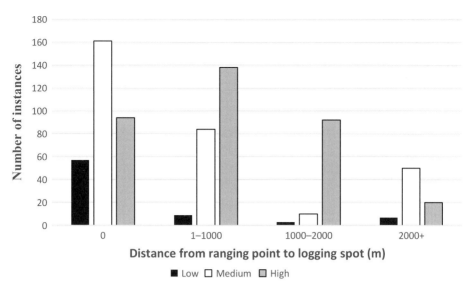

Figure 6.2 Changes in canopy level use by the study group of *Trachypithecus margarita* in relation to the distance of logging hotspots to the group in Veun Sai-Siem Pang National Park, Cambodia.

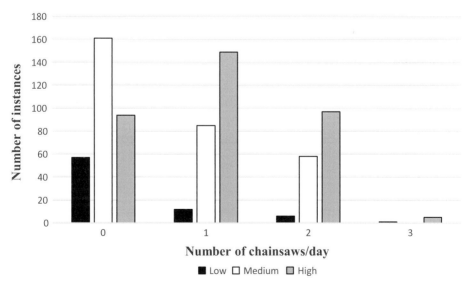

Figure 6.3 Changes in canopy level use by the study group of *Trachypithecus margarita* in relation to the daily number of chainsaws active in the area in Veun Sai-Siem Pang National Park, Cambodia.

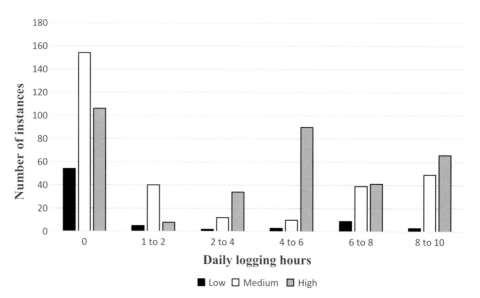

Figure 6.4 Changes in canopy level use by the study group of *Trachypithecus margarita* in relation to the total daily logging hours in the area in Veun Sai-Siem Pang National Park, Cambodia.

6.5   Discussion

6.5.1   Logging at VSSPNP

We found that both the number of active chainsaws and the length of logging bouts were substantially greater in 2013 than in 2014. The observed decline of logging activity in 2014 is most likely due to an increase in the intensity of law enforcement at the site during that time. These results suggest that logging is likely to continue at high rates if this sort of enforcement is not maintained. Such trends would be detrimental to the forest and its many inhabitants, as they would likely continue on a shift to other potentially important species as outlined below (Pye, 2015a).

 Pterocarpus macrocarpus was the tree species targeted most frequently for logging over the entire study period, likely due to its value in the international luxury wood market (Environmental Investigation Agency, 2016; Winfield et al., 2016). The fact that this species is able to grow in all kinds of forest means that logging damage in the study area was quite widespread. Due to logging intensity, *P. macrocarpus* was virtually absent from the area by early 2014, and loggers had already begun focusing on other species, such as *Dalbergia oliveri*, which was the second most commonly logged species in our study. This could also represent a reason why logging slowed down in 2014, although due to logging patterns in other areas of Cambodia, we think the change in pace is much more likely to be due to the aforementioned changes in enforcement. Other logged species in VSSPNP are fruiting trees, including *Nephelium melliferum* or *Baccaurea ramiflora*. Wood from these trees is not valuable, but locals target them during the fruiting season, cutting them down when they are in full fruit to pick some fruit to eat, leaving the cut tree and the remaining fruit to rot. This behaviour needs to be immediately addressed and curbed, because it not only disturbs birds, primates and small mammals, but also local people who depend on fruit as an additional resource to feed their families.

Given what is logged in other parts of Cambodia, it is likely that *Anisoptera costata*, *Xylia xylocarpa*, several *Hopea* species or *Dipterocarpus alatus* could become future targets for logging at VSSPNP (Peter & Pheap, 2015). This is of concern as *D. alatus* is frequently used by langurs for feeding and sleeping (Gonzalez-Monge, 2016) and is relied on by local people as a sustainable income source via the collection of resin. Thus, the removal of these large trees from the forest will have not only a large ecological impact, but also a harmful effect on the economy and society of local human populations.

6.5.2   Effects of Logging on Langurs

Similar to other langur studies (Grieser-Johns & Grieser-Johns, 1995; Guo et al., 2008; Li, 2004; Poirier, 1968), our results show that logging significantly impacts the ranging behaviour of silvered langurs. We observed that high amounts of logged trees in a particular section of the langur home range negatively impacted the amount of ranging points, denoting the presence of langurs in said section, in a significant manner.

Some areas of the home range that were commonly used by the langurs during 2013 were no longer used in 2014 and this seems to be associated with heavy logging activity in the area (Figure 6.1). This included the northern part of the home range, where 45 trees were lost in just 60.5 ha (0.74 logged trees per hectare). While it is possible this area was abandoned for another reason, the fact that the other areas of the home range that were not as heavily logged (44 trees in 195.75 ha for the remainder of the home range, 0.22 logged trees per hectare) were all revisited in 2014 suggest logging is playing a role in habitat use. It should be noted that due to the small r^2 value, there are likely other factors contributing to the langurs' change in habitat use from 2013 to 2014, such as changes in food availability, fruiting patterns or repeated human disturbance. However, as a large part of the abandoned area consists of mixed evergreen forest, which is known to be the preferred forest habitat type for this group (Gonzalez-Monge, 2016), it seems that logging is at least partly to blame for the change in home-range use.

While the group did not use the heavily logged northern section of their range in 2014, they might return in the future, especially if there is no further logging disturbance. In fact, colobine groups are often reported to return to logged areas after logging ceases (Guo et al., 2008; Leca et al., 2013; Tan et al., 2007), showing a certain degree of tolerance to this type of disturbance. Langurs in particular seem to be relatively resilient to forest disturbance if it occurs at a low intensity and is not combined with other anthropogenic forces (Chivers, 1985; Gupta & Kumar, 1994; Johns & Skorupa, 1987; Nijman, 2010; Plumptre & Reynolds, 1994; Poirier, 1968;

Umapathy & Kumar, 2003; Wich & Sterck, 2010; Workman & Le, 2010; Xiang et al., 2011).

Logging also impacted langur canopy use as the group was more frequently found in the higher canopy when logging was being carried out in the vicinity than when it was either absent or far away. This same trend is found when looking at the length of logging bouts and the number of chainsaws heard daily, both of which also resulted in animals using the high canopy more. Few studies have addressed the immediate impact of logging on primates, although previous studies have noted that chainsaw activity in the vicinity of langurs seems to cause distress (Li et al., 1999).

Removal of big trees reduces food availability (Heiduck, 2002; Johns & Skorupa, 1987; Li et al., 2008), and when coupled with the targeted logging of species of great importance to colobines for feeding and sleeping sites, will likely lead to a sharp decline in population numbers (Anderson et al., 2007). Furthermore, the lack of large trees will result in lower habitat connectivity, which will affect the langurs at our study site, because they tend to concentrate movement and behaviour in the middle and high canopy (Gonzalez-Monge, 2016). These issues have been observed in other primates in logged areas (Chapman et al., 2000; Felton et al., 2003; Ferrari & Diego, 1995; Johns, 1983; 1986; Li, 2004; Li et al., 2008; Menon & Poirier, 1996; Ruhiyat, 1983; Umapathy et al., 2011). Our results highlight this particular concern for VSSPNP as many of the recorded logged trees were species used as food or sleeping trees by the study group. Given that *Presbytis femoralis* and *Trachypithecus obscurus* saw increases in infant mortality and low recruitment numbers when faced with logging in their habitat (Grieser-Johns & Grieser-Johns, 1995), it seems that our study population may potentially be at risk of a similar fate. As described above, langurs are thought to be somewhat tolerant to a certain intensity of logging, but the threshold for this will be different at each site, depending on the environment and other ecological pressures. Logging data in Cambodia show a worrying trend in that once the most valuable tree species have been extirpated from an area, loggers will return to the logged sites and start focusing on the next most valuable species, and so on (Vrieze, 2014). This suggests that primates and other wildlife living at VSSPNP will experience increasing damage to their forest habitat and that increased efforts towards curbing these activities are needed to prevent further escalation and degradation.

Logging impacts on dipterocarps are important as the family is the most logged target taxon at VSSPNP and constitute a preferred food resource and offer sleeping sites to the study species (Gonzalez-Monge, 2016). The disappearance of this taxon could have potentially irreversible negative effects on langur populations in the area. In spite of this, dipterocarp seedlings and saplings can survive logging episodes and eventually be productive by flushing new leaves and fruiting, even if their numbers are smaller at first (Appanah & Manaf, 1994). Langurs can adapt to dipterocarp eradication by moving from logged areas to other sectors where dipterocarps or other important trees are still present until the former regenerate. Logging did not alter the original setup of the forest in habitats where dipterocarps were common and diverse (Cannon et al., 1998). However, those were lowland rainforests where dipterocarps are the dominant group, so they are not the same habitats as those in VSSPNP, where regeneration dynamics might work differently. Langurs are also dependent on other plant families that might not be able to withstand logging disturbance as well as dipterocarps, and special care should be taken to study the regeneration dynamics of other families of importance to langur diet, such as Fagaceae, Fabaceae or Apocynaceae. Further studies should look into any differences in langur use of particular plant species depending on the age of the plant, and also in regeneration dynamics of their habitats.

Managing logging at VSSPNP is of critical importance; to date there is still plenty of good langur habitat remaining, and populations will likely be able to remain healthy as long as there are enough trees to support them, even if some logging has been carried out (Grieser-Johns & Grieser-Johns, 1995; Hu, 2011; Johns & Skorupa, 1987; Knop et al., 2004; Kool, 1993; Marshall et al., 2006; Potts, 2011; Rijksen, 1978; Singh et al., 2001; Skorupa, 1985; Umapathy & Kumar, 2003; Umapathy et al., 2011; Xiang et al., 2011). Illegal logging for export purposes, however, must be stopped.

Forests in the area, although under human pressure, can still present very healthy populations of megafauna as long as extractive activities do not increase in intensity (Gonzalez-Monge, 2016). Studies on logging in Malaysian dipterocarp forests show that most vertebrate species present in a forest will persist or reappear a decade after logging was carried out in an area, and primates and other large-bodied vertebrates dependent on the same or similar resources, such as hornbills (Southeast Asian equivalents of toucans), will still retain their population numbers even after almost three-quarters of the forest have been logged (Johns, 1992). Limited-scale and low-intensity logging can be compatible with primate conservation (Chapman et al., 2000; Knop et al., 2004; Marshall et al., 2006; Salter et al., 1985; Skorupa, 1985; Xiang et al., 2011), although good management is needed so that it is sustainable and intensity is kept low; reduced proximity of logged areas to unexploited or protected areas would be of great help for conservation aims. Of great importance as well, especially in the light of the current global biodiversity crisis in the Indo-Burma region, should be the prevention of poaching and hunting, which probably will have a larger impact on local wildlife than selective logging once the original habitat is fragmented, as has already happened in other regions (Estrada & Coates-Estrada, 1984; Johns & Skorupa, 1987; Marshall et al., 2006; Nijman, 2004; 2005; Peres, 1997; Raemaekers & Chivers, 1980; Remis & Jost Robinson, 2012; Rosenbaum et al., 1998). Sadly, given the current state of affairs and the rate of forest loss in Cambodia (Global Witness, 2007; 2015; Hansen et al., 2008; 2013) it is hard to believe that the state of conservation in northeast Cambodia will be indefinitely healthy if nothing is done to curb illegal logging and other human disturbances.

6.6   Conclusions and Future Directions

The results of this study show that logging had an immediate effect on the way langurs range in their habitat and use of the forest canopy. It is vital to curb illegal logging at VSSPNP before remaining tree species that are of importance to langurs and other species are eradicated, which will compromise the langurs' survival. Langurs were not targeted by hunters, but it is also essential to prevent poaching to maintain healthy local wildlife populations and to prevent a further escalation in wildlife demand in the surrounding towns. As langurs are somewhat tolerant to human disturbances, it would be of interest to look at changes to group number and composition and their interspecific associations over time. Further changes in ranging behaviour, habitat use and diet should also be continually monitored to determine whether the results found here may have long-term impacts on the animals. It is only after studying animals for a long stretch of time that we can begin to understand all the impacts of human disturbance (Chapman et al., 2000; 2006; Decker, 1994; Johns, 1992).

It is our hope that these results will increase our knowledge of how primates are responding to the proximate threat of logging, which is likely to represent other human disturbances as well. The lead author found a path to conservation work through his experiences showing how the majority of human activities impact wildlife populations, making the results of this chapter pertinent to his continued goals and research agenda. Although logging at the site was selective and done at a relatively small scale, the animals were adjusting their behaviour and habitat use, suggesting even small changes that are deemed sustainable may impact animals. It has also highlighted the incredible importance of investment in law enforcement in these regions, as when law enforcement increased in 2014, logging activity decreased. With the addition of over a million hectares of protected areas by the Cambodian government in 2016, there is hope that this sort of logging may decrease and wildlife protection be effective. However, the fact that concessions continue to take precedence in many government decisions is unsettling. Research like this, on rarely studied species, is needed in order to truly understand the impacts of all human activity, regardless of scale. It is our hope that future primatologists will continue to collect these types of data as well as to monitor the health and life-histories of these populations to better understand how threats are dealt with as they occur. It is only then that we may be able to predict long-term consequences.

Acknowledgements

This study was made possible with the financial help of the Australian National University, Primate Conservation Inc. and Conservation International. We would also like to thank the Cambodian Forestry Administration and Conservation International Greater Mekong, particularly Tracy Farrell and Seng Bunra, for their support and assistance throughout the project. None of this work would have been possible without the help of the local research assistants, particularly Buntha Sitha and Lort Soulit, as well as the many local guides and law enforcement personnel. Eve Smeltzer provided invaluable help gathering data, and other field assistants we would like to thank are Camilla Brent and Elizabeth Coombs. Statistics assistance was given by Pauline Ding and Richard Farmer. We would like to thank Colin Groves and Ben Rawson for their input and support. We also thank the reviewers for their advice.

References

Anderson, J., Cowlishaw, G. & Rowcliffe, J. M. (2007). Effects of forest fragmentation on the abundance of *Colobus angolensis palliatus* in Kenya's coastal forests. *International Journal of Primatology*, **28**(3), 637–55.

Appanah, S. & Manaf, M. R. A. (1994). Fruiting and seedling survival of dipterocarps in a logged forest. *Journal of Tropical Forest Science*, **6**(3), 215–22.

Bain, R. H. & Hurley, M. M. (2005). A biogeographic synthesis of the amphibians and reptiles of Indochina. *Bulletin of the American Museum of Natural History*, **360**, 1–138.

Borgerson, C. (2015). The effects of illegal hunting and habitat on two sympatric endangered primates. *International Journal of Primatology*, **36**(1), 74–93.

Cannon, C. H., Peart, D. R. & Leighton, M. (1998). Tree species diversity in commercially logged Bornean rainforest. *Science*, **281**(5381), 1367–8

Chapman, C. A., Balcomb, S. R., Gillespie, T. R., Skorupa, J. P. & Struhsaker, T. T. (2000). Long-term effects of logging on African primate communities: a 28-year comparison from Kibale National Park, Uganda. *Conservation Biology*, **14**(1), 207–17.

Chapman, C. A., Wasserman, M. D. & Gillespie, T. R. (2006). Behavioral patterns of colobus in logged and unlogged forests: the conservation value of harvested forests. In Newton-Fisher, N. E., Notman, H., Patterson, J. D. & Reynolds, V. (eds) *Primates of Western Uganda*. New York: Springer, pp. 373–90.

Chapman, C. A., Naughton-Treves, L., Lawes, M. J., Wasserman, M. D. & Gillespie, T. R. (2007). Population declines of colobus in Western Uganda and conservation value of forest fragments. *International Journal of Primatology*, **28**(3), 513–28.

Chivers, D. J. (1977). The lesser apes. In Prince Rainier H. S. H. & Bourne G. H. (eds) *Primate Conservation*. New York: Academic Press, pp. 539–98.

Chivers, D. J. (1985). Southeast Asian primates. In Benirschke K. (ed) *Primates: The Road to Self-Sustaining Populations*. New York: Springer, pp. 57–70.

Critical Ecosystem Partnership Fund (2012). *Ecosystem Profile: Indo-Burma Biodiversity Hotspot*. Available at: www.cepf.net/Documents/final.indoburma_indochina.ep.pdf (accessed 13 July 2015).

de Almeida-Rocha, J. M., Peres, C. A. & Oliveira, L. C. (2017). Primate responses to anthropogenic habitat disturbance: a pantropic meta-analysis. *Biological Conservation*, **215**, 30–8.

de Lopez, T. T. (2002). Natural resource exploitation in Cambodia: an examination of use, appropriation and exclusion. *Journal of Environment and Development*, **11**(4), 355–79.

Decker, B. S. (1994). Effects of habitat disturbance on the behavioral ecology and demographics of the Tana River Red colobus (*Colobus badius rufomitratus*). *International Journal of Primatology*, **15**(5), 703–37.

Di Fiore, A. (2003). Ranging behavior and foraging ecology of lowland woolly monkeys (*Lagothrix lagotricha poeppigii*) in Yasuni National Park, Ecuador. *American Journal of Primatology*, **59**(2), 47–66.

Environmental Investigation Agency (2016). Analysis of the demand-driven trade in hongmu timber species: impacts of unsustainability and illegality in source regions. Paper presented at the Convention on International Trade in Endangered Species of Wild Fauna and Flora, Johannesburg, South Africa. Available at: https://cites.org/sites/default/files/eng/cop/17/InfDocs/E-CoP17-Inf-79.pdf.

Estrada, A. & Coates-Estrada, R. (1984). Some observations on the present distribution and conservation of *Alouatta* and *Ateles* in southern Mexico. *American Journal of Primatology*, **7**(2), 133–7.

Estrada, A. & Coates-Estrada, R. (1996). Tropical rain forest fragmentation and wild populations of primates at Los Tuxtlas, Mexico. *International Journal of Primatology*, **17**(5), 759–83.

Estrada, A., Garber, P. A. & Rylands, A. B., et al. (2017). Impending extinction crisis of the world's primates: why primates matter. *Science Advances*, **3**(1), 1–17.

Fan, P. F. & Jiang, X. L. (2008). Effects of food and topography on ranging behavior of black crested gibbon (*Nomascus concolor jingdongensis*) in Wuliang Mountain, Yunnan, China. *American Journal of Primatology*, **70**(9), 871–8.

Felton, A. M., Engström, L. M., Felton, A. & Knott, C. D. (2003). Orangutan population density, forest structure and fruit availability in hand-logged and unlogged peat swamp forests in West Kalimantan, Indonesia. *Biological Conservation*, **114**(1), 91–101.

Ferrari, S. F. & Diego, V. H. (1995). Habitat fragmentation and primate conservation in the Atlantic Forest of eastern Minas Gerais, Brazil. *Oryx*, **29**(3), 192–6.

Global Witness (2007). Cambodia's family trees: illegal logging and the stripping of public assets by Cambodia's elite. Available at: www.globalwitness.org/%85/cambodias_family_trees_low_res.pdf (accessed 13 July 2015).

Global Witness (2015). The cost of luxury: Cambodia's illegal trade in precious wood with China. Available at: www.globalwitness.org/documents/17847/globalwitnessthecostofluxurypress releaseenglish6feb15.pdf (accessed 7 September 2015).

Gonzalez-Monge, A. (2016). The socioecology, and the effects of human activity on it, of the Annamese silvered langur (*Trachypithecus margarita*) in northeastern Cambodia. PhD Thesis, Australian National University.

Grieser-Johns, A. & Grieser-Johns, B. (1995). Tropical forest primates and logging: long-term coexistence? *Oryx*, **29**(3), 205–11.

Guo, S. T., Ji, W. H., Li, B. G. & Li, M. (2008). Response of a group of Sichuan snub-nosed monkeys to commercial logging in the Qinling Mountains, China. *Conservation Biology*, **22**(4), 1055–64.

Gupta, A. K. & Kumar, A. (1994). Feeding ecology and conservation of Phayre's leaf monkey *Presbytis phayrei* in Northeast India. *Biological Conservation*, **69**(3), 301–6.

Hansen, M. C., Stehman, V., Potapov, P. V., et al. (2008). Humid tropical forest clearing from 2000 to 2005 quantified by using multitemporal and multiresolution remotely sensed data. *Proceedings of the National Academy of Sciences*, **105**(27), 9439–44.

Hansen, M. C., Potapov, P. V., Moore, R., et al. (2013). High-resolution global maps of 21st-century forest cover change. *Science*, **342**(850), 133–9.

Heiduck, S. (2002). The use of disturbed and undisturbed forest by masked titi monkeys *Callicebus personatus melanochir* is proportional to food availability. *Oryx*, **36**(2), 133–9.

Hu, G. (2011). Dietary breadth and resource use of François' langur in a seasonal and disturbed habitat. *American Journal of Primatology*, **73**(11), 1176–87.

Johns, A. D. (1983). Tropical forest primates and logging: can they coexist? *Oryx*, **17**, 114–18.

Johns, A. D. (1986). Effects of selective logging on the behavioral ecology of west Malaysian primates. *Ecology*, **67**(3), 684–94.

Johns, A. D. (1992). Vertebrate responses to selective logging: implications for the design of logging systems. *Philosophical Transactions of the Royal Society of London B*, **335**(1275), 437–42.

Johns, A. D. & Skorupa, J. P. (1987). Responses of rain-forest primates to habitat disturbance: a review. *International Journal of Primatology*, **8**(2), 157–91.

King, A., Behie, A. M., Rawson, B. M. & Hon, N. (2016). Patterns of salt lick use by mammal and bird species in Northeastern Cambodia. *Cambodian Journal of Natural History*, **1**, 40–50.

Knop, E., Ward, P. I. & Wich, S. A. (2004). A comparison of orang-utan density in a logged and unlogged forest on Sumatra. *Biological Conservation*, **120**(2), 183–8.

Kool, K. M. (1993). The diet and feeding behavior of the silver leaf monkey (*Trachypithecus auratus sondaicus*) in Indonesia. *International Journal of Primatology*, **14**(5), 667–700.

Leca, J. B., Gunst, N., Rompis, A., et al. (2013). Population density and abundance of ebony leaf monkey (*Trachypithecus auratus*) in West Bali National Park, Indonesia. *Primate Conservation*, **26**(1), 133–44.

Li, B. G., Ren, B. P. & Gao, Y. F. (1999). A change in the summer home range of Sichuan snub-nosed monkeys in Yuhuangmiao, Qinling Mountains. *Folia Primatologica*, **70**(5), 269–73.

Li, D. Y., Grueter, C. C., Ren, B. P., et al. (2008). Ranging of *Rhinopithecus bieti* in the Samage Forest, China: II. Use of land cover types and altitudes. *International Journal of Primatology*, **29**, 1147–73.

Li, Y. M. (2004). The effect of forest clear-cutting on habitat use in Sichuan snub-nosed monkey (*Rhinopithecus roxellana*) in Shennongja Nature Reserve, China. *Primates*, **45**(1), 69–72.

Marshall, A. J., Nardiyono, Engström, L. M., et al. (2006). The blowgun is mightier than the chainsaw in determining population density of Bornean Orangutans (*Pongo pygmaeus morio*) in the forests of East Kalimantan. *Biological Conservation*, **129**(4), 566–78.

Menon, S. & Poirier, F. E. (1996). Lion-tailed macaques (*Macaca silenus*) in a disturbed forest fragment: activity patterns and time budget. *International Journal of Primatology*, **17**(6), 969–85.

Nijman, V. (2004). Effects of habitat disturbance and hunting on the density and biomass of the endemic Hose's leaf monkey *Presbytis hosei* (Thomas, 1889) (Mammalia: Primates: Cercopithecidae) in East Borneo. *Contributions to Zoology*, **73**(4), 283–91.

Nijman, V. (2005). Decline of the endemic Hose's langur *Presbytis hosei* in Kayan Mentarang National Park, East Borneo. *Oryx*, **39**(2), 1–4.

Nijman, V. (2010). Ecology and conservation of the Hose's langur group (Colobinae: *Presbytis hosei*, *P. canicrus*, *P. sabana*): a review. In Gursky-Doyen, S. & Supriatna, J. (eds) *Indonesian Primates*. New York: Springer, pp. 269–84.

Onderdonk, D. A. & Chapman, C. A. (2000). Coping with forest fragmentation: the primates of Kibale National Park. *International Journal of Primatology*, **21**(4), 587–611.

Peres, C. A. (1997). Effects of habitat quality and hunting pressure on arboreal folivore densities in neotropical forests: a case study of howler monkeys (*Alouatta* spp.). *Folia Primatologica*, **68**(3–5), 199–222.

Peter, Z. & Pheap, A. (2015). (Un)protected areas. *The Cambodia Daily*, 1 August. Available at: www.cambodiadaily.com (accessed 7 September 2015).

Petersen, R., Sizer, N., Hansen, M., Potapov, P. & Thau, D. (2015). Satellites uncover 5 surprising hotspots for tree cover loss. World Resource Institute blog, 2 September. Available at: www.wri.org/blog/2015/09/satellites-uncover-5-surprising-hotspots-tree-cover-loss (accessed 4 September 2015).

Plumptre, A. J. & Reynolds, V. (1994). The effect of selective logging on the primate populations in the Budongo Forest Reserve, Uganda. *Journal of Applied Ecology*, **31**(4), 631–41.

Poirier, F. E. (1968). Analysis of a Nilgiri langur (*Presbytis johnii*) home range change. *Primates*, **9**(1), 29–43.

Potts, K. B. (2011). The long-term effect of timber harvesting on the resource base of chimpanzees in Kibale National Park, Uganda. *Biotropica*, **43**(2), 256–64.

Pye, D. (2013). Chainsaws stayed busy in last year. *Phnom Penh Post*, 26 December. Available at: www.phnompenhpost.com/national/chainsaws-stayed-busy-past-year (accessed 7 September 2015).

Pye, D. (2015a). Timber by the numbers. *Phnom Penh Post*, 7 April. Available at: www.phnompenhpost.com/national/timber-numbers (accessed 7 September 2015).

Pye, D. (2015b). Logging's roots deep. *Phnom Penh Post*, 23 June. Available at: www.phnompenhpost.com/national/loggings-roots-deep (accessed 7 September 2015).

Pye, D. & Titthara, M. (2014). The calculus of logging. *Phnom Penh Post*, 10 October. Available at: www.phnompenhpost.com/national/calculus-logging (accessed 7 September 2015).

Pye, D. & Titthara, M. (2015). The 'timber gangsters'. *Phnom Penh Post*, 6 February. Available at: www.phnompenhpost.com/national/timber-gangsters (accessed 7 September 2015).

Raemaekers, J. J. & Chivers, D. J. (1980). Socio-ecology of Malayan forest primates. In Chivers, D. J. (ed.) *Malayan Forest Primates: Ten Years' Study in Tropical Rain Forest*. New York: Springer, pp. 279–316.

Rawson, B. M. (2010). The status of Cambodian primates. In Nadler, T., Rawson, B. M. & Thinh, V. N., (eds) *Conservation of Primates in Indochina*. Hanoi: Frankfurt Zoological Society and Conservation International, pp. 17–329.

Remis, M. J. & Jost Robinson, C. A. (2012). Reductions in primate abundance and diversity in a multiuse protected area: synergistic impacts of hunting and logging in a Congo basin forest. *American Journal of Primatology*, **74**(7), 602–12.

Rijksen, H. D. (1978). A field study on Sumatran orang utans (*Pongo pygmaeus abelii* Lesson 1827): ecology, behaviour and conservation. PhD Thesis, Agricultural University, Wageningen.

Riley, E. P. (2008). Ranging patterns and habitat use of Sulawesi Tonkean macaques (*Macaca tonkeana*) in a human-modified habitat. *American Journal of Primatology*, **70**(7), 670–9.

Rosenbaum, B., O'Brien, T. G., Kinnaird, M. & Supriatna, J. (1998). Population densities of Sulawesi crested black macaques (*Macaca nigra*) on Bacan and Sulawesi, Indonesia: effects of habitat disturbance and hunting. *American Journal of Primatology*, **77**, 76–85.

Ruhiyat, Y. (1983). Socio-ecological study of *Presbytis aygula* in west Java. *Primates*, **24**(3), 344–59.

Salter, R. E., MacKenzie, N. A., Nightingale, N., Aken, K. M. & Chai, P. K. (1985). Habitat use, ranging behaviour, and food habits of the proboscis monkey, *Nasalis larvatus* (van Wurmb), in Sarawak. *Primates*, **26**(4), 436–51.

Singh, M., Kumara, H. N., Kumar, M. A. & Sharma, A. K. (2001). Behavioural responses of lion-tailed macaques (*Macaca silenus*) to a changing habitat in a tropical rain forest fragment in the Western Ghats, India. *Folia Primatologica*, **72**(5), 278–91.

Skorupa, J. P. (1985). Responses of rainforest primates to selective logging in Kibale Forest, Uganda: a summary report. In Benirschke, K. (ed.) *Primates: The Road to Self-Sustaining Populations*. New York: Springer, pp. 57–70.

Tan, C. L., Guo, S. T. & Li, B. G. (2007). Population structure and ranging patterns of *Rhinopithecus roxellana* in Zhouzhi National Nature Reserve, Shaanxi, China. *International Journal of Primatology*, **28**(3), 577–91.

Titthara, M. (2014). A logging free-for-all. *Phnom Penh Post*, 10 April. Available at: www.phnompenhpost.com (accessed 7 September 2015).

TRAFFIC (2008). *What's Driving the Wildlife Trade? A Review of Expert Opinion on Economic and Social Drivers of the Wildlife Trade and Trade Control Efforts in Cambodia, Indonesia, Lao PDR and Vietnam*. Washington, DC: East Asia and Pacific Region Sustainable Development Department, World Bank.

Umapathy, G. & Kumar, A. (2003). Impacts of forest fragmentation on lion-tailed macaque and Nilgiri langur in Western Ghats, South India. In Marsh, L. K. (ed.) *Primates in Fragments: Ecology and Conservation*. New York: Springer, pp. 163–89.

Umapathy, G., Hussain, S. & Shivaji, S. (2011). Impact of habitat fragmentation on the demography of lion-tailed macaque (*Macaca silenus*) populations in the rainforests of Anamalai Hills, Western Ghats, India. *International Journal of Primatology*, **32**(4), 889–900.

Vrieze, P. (2014). Extinction looms as notorious rosewood loggers set sights on Burma species, group warns. *The Irrawaddy*, 24 June. Available at: www.irrawaddy.com (accessed 30 November 2016).

Wallace, R. B. (2006). Seasonal variations in black-faced black spider monkey (*Ateles chamek*) habitat use and ranging behavior in a southern Amazonian tropical forest. *American Journal of Primatology*, **68**(4), 313–32.

Waltert, M., Faber, K. & Mühlenger, M. (2002). Further declines of threatened primates in the Korup Project Area, south-west Cameroon. *Oryx*, **36**(3), 257–65.

White, E. C., Dikangadissi, J. T. & Dimoto, E., et al. (2010). Home-range use by a large horde of wild *Mandrillus sphinx*. *International Journal of Primatology*, **31**(4), 627–45.

Wich, S. A. & Sterck, E. H. M. (2010). Thomas langurs: ecology, sexual conflict and social dynamics. In Gursky-Doyen, S. & Supriatna, J. (eds) *Indonesian Primates*. New York: Springer, pp. 285–308.

Winfield, K., Schott, M. & Grayson, C. (2016). Global status of *Dalbergia* and *Pterocarpus* rosewood producing species in trade. Paper presented at the Convention on International Trade in Endangered Species of Wild Fauna and Flora, Johannesburg, South Africa. Available at: www.global-eye.co/ge/wp-content/uploads/2016/09/CoP17-Inf-Doc-XXX-English-Exec-Summ-Global-Overview.pdf.

Wolf, H. A. (1996). Deforestation in Cambodia and Malaysia: the case for an international legal solution. *Pacific Rim Law and Policy Journal*, **5**(2), 429–55.

Workman, C. & Le, V. D. (2010). Seasonal effects on feeding selection by Delacour's langur (*Trachypithecus delacouri*) in Van Long Nature Reserve, Vietnam. In Nadler, T., Rawson, B. M. & Thinh, V. N. (eds) *Conservation of Primates in Indochina*. Hanoi: Frankfurt Zoological Society and Conservation International, pp. 143–56.

Xiang, Z. F., Huo, S. & Xiao, W. (2011). Habitat selection of black-and-white snub-nosed monkey (*Rhinopithecus bieti*) in Tibet: implications for species conservation. *American Journal of Primatology*, **73**(4), 347–55.

Zhang, D., Fei, H. L. & Yuan, S. D., et al. (2014). Ranging behavior of eastern hoolock gibbon (*Hoolock leuconedys*) in a northern montane forest in Gaoligongshan, Yunnan, China. *Primates*, **55**(2), 239–47.

Zunino, G. E., Kowalewski, M. M., Oklander, L. L. & Gonzalez, V. (2007). Habitat fragmentation and population size of the black and gold howler monkey (*Alouatta caraya*) in a semideciduous forest in Northern Argentina. *American Journal of Primatology*, **69**(9), 1–10.

7 The Immediate Impact of Selective Logging on Rwenzori Angolan Colobus (*Colobus angolensis ruwenzorii*) at Lake Nabugabo, Uganda

Julie A. Teichroeb, Gregory R. Bridgett, Amélie Corriveau and Dennis Twinomugisha

7.1 Personal Narrative

With my strong interest in animal behaviour, I (JAT) started my undergraduate career in biology, but ended up completing a Bachelor of Science in biological anthropology at the University of Calgary after my discovery that this was the area where primate behaviour was most intensively studied. I went on to do my Master of Arts with Jim Paterson and my PhD with Pascale Sicotte in primatology at the University of Calgary, engaging in fieldwork on ursine colobus monkeys (*Colobus vellerosus*) at the Boabeng-Fiema Monkey Sanctuary (BFMS) in Ghana for both degrees. Many questions interested me throughout my graduate career, especially understanding how an animal's resources influenced their grouping patterns and their relationships with other individuals in their group. This was, after all, the heyday of testing socioecological models. Though more difficult to study in long-lived animals like primates, I was also intrigued with how sexual selection had acted on primates and what the effects might be in terms of morphological adaptations in males, female mate choice and sexual conflict. My PhD dissertation ended up focusing on both the social and the ecological factors controlling group size and group composition in ursine colobus.

Working in West Africa over the 10 years it took to complete my graduate degrees, I became acutely aware of all the conservation challenges facing wildlife there. When I started travelling to Ghana in 2000, it was rare to see large forest trees still standing, and when you did find areas where forest had been preserved, large animals were never seen and even birds were relatively rare. The bushmeat trade was (and is) also a serious problem, decimating wildlife in the region. Hunters were found lining the roads near any forested area, holding up dead monkeys by their tails or displaying other animals, hoping that passing motorists would be interested in buying the meat. Larger animals were already so scarce that most hunters had only forest snails or grasscutters (bush rats) for sale.

BFMS seemed like a sanctuary to both humans and monkeys in comparison with what I would normally see driving through Ghana. The two monkey species present, the ursine colobus and Campbell's mona monkeys (*Cercopithecus campbelli lowei*), were protected by traditional religious beliefs that saw them as the children of two local gods. This hunting taboo was bolstered with laws prohibiting their killing and officers from the Ghana Wildlife Division stationed at the site. The forest surrounding the village, though less protected than the monkeys, contained a sacred grove area and still had many tall forest trees, including huge mahoganies (*Khaya grandifoliola*) and giant strangler figs (*Ficus ottoniifolia, F. polita*). It was a place where I could follow the monkeys without them fleeing due to past hunting pressure. I did not focus on questions of conservation while working there, but the fact that BFMS is made up of a series of relatively small forest fragments, hemmed in by agriculture, had to be a consideration in my work. Population density for the colobus was high within these forest fragments and dispersing beyond them was not really a viable option for the monkeys. On one particular day, while working in the forest in my first year in Ghana, Tania Saj and I saw two mona monkeys die because they were poisoned by proponents of a local Christian sect, who had hunted and eaten monkeys at BFMS in the past. It struck me at that moment that even where conservation seems to be working, changing circumstances and beliefs can reverse progress very quickly.

My postdoctoral work took me to McGill University to work with Colin Chapman at his new field site, Lake Nabugabo in Uganda. He chose this site specifically because it was not a national park and thus the vervet monkeys (*Chlorocebus pygerythrus*) could be studied for their abilities to survive in an anthropogenically modified landscape. The abundance of vervet monkeys and the unprotected status of the area also meant that we could get permission to do some foraging experiments on this population. I had begun to be quite interested in how animals detected food and chose their travel paths through their complicated habitat. By providing small amounts of food to the vervets in specific ways and patterns, I could begin to understand their perceptive abilities and their decision-making processes in greater detail.

It was difficult to watch the vervets interact in such varied ways with the people of Nabugabo. While tourists, the staff of the tourist lodges and fishermen often fed the monkeys, they would also act quite aggressively towards them. The vervets also raided local crops and came into direct conflict with farmers and the dogs of local people. Our field assistants watched many vervets die from violent assaults by both people and dogs, as well as incidents of mass poisoning. It was that first year at Nabugabo that I realised that my future research programme was always going to have to incorporate questions on how the monkeys were adapting to increasing anthropogenic pressure.

During my first year in Uganda, I became aware of a rare colobus monkey population living in the tall forest fragments around Nabugabo. This population was the montane subspecies of Rwenzori Angolan colobus (*Colobus angolensis ruwenzorii*) about which little was known, especially in low-altitude forest. I began to habituate part of this population in 2013 and continue to have students and a team of field assistants follow this fluid 'supertroop'. Again, my research was focused on a primate population living in forest fragments with a far from secure future.

My habituated animals were in a fragment, mostly contained in a forest reserve, and thus the government of Uganda could decide at any time to utilise the resources there. That is indeed what happened in March 2014, when logging began in the area. Despite the fact that most of my original research interests lay elsewhere, it has become impossible to study primates in the wild without some focus on how human impacts on the environment are affecting them.

7.2   Introduction

Habitat loss is the most pervasive threat facing primate populations today (Chapman & Peres, 2001; Estrada et al., 2017). Tropical forests, which contain 90 per cent of the world's primates, are specifically at risk (Hansen et al., 2013; Mittermeier & Cheney, 1987) and logging and wood harvesting now threaten 60 per cent of primate species (Estrada et al., 2017). Deforestation due to timber extraction is occurring at alarming rates worldwide and the threat is increasing as global demand for timber grows (Malhi et al., 2014). The subsequent habitat modifications after timber extraction will inevitably impact primates, forcing them to live in human-altered environments (Barbier et al., 1994; Lewis et al., 2015). It is understood that primate populations occupying tropical forest habitat will decrease following widespread deforestation. It has also been proposed by Cowlishaw (1999) that even primate populations that have survived the deforestation of their habitat may still incur an 'extinction debt', in that they are experiencing a lag-time until population collapse. Using the species/area curve and examining populations of forest primates across Africa, Cowlishaw (1999) found that current populations could be expected to decrease in size due to historical deforestation; however, as these populations are also experiencing ongoing deforestation, their extinction risk is exacerbated. The lag-time between habitat modification and eventual population extinction means that synergistic factors such as hunting, edge effects, fires, climate change and disease work together to decrease animal populations and cause their extinction in association with deforestation (Brook et al., 2008; Chapman & Peres, 2001).

Studies on the effects of selective logging on primates fail to present as clear a picture as studies on complete deforestation. Selective logging is typically defined as the harvesting of less than 10 per cent of trees in a forest, which allows for forest regeneration post-logging (Johns & Skorupa, 1987). Selective logging has become a common practice in the tropics (Asner et al., 2009); however, it often acts as a gateway leading to other forms of disturbance (Edwards et al., 2014; Lewis et al., 2015; Mayor et al., 2015). An extensive review of the effects of selective logging on various primate populations occupying a variety of forest habitats, conducted by Johns and Skorupa (1987), has shown idiosyncratic results, some of which may be due to logging defined as 'selective' showing great variability in the actual amount of destruction (from 5 to more than 70 per cent). Chapman and Peres (2001) point to the fact that trees not targeted for logging can still be damaged, impacting the actual number of trees lost. Furthermore, similar habitats with similar populations of primates experiencing equivalent rates of destruction have resulted in markedly different population effects of selective logging due to differences in initial primate densities and the levels of human impact on these populations pre- and post-logging. Primate responses to logging appear to be species-specific and dependent on the type and level of disturbance, as well as the responses of the ecosystem after logging (Fimbel, 1994; Johns & Skorupa, 1987). Multiple factors, including size and spacing of remaining forest fragments, availability and density of important food sources, the overall degree of damage, species' ability to move between fragments, and the amount of hunting pressure following disturbance, will all impact a species' ability to survive locally.

Despite the variation across populations, some general patterns of the impact of selective logging are evident. Body size and diet are typically assumed to be the most predictive of a primate's ability to survive habitat disturbance. However, Johns and Skorupa (1987) found that body size is only predictive when the effects of diet are controlled. Diet type alone was considered to be predictive as it was found that the level of frugivory in a primate's diet negatively correlated with a species' survival ratio following forest disturbance. These results indicate that large-bodied frugivores, particularly the members of the genera *Ateles*, *Pan* and *Pongo*, are most at risk following disturbance, while smaller-bodied primates and primates with more folivorous diets have an increased chance of survival in selectively logged habitats.

Based on the folivorous diet of colobine monkeys, one might expect these species to successfully inhabit selectively logged areas, but numerous studies have once again presented a more complicated picture. Guerezas (*Colobus guereza*) appear to maintain abundant populations in logged habitat (Skorupa, 1986), and this species was actually found at higher densities in lightly logged compared to unlogged areas, indicating that logged forest may be preferred habitat (Chapman et al., 2000; Plumptre & Reynolds, 1994). Johns and Skorupa (1987) describe guerezas as a 'light-loving' species that can benefit from the higher temperatures in logged habitats where more energy can be directed to digestion, allowing them to exploit a lower-quality leafy diet. Conversely, closely related black colobus (*C. satanus*) and red colobus monkeys (*Procolobus badius*) have been found to be more abundant in undisturbed forest and to respond negatively to logging, perhaps as a result of more specialised diets (Johns & Skorupa, 1987; McKey, 1978; Struhsaker, 1972). Unsurprisingly, the dietary flexibility of a species coupled with the abundance of specific food types post-logging can alter its ability to survive disturbances. Studies thus need to take into account local conditions to explain the responses of different species to selective logging. Colobus monkeys also typically face a great deal of hunting pressure due to their large size, and have been shown to be vulnerable to being hunted to depletion due to their conspicuous nature (Johns & Skorupa, 1987; Oates et al., 2000). With increased access by people to disturbed forests and the changes in canopy height and makeup (Bennett & Dahaban, 1995), colobus could be even more susceptible than other primate groups to hunting pressure following selective logging.

The difficulty of finding broad-scale patterns of the effect of selective logging on primates is compounded by variation in methodologies between studies and the fact that studies often lack comparable data on the same forest areas and primate populations both pre- and post-logging. It is common to compare primate popula- tions living in logged areas to those in nearby unlogged areas (e.g. Chapman et al., 2000; Plumptre & Reynolds, 1994). Johns and Johns (1995) point out the critical importance of studying single populations of the same species prior to logging, during logging, and throughout the regeneration of the forest post-logging.

In this study, we examined the immediate ecological changes caused by small- scale, selective logging in a forest fragment, Manwa Forest Reserve, at Lake Nabu- gabo, Uganda. We also determined the effect of logging on the density, activity budget, diet and subgroup sizes of Rwenzori Angolan colobus (*Colobus angolensis ruwenzorii*). This subspecies of Angolan colobus is vulnerable to extinction according to the IUCN (Kingdon et al., 2008). We collected pre- and post-logging data on the structure of the forest, the numbers of colobus present, and the behaviour of one large colobus group. We predicted that: (1) since logging does not usually kill primates (Struhsaker, 1997) and because the extraction was at low levels and done without heavy machinery, changes to colobus densities would not be apparent immediately after logging; (2) the colobus activity budgets would show more resting and less feeding and moving after selective logging due to lowered food availability, as has been seen in other primate populations immediately after selective logging (Johns, 1986); (3) the diet of the colobus would include fewer of the tree species targeted by logging (umbrella tree, *Maesopsis eminii*). Logging has been shown to decrease fruit availability but lead to increased young leaf growth (Johns, 1983); we therefore also predicted that (4) colobus would show a reduction in time spent feeding on fruit (Johns & Skorupa, 1987), with a corresponding increase in leaf eating (Ganzhorn, 1995; Johns, 1986) post-logging. (5) Finally, we also predicted that the colobus would form smaller subgroup sizes than in pre-logging periods because of reduced food availability (e.g. Johns, 1986; Johns & Johns, 1995). Though we are unable to test this hypothesis currently, we also propose that downstream effects of logging may be apparent after several years, with lowered recruitment of juveniles for the colobus ranging in logged areas, due to a loss of important food trees (Johns, 1992; Struhsaker, 1997).

7.3   Methods

This study was conducted at Lake Nabugabo, Masaka District, central Uganda (0°22′– 12°S and 31°54′E). Lake Nabugabo is a small lake (8.2 × 5 km) at an elevation of 1136 m, lying to the west of the large Lake Victoria. The landscape surrounding the lake consists mostly of swamps, with the north and west sides also including a mixed habitat of wetlands, grasslands, patches of tall forest, degraded forest, farmers' fields, and a few buildings (Chapman et al., 2016). One of these patches of tall forest adjacent to the trading centres of Bukumbula and Nabugabo is partly made up of the ~280 ha Manwa Forest Reserve. Rwenzori Angolan colobus inhabit this forest and the adjacent fragments. This subspecies forms large permanent groups of >300 individuals in montane areas (Fashing et al., 2007; Fimbel et al., 2001), but at lowland sites, like Nabugabo, subgroups of variable size show fission–fusion behaviour and have been referred to as 'supertroops' (Oates, 1974). Pre-logging data were collected on the structure of the forest, the numbers of colobus present and the behaviour of a large fluid supertroop of colobus in 2013 and the beginning of 2014. Selective logging took place in Manwa Forest Reserve beginning on 26 March 2014. Ninety loggers in six teams entered the forest to log *Maesopsis eminii* trees $\geq$40 cm diameter at breast height (DBH) using hand and pit saws. The local community protested the logging, with representatives travelling to Kampala to discuss the issue with the Ugandan environment minister. After these protests, logging ceased after only one month. We collected post-logging data on changes to the forest, colobus numbers and behaviour beginning in July 2014.

7.3.1   Ecological Survey

As part of a long-term study on the behavioural ecology of Rwenzori Angolan colobus, pre-logging data were collected on the structure of the forest and the numbers of colobus present in the large forest fragment (140 ha were sampled, of which just over half is within the forest reserve boundary) at Lake Nabugabo from 19 April to 29 June 2013. Though the entire forest fragment is not included within Manwa Forest Reserve where logging occurred, to consistently compare pre- and post-logging data we include data from the whole 140 ha that we sampled (Table 7.1). Colobus subgroups were found throughout the entire forest fragment and the ones studied (Troop FG) were usually found within the reserve.

Line-transect surveys (Whitesides et al., 1988) were used to assess both the ecology of the forest and the abundance of primate populations. First, the perimeter of the forest was mapped using a GPS, then 32 parallel, straight-line transects were cut at 100 m intervals through the forest fragment. Transects varied in length (Table 7.1) and were cut either until the edge of the fragment was reached or we moved into the swamp on the northwest side of the forest and standing water became more than 30 cm deep. Ecological assessment was done by identifying and measuring all trees $\geq$10 cm DBH within 5 m on each side of the transects. For trees with multiple stems $\geq$10 cm DBH, we measured all stems and consolidated them by taking the square root of the sum of all squared DBHs (Nature Conservation Practice, 2006). Trees were identified to the species level with the assistance of a knowledgeable local botanist (Matovu Ponsiano). The percentage of canopy cover was estimated every 50 m along transects. On each transect, a scan was taken to assess average canopy height and one tree that represented this height was measured using a clinometer. In addition to the ecological survey, we examined the amount of disturbance to the forest by noting all instances of human activity (stumps, charcoal pits, cut branches, etc.) present within 5 m on either side of all transects.

Post-logging ecological surveys were carried out in July 2014 by rewalking the existing 32 pre-logging transects and noting any new disturbance caused by the loggers. We recorded, measured and identified the species of new stumps within 5 m on either side of transects, determining whether the trees were cut by loggers or by

Table 7.1 Pre-logging tree composition and occurrence of logging on transects at Lake Nabugabo, Uganda

Transect	Length (m)	Number of stems ≥10 cm DBH*	Mean DBH (cm)	Logging?	# Trees logged	Mean stump diameter (cm)
1	73	39	18.6	N		
2	86	42	24.3	N		
3	67	27	27.3	N		
4	527	236	23.7	N		
5	98	21	23.6	N		
6	190	61	21.7	N		
7	120	61	22.5	N		
8	73	76	20.1	N		
9	43	37	21.9	N		
10[‡]	140	36	22	N		
11	170	55	26.9	Y	5	32.4
12	626	216	25	Y	†	
13	337	105	25.8	Y	†	
14	29	13	22.5	Y	1	39
15	140	61	22.9	Y	†	
16	110	52	26	N		
17	100	39	28.1	N		
18	290	105	22.4	Y	†	
19	300	103	22.7	N		
20	359	116	23.4	Y	5	34.7
21	459	167	26.1	Y	†	
22	498	212	27.7	Y	12	33.5
23	548	208	25.5	N		
24	615	285	25.3	Y	†	
25	671	259	29.9	Y	3	30.3
26	509	234	27.8	Y	9	35.7
27	602	199	27.5	Y	†	
28	524	173	28.8	Y	1	51.6
29	527	149	31.4	Y	7	30.8
30	432	128	32.3	Y	2	29
31	252	73	31.8	Y	1	40
32	187	43	33.3	N		

* Pre-logging stems within 5 m of either side of the transect.
† Logging just off transect.
‡ Transects 1–10 were located outside of Manwa Forest Reserve where no logging took place.

local people gathering firewood and building supplies. We additionally noted when logging had occurred just off transects (Table 7.1). Incidental damage to living trees caused by the felling of large trees for timber and damage caused by the construction of logging camps were also recorded when possible. Canopy coverage was again estimated every 50 m along transects in post-logging surveys.

7.3.2 Primate Surveys

Pre-logging primate surveys were done in a single day using the 32 parallel transects. Beginning early in the morning on 5 June 2013, researchers, in four teams of two, walked slowly (~1 kmh) and quietly along parallel transects at the same time until the end was reached. Observers then turned around and walked quietly back to the starting point so that two sweeps of each transect were done to identify and count the primates seen. When primate groups were detected, their location along the transect was noted, as well as the time, species, distance from the observer, sighting angle, approximate distance to the first animal encountered and the average height of the group (Anderson et al., 2007a; Buckland et al., 2001; Whitesides et al., 1988). Additional data gathered included the main group behaviour when encountered, number of animals seen, age and sex class of animals observed, approximate group spread, presence of other species, which side of the transect the group was encountered on and whether the count was considered accurate or incomplete. After each set of sweeps along transects, the research teams met outside the forest to collate results and discuss observations to ensure the accuracy of the data and avoid the double-counting of groups (Anderson et al., 2007b). The four teams of observers then moved to the next four parallel transects and began walking them at the same time. This process was repeated until all transects had been walked.

A post-logging primate survey was carried out over several days in July 2014. Due to time constraints, a large team was not assembled in post-logging surveys and two observers concurrently completed the primate survey and the ecological survey. Two observers walked quietly at about 1 kmh on the existing 32 parallel transects, recording both damage to the forest and any primates seen. Two sweeps were again done for each transect, and when primates were encountered the same information was recorded as for the pre-logging survey. Sampling effort, in terms of walks along transects, was the same in pre- and post-logging surveys; however, because post-logging primate surveys were done over a number of days rather than all on the same day, the possibility of double-counting the same groups was higher. We do not think that this affected our results because the groups that were encountered on successive days in the post-logging survey were in areas of the forest fragment that were distant from one another. Though vervet monkeys and red-tailed monkeys (*Cercopithecus ascanius*) were also encountered in both primate surveys, here we only report data on Rwenzori Angolan colobus.

7.3.3 Behavioural Data

After the initial primate survey in 2013, a large, fluid supertroop of Rwenzori Angolan colobus was chosen for habituation and continued behavioural monitoring (Troop FG). Local field assistants were trained in teams of two to conduct follows of this supertroop (often found in subgroups of differing size) for six days per month. Follows began in July 2013 and continued until March 2014, when logging began. Follows started again in July 2014 after the loggers had left the forest and the monkeys had returned to their former range. With some variability, follows generally began at 7:30 a.m. and continued until 4:30 p.m. Field assistants collected scan samples (Altmann, 1974) via the frequency method (Struhsaker, 1975) every 30 minutes for up to five individuals, recording age and sex class, identity (if known), activity, food item and species (if feeding), distance and age and sex class of the nearest-neighbour, and a GPS point of the subgroup location. Observers moved around the subgroup between scans in an attempt to ensure that the same individuals were not scanned in successive samples. A count of the subgroup and the age and sex class composition was recorded at least once during each follow, as well as whether or not it was deemed a good count. Observers noted any fission and fusion events with other subgroups *ad libitum*. When the subgroup being followed underwent fissioning, observers stayed with either the largest subgroup or the one that contained the most known individuals.

We compared the behaviour of the Rwenzori Angolan colobus supertroop pre- and post-logging by examining data on activity budget, diet and subgroup sizes. To ensure a valid comparison and avoid both seasonal effects on these behaviours and interindividual differences in data collection between researchers, we used a matched sample of data from July to September 2013 (pre-logging) and July to September 2014 (post-logging) that was collected by the same observation team (M. Ponsiano and L. Katwere). After these restrictions to ensure comparable samples, we were left with 11 days of pre-logging data (835 scans of individuals) to compare with 11 days of post-logging data (815 scans of individuals).

7.3.4   Data Analyses

For our pre-logging ecological assessment of the forest, we calculated the total stems present, number of tree species, dominant tree species, average tree height (m), mean DBH (cm), stem density (#/ha), basal area (m^2/ha) and canopy cover. Total stems were calculated by adding up all the trees enumerated along our 10 m wide transects (total area covered 9.702 ha) and extrapolating this to the entire 140 ha sampled. The dominant tree species was the most common species ($\geq$10 cm DBH) enumerated along transects. The basal area for the forest was calculated by determining the area covered by each sampled tree ($A = \pi r^2$), then adding these together and dividing by the number of hectares sampled. Canopy cover estimates were averaged for each transect. Comparisons between pre- and post-logging data were possible for total stems, stem density, and canopy cover, so these were recalculated for our post-logging ecological survey. Statistical comparisons of these three measures were done with data from each transect using Wilcoxon signed rank tests and paired t-tests, with use of parametric and non-parametric tests dependent on sample size.

From the primate survey data, we calculated the group density of colobus seen along the transects in the pre- and post-logging periods for comparison. Colobus group densities were calculated using the reliable distance-to-animal method, where the width of the transect was the maximum reliable observer–animal distance from the transect (Struhsaker, 1981; equation 7.1).

$$\text{Group density} = \frac{\Sigma \text{ group sightings}}{2(\text{length} \times \text{width of one side of transect in km})} \qquad (7.1)$$

Though the Whitesides method (Whitesides et al., 1988) has been shown to be more accurate for primate survey data (Fashing & Cords, 2000), this method could not be used here because it requires species- and site-specific mean group spreads and group sizes, of which samples of ≥ 30 are considered reasonable (Whitesides et al., 1988). Our colobus surveys led to 26 sightings where group spread and size values were attained. Given that we are comparing group densities at the same site over time, rather than between sites and researchers, the reliable distance-to-animal method should be sufficient. We acknowledge, however, that the main issue with the calculation of group density for Rwenzori Angolan colobus at Nabugabo is that the fission–fusion behaviour of this subspecies makes different size groupings possible over short time periods.

Activity budget was analysed by comparing daily proportions of scans spent feeding, resting, moving or socialising with Mann–Whitney U tests between pre- and post-logging periods. Subgroup size counts each day that were deemed 'good counts' by observers were also compared for these two periods with Mann–Whitney U tests. We extracted diet data on plant part and species from scans in which individuals were feeding. The daily proportions of scans spent feeding on different plant parts were compared for the pre- and post-logging periods with Mann–Whitney U tests. Data were analysed using R version 3.2.0 (R Core Team, 2015).

7.4   Results

7.4.1   Changes to the Forest as a Result of Logging

In the pre-logging ecological survey, the forest was found to contain 60 tree species with an average height of 22.95 m, and the dominant tree species was *Pseudospondias microcarpa*. Logging should not have changed these characteristics because *Maesopsis eminii* was targeted and a small percentage of trees were logged. Pre-logging analyses showed that the total stems (≥ 10 cm DBH) present within the 140 ha sampled was 53 471. Post-logging, the number of stems logged along transects (9.702 ha) was 46, for an estimated loss of 664 trees within the 140 ha (Table 7.1). Thus, post-logging, total stem number was estimated at 52 807 for a loss of only 1.2 per cent; however, statistical comparison of the number of stems ≥ 10 cm DBH along logged transects showed that this was a significant decrease (Wilcoxon signed rank: $N = 17$, $Z = 2.78$, $p = 0.005$). Mean DBH in the forest in the pre-logging period was 26.31 cm and basal area was 26.96 m^2/ha. Larger trees were the ones removed by loggers (mean stump diameter: 33.97 cm), so presumably mean DBH and basal area had decreased slightly in the post-logging period; however, we did not reassess the DBH of all trees along transects post-logging due to time constraints. Logging led to an overall reduction in stem density from 374.3 stems/ha in the pre-logging period to 371.9 stems/ha post-logging, which was not significantly different when including logged and unlogged transects (paired t-test: $N = 32$, $t = 0.11$,

$p = 0.91$). Mean canopy cover in the pre-logging period was 77.4 per cent and post-logging it was 73.6 per cent. Canopy coverage decreased on most transects where logging occurred compared to pre-logging coverage, leading to a significant difference (Wilcoxon signed rank: $N = 14$, $Z = 3.03$, $p = 0.002$), while there was no difference on transects without logging ($N = 14$, $Z = -1.37$, $p = 0.17$).

This logging operation was supposed to exclusively target *M. eminii* trees $\geq$40 cm DBH; however, only 42.9 per cent of logged stumps enumerated on transects (18/42) were identified as this species, with a mean stump diameter of 44.5 cm. A stump diameter of just over 44 cm indicates that the DBH of these trees was likely often less than 40 cm. At least five species other than *M. eminii* were also cut (including *Funtumia latifolia*, *Newtonia buchananii*, *Pycnanthus angolensis*, *Beilschmiedia ugandensis* and *Sieberiena holckii*; mean stump diameter 35.8 cm) and the loggers damaged several areas building camps (Figure 7.1a). Since some of these trees may have been cut for the building of pit saws and camps (Figure 7.1a, b), it is not known whether the boles of trees other than *M. eminii* were removed for timber. However, the larger size of the *F. latifolia* stems (mean stump diameter = 40 cm) suggests that this species was removed for timber. The felling of the largest trees ($N = 3$) did a fair amount of incidental damage, with a mean of 3.33 other large trees damaged by being either knocked down or having most of their canopies ripped off.

7.4.2   Colobus Densities Pre-Logging and Post-Logging

Local field assistants at Nabugabo reported that Rwenzori Angolan colobus were not seen, nor was any loud calling heard, during the logging operation. Colobus had returned to their former range in the logged areas of the forest by July 2014, two and a half months after logging ceased, which we confirmed with the observation of 14 known individuals. Due to the fission–fusion of subgroups and the transient nature of groups in this population, comparing pre- and post-logging group densities is difficult, but we did see a change from 4.37 groups/km^2 to 2.43 groups/km^2. In the

Figure 7.1 (a) Logger camp and (b) pit saws abandoned after logging at Lake Nabugabo.

pre-logging survey we counted 93 colobus in nine groups, while in the post-logging survey we counted 54 individuals in five groups.

7.4.3   Post-Logging Impacts on Colobus Behaviour

The mean daily subgroup size for supertroop FG in the pre-logging period from July to September 2013 was 153.3 individuals ($N = 8$ days with good group counts), while in the post-logging period from July through September 2014, it was 166 ($N = 7$ days). There was no significant difference in daily totals for subgroup size between these two periods (Mann–Whitney U: $N_{pre} = 8$, $N_{post} = 7$, $U = 38$, $p = 0.27$).

Activity budget in the pre-logging period was 23.7 per cent feeding, 41.8 per cent resting, 24.7 per cent moving, 4.6 per cent socialising and 4.8 per cent other. In the post-logging period the activity budget changed to 17.4 per cent feeding, 48.1 per cent resting, 20.6 per cent moving, 9.6 per cent socialising, and 4.3 per cent other (Figure 7.2). This resulted in less feeding and moving and more resting and socialising than in the pre-logging period (Mann–Whitney U: feeding, $N_{pre} = 11$, $N_{post} = 11$, $U = 19$, $p = 0.007$; moving, $N_{pre} = 11$, $N_{post} = 11$, $U = 30$, $p = 0.049$; resting, $N_{pre} = 11$, $N_{post} = 11$, $U = 97$, $p = 0.018$; social, $N_{pre} = 11$, $N_{post} = 11$, $U = 100$, $p = 0.011$; other, $N_{pre} = 11$, $N_{post} = 11$, $U = 49.5$, $p = 0.49$).

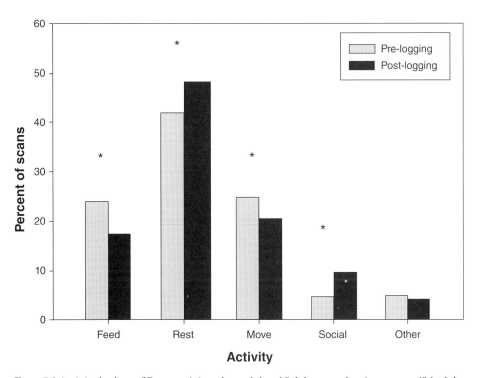

Figure 7.2 Activity budget of Rwenzori Angolan colobus (*Colobus angolensis ruwenzorii*) in July to September 2013 (pre-logging) and July to September 2014 (post-logging) at Lake Nabugabo. Stars indicate significant differences.

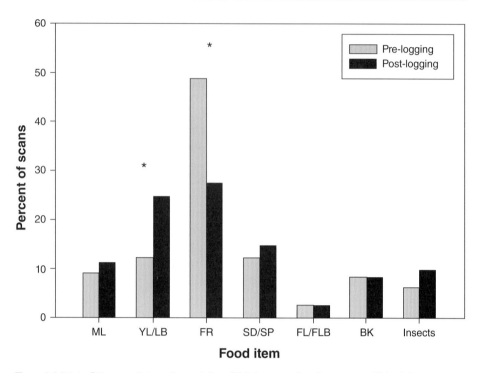

Figure 7.3 Diet of Rwenzori Angolan colobus (*Colobus angolensis ruwenzorii*) in July to September 2013 (pre-logging) and July to September 2014 (post-logging) at Lake Nabugabo. Abbreviations: ML mature leaves, YL/LB young leaves/leaf buds, FR fruit, SD/SP seeds/seed pods, FL/FLB flowers/flower buds, BK bark. Stars indicate significant differences.

The diet in the pre-logging period was made up of 8.9 per cent mature leaves, 12.1 per cent young leaves/leaf buds, 48.9 per cent fruit, 12.1 per cent seeds/seed pods, 2.6 per cent flowers/flower buds, 8.4 per cent bark and 6.3 per cent insects. In the post-logging period, the diet consisted of 11.3 per cent mature leaves, 24.8 per cent young leaves/leaf buds, 27.7 per cent fruit, 14.9 per cent seeds/seed pods, 2.8 per cent flowers/flower buds, 8.5 per cent bark and 9.9 per cent insects (Figure 7.3). Significant differences were seen in the greater post-logging intake of young leaves/leaf buds and smaller consumption of fruit compared to the pre-logging period (Mann–Whitney U: mature leaves, $N_{pre} = 11$, $N_{post} = 11$, $U = 77.5$, $p = 0.28$; young leaves/leaf buds, $N_{pre} = 11$, $N_{post} = 11$, $U = 105$, $p = 0.004$; fruit, $N_{pre} = 11$, $N_{post} = 11$, $U = 3$, $p = 0.0002$; seeds/seed pods, $N_{pre} = 11$, $N_{post} = 11$, $U = 74.5$, $p = 0.37$; flowers/flower buds, $N_{pre} = 11$, $N_{post} = 11$, $U = 64.5$, $p = 0.82$; bark, $N_{pre} = 11$, $N_{post} = 11$, $U = 56$, $p = 0.79$; insects, $N_{pre} = 11$, $N_{post} = 11$, $U = 88.5$, $p = 0.07$).

In terms of important tree species in the diet, there were five species that each made up at least 5 per cent of the diet in the pre-logging period, with *M. eminii* the most eaten at 21.5 per cent of the diet. Post-logging this increased to six species each making up at least 5 per cent of the diet, and while *M. eminii* was still important, its contribution to the diet dropped to 7.8 per cent (Table 7.2). In pre-logging feeding on

Table 7.2 Food species most frequently eaten* by Rwenzori Angolan colobus July through September 2013 and 2014 (before and after logging) at Lake Nabugabo, Uganda

Pre-logging food species	Percentage of diet	Post-logging food species	Percentage of diet
Maesopsis eminii	21.5	*Maesopsis eminii*	7.8
Antiaris toxicaria	9.1	*Antiaris toxicaria*	7.8
Pseudospondias microcarpa	6.5	*Pseudospondias microcarpa*	7.0
Newtonia buchananii	5.9	*Newtonia buchananii*	5.5
Pycnanthus angolensis	5.4	*Pycnanthus angolensis*	5.5
		Macaranga schweinfurthii	5.5

* Species making up at least 5 per cent of the diet.

M. eminii, 86.8 per cent of samples were fruit, 7.9 per cent were young leaves and 5.3 per cent were mature leaves. In the post-logging period, 50 per cent of feeding on *M. eminii* was on fruits, 40 per cent was on young leaves and 10 per cent was on mature leaves. Overall, 36.3 per cent of fruit feeding in the pre-logging period was on *M. eminii* and this dropped to 13.5 per cent post-logging.

7.5   Discussion

The small scale of the logging that was done at Nabugabo in March 2014 was likely due to both community protests that halted logging prematurely and the small size of the forest reserve. Had the forest been larger, it is unlikely that traditional logging methods would have been employed and roads and heavy logging machinery would have led to much greater damage (e.g. Cannon et al., 1994; Douglas et al., 1992; Gullison & Hardner, 1993; Uhl & Vieira, 1989). Logging done by hand is usually much less damaging than that done with heavy machinery (Putz et al., 2001); loggers at Nabugabo cut logs into planks at pit saws before carrying them out of the forest on foot, so large trees were not hauled out on roads. Subsequent attempts to collect firewood on a commercial scale from the forest (by firewood dealers from the nearest town, Masaka), which would have aggravated degradation, were also foiled by the local community.

The behaviour of the Rwenzori Angolan colobus at Nabugabo during logging conformed to that observed in other primates: the animals fled the area of active logging but returned to their former range once logging ceased (Arnhem et al., 2008; Johns, 1986; White & Tutin, 2001). We suspect that the colobus at Nabugabo fled to safe spots in adjoining forest along the Juma River (just outside of the forest reserve boundaries) where no logging occurred. The tendency for animals to flee areas where active habitat disturbance is occurring can cause them to move into ranges that are already occupied by conspecifics, leading to increased territorial aggression (White & Tutin, 2001). Given the large-scale fission–fusion events that we have observed among subgroups of Rwenzori Angolan colobus and the extremely large groups seen in montane areas (Fashing et al., 2007), we suspect that, despite temporal variation in which individuals maintain association, the whole population of the forest fragment may sometimes coalesce. If this is the case, it would mean that the colobus could gather together, for a period of time, in one part of the forest without suffering heightened territorial aggression.

Two and a half months after logging at Lake Nabugabo, our results suggest a decrease in the numbers of Rwenzori Angolan colobus. Though our study group had returned to its previous range, the overall population size may have decreased or some colobus that fled logging may have yet to return. It is also possible that the colobus densities had not changed but that there were more group fissions in the pre-logging period or that our slightly different survey methods between the pre- and post-logging periods led to spurious results. Although counting the overall number of individuals is difficult in fission–fusion species (Chapman et al., 1993), we found that colobus subgroup sizes remained the same compared to a matched pre-logging sample. This may be an indication that colobus densities did not change; however, primates tend to maintain their species-specific social organisation (i.e. group sizes and compositions) even in the face of substantial decreases in population density (Cowlishaw & Dunbar, 2000).

Direct mortality due to logging is not common in primates, but a decreased food supply after logging could potentially lead to lowered recruitment of infants in the long term (Johns, 1992; Struhsaker, 1997). Even when species targeted by selective logging are not key food resources, primate food sources can be negatively affected due to a high degree of unintended incidental damage (Skorupa, 1986). At Nabugabo, the targeted tree species (*M. eminii*) was actually the top food item in the colobus diet. Thus, despite the relatively small amount of damage that was done by the logging, we still saw some of the predicted changes in colobus behaviour. Compared to the pre-logging period, our focal supertroop of colobus changed their diet in the post-logging period. The logged tree species, *M. eminii*, decreased in importance in the diet, likely due to the reduction in the availability of this species caused by logging. The consumption of fruit decreased after logging while young leaves/buds and mature leaves became more important. While phenology data are not available, young leaves were observed in abundance after logging due to the opening up of some areas of the canopy. Fruit may also have been less available due to the felling of important fruit trees and subsequent disturbance (Felton et al., 2003; Johns, 1983; 1986; Johns & Skorupa, 1987). The targeted tree species, *M. eminii*, made up a lot of the fruit feeding before logging, but far less afterwards when young leaves were eaten more from this species and, overall, it was consumed less. That being said, without phenology data we cannot be entirely certain that dietary changes were an effect of logging and not just due to changes in overall food availability; however, we tried to mitigate this potential issue by analysing matching seasonal samples from before and after logging.

It is difficult to say whether these changes in the diet of our study troop will have eventual detrimental effects on infant recruitment. Fruit is considered a high-quality food source (Felton et al., 2009; Isbell, 1991; Wrangham, 1980) that allows population growth. However, young leaves are also often easily digested and have high amounts of protein (Ganzhorn, 1995; Ganzhorn & Wright, 1994; Rothman et al., 2006). The increased availability of new leaves provided by more sun exposure and colonising plants after logging has been cited as the reason that the guereza populations at Kibale National Park and Budongo Forest Reserve in Uganda have responded positively to logging (Chapman et al., 2000; Plumptre & Reynolds, 1994; Skorupa, 1986). After some disturbance, even mature leaves may become higher quality because sun exposure can increase protein and simple sugars, while fibre remains the same (Behie & Pavelka, 2012; Ganzhorn, 1995). Indeed, folivores often fare better than frugivores when their habitat is disturbed (Johns & Skorupa, 1987), though there is a lot of variability in the responses of folivores to logging (Struhsaker, 1972). Thus, the possibility remains that Rwenzori Angolan colobus at Nabugabo will not be affected negatively by the little logging that was done and, in fact, that they may respond positively.

We did find that the activity budget of Rwenzori Angolan colobus at Nabugabo showed all of the changes that were predicted by prior research on the effect of logging in other species. Johns (1986) found that white-handed gibbons (*Hylobates lar*) and banded leaf monkeys (*Presbytis melalophos*) both decreased the time that they fed and travelled and increased the time spent resting following selective logging in Malaysia. Notably, the percentage of trees cut at the site studied by Johns (1986) was also low (3.3 per cent), but incidental damage due to felling and mechanised log transportation caused a total loss of 50.9 per cent of the trees $\geq$30 cm DBH, much greater than the damage done at Nabugabo. Based on Johns' (1986) findings, we predicted a decrease in moving and feeding and an increase in resting after logging for Rwenzori Angolan colobus, all of which we found. We also saw an increase in social behaviour after logging, though subgroup sizes were not any larger. Decreased moving and feeding for the colobus after logging at Nabugabo could be explained by several factors: (1) given that their top food species was the target of loggers, lowered overall food availability may have led to less feeding and decreased energy output (Milton, 1980; Raemaekers, 1978; Waser, 1975); (2) the greater proportion of leaves in the diet post-logging may have necessitated greater resting to digest the associated cellulose and hemicellulose (Dasilva, 1992; Waterman & Choo, 1981); (3) alternatively, if fewer trees were producing high-quality leaves after logging, the monkeys may have been able to get enough food in fewer locations without searching widely (Behie & Pavelka, 2005); and/or (4) the decreased canopy cover in the post-logging period could have disrupted travel routes for this arboreal species (Cheyne et al., 2013; Johns, 1986; Putz et al., 2001).

The increased social behaviour that we found post-logging could be a reflection of the animals having more time available for grooming and playing due to the decrease in moving and feeding. Alternatively, the stress caused by the logging and the subsequent decrease in food could have triggered an increase in social grooming. In several other animal species, females increased their grooming of infants and one another after stressful events (reviewed by Liu et al., 1997 and Taylor et al., 2000). Our data support the idea that increased sociality in Rwenzori Angolan colobus at

Nabugabo post-logging was simply a result of having more time available. Time spent grooming pre- and post-logging was the same and the increase in social behaviour post-logging was actually due to an increase in time spent playing.

Selectively logged forests tend to retain high conservation value (Mayor et al., 2015), and if logging is not resumed at Nabugabo recovery from this episode of logging will likely be relatively fast. Twenty-five years after logging at Kibale National Park, Uganda, Chapman and Chapman (1997) found that, compared with unlogged areas, lightly logged areas showed similar growth of small trees and greater growth rates for large trees. Another ten years after this initial study, lightly logged areas also had greater tree recruitment than either unlogged or heavily logged areas (Chapman & Chapman, 2004). At Nabugabo, the current dominance of a pioneer species, *M. eminii*, and other species like *Funtumia latifolia* strongly suggests that the forest is under recovery from a past destructive episode. The presence of these species may facilitate forest recovery.

One of the main reasons why primate populations often do not recover after logging, despite being relatively resilient to changes in their habitat (Johns, 1992; Plumptre & Reynolds, 1994), is that logging opens up the forest to access by hunters (Bennett & Dahaban, 1995; Remis & Jost Robinson, 2012). Hunting can actually be a greater threat than logging because it can persist long after logging has ceased (Brodie et al., 2014). At Nabugabo, the location and fragmented nature of the forest means that it is already open to hunters, but luckily primates are not currently targeted in this area as ungulates are the preferred bushmeat species.

7.6   Conclusions and Future Directions

This study shows that even a short logging episode, in which a small number of trees are targeted and logs are removed without the use of machinery, can still cause significant changes to the behaviour of an arboreal primate species. Though the damage done did not appear to have a great immediate effect on colobus numbers and survival, the animals changed their diet and their activity budget in the post-logging period. Our long-term study of Troop FG and the forest at Nabugabo will allow us to document whether these changes have future impacts on this population. Will the dietary change and the activity budget modifications eventually influence infant recruitment? How will the forest recover from this episode of selective logging? These are questions we aim to tackle. In addition, the small nature of the forest fragment that we work in and the increasing anthropogenic pressure from local people that need fuelwood and other resources is a constant threat. What does the future hold for animals impacted by humans to such a degree? Almost all zoologists are facing this question and current and future primatologists will need to adapt their interests to understand primate responses to a multitude of threats. Only by understanding species-specific responses to varied conditions can we begin to reverse the situation. Given the response of the community at Nabugabo to the threats to the forest, we are very hopeful for the future of the forest wildlife there. We hope to build positive community attitudes by expanding our team of local field assistants in the next few years and training others to identify birds and butterflies, which will give them employment leading tourists into the forest. In addition, we hope to further build the skills of promising residents of Nabugabo and surrounding areas by helping them further their education. Conservation has been truly positively impacted in primate-habitat countries when nationals have gone on to get PhDs in related fields and make a difference in their own countries (e.g. Strier & Boubli, 2006).

Acknowledgements

Funding for this research was provided by Primate Conservation Inc. and the American Association of Physical Anthropology. We thank the Uganda Wildlife Authority, the Uganda National Council for Science and Technology and the University of California Santa Cruz IACUC for permission to conduct this research. Colin Chapman and Lauren Chapman provided assistance both in and out of the field. This project would not have been possible without the research assistance of Sofia Poonawala, Gabriella Fanous, Katwere Livingstone, Henry Kirabira, Jackson Mutebi, Jeofrey Kiberu, Frederick Sseguya, Dalal Hanna and Logan Smith. We are particularly grateful for the hard work and encyclopaedic knowledge of tree species provided by Matovu Ponsiano. This manuscript benefited from the helpful comments of Alison Behie and Steig Johnson.

References

Altmann, J. (1974). Observational study of behaviour: sampling methods. *Behaviour*, **49**, 227–67.

Anderson, J., Rowcliffe, J. M. & Cowlishaw, G. (2007a). The Angola black-and-white colobus (*Colobus angolensis palliatus*) in Kenya: historical range contractions and current conservation status. *American Journal of Primatology*, **69**, 664–80.

Anderson, J., Cowlishaw, G. & Rowcliffe, J. M. (2007b). Effects of forest fragmentation on the abundance of *Colobus angolensis palliatus* in Kenya's coastal forests. *International Journal of Primatology*, **28**, 637–55.

Arnhem, E., Dupain, J., Vercauteren Drubbel, R., Devos, C. & Vercauteren, M. (2008). Selective logging, habitat quality and home range use by sympatric gorillas and chimpanzees: a case study from an active logging concession in southeast Cameroon. *Folia Primatologica*, **79**, 1–14.

Asner, G. P., Rudel, T. K., Aide, T. M., DeFries, R. & Emerson, R. (2009). A contemporary assessment of change in humid tropical forests. *Conservation Biology*, **23**, 1386–95.

Barbier, E. B., Burgess, J. C., Bishop, J. & Aylward, B. (1994). *The Economics of the Tropical Timber Trade*. London: Earthscan.

Behie, A. M. & Pavelka, M. S. M. (2005). The short-term effects of a hurricane on the diet and activity of black howlers (*Alouatta pigra*) in Monkey River, Belize. *Folia Primatologica*, **76**, 1–9.

Behie, A. M. & Pavelka, M. S. M. (2012). Food selection in the black howler following habitat disturbance: implications for the importance of mature leaves. *Journal of Tropical Ecology*, **28**, 153–60.

Bennett, E. L. & Dahaban, Z. (1995). Wildlife responses to disturbances in Sarawak and their implications for forest management. In Primack, R. & Lovejoy, T. E. (eds) *Ecology, Conservation, and Management of Southeast Asian Rainforests*. New Haven, CT: Yale University Press, pp. 66–86.

Brodie, J. F., Girodano, A. J., Zipkin, E. F., et al. (2014). Correlation and persistence of hunting and logging impacts on tropical rainforest mammals. *Conservation Biology*, **29**, 110–21.

Brook, B. W., Sodhi, N. S. & Bradshaw, C. J. A. (2008). Synergies among extinction drivers under global change. *Trends in Ecology and Evolution*, **23**, 453–60.

Buckland, S. T., Anderson, D. R., Burnham, K. P., et al. (2001). *Introduction to Distance Sampling: Estimating Abundance of Biological Populations*. Oxford: Oxford University Press.

Cannon, C. H., Peart, D. R., Leighton, M. & Kartawinata, K. (1994). The structure of lowland rainforest after selective logging in West Kalimantan, Indonesia. *Forest Ecology and Management*, **68**, 49–68.

Chapman, C. A. & Chapman, L. J. (1997). Forest regeneration in logged and unlogged forests of Kibale National Park, Uganda. *Biotropica*, **29**, 396–412.

Chapman, C. A. & Chapman, L. J. (2004). Unfavorable successional pathways and the conservation value of logged tropical forest. *Biodiversity and Conservation*, **13**, 2089–105.

Chapman, C. A. & Peres, C. A. (2001). Primate conservation in the new millennium: the role of scientists. *Evolutionary Anthropology*, **10**, 16–33.

Chapman, C. A., White, F. J. & Wrangham, R. W. (1993). Defining subgroup size in fission–fusion societies. *Folia Primatologica*, **61**, 31–4.

Chapman, C. A., Balcomb, S. R., Gillespie, T. R., Skorupa, J. & Struhsaker, T. T. (2000). Long-term effects of logging on African primate communities: a 28 year comparison from Kibale National Park, Uganda. *Conservation Biology*, **14**, 207–17.

Chapman, C. A., Twinomugisha, D., Teichroeb, J. A., et al. (2016). How do primates survive among humans? Mechanisms employed by vervet monkeys at Lake Nabugabo, Uganda. In Waller, M. T. (ed.) *Ethnoprimatology, Primate Conservation in the 21st Century*. New York: Springer, pp. 77–94.

Cheyne, S. M., Thompson, C. J. H. & Chivers, D. J. (2013). Travel adaptations of Bornean agile gibbons *Hylobates albibarbis* (Primates: Hylobatidae) in a degraded secondary forest, Indonesia. *Journal of Threatened Taxa*, **5**, 3963–8.

Cowlishaw, G. (1999). Predicting the pattern of decline of African primate diversity: an extinction debt from historical deforestation. *Conservation Biology*, **13**, 1183–93.

Cowlishaw, G. & Dunbar, R. I. M. (2000). *Primate Conservation Biology*. Chicago, IL: University of Chicago Press.

Dasilva, G. L. (1992). The western black-and-white colobus as a low-energy strategist: activity budgets, energy expenditure and energy intake. *Journal of Animal Ecology*, **61**, 79–91.

Douglas, I., Spencer, T., Greer, T., et al. (1992). The impact of selective commercial logging on stream hydrology, chemistry and sediment loads in Ulu Segama rain forest, Sabah, Malaysia. *Philosophical Transactions of the Royal Society London: Biological Sciences*, **335**, 397–406.

Edwards, D. P., Tobias, J. A., Sheil, D., Meijaard, E. & Laurance, W. F. (2014). Maintaining ecosystem function and services in logged tropical forests. *Trends in Ecology and Evolution*, **29**, 511–20.

Estrada, A., Garber, P. A., Rylands, A. B., et al. (2017). Impending extinction crisis of the world's primates: why primates matter. *Science Advances*, **3**, e600946.

Fashing, P. J. & Cords, M. (2000). Diurnal primate densities and biomass in the Kakamega Forest: an evaluation of census methods and a comparison with other forests. *American Journal of Primatology*, **50**, 139–52.

Fashing, P. J., Mulindahabi, F., Gakima, J. B., et al. (2007). Activity and ranging patterns of *Colobus angolensis ruwenzorii* in Nyungwe Forest, Rwanda: possible costs of large group size. *International Journal of Primatology*, **28**, 529–50.

Felton, A. M., Engström, L. M., Felton, A. & Knott, C. D. (2003). Orangutan population density, forest structure and fruit availability in hand-logged peat swamp forests in West Kalimantan, Indonesia. *Biological Conservation*, **114**, 91–101.

Felton, A. M., Felton, A., Wood, J. T., et al. (2009). Nutritional ecology of *Ateles chamek* in lowland Bolivia: how macronutrient balancing influences food choices. *International Journal of Primatology*, **30**, 675–96.

Fimbel, C. C. (1994). Ecological correlates of species success in modified habitats may be disturbance- and site-specific: the primates of Tiwai Island. *Conservation Biology*, **8**, 106–13.

Fimbel, C., Vedder, A., Dierenfeld, E. & Mulindahabi, F. (2001). An ecological basis for large group size in *Colobus angolensis* in the Nyungwe Forest, Rwanda. *African Journal of Ecology*, **39**, 83–92.

Ganzhorn, J. U. (1995). Low-level forest disturbance effects on primary production, leaf chemistry, and lemur populations. *Ecology*, **76**, 2084–96.

Ganzhorn, J. U. & Wright, P. C. (1994). Temporal patterns in primate leaf eating: the possible role of leaf chemistry. *Folia Primatologica*, **63**, 203–8.

Gullison, R. E. & Hardner, J. J. (1993). The effects of road design and harvest intensity on forest damage caused by selective logging: empirical results and a simulation model. *Forest Ecology and Management*, **59**, 1–14.

Hansen, M. C., Potapov, P. V., Moore, R., et al. (2013). High-resolution global maps of 21st-century forest cover change. *Science*, **342**, 850–3.

Isbell, L. A. (1991). Contest and scramble competition: patterns of female aggression and ranging behavior among primates. *Behavioral Ecology*, **2**, 143–55.

Johns, A. D. (1983). Ecological effects of selective logging in a West Malaysian rainforest. PhD Thesis, University of Cambridge.

Johns, A. D. (1986). Effects of selective logging on the behavioral ecology of West Malaysian primates. *Ecology*, **67**, 684–94.

Johns, A. D. (1992). Vertebrate responses to selective logging: implications for the design of logging systems. *Philosophical Transactions of the Royal Society London: Biological Sciences*, **335**, 437–42.

Johns, A. D. & Skorupa, J. P. (1987). Responses of rain-forest primates to habitat disturbance: a review. *International Journal of Primatology*, **8**, 157–91.

Johns, A. G. & Johns, B. G. (1995). Tropical forest primates and logging: long-term coexistence? *Oryx*, **29**, 205–11.

Kingdon, J., Struhsaker, T., Oates, J. F., Hart, J. & Groves, C. P. (2008). *Colobus angolensis* ssp. *ruwenzorii*. *The IUCN Red List of Threatened Species*. Available at: http://dx.doi.org/10.2305/IUCN.UK.2008.RLTS.T5147A11117676.en (accessed 20 June 2017).

Lewis, S. L., Edwards, D. P. & Galbraith, D. (2015). Increasing human dominance of tropical forests. *Science*, **349**, 827–32.

Liu, D., Diorio, J., Tannenbaum, B., et al. (1997). Maternal care, hippocampal glucocorticoid receptors, and hypothalamic–pituitary–adrenal responses to stress. *Science*, **277**, 1659–62.

Malhi, Y., Gardner, T. A., Goldsmith, G. R., Silman, M. R. & Zelazowski, P. (2014). Tropical forests in the Anthropocene. *Annual Review of Environment and Resources*, **39**, 125–59.

Mayor, P., Pérez-Peña, P., Bowler, M., et al. (2015). Effects of selective logging on large mammal populations in a remote indigenous territory in the northern Peruvian Amazon. *Ecology and Society*, **20**, 36.

McKey, D. (1978). Soils, vegetation, and seed-eating by black colobus monkeys. In Montgomery, G. G. (ed.) *Arboreal Folivores*. Washington, DC: Smithsonian Institution Press, pp. 423–37.

Milton, K. (1980). *The Foraging Strategy of Howler Monkeys: A Study in Primate Economics*. New York: Columbia University Press.

Mittermeier, R. A. & Cheney, D. L. (1987). Conservation of primate and their habitats. In Smuts, B. B., Cheney., D. L., Seyfarth R., Wrangham, R. W. & Struhsaker, T. T. (eds) *Primate Societies*. Chicago, IL: University of Chicago Press, pp. 477–90.

Nature Conservation Practice (2006). Measurement of diameter at breast height (DBH). Technical note. Agriculture, Fisheries and Conservation Department, Conservation Branch.

Oates, J. F. (1974). The ecology and behaviour of the black-and-white colobus monkey (*Colobus guereza* Ruppell) in East Africa. PhD Thesis, University of London.

Oates, J. F., Abedi-Lartey, M., McGraw, W. S., Struhsaker, T. T. & Whitesides, G. H. (2000). Extinction of a West Africa red colobus monkey. *Conservation Biology*, **14**, 1526–32.

Plumptre, A. J. & Reynolds, V. (1994). The effect of selective logging on the primate populations in the Budongo Forest Reserve, Uganda. *Journal of Applied Ecology*, **31**, 631–41.

Putz, F. E., Sirot, L. K. & Pinard, M. A. (2001). Tropical forest management and wildlife: silvicultural effects on forest structure, fruit production, and locomotion of arboreal animals. In Fimbel, R. A., Grajal, A. & Robinson, J. G. (eds) *The Cutting Edge: Conserving Wildlife in Logged Tropical Forest.* New York: Columbia University Press, pp. 11–34.

R Core Team (2015). *R: a Language and Environment for Statistical Computing.* Vienna: R Foundation for Statistical Computing.

Raemaekers, J. J. (1978). Changes through the day in the food choice of wild gibbons. *Folia Primatologica*, **30**, 194–205.

Remis, M. J. & Jost Robinson, C. A. (2012). Reductions in primate abundance and diversity in a multiuse protected area: synergistic impacts of hunting and logging in a Congo Basin forest. *American Journal of Primatology*, **74**, 602–12.

Rothman, J. M., Dierenfeld, E. S., Molina, D. O., et al. (2006). Nutritional chemistry of foods eaten by gorillas in Bwindi Impenetrable National Park, Uganda. *American Journal of Primatology*, **68**, 675–91.

Skorupa, J. P. (1986). Responses of rainforest primates to selective logging in Kibale Forest, Uganda: a summary report. In Benirschke, K. (ed.) *Primates: The Road to Self-Sustaining Populations.* New York: Springer Verlag, pp. 57–70.

Strier, K. B. & Boubli, J. P. (2006). A history of long-term research and conservation of northern muriquis (*Brachyteles hypoxanthus*) at the Esatção Biológica de Caratinga/RPPN-FMA. *Primate Conservation*, **20**, 53–63.

Struhsaker, T. T. (1972). Rainforest conservation in Africa. *Primates*, **13**, 103–9.

Struhsaker, T. T. (1975). *The Red Colobus Monkey.* Chicago, IL: University of Chicago Press.

Struhsaker, T. T. (1981). Census methods for estimating densities. In Assembly of Life Sciences (U.S.), Committee on Nonhuman Primates, Subcommittee on Conservation of Natural Populations (ed.) *Techniques for the Study of Primate Population Ecology.* Washington, DC: National Academy Press, pp. 36–80.

Struhsaker, T. T. (1997). *Ecology of an African Rainforest.* Gainesville, FL: University of Florida Press.

Taylor, S. E., Cousino Klein, L., Lewis, B. P., et al. (2000). Biobehavioral responses to stress in females: tend-and-befriend, not fight-or-flight. *Psychological Review*, **107**, 411–29.

Uhl, C. & Vieira, I. C. G. (1989). Ecological impacts of selective logging in the Brazilian Amazon: a case study from the Paragominas region in the state of Para. *Biotropica*, **21**, 98–106.

Waser, P. M. (1975). Monthly variations in feeding and activity patterns of the mangabey, *Cercocebus albigena* (Lydekker). *East African Wildlife Journal*, **13**, 249–63.

Waterman, P. G. & Choo, G. M. (1981). The effects of digestibility-reducing compounds in leaves on food selection by some colobines. *Malaysian Applied Biology*, **10**, 147–62.

White, L. J. T. & Tutin, C. E. G. (2001). Why chimpanzees and gorillas respond differently to logging: a cautionary tale from Gabon. In Weber, B., White, L. J. T., Vedder, A. & Simons Morland, H. (eds) *African Rain Forest Ecology and Conservation.* New Haven, CT: Yale University Press, pp. 449–62.

Whitesides, G. H., Oates, J. F., Green, S. M. & Kluberdanz, R. P. (1988). Estimating primate densities from transects in a West African rain forest: a comparison of techniques. *Journal of Animal Ecology*, **57**, 345–67.

Wrangham, R. W. (1980). An ecological model of female-bonded primate groups. *Behaviour*, **75**, 262–300.

8 Threatened Hosts, Threatened Parasites?

Parasite Diversity and Distribution in Red-Listed Primates

Liesbeth Frias and Andrew J. J. MacIntosh

8.1 Personal Narrative

I (AJJM) entered the University of Manitoba planning to become a marine biologist. Why a teenager from the frozen prairies, thousands of kilometres away from any coastline, landed on that trajectory is anyone's guess, but there I was at 16 completing my open-water diving certification in the frigid waters of West Hawk Lake in the Canadian Shield, marvelling at the northern pike and sunken snowmobiles. Upon entering university, however, two factors intervened to change my course. First, U of M professors went on strike in the fall of 1995, interrupting my nascent scientific education. Some continued to teach, however, and this brings me to the second reason for my shift in focus; the one course I managed to retain was *Human Origins and Antiquity*, a physical anthropology course on human evolution with a module on primate evolution and behaviour. That was enough for me to throw in my lot with the anthropologists, and later the primatologists, and trade dreams of oceans for jungles.

I eventually moved to the University of Calgary to complete my undergraduate degree, joining a vibrant department with arguably the best options for studying primatology in Canada. As an undergraduate, in addition to learning about primate behaviour, ecology and evolution in the classroom and laboratory, I was able to join field courses with Mary Pavelka in Belize studying howling monkeys (*Alouatta pigra*) and with Agustín Fuentes (then at Central Washington University) in Bali studying temple macaques (*Macaca fascicularis*). Those experiences stood in stark contrast to one another, with the howlers existing relatively free of direct human interference along the banks of Monkey River, and the macaques having become dependent on humans for food in Padangtegal's 'Sacred Monkey Forest Sanctuary'. Agustín's Ethnoprimatology movement hit home for me here, as nowhere else are human–animal interactions more salient that in such heavily touristed, locally managed temple monkey forests, where every aspect of the lives of the monkeys is affected by humans.

The human–non-human primate interface again became salient to me when I embarked on my Master's degree research with Pascale Sicotte at the Boabeng-Fiema Monkey Sanctuary in Ghana. Though not the focus of my research, the site is rich in issues relevant to primate conservation. The two local primates (Campbell's mona monkeys, *Cercopithecus campbelli lowei*, and ursine colobus, *Colobus vellerosus*) inhabit a small forest fragment surrounded by the villages and agricultural lands of Boabeng and Fiema. Fortunately, the primates are protected via local traditions that hold the animals sacred, though hunters are commonly seen within the sanctuary, presumably with other targets in mind. Through a local initiative, with the support of the Ghanaian Wildlife Division, the area was formalised in the 1970s as a nature sanctuary and has maintained an active ecotourism operation since. At the same time, local development still threatens the forest, and I saw first-hand how local demands can supersede nature preservation when a swath of forest was cut virtually overnight to make room for electricity poles.

But it wasn't until the beginning of my PhD research, years later, that issues of wildlife health and conservation became the foci of my research. As an undergraduate, I formed a keen interest in the behavioural ecology of primates, and particularly in the ecological interactions between primate hosts and parasites. That's how I ended up in Japan at Kyoto University's Primate Research Institute, doing a PhD with Mike Huffman, who pioneered studies of primate responses to parasite infection, most famously through self-medication. Since then, I've done a fair amount of work with Japanese macaques (*Macaca fuscata*) and their gastrointestinal parasites as a model system to learn about primate–parasite relationships, asking questions such as: who is likely to be infected and with what? How do parasites spread between hosts? What impacts might they have on primate host behaviour, physiology, health and fitness? And can we detect these effects using available methods? While my focus has generally been ecological, all of these are now critical questions facing primate conservationists concerned with how parasites and infectious diseases might contribute to further population declines, particularly with the expanding human–non-human primate interface.

In recent years, I have been developing a project investigating primate and parasite communities in a transitioning ecosystem along the Kinabatangan River in Sabah, Malaysian Borneo, along with my graduate student and co-author Liesbeth Frias. The continuous expansion of the oil palm industry adds a distinct and current flavour to this research, but although the situation for most primates across the globe differs in both degree and kind, the results are often the same: human pressures continue to marginalise wildlife everywhere, disrupting natural ecological associations and thereby opening the door for novel or resurgent pathogen exchange. The expanding human–domestic animal–wildlife interface provides myriad opportunities for the agents of disease to shift hosts, while habitat loss, fragmentation and degradation interrupt natural processes involving hosts and parasites in ways we do not yet fully comprehend. It is my sincere hope that my work can contribute in some small way to inform primate health and conservation.

Whether of oceans or of jungles, it is now eminently clear that our dreams of nature must be coupled with conservation awareness and action, or the dreams of future generations will remain as such, forever.

8.2   Introduction

With over 500 species now recognised, non-human primates are one of the most biodiverse groups of mammals on the planet, following only rodents and bats (over

2200 and 1100 species, respectively) (IUCN, 2017; Mittermeier et al., 2013), and they are also one of the most threatened (Estrada et al., 2017; Wich & Marshall, 2016). Their high dependence on tropical forest ecosystems makes them especially vulnerable to habitat loss, fragmentation and degradation (Isaac & Cowlishaw, 2004). While habitat loss is the major driver of primate population declines globally (Estrada et al., 2017), the spread of infectious disease, particularly that resulting from increased contact with humans and domestic livestock, has emerged as an important stochastic process of concern (Chapman et al., 2005; Gillespie et al., 2008; Leendertz et al., 2006; Nunn & Gillespie, 2016).

Numerous cases now illustrate the potential dangers of infectious diseases for wild primate populations, and how anthropogenic factors might mediate their influence. Ebola virus and human respiratory paramyxoviruses have led to dramatic decreases in African great ape populations (Bermejo et al., 2006; Kaur et al., 2008; Köndgen et al., 2008; Leroy et al., 2004), and bacterial pathogens causing anthrax (*Bacillus anthracis*, *B. cereus*) are a growing concern for great apes and other wildlife in Africa (Hoffmann et al., 2017; Leendertz et al., 2004). The detection of *Treponema pallidum* subsp. *pertenue* in African primates suggests that the etiological agent of yaws, a disease previously thought to be restricted to humans, may have a non-human reservoir (Knauf et al., 2013; 2017). Furthermore, human infections with zoonotic malaria (*Plasmodium knowlesi*) in Southeast Asia suggest environmental change as a key factor driving a parasite species previously thought only to infect free-living macaques into human populations (Barber et al., 2017; Cox-Singh, 2012; Cox-Singh & Singh, 2008). Finally, recent studies highlight the bidirectional exchange of harmful parasitic nematodes (e.g. hookworms) between humans, including researchers, and great apes (Hasegawa et al., 2014; Kalousová et al., 2016). These examples highlight the diversity of threats from infectious diseases facing wild primates globally, as well as the need to monitor their dynamics.

With the majority of emerging infectious diseases in humans originating in domestic animals and wildlife, particularly primates (Wolfe et al., 2007), and the acknowledgement that non-human primates can be just as vulnerable (Leendertz et al., 2006), the human–non-human primate interface has become a focal point in primate infectious disease research. Indeed, numerous studies have attempted to test whether anthropogenic factors can influence associations between primates and the organisms that infect them, by sampling groups or populations that vary in their degree of exposure to human influence (Bublitz et al., 2014; Chapman et al., 2006; Gillespie et al., 2005; Goldberg et al., 2008; Kowalewski et al., 2011; Salzer et al., 2007). Human encroachment is thought to impact primate disease dynamics by putting primate populations under stress and therefore increasing their susceptibility to infection or by exposing them to novel sources and types of infection. While evidence for a relationship between habitat degradation or fragmentation and both physiological stress and parasite infection seems equivocal (Behie & Pavelka, 2013; Chapman et al., 2007; Snaith et al., 2008), there is a growing body of evidence suggesting that close contact between human and non-human primates can influence the flow of parasites between them, sometimes even involving domestic animals

(Bublitz et al., 2014; Goldberg et al., 2008; Hasegawa et al., 2014; Kalousová et al., 2016; Rwego et al., 2008; Salyer et al., 2012). How anthropogenic change might influence parasitism and infectious disease dynamics in primates has therefore emerged as a critical question concerning their conservation (Chapman et al., 2005; Gillespie et al., 2008; Nunn & Gillespie, 2016).

At the same time, there is some evidence that parasite biodiversity may actually decline in primates threatened with extinction (Altizer et al., 2007). Using the Global Mammal Parasite Database (GMPD) (Nunn & Altizer, 2005), Altizer et al. (2007) performed a broad, comparative analysis and demonstrated that primate threat status – according to the 2004 IUCN Red List of Threatened Species – was negatively associated with parasite species diversity (richness). Although their findings disappeared when controlling for other influential host attributes in statistical models, these results suggested that declining primate populations with shrinking and fragmented geographic ranges might be unable to support intact parasite communities. While it may be challenging to identify mechanisms from such large, comparative studies, large databases summarising information currently existing in the literature can help elucidate broader patterns in ecology and provide avenues for more intensive research at smaller scales.

Since its inception, the GMPD has been used to test numerous evolutionary hypotheses about parasite infection in primates (e.g. Nunn & Dokey, 2006; Nunn et al., 2003; 2005; Pedersen et al., 2005; Vitone et al., 2004; Young et al., 2013). With a new version of the database recently introduced (Stephens et al., 2017), this chapter revisits the work done by Altizer et al. (2007), building on a growing body of work and an intervening decade's worth of primate–parasite literature and primate conservation assessment, to reexamine the relationship between host threat status and both parasite prevalence and species richness. We make no excuses for 'standing on the shoulders of giants' in this endeavour, but felt that the time was right and the availability of data sufficiently padded to warrant such a reassessment, particularly given the growing need to better understand threats from infectious diseases in endangered primates.

We focus on the relationship between host threat status, parasite host range, and two indices of parasite infection: *prevalence*, which indicates the number of infected individuals among a sample; and *species richness*, which indicates the number of unique parasite species infecting a given host. We restrict our analyses to the two most commonly reported parasite groups in primate–parasite biodiversity studies: helminths and protists. In addition, we examine *parasite host range*, defined by whether a parasite can infect a small versus a large number of host species, as this was targeted by Altizer et al. (2007) as an area needing further assessment. In their study, Altizer et al. (2007) found little evidence that parasite host range, or transmission mode for that matter, affects the relationship they found between parasite richness and host threat status, i.e. diversity of both generalist and specialist parasites was lower in threatened primates. Following the earlier study, we predicted that parasite prevalence and species richness would be lower in threatened primates, but also that host range should mediate this relationship. More specifically, we predicted stronger reductions in the prevalence and richness of specialist parasites in threatened primates because generalist parasites may be better buffered against declines in specific host populations within the overall host community. The goal of this study was therefore to update our understanding of the relationship between host threat status, parasite prevalence and parasite biodiversity, using an enhanced dataset to test whether the findings of Altizer et al. (2007) hold up to further scrutiny.

8.3   Methods

8.3.1   The Primate Phylogeny

We used the consensus phylogeny found in version 3 of the 10k Trees database (http://10ktrees.nunn-lab.org; Arnold et al., 2010), which incorporates tree topologies that reflect levels of uncertainty about nodes and branch lengths. For species classification, we followed the primate taxonomy found in Wilson and Reeder (2005).

8.3.2   The Global Mammal Parasite Database

We used the recently updated version 2.0 of the GMPD (Stephens et al., 2017), containing over 24 000 host–parasite entries collected from the scientific literature from wild mammals and their parasites (both micro- and macroparasites). We restricted our analyses to helminths and protists (hereafter, 'parasites'), and assigned host range for all parasites listed to the species level, following Pedersen et al. (2005), with parasites specific to a single species or genus of host classified as 'specialists' and those that can infect multiple host genera classified as 'generalists'. Figure 8.1

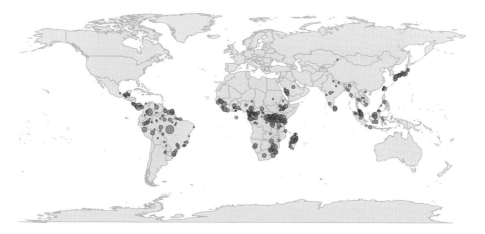

Figure 8.1 Global distribution of parasite species richness in primates, focusing on helminth and protistan parasites used in the present study. Circles represent 343 individual study sites recorded in the GMPD, from where richness data were reported, and circle size represents total richness values gleaned from these studies. Note that richness counts largely reflect sampling effort plus other sources of variation as described in the text.

illustrates the global distribution of parasite species richness in primates at sampling sites reporting latitude and longitude information.

8.3.3   The IUCN Red List of Threatened Species

To determine primate threat level, we used the updated IUCN Red List of Threatened Species (IUCN, 2017). Following Altizer et al. (2007), we combined IUCN status into two variables, where species listed as least concern (LC) or near threatened (NT) were considered 'non-threatened' and species listed as vulnerable (VU), endangered (EN) or critically endangered (CR) were considered 'threatened'. We did not consider data for primates in the categories extinct in the wild (EW), extinct (EX) or data deficient (DD).

8.3.4   Additional Datasets Used for Primate Traits

The GMPD and IUCN data were merged with host traits retrieved from: (1) the PanTHERIA database, which includes species life-history, ecological and geographical traits (Jones et al., 2009); and (2) the EDGE of Existence programme database, which includes similar information to identify evolutionarily distinct and globally endangered species for conservation prioritisation (Redding et al., 2010). We extracted mean adult body mass (g), group size, home-range size (km^2), population density (individuals/km^2) and geographic range size (km^2), geographic range latitudinal midpoint (decimal degrees) and whether or not the species is largely arboreal or terrestrial. Where numerical data were available in each database, we first ensured that values correlated strongly between each (data not shown), and then combined the sets of data, defaulting to the PanTHERIA database, which generally contained more data points.

8.3.5   Controlling for Sampling Effort

Sampling effort can dramatically influence diversity studies. One way to limit its influence on species richness results is by including a sampling effort parameter in statistical models (Altizer et al., 2007; Nunn et al., 2003). We therefore set the number of published studies appearing in the GMPD for each primate species as a fixed effect in our richness models. Our measure of sampling effort included between 1 and 37 studies per host species examined, with a mean $\pm$ SD of 5.4 $\pm$ 5.6 and a highly left-skewed distribution.

8.3.6   Statistical Models

We used generalised linear mixed-effects modelling of both parasite prevalence and species richness data. We incorporated the primate phylogeny into a Bayesian mixed-effects modelling framework implemented using the package MCMCglmm (Hadfield, 2010) in R version 3.4.1 (R Core Team, 2017). We used the weakly informative inverse-gamma prior with shape and scale parameters set to 0.002 (Hadfield, 2010) in all models to restrict prior assumptions from influencing our results. We set the number of Monte Carlo simulations to 5 000 000, with a burn in of 5000 and a thinning interval of 500 to reduce sampling autocorrelation. The number of MCMC samples for all models was thus 9990, as we aimed for an effective sample size for each of our model parameters of approximately 10 000 (range 6926–11 517). We also ensured model convergence, proper mixing of the Markov chains, and that there was no autocorrelation of residuals (all <0.1). Furthermore, we ensured there was no multicollinearity in our fixed-effects structure.

Because we extracted information from five separate databases, the number of primate species that could be included in any given analysis depended on which variables were included in each statistical model. The overall dataset we used included 3411 host–parasite interactions, representing 141 host species and 441 parasite species. To manage such discrepancies, we constructed a series of models using four different datasets: full and reduced models for both prevalence and species richness (see Table 8.1 for model descriptions). Full models incorporated the primate-specific attributes described in Section 8.3.4, while parameter-reduced models included only the interaction between primate threat status and parasite host range, allowing for a larger number of host species to be included because the primate attribute data were limited. While the full models are at once more conservative and more robust, given their ability to account for the potential confounding effects of host traits on variation in parasitism across primates, the parameter-reduced models included a larger number of primate species and may therefore remain informative. Note that where interaction terms did not produce significant results, and models containing them did not outperform models without them, interactions were removed and main effects were tested individually for clarity and parsimony.

Parasite prevalence consisted of an observation of prevalence for a given parasite infecting a given primate host at a given site. We converted prevalence in the GMPD (expressed as a percentage of infected hosts or positive samples per parasite species) to an integer by multiplying it by the study's reported sample size (sample number rather than the number of individuals sampled). Our response variable for prevalence was therefore modelled as the number of infected individuals or samples given the number of individuals or samples in the study, using a binomial error distribution. Parasite species richness values were compiled for each unique combination of parasite type (helminth, protist), host IUCN threat status (threatened, non-threatened) and parasite host range (specialist, generalist). We used only cases in which parasites were identified to the species level in the GMPD. We modelled parasite species richness with a zero-truncated Poisson error distribution, as inclusion in the species richness dataset required the presence of at least one parasite.

While p-values are not typically reported using Bayesian inference, standard MCMCglmm model output does include them and we therefore report them here to

Table 8.1 Statistical model formulations used in this study

Model sets		Fixed effects	Random effects	Sample sizes
Parasite prevalence	*Full models*	(1) IUCN status * parasite host range; (2) adult body mass; (3) group size; (4) home–range size; (5) population density; (6) geographic range size; (7) latitudinal midpoint; (8) terrestriality	(1) Primate phylogeny; (2) host species identity (for multiple entries); (3) citation identity; (4) parasite taxonomy (parasite genus nested within class nested within phylum nested within type, except when helminths and protists were separated)	1345 observations from 104 host species and 227 parasite species
	Reduced models	(1) IUCN status * parasite host range	Same as above	832 observations from 70 host species and 186 parasite species
Parasite species richness	*Full models*	(1) IUCN status * parasite host range; (2) adult body mass; (3) group size; (4) home–range size; (5) population density; (6) geographic range size; (7) latitudinal midpoint; (8) terrestriality; (9) parasite type; (10) GMPD citation counts	(1) Primate phylogeny; (2) host species identity (for multiple entries)	342 observations from 131 host species and 327 parasites
	Reduced models	(1) IUCN status * parasite host range	Same as above	217 observations from 80 host species and 266 parasites

facilitate rapid understanding of the results. We also report the posterior means and credible intervals (CI) for each parameter and take any parameter with CI that do not overlap 0 ($p < 0.05$) as 'statistically significant'. For all models, any numerical variables included in the fixed-effects structure were scaled for the analysis to improve model convergence and to allow for direct comparisons between parameter estimates; i.e. all estimates appear at the same scale.

8.4   Results

Our phylogenetic hypothesis (the consensus tree downloaded from the 10k Trees website) is shown in Figure 8.2, along with a representation of raw parasite species richness counts for each primate species in our dataset. The phylogenetic signals (conventionally represented by the parameter λ) from this consensus tree estimated in our models of both parasite prevalence ($\lambda \cong 0.002$) and species richness ($\lambda \cong 0.02$) were both low, and therefore unlikely to have significantly influenced the results.

8.4.1   Models of Parasite Prevalence

The median and interquartile range (IQR) for parasite prevalence across the dataset used was 0.22 (IQR = 0.08–0.50), while that for helminths was 0.23 (IQR = 0.08–0.59) and that for protists was 0.25 (IQR = 0.10–0.50). In the full statistical models for prevalence, we observed an interaction between host threat status and parasite host range, suggesting that the relationship between host threat status and parasite prevalence is mediated by parasite host range (Table 8.2). Specifically, it appears that specialist parasites exhibit a slightly higher median prevalence than generalist parasites in non-threatened hosts (0.21 (IQR = 0.09–0.50) versus 0.18 (IQR = 0.07–0.46)), whereas median prevalence was considerably greater for generalist than specialist parasites in threatened hosts (0.33 (IQR = 0.12–0.67) versus 0.20 (IQR = 0.08–0.45); Figure 8.3a). None of the other variables in the model predicted variation in parasite prevalence. We observed similar results in the reduced model that lacked controls for host traits but incorporated a significantly larger number of data points (Table 8.3).

When models were repeated for helminths and protists separately, the above relationships held for helminths but not for protists. In the helminth models, the interaction between threat status and parasite host range was again significant in both the full (post. mean = –2.667, CI = –3.197 to –2.099, pMCMC < 0.001) and reduced (post. mean = –1.203, CI = –1.633 to –0.753, pMCMC < 0.001) models. In addition, geographic range area was negatively associated with helminth prevalence in the full model (post. mean = –0.337, CI = –0.658 to –0.029, pMCMC = 0.039). In contrast, we did not observe a significant interaction between threat status and parasite host range in our models of protist prevalence (post. mean = –0.384, CI = –1.070–0.338, pMCMC = 0.279). When the interaction term was removed to better interpret main effects, prevalence of specialist protists was

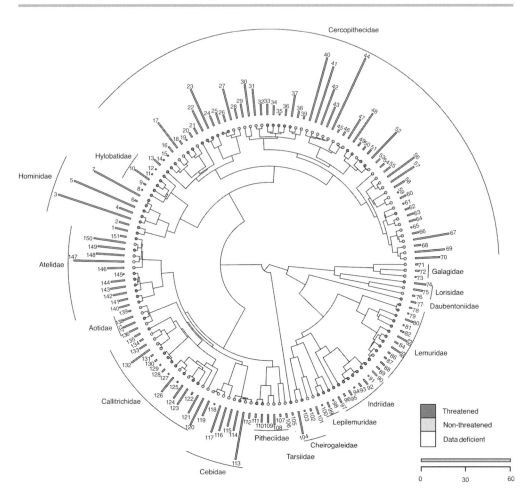

Figure 8.2 Parasite species richness across the primate phylogeny. The primate phylogeny represents a subset of the consensus tree downloaded from the 10k Trees website. Bars represent summed values for helminth and protistan parasite species richness as reported in the GMPD. The scale bar indicates the largest richness value in the dataset (59, *Pan troglodytes*, *Papio anubis*). Primate species are identified by a numeric tag shown above each bar, and listed numerically in a footnote. IUCN listings were combined into three status levels: threatened, non-threatened, and data deficient.

Hominidae. 1. *Pongo pygmaeus*; 2. *Pongo abelii*; 3. *Pan troglodytes troglodytes*; 4. *Pan paniscus*; 5. *Gorilla gorilla gorilla*; 6. *Gorilla beringei graueri*; 7. *Gorilla beringei*. **Hylobatidae.** 8. *Nomascus leucogenys*; 9. *Symphalangus syndactylus*; 10. *Hylobates lar*; 11. *Hylobates moloch*; 12. *Bunopithecus hoolock*. **Cercopithecidae.** 13. *Presbytis melalophos*; 14. *Trachypithecus phayrei*; 15. *Trachypithecus delacouri*; 16. *Trachypithecus obscurus*; 17. *Trachypithecus cristatus*; 18. *Trachypithecus vetulus*; 19. *Trachypithecus pileatus*; 20. *Semnopithecus entellus*; 21. *Rhinopithecus bieti*; 22. *Piliocolobus thephrosceles*; 23. *Piliocolobus rufomitratus*; 24. *Piliocolobus badius*; 25. *Colobus vellerosus*; 26. *Colobus polykomos*; 27. *Colobus guereza*; 28. *Colobus angolensis*; 29. *Macaca mulatta*; 30. *Macaca fascicularis*; 31. *Macaca fuscata*; 32. *Macaca cyclopis*;

significantly lower than that for generalist protists, irrespective of host threat status, for both the full (post. mean = –0.580, CI = –1.016 to –0.163, pMCMC = 0.010) and reduced (post. mean = –0.622, CI = –2.025 to –0.228, pMCMC = 0.002) models. There was no significant difference in protist prevalence between threatened and non-threatened hosts in either the full (post. mean = –0.577, CI = –0.281–1.369, pMCMC = 0.166) or reduced (post. mean = 0.077, CI = –0.516–0.700, pMCMC = 0.804) model.

Figure 8.2 Cont.

33. *Macaca nemestrina*; 34. *Macaca silenus*; 35. *Macaca nigra*; 36. *Macaca hecki*; 37. *Macaca sinica*; 38. *Macaca radiata*; 39. *Macaca assamensis*; 40. *Papio ursinus*; 41. *Papio cynocephalus*; 42. *Papio papio*; 43. *Papio hamadryas*; 44. *Papio anubis*; 45. *Theropithecus gelada*; 46. *Lophocebus aterrimus*; 47. *Lophocebus albigena*; 48. *Mandrillus sphinx*; 49. *Mandrillus leucophaeus*; 50. *Cercocebus atys*; 51. *Cercocebus torquatus*; 52. *Cercocebus galeritus*; 53. *Cercocebus agilis*; 54. *Miopithecus talapoin*; 55. *Chlorocebus sabaeus*; 56. *Chlorocebus pygerythrus*; 57. *Chlorocebus aethiops*; 58. *Erythrocebus patas*; 59. *Cercopithecus preussi*; 60. *Cercopithecus lhoesti*; 61. *Cercopithecus neglectus*; 62. *Cercopithecus diana*; 63. *Cercopitecus mona*; 64. *Cercopithecus campbelli*; 65. *Cercopithecus petaurista*; 66. *Cercopithecus cephus*; 67. *Cercopithecus ascanius*; 68. *Cercopithecus nictitans*; 69. *Cercopithecus mitis*; 70. *Cercopithecus albogularis*. **Galagidae.** 71. *Galago demidoff*; 72. *Otolemur crassicaudatus*; 73. *Galago moholi*. **Lorisidae.** 74. *Nycticebus coucang*; 75. *Perodicticus potto*; 76. *Arctocebus calabarensis*. **Daubentoniidae.** 77. *Daubentonia madagascariensis*. **Lemuridae.** 78. *Varecia variegata variegata*; 79. *Varecia rubra*; 80. *Lemur catta*; 81. *Prolemur simus*; 82. *Hapalemur griseus*; 83. *Eulemur macaco macaco*; 84. *Eulemur mongoz*; 85. *Eulemur rufus*; 86. *Eulemur rubriventer*; 87. *Eulemur collaris*; 88. *Eulemur fulvus*; 89. *Eulemur albifrons*. **Indriidae.** 90. *Propithecus edwardsi*; 91. *Propithecus diadema*; 92. *Propithecus verreauxi*; 93. *Propithecus deckenii*; 94. *Propithecus tattersalli*; 95. *Propithecus coquereli*; 96. *Avahi occidentalis*; 97. *Indri indri*. **Lepilemuridae.** 98. *Lepilemur microdon*; 99. *Lepilemur ruficaudatus*; 100. *Lepilemur edwardsi*. **Cheirogaleidae.** 101. *Cheirogaleus medius*; 102. *Cheirogaleus major*; 103. *Microcebus rufus*; 104. *Microcebus murinus*. **Tarsiidae.** 105. *Tarsius bancanus*. **Pitheciidae.** 106. *Callicebus torquatus*; 107. *Callicebus moloch*; 108. *Pithecia pithecia*; 109. *Pithecia irrorata*; 110. *Chiropotes satanas*; 111. *Cacajao calvus*. **Cebidae.** 112. *Saimiri ustus*; 113. *Saimiri sciureus*; 114. *Saimiri oerstedii*; 115. *Saimiri boliviensis*; 116. *Cebus paella*; 117. *Cebus capucinus*; 118. *Cebus olivaceus*; 119. *Cebus albifrons*. **Callitrichidae.** 120. *Saguinus fuscicollis*; 121. *Saguinus mystax*; 122. *Saguinus leucopus*; 123. *Saguinus oedipus*; 124. *Saguinus geoffroyi*; 125. *Saguinus niger*; 126. *Saguinus midas*; 127. *Saguinus bicolor*; 128. *Leontopithecus rosalia*; 129. *Leontopithecus chrysopygus*; 130. *Leontopithecus chrysomelas*; 131. *Callithrix penicillate*; 132. *Callithrix jacchus*; 133. *Callithrix pygmaea*; 134. *Callithrix argentata*; 135. *Callimico goeldii*; **Aotidae.** 136. *Aotus trivirgatus*; 137. *Aotus nancymae*; 138. *Aotus vociferans*; 139. *Aotus azarae*. **Atelidae.** 140. *Lagothrix lagotricha*; 141. *Brachyteles arachnoides*; 142. *Ateles paniscus*; 143. *Ateles geoffroyi*; 144. *Ateles fusciceps*; 145. *Ateles belzebuth*; 146. *Alouatta guariba*; 147. *Alouatta seniculus*; 148. *Alouatta caraya*; 149. *Alouatta pigra*; 150. *Alouatta palliata*; 151. *Alouatta belzebul*.

Table 8.2 MCMCglmm model output for variation in parasite prevalence (full models)

Model term	Posterior mean	Lower 95%CI	Upper 95%CI	Effective sample size	pMCMC
(Intercept)	−1.610	−3.326	−0.155	9990	0.048*
Host threat status (threatened versus not-threatened)	–	–	–	–	–
Parasite host range (specialist versus generalist)	–	–	–	–	–
Scaled home-range size	0.042	−0.109	0.183	9990	0.575
Scaled adult body mass	−0.246	−0.576	0.092	10381	0.133
Scaled population density	−0.201	−0.488	0.069	9990	0.152
Scaled group size	−0.093	−0.342	0.178	9990	0.493
Scaled geographic range size	−0.180	−0.406	0.053	9990	0.130
Scaled latitudinal midpoint	0.118	−0.167	0.392	10004	0.403
Terrestriality (terrestrial versus arboreal)	0.299	−0.327	0.952	9990	0.363
Threat status [×] parasite host range	**−1.330**	**−1.767**	**−0.889**	**9990**	**<1e−04*****

Note: data for this model include 1345 observations representing 104 host species and 227 parasite species. Reference levels for each factor appear as the second of two levels listed in parentheses. Emboldened estimates reflect statistically significant results for which the credible intervals did not overlap 0. Estimates for main effects involved in significant interactions not shown to avoid misinterpretation.
*$p < 0.05$; ***$p < 0.0001$.

Table 8.3 MCMCglmm model output for variation in parasite prevalence (reduced models)

Model term	Posterior mean	Lower 95%CI	Upper 95%CI	Effective sample size	pMCMC
(Intercept)	−1.141	−3.135	0.959	9990	0.114
Host threat status (threatened versus not-threatened)	–	–	–	–	–
Parasite host range (specialist versus generalist)	–	–	–	–	–
Threat status [×] parasite host range	**−0.637**	**−0.973**	**−0.287**	**9990**	**<1e−04*****

Note: data for this model include 832 observations representing 70 host species and 186 parasite species. Reference levels for each factor appear as the second of two levels listed in parentheses. Emboldened estimates reflect statistically significant results for which the credible intervals did not overlap 0. Estimates for main effects involved in significant interactions not shown to avoid misinterpretation.
***$p < 0.0001$.

8.4.2 Models of Parasite Species Richness

The median value for each of total parasite species richness (IQR = 1–4), helminth richness (IQR = 1–4) and protist richness (IQR = 1–3.5) was two. We observed no significant interactions between threat status and parasite host range in either the

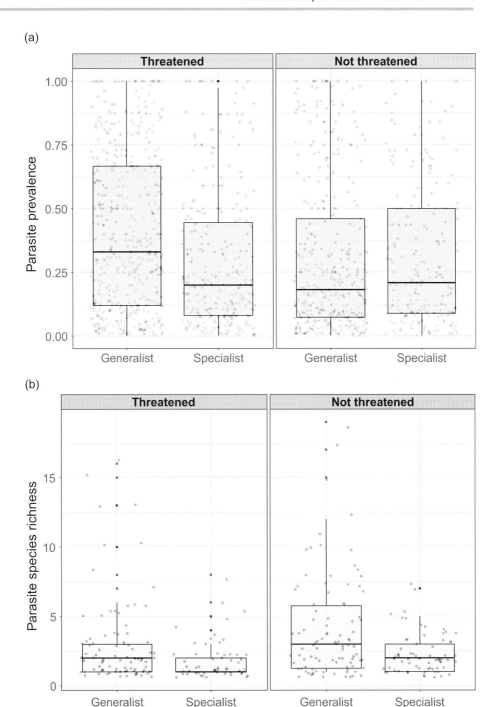

Figure 8.3 Parasite prevalence and species richness in relation to host threat status and parasite host range. Boxplots indicating the median parasite prevalence (a) and species richness (b), along with 25 per cent and 75 per cent quartiles (boxes) and 1.5 * IQR whiskers, for generalist and specialist parasite species infecting threatened (left panels) and non-threatened (right panels) hosts. Data clouds are presented for transparency, and jittered horizontally for clarity.

full (post. mean = −0.238, CI = −0.858–0.389, pMCMC = 0.458) or reduced (post. mean = −0.187, CI = −0.631 to −0.272, pMCMC = 0.429) models (Figure 8.3b). However, models show that parasite species richness was significantly lower in specialists (median = 2, IQR = 1–3) than in generalists (median = 2, IQR = 1–4.5) in both the full (Table 8.3) and reduced (Table 8.4) models. Moreover, in reduced models only, parasite richness was also lower in threatened (median = 2, IQR = 1–3) than in non-threatened (median = 2, IQR = 1–5) primates (Table 8.5). Full models also show a positive correlation between parasite species richness and primate body mass, but no other relationships involving host-centric traits (Table 8.4). As predicted, sampling effort was significantly associated with richness counts in both models, with increasing effort resulting in higher counts. Finally, there were no significant differences between richness of helminths and protists in either model.

For helminths, we again observed no significant interactions between threat status and parasite host range in either the full (post. mean = 0.002, CI = −1.162–1.094, pMCMC = 0.986) or reduced (post. mean = −0.187, CI = −0.652–0.262, pMCMC = 0.431) models. We found the same pattern for protists in both full (post. mean = −0.211, CI = −0.889–0.424, pMCMC = 0.526) and reduced (post. mean = −0.187, CI = −0.651–0.273, pMCMC = 0.424) models. In general, models for helminths and protists mimicked the combined models, except that the effect of parasite host range in protistan parasites was not significant in the full model

Table 8.4 MCMCglmm model output for variation in parasite richness (full models)

Model term	Posterior mean	Lower 95% CI	Upper 95% CI	Effective sample size	pMCMC
(Intercept)	0.749	0.051	1.372	8440	0.044
Scaled sampling effort	**0.450**	**0.299**	**0.599**	**9950**	**<1e−04***
Host threat status (threatened versus not-threatened)	−0.234	−0.665	0.188	9621	0.270
Parasite host range (specialist versus generalist)	**−0.629**	**−0.924**	**−0.318**	**10355**	**<1e−04***
Parasite type (protist versus helminth)	−0.072	−0.363	0.219	9950	0.621
Scaled home-range size	−0.087	−0.304	0.126	9950	0.428
Scaled adult body mass	**0.238**	**0.022**	**0.456**	**8242**	**0.027***
Scaled population density	0.096	−0.076	0.274	9950	0.274
Scaled group size	0.032	−0.160	0.231	9950	0.744
Scaled geographic range size	0.026	−0.153	0.197	9662	0.764
Scaled latitudinal midpoint	−0.055	−0.235	0.124	9950	0.541
Terrestriality (terrestrial versus arboreal)	−0.182	−0.697	0.340	9455	0.503

Note: data for this model include 342 observations representing 131 hosts. Reference levels for each factor appear as the second of two levels listed in parentheses. Emboldened estimates reflect statistically significant results for which the credible intervals did not overlap 0.
*$p < 0.05$; ***$p < 0.0001$.

Table 8.5 MCMCglmm model output for variation in parasite richness (reduced models)

Model term	Posterior mean	Lower 95%CI	Upper 95%CI	Effective sample size	pMCMC
(Intercept)	0.793	0.225	1.308	9112	0.015
Scaled sampling effort	0.432	0.324	0.543	6926	**<1e-04*****
Host threat status (threatened versus not-threatened)	−0.320	−0.601	−0.050	9950	**0.024***
Parasite host range (specialist versus generalist)	−0.551	−0.778	−0.321	8953	**<1e-04*****
Parasite type (protist versus helminth)	−0.041	−0.246	0.172	9628	0.701

Note: data for this model include 217 observations representing 57 hosts. Reference levels for each factor appear as the second of two levels listed in parentheses. Emboldened estimates reflect statistically significant results for which the credible intervals did not overlap 0.
***$p < 0.0001$.

(post. mean = −0.017, CI = −0.344–0.310, pMCMC = 0.912) but it was in the reduced model (post. mean = −0.321, CI = −0.601 to −0.053, pMCMC = 0.022).

8.5 Discussion

We found both similarities and differences with the Altizer et al. (2007) study we set out to replicate. In general, patterns of parasite species richness were similar between the studies, as we observed reduced parasite species richness in threatened primates only when potentially confounding host attributes were excluded from statistical models. Also, like the earlier study, parasite host range did not mediate this relationship; i.e. richness was lower overall in threatened hosts (at least in reduced models). That said, the fact that models including host traits masked the effect of threat status on parasite richness, in both the earlier study and in our own, suggests that we should take this result with caution. On the other hand, and in contrast to previous findings, we observed a significant relationship between parasite prevalence and primate threat status, and this was mediated by parasite host range. Since this result was evident in models both with and without potentially confounding host attributes, this relationship appears to be robust (at least overall and for helminths, if not for protists). Thus, the present study suggests that elements of both parasite distribution (prevalence) and parasite diversity (species richness) differ between threatened and non-threatened primates.

For parasites, well-distributed species are those with high prevalence in the host population (Morand & Guégan, 2000). In the present study, we observed that the prevalence of specialist parasites may be slightly biased towards non-threatened hosts, but this result was emphasised through an interaction in which the prevalence of generalist parasites exhibited a comparatively larger bias towards threatened hosts. This interaction indicates that the structure of parasite communities differs in threatened and non-threatened primate hosts, with generalists seemingly able to maintain larger populations than specialists in threatened hosts. These results might also suggest that more specialised parasites are at higher risk of population declines than generalist parasites in threatened hosts, either through increased competition with more opportunistic (generalist) parasites or through decreased connectivity (i.e. increased fragmentation) in the host population. However, we found no evidence to suggest that parasite species diversity in threatened and non-threatened hosts depends on parasite host range. There is in fact considerable debate about whether we should expect specialist parasites to be at greater risk of extinction (Dobson et al., 2008; Dunn et al., 2009; Strona, 2015; Vázquez & Simberloff, 2002), or whether generalist parasites should thrive in anthropogenic environments. Whether our prevalence results are an indication that specialist parasite populations are trending downward, or that generalist parasites are trending upward in threatened hosts, and thereby increasing the likelihood of specialist parasite species losses in the future, can only be determined through careful and continued monitoring.

From a host's perspective, irrespective of changes in the prevalence of specialist parasites, increases in the prevalence of generalist parasites might be an undesirable outcome of disrupted host–parasite associations. Considerable theoretical work suggests that generalist parasites are much more likely than specialist parasites to drive hosts towards extinction because they can persist in alternative hosts when endangered hosts become less abundant (Castro & Bolker, 2005; Gog et al., 2002; McCallum & Dobson, 2002). Moreover, a quick examination of the infectious diseases that have caused large population declines in wildlife confirms this to be the case (e.g. rinderpest: Plowright, 1982; Ebola: Leroy et al., 2004; anthrax: Hoffmann et al., 2017). While we focused on helminths and protists, which in comparison to viral and bacterial pathogens tend to be endemic and seldom have such dramatic impacts on host health, there is compelling evidence that such parasites can nonetheless regulate host populations (Albon et al., 2002; Dobson & Foufopoulos, 2001; Dobson & Hudson, 1986; Grenfell & Gulland, 1995; Nguyen et al., 2015; Tompkins & Begon, 1999). For macroparasites such as intestinal helminths and arthropods, which reproduce outside of their hosts, potential fitness costs are intricately tied to the intensity of infection experienced, i.e. how many parasite individuals are present in an infected host (Hudson & Dobson, 1995; Tompkins et al., 2002), which itself depends largely on the parasite's abundance in the host community. Therefore, increased prevalence of generalist parasites, inasmuch as it likely indicates increased generalist parasite abundance (Barger & Esch, 2002; Morand & Guégan, 2000; Poulin, 1998; 1999), may represent an additional challenge for endangered primates.

It is perhaps less clear how we should interpret lower parasite species richness in threatened primates. While dealing with a smaller range of parasites might sound advantageous, it remains unknown how or if parasite biodiversity and parasite-related threats to primate health and fitness are correlated. Co-infecting parasites within a host can interact in multiple ways (Pedersen & Fenton, 2007), having either detrimental or beneficial effects, or a combination of the two (Vaumourin et al., 2015). Moreover, the risks associated with endemic versus emerging or resurging infections should mediate this relationship significantly (Hosseini et al., 2017), and it is possible that the loss of certain endemic parasites increases the risk of contracting novel or rarer parasites that may have more adverse health effects (Quigley et al., 2017). For example, Ezenwa and Jolles (2015) demonstrated that removing helminth parasites increased survival in African buffalo infected with bovine tuberculosis and significantly increased its incidence in the population. Another possibility relates to the fact that parasites can induce *apparent competition* – competition for 'enemy-free space' – between hosts in a community (Hudson & Greenman, 1998). For example, white-tailed deer exclude other ungulates because they are infected with a meningeal nematode fatal to other ungulate species (Anderson & Prestwood, 1981). Therefore, losses in endemic parasite fauna may profoundly influence wildlife populations in multiple ways.

We should, however, view these richness results with caution, and not only because the association between richness and threat status was masked when incorporating host traits into the models. It is also worth considering that rarer host species may at once be the most vulnerable to becoming extinct and harbour the least diverse parasite communities. Indeed, among a wide array of host species, including primates, higher population densities and larger geographic ranges typically facilitate increased diversity and abundance in parasite communities (Arneberg et al., 1998; Gregory, 1990; Nunn et al., 2003). As a result, it may be challenging to dissociate mechanisms directly related to primate threat status from mechanisms such as *passive sampling*, which is a purely stochastic process in which parasite diversity would increase simply through increased opportunities for unique host–parasite interactions, e.g. by hosts covering a large geographic area. Longitudinal studies documenting changes in both host and parasite population processes are required to distinguish effects of passive sampling from those related to host threat status.

8.6   Future Directions

In the context of the Anthropocene, in which rapid global changes are already inducing changes in the dynamics and distribution of infectious diseases, understanding host–parasite interactions across scales from individual hosts to communities is particularly important. Yet, the interactions between hosts and their parasite communities are still largely unknown. Comprehensive comparative studies such as ours and others using common data repositories can facilitate the exploration and description of host–parasite interactions across a wide array of natural systems, but what is really lacking are robust empirical studies testing the predictions born of the numerous theoretical and comparative analyses. Myriad promising avenues could move us closer to such a goal, but we highlight three that are currently important to our own work. This is not an exhaustive list, and we do not claim that these are the most important tasks at hand, but we believe that increasing our efforts in these three areas will go a long way towards enhancing our ability to predict outcomes of changing host–parasite associations as the Anthropocene trundles on. The three areas discussed in the concluding paragraphs are: (1) cryptic parasite species diversity; (2) parasites in primate communities; and (3) parasite regulation of primate populations.

Ernst Mayr once wrote that, 'Hardly any aspect of life is more characteristic than its almost unlimited diversity' (Mayr, 1982: 133). He continues, 'Wherever we look, we find uniqueness, and uniqueness spells diversity.' This is as true for parasites as it is for free-living species, though owing to their lifestyles and various other characteristics, it can be especially challenging to register the true diversity of parasitic organisms (Dobson et al., 2008). Despite the recent expansion of the GMPD, as foreseen by Mayr, we continue to find new parasites of all major taxa in primate hosts (Cooper & Nunn, 2013). We also have exceptionally poor coverage in our sampling for primate parasites across the world with clear geographic and species biases (Hopkins & Nunn, 2007; 2010), and even where coverage is ample, a new wave of molecular investigations has begun to uncover unprecedented cryptic species diversity in primate parasites (Frias et al., 2018; Ghai et al., 2014; Lauck et al., 2013; Sibley et al., 2014). It is only when we have a better command of the real diversity of parasites infecting primates that we can truly begin to tackle community-level ecological dynamics.

It perhaps goes without saying, then, that increasing our sampling efforts and identifying cryptic species of parasites is a prerequisite to the second area we wish to highlight: parasites in primate communities. Host community structure can either up- or down-regulate exposure to parasites and infectious diseases for members of the community. On the one hand, intact communities can buffer exposure to infectious agents through a 'dilution effect' – i.e. biodiverse communities include a higher proportion of less competent hosts acting as ecological sinks for parasites (Civitello et al., 2015; Keesing et al., 2006; 2010; Schmidt & Ostfeld, 2001). On the other hand, intact communities might also include 'amplifier' hosts which disproportionately spread infectious agents throughout the community (Dunn et al., 2009; Hechinger & Lafferty, 2005; Hudson et al., 2006; Koh et al., 2004). Most primates live in communities with closely related species capable of sharing their parasites and pathogens, so until we begin to understand such dynamics, we will be unable to determine to what extent parasite pressures, such as host regulation or parasite-mediated apparent competition, might further threaten endangered primates.

Lastly, it is perhaps somewhat surprising that we still have very little idea about how and whether most parasites influence primate health, fitness and, ultimately, abundance. We know from a handful of dramatic cases that infectious diseases can have profound effects on primate populations: e.g. Ebola in Central African great apes (Bermejo et al., 2006; Leroy et al., 2004), persistent anthrax in chimpanzees and other wildlife (Hoffmann et al., 2017; Leendertz et al., 2004), and yellow fever in howler monkeys (Almeida et al., 2012; Holzmann et al., 2010). Such events are typically triggered by an outbreak of a generalist pathogen with little evidence for endemicity in the host population. Influences of endemic parasites, on the other hand, i.e. those that persist at stable or dynamic equilibria in the host population over time, are considerably harder to pin down. Examples might include bot flies causing mortality in howler monkeys (Milton, 1996) and tapeworm coenurosis increasing mortality and inhibiting reproduction in gelada monkeys (Nguyen et al., 2015), but much more work is required before we understand under what conditions regulation is likely or even possible, to what extent regulation is driven by one or a retinue of co-infecting parasites, and how host communities, or changes therein, might influence these relationships.

We thus end with a plea to increase our efforts and target parasite biodiversity as a fundamental component of primate conservation assessment. This is in fact already ongoing, but a quick referral to Hopkins and Nunn (2007; 2010), or a perusal of the GMPD itself, will show that there are still huge gaps in our knowledge. A little stamp-collecting like the great naturalists of old will go a long way towards allowing for better community-level assessments, and will significantly improve the value of comparative studies like the one presented here. Longitudinal and even experimental (where appropriate) studies can then bring into focus the potential roles of parasites in regulating primate populations and structuring their communities, information critical to our ability to predict the outcomes of altered community dynamics in the face of anthropogenic change. This is by no means an easy task, but it is an essential one, because how such changes impact endangered primates might be a deciding factor in determining their future in this anthropocentric world.

Acknowledgements

First and foremost, we would like to thank the editors of this volume for the invitation to be a part of this important discussion: Alison Behie, Nick Malone and Julie Teichroeb. Second, our contribution would not exist without the ingenious original study published in 2007 by Sonia Altizer, Charlie Nunn and Patrick Lindenfors. We also thank Charlie Nunn for his valuable advice regarding parts of the analyses conducted here, and for his general commentary on our work. Many of the ideas presented here stem from our work in Sabah, Malaysian Borneo, so we would also like to acknowledge our collaborators there: Benoit Goossens, Milena Salgado-Lynn, Danica Stark, Sergio Guerrero and Sen Nathan. We would also like to express our thanks to Yoshi Kawamoto for discussions about primate phylogeny, and to Munehiro Okamoto for the lively debates about parasite diversity and distribution in primates. AJJM additionally thanks Mike Huffman for his endless support and encouragement, and Pascale Sicotte, Mary Pavelka and Agustín Fuentes for the inspiration early on.

References

Albon, S., Stien, A., Irvine, R., et al. (2002). The role of parasites in the dynamics of a reindeer population. *Proceedings of the Royal Society of London Series B: Biological Sciences*, **269**(1500), 1625–1632.

Almeida, M. A. B. d., Dos Santos, E., da Cruz Cardoso, J., et al. (2012). Yellow fever outbreak affecting *Alouatta* populations in southern Brazil (Rio Grande Do Sul State), 2008–2009. *American Journal of Primatology*, **74**(1), 68–76.

Altizer, S., Nunn, C. L. & Lindenfors, P. (2007). Do threatened hosts have fewer parasites? A comparative study in primates. *Journal of Animal Ecology*, **76**(2), 304–14.

Anderson, R. C. & Prestwood, A. K. (1981). Lungworms. In: Davidson, W. R., Hayes, F. A., Nettles, V. F. & Kellogg, F. E. (eds) *Diseases and Parasites of the White-Tailed Deer*. Tallahasse, FL: Tall Timbers Research Station, pp. 266–317.

Arneberg, P., Skorping, A., Grenfell, B. & Read, A. F. (1998). Host densities as determinants of abundance in parasite communities. *Proceedings of the Royal Society of London Series B: Biological Sciences*, **265**, 1283–9.

Arnold, C., Matthews, L. J. & Nunn, C. L. (2010). The 10k Trees website: a new online resource for primate phylogeny. *Evolutionary Anthropology*, **19**(3), 114–18.

Barber, B. E., Rajahram, G. S., Grigg, M. J., William, T. & Anstey, N. M. (2017). World malaria report: time to acknowledge *Plasmodium knowlesi* malaria. *Malaria Journal*, **16**(1), 135.

Barger, M. A. & Esch, G. W. (2002). Host specificity and the distribution–abundance relationship in a community of parasites infecting fishes in streams of North Carolina. *Journal of Parasitology*, **88**(3), 446–53.

Behie, A. & Pavelka, M. M. (2013). Interacting roles of diet, cortisol levels, and parasites in determining population density of Belizean howler monkeys in a hurricane damaged forest fragment. In: Marsh, L. K. & Chapman, C. A. (eds) *Primates in Fragments*. New York: Springer, pp. 447–456.

Bermejo, M., Rodríguez-Teijeiro, J. D., Illera, G., et al. (2006). Ebola outbreak killed 5000 gorillas. *Science*, **314**(5805), 1564.

Bublitz, D. C., Wright, P. C., Rasambainarivo, F. T., et al. (2014). Pathogenic enterobacteria in lemurs associated with anthropogenic disturbance. *American Journal of Primatology*, **77**(3), 330–7.

Castro, F. D. & Bolker, B. (2005). Mechanisms of disease-induced extinction. *Ecology Letters*, **8**(1), 117–26.

Chapman, C. A., Gillespie, T. R. & Goldberg, T. L. (2005). Primates and the ecology of their infectious diseases: how will anthropogenic change affect host–parasite interactions? *Evolutionary Anthropology*, **14**(4), 134–44.

Chapman, C. A., Speirs, M. L., Gillespie, T. R., Holland, T. & Austad, K. M. (2006). Life on the edge: gastrointestinal parasites from the forest edge and interior primate groups. *American Journal of Primatology*, **68**(4), 397–409.

Chapman, C. A., Saj, T. L. & Snaith, T. V. (2007). Temporal dynamics of nutrition, parasitism, and stress in colobus monkeys: implications for population regulation and conservation. *American Journal of Physical Anthropology*, **134**(2), 240–50.

Civitello, D. J., Cohen, J., Fatima, H., et al. (2015). Biodiversity inhibits parasites: broad evidence for the dilution effect. *Proceedings of the National Academy of Sciences*, **112**(28), 8667–8671.

Cooper, N. & Nunn, C. L. (2013). Identifying future zoonotic disease threats: where are the gaps in our understanding of primate infectious diseases? *Evolution, Medicine, and Public Health*, **2013**(1), 27–36.

Cox-Singh, J. (2012). Zoonotic malaria: *Plasmodium knowlesi*, an emerging pathogen. *Current Opinion in Infectious Diseases*, **25**(5), 530–6.

Cox-Singh, J. & Singh, B. (2008). Knowlesi malaria: newly emergent and of public health importance? *Trends in Parasitology*, **24**(9), 406–10.

Dobson, A. & Foufopoulos, J. (2001). Emerging infectious pathogens of wildlife. *Philosophical Transactions of the Royal Society of London. Series B: Biological Sciences*, **356**(1411), 1001–12.

Dobson, A. P. & Hudson, P. J. (1986). Parasites, disease and the structure of ecological communities. *Trends in Ecology & Evolution*, **1**(1), 11–15.

Dobson, A., Lafferty, K. D., Kuris, A. M., Hechinger, R. F. & Jetz, W. (2008). Homage to Linnaeus: how many parasites? How many hosts? *Proceedings of the National Academy of Sciences of the United States of America*, **105**, 11482–9.

Dunn, R. R., Harris, N. C., Colwell, R. K., Koh, L. P. & Sodhi, N. S. (2009). The sixth mass coextinction: are most endangered species parasites and mutualists? *Proceedings of the Royal Society B: Biological Sciences*, **276**(1670), 3037–45.

Estrada, A., Garber, P. A., Rylands, A. B., et al. (2017). Impending extinction crisis of the world's primates: why primates matter. *Science Advances*, **3**(1), e1600946.

Ezenwa, V. O. & Jolles, A. E. (2015). Opposite effects of anthelmintic treatment on microbial infection at individual versus population scales. *Science*, **347**(6218), 175–7.

Frias, L., Stark, D. J., Salgado-Lynn, M., et al. (2018). Lurking in the dark: cryptic *Strongyloides* in a Bornean slow loris. *International Journal for Parasitology: Parasites and Wildlife*, **7**(2), 141–6.

Ghai, R. R., Simons, N. D., Chapman, C. A., et al. (2014). Hidden population structure and cross-species transmission of whipworms (*Trichuris* sp.) in humans and non-human primates in Uganda. *PLoS Neglected Tropical Diseases*, **8**(10), e3256.

Gillespie, T. R., Chapman, C. A. & Greiner, E. C. (2005). Effects of logging on gastrointestinal parasite infections and infection risk in African primates. *Journal of Applied Ecology*, **42**(4), 699–707.

Gillespie, T. R., Nunn, C. L. & Leendertz, F. H. (2008). Integrative approaches to the study of primate infectious disease: implications for biodiversity conservation and global health. *American Journal of Physical Anthropology*, **137**(S47), 53–69.

Gog, J., Woodroffe, R. & Swinton, J. (2002). Disease in endangered metapopulations: the importance of alternative hosts. *Proceedings of the Royal Society of London. Series B: Biological Sciences*, **269**(1492), 671–6.

Goldberg, T. L., Gillespie, T. R., Rwego, I. B., Estoff, E. L. & Chapman, C. A. (2008). Forest fragmentation as cause of bacterial transmission among nonhuman primates, humans, and livestock, Uganda. *Emerging Infectious Diseases*, **14**(9), 1375–82.

Gregory, R. D. (1990). Parasites and host geographic range as illustrated by waterfowl. *Functional Ecology*, **4**(5), 645–54.

Grenfell, B. T. & Gulland, F. M. D. (1995). Introduction: ecological impact of parasitism on wildlife populations. *Parasitology*, **111**(51), S3–S14.

Hadfield, J. D. (2010). MCMC methods for multi-response generalized linear mixed models: the MCMCglmm R package. *Journal of Statistical Software*, **33**(2). DOI: 10.18637/jss.v003.102.

Hasegawa, H., Modrý, D., Kitagawa, M., et al. (2014). Humans and great apes cohabiting the forest ecosystem in Central African Republic harbour the same hookworms. *PLoS Neglected Tropical Diseases*, **8**(3), e2715.

Hechinger, R. F. & Lafferty, K. D. (2005). Host diversity begets parasite diversity: bird final hosts and trematodes in snail intermediate hosts. *Proceedings of the Royal Society B: Biological Sciences*, **272**(1567), 1059–66.

Hoffmann, C., Zimmermann, F., Biek, R., et al. (2017). Persistent anthrax as a major driver of wildlife mortality in a tropical rainforest. *Nature*, **548**(7665), 82–6.

Holzmann, I., Agostini, I., Areta, J. I., et al. (2010). Impact of yellow fever outbreaks on two howler monkey species (*Alouatta guariba clamitans* and *A. caraya*) in Misiones, Argentina. *American Journal of Primatology*, **72**(6), 475–80.

Hopkins, M. E. & Nunn, C. L. (2007). A global gap analysis of infectious agents in wild primates. *Diversity and Distributions*, **13**(5), 561–72.

Hopkins, M. E. & Nunn, C. L. (2010). Gap analysis and the geographical distribution of parasites. In: Morand, S. & Krasnov, B. (eds) *The Biogeography of Host–Parasite Interactions*. Oxford: Oxford University Press, pp. 129–42.

Hosseini, P. R., Mills, J. N., Prieur-Richard, A.-H., et al. (2017). Does the impact of biodiversity differ between emerging and endemic pathogens? The need to separate the concepts of hazard and risk. *Philosophical Transactions of the Royal Society B: Biological Sciences*, **372**(1722), 20160129.

Hudson, P. J. & Dobson, A. P. (1995). Macroparasites: observed patterns. In: Grenfell, B. T. & Dobson, A. P. (eds) *Ecology of Infectious Diseases in Natural Populations*. Cambridge: Cambridge University Press, pp. 144–76.

Hudson, P. & Greenman, J. (1998). Competition mediated by parasites: biological and theoretical progress. *Trends in Ecology & Evolution*, 13(10), 387–90.

Hudson, P. J., Dobson, A. P. & Lafferty, K. D. (2006). Is a healthy ecosystem one that is rich in parasites? *Trends in Ecology and Evolution*, 21(7), 381–5.

Isaac, N. J. B. & Cowlishaw, G. (2004). How species respond to multiple extinction threats. *Proceedings of the Royal Society B: Biological Sciences*, 271(1544), 1135–41.

IUCN (2017). *IUCN Red List of Threatened Species*. Version 2017.3. Available at: www.iucnredlist.org (accessed 26 September 2017).

Jones, K. E., Bielby, J., Cardillo, M., et al. (2009). PanTHERIA: a species-level database of life history, ecology, and geography of extant and recently extinct mammals. *Ecology*, 90(9), 2648.

Kalousová, B., Hasegawa, H., Petrželková, K. J., et al. (2016). Adult hookworms (*Necator* spp.) collected from researchers working with wild western lowland gorillas. *Parasites & Vectors*, 9(1), 75.

Kaur, T., Singh, J., Tong, S. X., et al. (2008). Descriptive epidemiology of fatal respiratory outbreaks and detection of a human-related metapneumovirus in wild chimpanzees (*Pan troglodytes*) at Mahale Mountains National Park, western Tanzania. *American Journal of Primatology*, 70(8), 755–65.

Keesing, F., Holt, R. D. & Ostfeld, R. S. (2006). Effects of species diversity on disease risk. *Ecology Letters*, 9(4), 485–98.

Keesing, F., Belden, L. K., Daszak, P., et al. (2010). Impacts of biodiversity on the emergence and transmission of infectious diseases. *Nature*, 468, 647.

Knauf, S., Liu, H. & Harper, K. N. (2013). Treponemal infection in nonhuman primates as possible reservoir for human yaws. *Emerging Infectious Diseases*, 19(12), 2058–60.

Knauf, S., Gogarten, J., Schuenemann, V. J., et al. (2017). African nonhuman primates are infected with the yaws bacterium *Treponema pallidum* subsp. *pertenue*. bioRxiv.

Koh, L. P., Dunn, R. R., Sodhi, N. S., et al. (2004). Species coextinctions and the biodiversity crisis. *Science*, 305(5690), 1632–4.

Köndgen, S., Kühl, H., N'Goran, P. K., et al. (2008). Pandemic human viruses cause decline of endangered great apes. *Current Biology*, 18(4), 260–4.

Kowalewski, M. M., Salzer, J. S., Deutsch, J. C., et al. (2011). Black and gold howler monkeys (*Alouatta caraya*) as sentinels of ecosystem health: patterns of zoonotic protozoa infection relative to degree of human–primate contact. *American Journal of Primatology*, 73(1), 75–83.

Lauck, M., Sibley, S. D., Hyeroba, D., et al. (2013). Exceptional simian hemorrhagic fever virus diversity in a wild African primate community. *Journal of Virology*, 87(1), 688–91.

Leendertz, F. H., Ellerbrok, H., Boesch, C., et al. (2004). Anthrax kills wild chimpanzees in a tropical rainforest. *Nature*, 430(6998), 451–2.

Leendertz, F. H., Pauli, G., Maetz-Rensing, K., et al. (2006). Pathogens as drivers of population declines: the importance of systematic monitoring in great apes and other threatened mammals. *Biological Conservation*, 131(2), 325–37.

Leroy, E. M., Rouquet, P., Formenty, P., et al. (2004). Multiple ebola virus transmission events and rapid decline of central African wildlife. *Science*, 303(5656), 387–90.

Mayr, E. (1982). *The Growth of Biological Thought: Diversity, Evolution and Inheritance*. Cambridge, MA: Belknap Press.

McCallum, H. & Dobson, A. (2002). Disease, habitat fragmentation and conservation. *Proceedings of the Royal Society B: Biological Sciences*, 269(1504), 2041–9.

Milton, K. (1996). Effects of bot fly (*Alouattamyia baeri*) parasitism on a free-ranging howler monkey (*Alouatta palliata*) population in Panama. *Journal of Zoology*, 239, 39–63.

Mittermeier, R. A., Rylands, A. B. & Wilson, D. E. (eds) (2013). *Handbook of Mammals of the World. Vol. 3. Primates*. Barcelona: Lynx Edicions.

Morand, S. & Guégan, J.-F. (2000). Distribution and abundance of parasite nematodes: ecological specialisation, phylogenetic constraint or simply epidemiology? *Oikos*, 88(3), 563–73.

Nguyen, N., Fashing, P. J., Boyd, D. A., et al. (2015). Fitness impacts of tapeworm parasitism on wild gelada monkeys at Guassa, Ethiopia. *American Journal of Primatology*, **77**(5), 579–94.

Nunn, C. L. & Altizer, S. M. (2005). The global mammal parasite database: an online resource for infectious disease records in wild primates. *Evolutionary Anthropology*, **14**(1), 1–2.

Nunn, C. L. & Dokey, A. T. W. (2006). Ranging patterns and parasitism in primates. *Biology Letters*, **2**(3), 351–4.

Nunn, C. L. & Gillespie, T. R. (2016). Infectious disease and primate conservation. In: Wich, S. A. & Marshall, A. J. (eds) *An Introduction to Primate Conservation*. Oxford: Oxford University Press, pp. 157–73.

Nunn, C. L., Altizer, S., Jones, K. E. & Sechrest, W. (2003). Comparative tests of parasite species richness in primates. *American Naturalist*, **162**(5), 597–614.

Nunn, C. L., Altizer, S. M., Sechrest, W. & Cunningham, A. A. (2005). Latitudinal gradients of parasite species richness in primates. *Diversity and Distributions*, **11**(3), 249–56.

Pedersen, A. B. & Fenton, A. (2007). Emphasizing the ecology in parasite community ecology. *Trends in Ecology & Evolution*, **22**(3), 133–9.

Pedersen, A. B., Altizer, S., Poss, M., Cunningham, A. A. & Nunn, C. L. (2005). Patterns of host specificity and transmission among parasites of wild primates. *International Journal for Parasitology*, **35**(6), 647–57.

Plowright, W. (1982). The effects of rinderpest and rinderpest control on wildlife in Africa. *Symposium of the Zoological Society of London*, **50**, 1–28.

Poulin, R. (1998). Large-scale patterns of host use by parasites of freshwater fishes. *Ecology Letters*, **1**(2), 118–28.

Poulin, R. (1999). The intra- and interspecific relationships between abundance and distribution in helminth parasites of birds. *Journal of Animal Ecology*, **68**(4), 719–25.

Quigley, B. J. Z., Brown, S. P., Leggett, H. C., Scanlan, P. D. & Buckling, A. (2017). Within-host interference competition can prevent invasion of rare parasites. *Parasitology*, **145**(6), 770–4.

R Core Team (2017). *R: a Language and Environment for Statistical Computing*. Vienna: R Foundation for Statistical Computing.

Redding, D. W., DeWolff, C. V. & Mooers, A. Ø. (2010). Evolutionary distinctiveness, threat status, and ecological oddity in primates. *Conservation Biology*, **24**(4), 1052–8.

Rwego, I. B., Isabirye-Basuta, G., Gillespie, T. R. & Goldberg, T. L. (2008). Gastrointestinal bacterial transmission among humans, mountain gorillas, and livestock in Bwindi Impenetrable National Park, Uganda. *Conservation Biology*, **22**(6), 1600–7.

Salyer, S. J., Gillespie, T. R., Rwego, I. B., Chapman, C. A. & Goldberg, T. L. (2012). Epidemiology and molecular relationships of *Cryptosporidium* spp. in people, primates, and livestock from Western Uganda. *PLoS Neglected Tropical Diseases*, **6**(4), e1597.

Salzer, J. S., Rwego, I. B., Goldberg, T. L., Kuhlenschmidt, M. S. & Gillespie, T. R. (2007). *Giardia* sp. and *Cryptosporidium* sp. infections in primates in fragmented and undisturbed forest in western Uganda. *Journal of Parasitology*, **93**(2), 439–40.

Schmidt, K. A. & Ostfeld, R. S. (2001). Biodiversity and the dilution effect in disease ecology. *Ecology*, **82**(3), 609–19.

Sibley, S. D., Lauck, M., Bailey, A. L., et al. (2014). Discovery and characterization of distinct simian pegiviruses in three wild African Old World Monkey species. *PLoS One*, **9**(6), e98569.

Snaith, T. V., Chapman, C. A., Rothman, J. M. & Wasserman, M. D. (2008). Bigger groups have fewer parasites and similar cortisol levels: a multi-group analysis in red colobus monkeys. *American Journal of Primatology*, **70**, 1–9.

Stephens, P. R., Pappalardo, P., Huang, S., et al. (2017). Global mammal parasite database version 2.0. *Ecology*, **98**(5), 1476.

Strona, G. (2015). Past, present and future of host–parasite co-extinctions. *International Journal for Parasitology: Parasites and Wildlife*, **4**(3), 431–41.

Tompkins, D. M. & Begon, M. (1999). Parasites can regulate wildlife populations. *Parasitology Today*, **15**(8), 311–13.

Tompkins, D. M., Dobson, A. P., Arneberg, P., et al. (2002). Parasites and host population dynamics. In: Hudson, P. J., Rizzoli, A., Grenfell, B. T., Heesterbeek, J. A. P. & Dobson, A. P. (eds) *The Ecology of Wildlife Diseases*. Oxford: Oxford University Press, pp. 45–62.

Vaumourin, E., Vourc'h, G., Gasqui, P. & Vayssier-Taussat, M. (2015). The importance of multiparasitism: examining the consequences of co-infections for human and animal health. *Parasites & Vectors*, **8**, 545.

Vázquez, D. P. & Simberloff, D. (2002). Ecological specialization and susceptibility to disturbance: conjectures and refutations. *The American Naturalist*, **159**(6), 606–23.

Vitone, N. D., Altizer, S. & Nunn, C. L. (2004). Body size, diet and sociality influence the species richness of parasitic worms in anthropoid primates. *Evolutionary Ecology Research*, **6**(2), 183–99.

Wich, S. A. & Marshall, A. J. (eds) (2016). *An Introduction to Primate Conservation*. Oxford: Oxford University Press.

Wilson, D. E. & Reeder, D. M. (eds) (2005). *Mammal Species of the World: A Taxonomic and Geographic Reference*, 3rd edn. Baltimore, MD: Johns Hopkins University Press.

Wolfe, N. D., Dunavan, C. P. & Diamond, J. (2007). Origins of major human infectious diseases. *Nature*, **447**(7142), 279.

Young, H., Griffin, R. H., Wood, C. L. & Nunn, C. L. (2013). Does habitat disturbance increase infectious disease risk for primates? *Ecology Letters*, **16**(5), 656–63.

9 Lemurs in Fragmented Forests

A Conservation and Research Collaboration

Sheila M. Holmes, Edward E. Louis Jr and Steig E. Johnson

9.1 Personal Narrative

I (SMH) first decided that I wanted to visit Madagascar in grade school, when I saw a slide show of its incredible biodiversity. My passion for science later led me to a biology field school in Kenya. While in Kenya, I saw a presentation by a local biologist that left a lasting impression; the talk detailed the daily struggle between people and the elephants who raided their crops. Thus, while initially taken as an option, this field school changed my career trajectory as it led me to discover the fields of behavioural ecology and conservation. I completed my Bachelor of Science at the University of Alberta, where a course in conservation biology also had a particularly strong influence on me. These experiences strengthened my belief that the real problem was not just that species were endangered, but that there were conflicts in the very conservation actions that were needed for different species to survive, and for natural and human communities to coexist.

After taking some time to gain fieldwork experience, I started looking into graduate biological research programmes. Steig Johnson's interests in the ecological adaptations of lemurs, and how these might shape evolutionary trajectories, appealed to my interests in behavioural ecology. I received my chance to finally see Madagascar when Steig arranged for me to volunteer with a colleague to find out if I wanted to pursue graduate research there. During this first trip, I was struck by how little forest was actually left. I had had the impression of Madagascar as a vast, unspoiled wilderness, and it shocked me to see both the extent of the deforestation and the conditions that people lived in. At that point, I knew I wanted to continue to work in Madagascar and that my research needed to have a conservation influence.

I decided to pursue research at a new study site, near Kianjavato, Madagascar. This site was being established by the Madagascar Biodiversity Partnership (MBP), founded by Edward Louis. Ed's initial interests in Madagascar island biogeography had shifted as he witnessed the endangerment of many species through human activities. In line with this new focus on conservation and the coexistence of local subsistence communities with wildlife, the new research station was to become a base for reforestation programmes that would benefit both natural and human communities.

Working with Steig and Ed reinforced my initial impressions that the diminishing capacity of Madagascar, both for primates and people, required that as researchers we could not merely be spectators while pursuing our own research interests. We had to become involved in the conservation of natural habitats and species, in a way that also benefited local communities. This common goal, bolstered by past collaborations between Ed and Steig, formed the basis for the black-and-white ruffed lemur (*Varecia variegata*) monitoring project in the Kianjavato-Vatovavy forest fragment network. The project began with research that would form a baseline of knowledge for this critically endangered species to help inform conservation action by MBP. In particular, the trees used by these lemurs would be the foundation for the reforestation programmes at the site, and the health of these populations would be a barometer for conservation success.

9.2   Introduction

There is increasing recognition in the discipline of biology that, as organisms are threatened by human impacts, we have a responsibility to investigate these threats and share our results and insights with relevant parties (Lovejoy, 2009; Meijaard & Sheil, 2007). The first responsibility of investigators wanting to contribute to conservation action is thus to increase the relevance of current research. Many research projects that claim to be conservation-based do not adequately invoke conservation action. In Bornean vertebrate research, for example, there is a bias towards descriptive studies that do not explicitly examine threats (Meijaard & Sheil, 2007). Biologists should thus focus more on measuring the quantitative impacts of threats to species and biological communities. Characterising and countering the often-unpredictable events that threaten natural systems requires long-term research and funding and therefore these are more easily accomplished by multiple parties (Meijaard & Sheil, 2007). Additionally, while single-species research is important for determining the basic requirements and particular factors leading to the decline of target species, interdisciplinary questions that span multiple organisms and their interactions are also essential. These may include investigating how to manage exploited ecosystems and resources to find a balance between biodiversity conservation and economics, how to inform and engage the public in biodiversity issues, and how to reconcile conservation and human land use requirements (Braunisch et al., 2012).

Incorporating conservation-relevant questions into research programmes is inadequate without effective information transfer between researchers and conservation practitioners. Peer-reviewed articles that target other scientists are the main form of communication for many researchers (Lovejoy, 2009; Shanley & López, 2009) but recommendations from these outputs are not commonly implemented in conservation policy (Schindler et al., 2011). Management plans, unpublished reports and dialogue with NGOs and experts may be more relevant to conservation practitioners (Schindler et al., 2011); communication with public officials, the general public and people in close proximity to the research and conservation efforts, while pertinent, is underused (Lovejoy, 2009). This lack of information transfer to local policy makers and the public leads to conservation decisions being made in the absence of scientific evidence (Shanley & López, 2009).

One reason for this communication bias is that institutions provide incentives for peer-reviewed journal articles and discourage diverse content and formats, making the application of research efforts to conservation costly to researchers (Shanley & López, 2009). However, diverse output formats are necessary as there are several barriers to knowledge uptake from peer-reviewed sources in developing countries (Sunderland et al., 2009), where much primatological research and conservation takes place. For example, researchers and conservation practitioners in habitat countries may be hindered by language barriers or by the prohibitive costs of accessing scientific literature (Schindler et al., 2011; Sunderland et al., 2009). When it is available, research may still be too broad and have little relevance to local realities, as studies may not consider the integration of social, economic and political situations (Berkes, 2007; Sunderland et al., 2009).

When they are accessible, scholarly publications can be valuable to conservation efforts as they may contribute to policy (Gezon, 2000). The sharing of relevant knowledge among scientists and non-scientist stakeholders increases the effectiveness and cultural appropriateness of policy implementation (Born et al., 2009) in multiple ways. Scientists can foster early stages of engagement by disseminating research results to relevant parties (Duchelle et al., 2009; Kainer et al., 2009). They can train local university students and technicians and help build local research capacity (Duchelle et al., 2009; Meijaard & Sheil, 2007; Sunderland et al., 2009). Finally, they can generate new knowledge through collaboration with local conservation practitioners and stakeholders (Duchelle et al., 2009). These kinds of partnerships, with two-way knowledge exchange, can increase the relevance of conservation recommendations (Sunderland et al., 2009).

Local conservation NGOs can help bridge the knowledge gap between science and management. Environmental NGOs have two main roles: they identify environmental needs and implement programmes to fulfil those needs (Gezon, 2000). Increased information exchange between academics and local NGOs can help focus research and expertise (da Fonseca, 2003; Smith et al., 2009). In addition, while the global benefits of conservation of tropical forests (e.g. carbon sequestration; McAlpine et al., 2010; Rudel, 2001) tend to exceed the international expenses, the opportunity costs borne by local communities may outweigh local benefits (Balmford & Whitten, 2003). To help mediate these high costs, researchers and NGOs have an obligation to involve local communities in research and decision-making (Kainer et al., 2009).

This realisation seems to be a reversal of early conservation policy. The traditional views that conservation required the exclusion of local people (Duffy, 2006), and that conservation goals could not be met except at the expense of human needs (Gezon, 2000), led to conservation plans being imposed on local resource users (stakeholders). This exclusion negatively impacted the livelihoods of many local people (Duffy, 2006) and authorities have since realised that these types of unilateral decisions foster resentment of conservation authorities and non-cooperation among stakeholders (Smith et al., 2009). Conservation success is more likely if the major users have a stake in conserving a target resource (Berkes, 2007), and when conservation plans incorporate local human needs (Duffy, 2006). Thus, it is necessary to engage those who rely heavily on tropical forests, and who may impact the use of resources (Kainer et al., 2009). An important caveat here is that local communities are not always the major users of tropical forests, as has been seen in some areas of Madagascar, where local populations are excluded from international mining zones and associated compensatory protected areas (e.g. Seagle, 2012). Nonetheless, in many cases local communities can have important impacts on tropical forests. Both academics and international NGOs have limitations and priorities (imposed by members, donors or institutional rewards, for example) and do not always fully comprehend local limitations and constraints (Smith et al., 2009), so the contribution of local knowledge can increase local engagement, research relevance and the likelihood of project success by placing research and conservation within the context of local culture, politics and economics (Garnett et al., 2009; Kainer et al., 2009; Smith et al., 2009).

This chapter investigates the promise and challenges of having a closer integration of research, conservation and local stakeholder interests through one case study: our own collaborative research in Madagascar. The ruffed lemur monitoring programme of MBP and researchers at the University of Calgary creates opportunities for scientists to ask research questions that will be relevant to conservation efforts and to convey those results to policy makers within MBP and the local community. This chapter will share the path to our current work, and the research questions and conservation needs that are our focus. It will then discuss our successes, challenges and the lessons we have learned through our experiences within the context of other research, and our goals for the future. As this is an ongoing process of knowledge exchange and lessons learned, we feel it is important to share our experiences on this collaborative project with other primatologists and conservation practitioners who are also aiming to increase the relevance of their research for conservation.

9.3   The Making of a Collaboration

Madagascar is well suited for collaborations between academics and local NGOs. The extreme poverty of the country and its high levels of biodiversity and endemism have led to a strong role of defining and facilitating environmental policies by NGOs (Duffy, 2006; Hannah et al., 1998). Additionally, Madagascar is in need of conservation action, as it houses the entire natural range of the lemurs, recognised as the most endangered group of mammals (Schwitzer et al., 2013). Approximately 90 per cent of lemur species with sufficient data to evaluate are vulnerable, endangered or critically endangered (Schwitzer et al., 2013). Much of this is due to habitat loss through logging for timber and fuelwood, slash-and-burn shifting agriculture and other human activities, including mining (both industrial and artisanal) and charcoal production – thus, mostly small-scale subsistence pursuits rather than large-scale industrial activities (Schwitzer et al., 2013).

Kianjavato is located in the lowland evergreen forests of southeastern Madagascar (Figure 9.1). The site, as elsewhere in Madagascar, experienced heavy forest loss between 1950 and 1970 (Harper et al., 2007), a loss which continues. Ed Louis first visited the Kianjavato area while collecting samples for genetic analysis in 2000. He was able to draw on his experiences there when deciding to found both a Malagasy NGO, MBP, and a research station in 2009. The Kianjavato Ahmanson Field Station

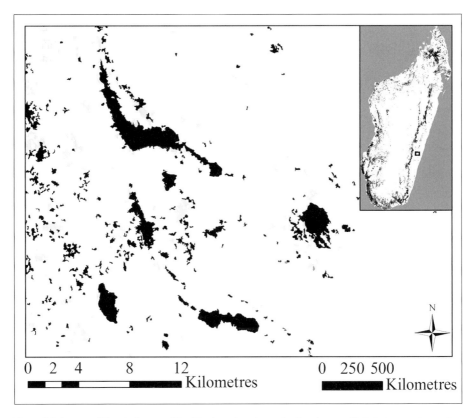

Figure 9.1 A map of the study area. The black rectangle on the inset map of Madagascar shows the location of the study area. Madagascar GIS layers were provided by Conservation International. The forest extent has been modified based on Google Inc. (2009) and ground-truthing of five of the seven visible forest fragments, completed in 2014 and 2015. Black represents forest, dark grey denotes water, light grey depicts cloud or shade (interference in satellite signal) and white is non-forest land cover. This figure was created in ArcGIS 10.4.1 (ESRI, 2016).

(KAFS) was built to support reforestation, community-based conservation, research and education. It was founded on the premise that stewardship of the forests should ultimately be in the hands of the surrounding communities; thus, the land for the station was leased for 25 years, to be returned to the Commune (local government administrative unit) at that point in time. Reforestation and related research, including the impact of lemurs on seed germination, also started in 2009 (Manjaribe et al., 2013).

The remaining forest fragments in the Kianjavato area were embedded in a network of human communities, creating a physical patchiness not seen in previous studies from national parks like Ranomafana and Andringitra. This landscape structure clearly conveyed a sense of human and wildlife connections and conflicts. We quickly recognised the opportunity to observe these conflicts, and to work to seek a balance of land use that would favour both humans and wildlife.

Our original interest in black-and-white ruffed lemur distribution and habitat selectivity built upon Johnson and colleagues' (2004; 2005) surveys in the largely intact forest of Ranomafana National Park. Those surveys showed that the critically endangered (Andriaholinirina et al., 2014) ruffed lemurs were hemmed in by elevation and forest edge – preferring lowland forest, which was mostly lost to human land use (Johnson et al., 2004; 2005). Ruffed lemurs are known to have a patchy distribution (being found in some areas but not in other contiguous, seemingly habitable forest (Irwin et al., 2005; Vasey, 2005)). These results led us to imagine that landscape variables may impose this patchiness. We thus began to investigate the distribution of ruffed lemurs in some of the few remaining lowland rainforests. These forests were heavily disturbed, but within the reported elevation zone of ruffed lemurs (Goodman & Ganzhorn, 2004). They were also prioritised for protection at scientific and conservation priority-setting meetings in Madagascar in 1995 (Hannah et al., 1998). Given their sensitivity to logging (Balko, 1998; White et al., 1995), we expected ruffed lemurs to show limited dispersal across disturbed areas and therefore genetic distinction among forest fragments. We also wanted to determine which landscape variables imposed species distribution *within* fragments (Holmes, 2012) and which habitat features proved important for the species to use an area (Holmes, 2012).

When we started our joint research in Kianjavato, ruffed lemurs were already being followed by students from the University of Antananarivo and local MBP employees to collect seeds from lemur faeces that would be used to rebuild forests for the benefit of both humans and biodiversity. We thus decided to add an ecological research component that could both study the ecology of this species and be used to inform conservation efforts. To those ends, researchers and conservation practitioners at MBP and the University of Calgary began a joint monitoring programme of black-and-white ruffed lemurs, employing local technicians and supporting a rotating set of international volunteers. This team has engaged in daily monitoring of ruffed lemurs through focal animal sampling of collared individuals in two forests since May 2010. We added ongoing population surveys of all nine lemur species (*V. variegata, Eulemur rufifrons, E. rubriventer, Hapalemur griseus, Prolemur simus, Daubentonia madagascariensis, Cheirogaleus major, Microcebus jollyae, Avahi peyrierasi*) to the programme in mid-2014. Nocturnal surveys were conducted for seven months in 2014–15 to establish a baseline for future nocturnal studies. Day-active (diurnal and cathemeral) lemurs continue to be surveyed in five forest fragments each month. Finally, the team undertook a month-long survey expedition to two more-remote forest fragments in April 2015 to obtain preliminary information on lemur distributions and conservation threats in those areas.

To date, our research has mainly focused on conservation genetics and behavioural ecology of ruffed lemurs. We have examined the genetic diversity and differentiation of lemurs across forests of different sizes and isolation distances, determining that both factors appear to impact ruffed lemurs on a genetic level (Holmes et al., 2013). This research has a couple of uses. First, it acts as a baseline against which to measure future changes due to anthropogenic activities or conservation successes. Additionally, if any interventions (e.g. translocations) are required, information on genetic diversity and differentiation of populations across forest fragments could inform such actions. We have also assessed influences on the high degree of fission–fusion dynamics in ruffed lemurs (Holmes et al., 2016) and the distribution and habitat use of the species in the heavily deforested landscape (Holmes, 2012; Holmes et al., 2015). These studies help clarify the relative impact of anthropogenic features (e.g. forest edge) in ranging and grouping patterns and confirm the importance of large trees to this species (Holmes, 2012; Holmes et al., 2015). We have also undertaken brief studies of movement ecology (Johnson et al., 2011) and activity patterns (Guthrie et al., 2017). Finally, we have contributed to broader studies, including comparing the characteristics of vegetation and lemur populations across field sites under different disturbance levels (e.g. Baden et al., 2013; Brown et al., 2013).

9.4   Successes

Previous studies have measured success as positive changes in the behaviour and attitudes of local stakeholders, biodiversity conservation and economics. Due to a lack of baseline data (see Section 9.5), however, we are gauging success in terms of community engagement and motivation relative to the recommendations of other studies.

9.4.1   Community Engagement

Results from conservation research suggest that attitudes change more when the knowledge and values of stakeholders are incorporated into decision-making, and when there is greater transparency and trust among parties (Sterling et al., 2017). For example, in the Taita Hills, Kenya, researchers presented to an audience of government officials, staff from socioeconomic NGOs and community members the results of a study showing how forest fragmentation and degradation impacts bird species, and ways to mitigate these impacts (Githiru & Lens, 2007). All members were given the opportunity to voice their priorities for forest resources, to identify issues and to present possible solutions (Githiru & Lens, 2007). The presentation and discussion were translated into local dialects, which increased community member participation and appreciation for the issues, as the information presented challenged potentially long-held false beliefs about the ecosystem (Githiru & Lens, 2007). The socioeconomic presentations by NGO staff highlighted the connection between the environment, biodiversity and human livelihoods (Githiru & Lens, 2007). When reforestation scenarios were compared, the group started with a number of scenarios that would equally benefit local communities, so they were able to then pick the one that simultaneously gave the most environmental benefits (Githiru & Lens, 2007). This example shows that using scientific research to inform conservation efforts can be improved by taking the extra step of providing alternative solutions so that the best option can be selected by consensus based on the needs of all (Githiru & Lens, 2007).

In general, active participation seems to have better results than simple one-way communication of research-based conservation practice to stakeholders (Cardoso et al., 2001; Githiru & Lens, 2007; Sterling et al., 2017). Engaging stakeholders as early as possible in the process with clear goals, along with regular updates on progress, can increase motivation (Sterling et al., 2017). In addition, meeting with a representative group of stakeholders, rather than entire communities, can help focus discussions (Sterling et al., 2017). Selecting leaders among representatives that have charisma, experience and strong ties to the community can increase community trust and participation (Sterling et al., 2017). Before our collaboration began, and even before any research or reforestation work began, MBP met with local representatives (Manjaribe et al., 2013). These included men and women, administrative officials, traditional people of influence and school employees (Manjaribe et al., 2013). By meeting as early as possible to share their goals and the science behind them, MBP staff were able to communicate the benefits of intact forests to community members, gauge enthusiasm for the conservation and research efforts and obtain feedback (Manjaribe et al., 2013). Whenever new researchers or volunteers start at KAFS, they meet with both local government officials and administrators from the National Center for Applied Research and Rural Development (FOFIFA), who have an office adjacent to one of the remaining forest fragments; this occurs before any research or conservation activities are pursued.

Much of the community engagement has been facilitated by the NGO Conservation Fusion. These educators have played a major role in linking the community to MBP's conservation efforts. These efforts include assigning endemic species mascots to each school, conducting community functions and tree-planting events with conservation and sustainability messages, supporting the initiatives of local groups and individuals and introducing research results into the school curriculum.

9.4.2   Motivation

A major source of motivation among stakeholders in the Kianjavato area is the diversification of income created by the training and subsequent employment of local technicians. Community-run ecotourism will also further economic expansion in communities. Technicians have developed English-language skills through interaction with international volunteers and are now sharing their insights and experiences with tourists who have begun visiting Kianjavato. Visitors are also encouraged to participate by planting trees with reforestation technicians. Tourists give a donation to an employee-run association so that all employees benefit, not just the tour guides. These kinds of income diversification options reduce poverty in communities (Garnett et al., 2009), and in this way conservation can help support human livelihoods. While tourism in Kianjavato does not yet generate sufficient income to make programmes self-sustainable, it is slowly growing each year.

When offering economic incentives for conservation, one must take into account the diversity of communities, and try to avoid exacerbating inequalities (Sterling et al., 2017). For example, while ecotourism benefits those involved, it can also pose costs and challenges for local communities, such as restricting land for growth and development (Eshun & Tonto, 2014). Conservation that becomes associated with economic stimulus may also attract outsiders, increasing pressure on the environments needing protection (Duffy, 2006). We have experienced this at our site, where the recent economic improvements have attracted newcomers looking for work. The population of the Kianjavato Commune has increased from approximately 12 000 to approximately 14 000 people. Unfortunately, these newcomers have not experienced the educational programmes or the conservation planning process, so they are less likely to follow good practices. This has led to some difficult situations, including a recent fire in one of the forest fragments. MBP is attempting to minimise these situations through proactive programmes that establish a connection with the community and through maintaining flexibility to react to issues that arise. Finally, monetary incentives can lead to a lower valuation of the non-economic benefits of nature, and a lack of motivation in the absence of economic stimulus (Sterling et al., 2017). Having both short- and long-term benefits and objectives can thus help maintain motivation (Cardoso et al., 2001; Sterling et al., 2017). MBP's short-term incentives include conservation credits for planting trees, which can be redeemed for green technologies (e.g. solar panels, water filters). Credits can be accumulated individually or pooled for community resources, such as solar panels for schools. Eventually, long-term benefits will replace short-term stimulus; ecotourism will likely increase, and nursery managers will have honed their botanical skills to maintain self-sustaining nurseries that will sell trees to community members to replace those selectively harvested. MBP is working with stakeholders to increase local production of important commercial crops, including bamboo, lychee, coffee, cocoa and cinnamon. The research station will be community-run as well, and in the meantime green-technology jobs continue to diversify the small economy, including a solar charging station that rents out lights to community members.

There is a strong social component to participatory conservation, and many individuals may be more motivated by social benefits and community solidarity than environmental goals (Sterling et al., 2017). Researchers and conservationists can make use of established motivations and mechanisms to accomplish tasks. For example, Strier and Boubli (2006) report making use of the familiar mechanism of community interest volunteering to extend muriqui habitat. They discussed with community members the benefits of creekside forest to the watershed. Realising the shared benefits, farmers volunteered to reforest areas of their land for the mutual well-being of the community and the monkeys (e.g. Strier & Boubli, 2006). At Kianjavato, celebrations are embraced by the surrounding communities, so associating volunteer planting events (where the planting area is prepared by employees but seedlings are planted by volunteers from the community) with celebrations of World Environmental Day, Arbor Day and World Lemur Day have drawn much interest and helped plant tens of thousands of trees.

There is also a strong trust component to participatory conservation. Trust can be built through communication, transparency and an awareness of the local culture and perceptions (Sterling et al., 2017). When trying to maintain equality in collaboration, where problems, priorities and solutions come from all parties, it may also require some compromise between scientific rigour and local needs (Cardoso et al., 2001). In the case of MBP's reforestation project, there is a compromise in the composition of the corridor being planted. The higher elevation component (top 50 per cent) of the new forest will be permanent habitat for rainforest-dwelling species, and will not be subject to harvest (Manjaribe et al., 2013). The lower, adjacent 35 per cent will be timber species with some overlap in species composition with the permanent forest, but will be sustainably harvested (Manjaribe et al., 2013). The lowest 15 per cent of the hillsides, the area adjacent to the rice fields, will be composed of commercially valuable species, like fruit trees (Manjaribe et al., 2013). This composition represents a compromise between the optimal tree species composition desired by local communities for economic reasons and that required for conservation goals.

9.4.3   Direct Conservation Actions

The largest conservation initiative at the site is MBP's reforestation programme. This programme has successfully planted 1 273 071 trees at the site as of 30 June 2017, with yields increasing by more than 100 000 trees each year since 2013. As seeds that have passed through the gut of a lemur germinate more successfully than those that have not (Manjaribe et al., 2013), one direct conservation input of the lemur research includes the collection of seeds from lemur faeces for the reforestation programme. This activity both increases conservation awareness and manages threats. The simple presence of people in the forest each day allows early detection of illegal activities like lemur trapping, logging and forest fires. This demonstrates how stakeholders can be powerful advocates for the conservation of resources (Lovejoy, 2009).

9.4.4   Mentoring and Education

One role we play as researchers is helping to train the next generation of local scientists. It is policy in Madagascar that foreign researchers are paired with international university students with the objective of facilitating local graduate research (Wright & Andriamihaja, 2002). While researchers often maintain contact with their collaborating students after leaving the country, the benefit of collaboration with a local NGO is that students maintain a network of local support as they complete their theses and work towards publishing their studies. Students also gain experience in practical conservation as well as research, which further builds their capacity.

9.4.5   Applicable Research Findings

While we are still finding ways to increase the relevance of our research for conservation actions, we have made some preliminary efforts at conducting conservation-related population assessments. First, lemur surveys across forest fragments showed early indicators that conservation efforts by MBP in Kianjavato may be positively impacting lemur presence and abundance (Frasier et al., 2015; Holmes et al., 2015). Lemur encounter rates are highest near communities with the most conservation education and outreach activity (Holmes et al., 2015). Second, current surveys are identifying areas of species extirpation and low population density, as well as areas of greater disturbance since the placement of survey transects in 2014. The combination of these survey data with genetic data will inform conservation activities by giving a more complete picture of lemur distribution and mobility across the landscape, indicating which areas should be prioritised for conservation education and reforestation. Conservation activities are also starting to direct research activities. We have realised that we need a greater emphasis on quantifying the effects of various forms of disturbance on lemurs. We have also recognised the need to compare our heavily deforested site with other sites to look for general patterns.

9.5   Challenges

In general, successful conservation projects tend to have the following key components: building capacity in local communities and institutions; invoking local participation; making use of environmental education; incorporation of multiple sources of knowledge; and self-evaluation (Cardoso et al., 2001; Githiru & Lens, 2007; Sterling et al., 2017; Strier & Boubli, 2006). The last element is an important reminder that conservation is a dynamic learning process, and self-evaluation improves accountability and allows for the reassessment of goals and methods (Cardoso et al., 2001). Conservation lessons and failures are not often reported or shared, in some cases because of feared loss of funding and/or support (Sunderland et al., 2009). However, not sharing issues that arise may result in the duplication of mistakes and effort (Sunderland et al., 2009). As such, we felt it important to discuss some of the difficulties we have encountered, and challenges we still face.

9.5.1   Baseline Data

We were unable to collect sufficient baseline data prior to the start of conservation activities. For example, surveys did not start until four years after initial behavioural research, and almost five years after the start of conservation activities. This means we have missed out on quantifying a notable population increase in ruffed lemurs in at least one forest fragment (observed during behavioural follows). Though we were unable to complete these baseline assessments prior to the initiation of conservation efforts, finishing them now is vital to measuring the success of the conservation programmes in the future. Presently, we have conducted at least preliminary surveys of all nine lemur species in all seven forest fragments, with the exception of nocturnal data that were not collected in one fragment due to topographical constraints. In addition to ongoing behavioural data collection for ruffed lemurs, we have 11 months of behavioural data for red-bellied (*Eulemur rubriventer*) and red-fronted (*E. rufifrons*) lemurs in two forest fragments. We have collected genetic samples from three species of lemur (ruffed, red-bellied and red-fronted) across 3–5 forest fragments. We have also collected vegetation data and have ground-truthed the forest edge for five of seven forest fragments in each case.

Socioeconomic surveys are also important to accurately gauge changes in attitudes and behaviours among stakeholders. However, these studies require permits from the Institutional Review Board of a qualified post-secondary institution, and the government of Madagascar prior to interview implementation. The review board plays a vital role in ensuring the appropriateness of questions and interview protocols; however, obtaining affiliation with a qualified institution to obtain such a review can be a limiting factor. These reviews are also mandatory if results are to be published in peer-reviewed journals; this is desirable to maximise the opportunities to disseminate important conservation-related results. Some of these types of independent surveys have been done by researchers in the area, starting a few years after reforestation began. Some of these have also targeted communities outside of contemporary conservation efforts, which would give some idea of the attitudes and behaviours in the area prior to conservation outreach, though we do not yet have access to the exact methods or results of those studies.

9.5.2   Determining Anthropogenic Effects

It can be difficult to tease apart anthropogenic effects from basic ecology and evolution. The behaviour of our study individuals does not always conform to that predicted based on other studies (e.g. relationship between subgroup size and food availability; Holmes et al., 2016). It is difficult to determine the full extent of the impacts of fragmentation and other anthropogenic factors on this biological community. However, it is necessary to isolate factors as much as possible to inform conservation practices and determine evolutionary mechanisms for behavioural patterns. To date, we are using three different methods to try to distinguish anthropogenic impacts. The first is the use of comparative studies, where we collaborate with other researchers to include less disturbed areas in our studies (e.g. Holmes et al., 2013). While this allows a straight comparison between areas, it does require that other differences, such as elevation, be taken into consideration. Additionally, there are few, if any, sites not impacted by some form of human disturbance, which makes it more difficult to isolate these factors.

A second method we have used is the common method of using the literature to compare to other studies in nearby sites (e.g. Holmes et al., 2016). This tactic is even less satisfactory, as often methods used are slightly different, making comparison more difficult. To improve upon these methods, we have started to record major disturbance events (e.g. forest fires) with the goal of quantifying their future impact on lemur communities. Regardless, when looking at ecology and evolution, we always need to consider the potential impact that the heavy forest loss and fragmentation may have on our results. For habitat selectivity, for example, this means that we acknowledge that individuals may be using the best of a limited set of choices, which may not be optimal for the species of interest.

9.5.3   Conservation–Research Balance

Another challenge is finding a balance between research for conservation purposes and research on broader theoretical concepts. Ecological research typically makes recommendations and conclusions that are too broad and vague to be of use to conservation practitioners (Sunderland et al., 2009). When focusing on the conservation applications of research, it is possible that results will be too narrowly focused, and will lose applicability to areas that are less disturbed or disturbed in different ways. This struggle is one that all academics interested in establishing conservation best practices will face.

9.5.4   Other Challenges

One major challenge associated with collaborations is communication. We are constantly working to overcome language barriers, diversify outputs and share our results more effectively. We would also like to further increase the contributions of local stakeholders and students to research themes. Currently, all Malagasy graduate students have substantial input on research in that they design their thesis projects with the input of their supervisor and project researchers. While they do address themes related to ongoing or proposed research, they carve out an independent niche and sometimes take the research in directions that the project researchers had not anticipated. This establishes student independence as investigators and brings new ideas to the overall programme of research and conservation. Information and results from student projects and monitoring programmes are used by Conservation Fusion in creating educational programmes for local schools. Additionally, training manuals created by Conservation Fusion in collaboration with local technicians are spreading information and allowing guides to be better ambassadors of conservation and biodiversity. Technicians, supported by Conservation Fusion, have also begun conducting weekend camping trips in the forest with students from the community schools to pass on their knowledge. We would like to continue to encourage knowledge-sharing initiatives and also to increase communication between researchers, conservation workers, educators, students, technicians and community members.

9.6   Future Directions

9.6.1   Research

While we were unable to establish a baseline prior to commencement of conservation efforts, we are expanding monitoring efforts and plan to incorporate disturbance measures in the future. We also believe that the longer this partnership continues, with monitoring being funded by both conservation and research partners, the more research will benefit through the accumulation of demographic data and the ability to view population dynamics and behaviour in response to disturbance and also to reforestation and conservation education. In this way, we hope research can be used to better assess threats and the effectiveness of conservation methods.

9.6.2   Community and Sustainability

While research is important to us, a large function of the ruffed lemur monitoring project is to monitor lemur populations for conservation purposes, and it is one of many pieces in MBP's overall conservation programme. We want to support this programme to continue to benefit local people through education, sustainable technology, and jobs in research and ecotourism.

While much of the community participates in conservation activities, it may be beneficial to start to promote discussion over research priorities. We routinely discuss data collection methods with our local technicians to try to optimise the information we collect; however, it would be interesting to see how other kinds of local knowledge might inform our research. While MBP bridges research activities and participatory conservation, it may also be beneficial for researchers to more directly present our findings to the local communities and to hear feedback.

A large degree of credit for community involvement goes to conservation educators from the NGO Conservation Fusion. We have observed communities meeting to discuss illegal activities, increased cooperation of government authorities in monitoring and law enforcement and community-led conservation education activities. Collaboration with educators has facilitated this community support, and as researchers we need to step up to maintain that trust and motivation.

Sustainability is foremost in our minds. MBP has the goal of making the nurseries and research station self-sustaining for the community in the long term, and green technology is one of the ways they promote sustainable use of resources, including the forest. This aim towards sustainability that will benefit the community in the future is necessary if we want the impacts of our conservation-related research and actions to survive beyond our presence in Kianjavato.

9.6.3   Mentoring and Capacity Building

Our experience in Madagascar shows the importance of building local capacity and training the next generation of local scientists and conservationists. These scientists, whether they study primates or other organisms, can more readily incorporate economic, social, political and cultural factors into the biological and ecological data that they collect and better ensure that it is used to inform conservation efforts. While the majority of conservation in Madagascar is accomplished by Malagasy nationals as staff, and some Malagasy-run NGOs, there is room for improvement, and Madagascar is not yet in the position where the majority of science is done by nationals. This is a hugely important next step, which will require training, as is the case in many tropical countries (Born et al., 2009). More importantly, it requires foreign researchers to give collaborating students opportunities to take responsibility for leadership roles. Access to conservation tools and literature is also valuable (Meijaard & Sheil, 2007), as is sufficient training in manuscript and grant-application writing (Sunderland et al., 2009), particularly since much of this occurs in English. Continuing to support these students is high on our list of priorities.

9.7   Closing Remarks

In today's world, conservation is necessary in many geographical areas to preserve the species and ecosystems we study as researchers. Finding ways to improve both the relevance of our conservation-related research and the transmission of that knowledge are priorities. This often means working together with local conservation organisations and local communities to share research and hopefully inspire conservation action. Communication and knowledge exchange, while time-consuming and at times challenging, are vital to preserving the species we study. In order to successfully use research to inform conservation, researchers need to implement results in a way that incorporates biological research with knowledge of local customs, culture, politics and economics, and ideally in a way that builds local research and conservation capacity, and that benefits local communities that bear the costs of conservation actions.

Acknowledgements

We thank our long-time ruffed lemur technicians: Cressant Razafindravelo, Ferdinah Mbana, Jean Pierre Marolahy and Emilys Edgarçon Rakotoson. We also thank the many temporary technicians, students and international volunteers who have contributed to this programme over the years. We are grateful for funding provided by the American Association of Zoo Keepers (Omaha chapter), American Genetics Association, Ahmanson Family Foundation, the Arbour Day Foundation, the Association of Zoo and Aquarium Docents (Omaha chapter), the Association of Zoological Horticulture, the Association of Zoo and Aquarium's Conservation Endowment Fund, Calgary Zoo, Conservation International's Primate Action Fund, Denver Zoo, Disney Animal Kingdom's Worldwide Conservation Fund, Gladys Porter Zoo, Goggio Family Foundation, Government of Alberta, Houston Zoological Park, International Primatological Society, Irwin Andrew Porter Foundation, IUCN's Save Our Species initiative and its partner, the Fondation Segré Funding for Lemur Protection, Margot Marsh Biodiversity Foundation, Mohamed bin Zayed Species Conservation Fund, NSERC, Primate Conservation Inc., San Diego Zoo, Seaworld & Bush Gardens Conservation Fund, Theodore and Claire Hubbard Family Foundation, University of Calgary, V.J. and Angela Skutt Catholic High School, and Zoo Boise.

References

Andriaholinirina, N., Baden, A., Blanco, M., et al. (2014). *Varecia variegata. The IUCN Red List of Threatened Species 2014*. Available at: http://dx.doi.org/10.2305/IUCN.UK.2014-1.RLTS .T22918A16121857.en (accessed 27 August 2018).

Baden, A. L., Wright, P. C., Louis, E. E. & Bradley, B. J. (2013). Communal nesting, kinship, and maternal success in a social primate. *Behavioral Ecology and Sociobiology*, **67**, 1939–50.

Balko, E. A. (1998). A behaviorally plastic response to forest composition and logging disturbance by *Varecia variegata variegata* in Ranomafana National Park, Madagascar. PhD dissertation, State University of New York College of Environmental Science and Forestry.

Balmford, A. & Whitten, T. (2003). Who should pay for tropical conservation, and how could the costs be met? *Oryx*, **37**, 238–50.

Berkes, F. (2007). Community-based conservation in a globalized world. *PNAS*, **104**, 15188–93.

Born, J., Boreaux, V. & Lawes, M. J. (2009). Synthesis: sharing ecological knowledge – the way forward. *Biotropica*, **41**, 586–8.

Braunisch, V., Home, R., Pellet, J. & Arlettaz, R. (2012). Conservation science relevant to action: a research agenda identified and prioritized by practitioners. *Biological Conservation*, 153, 201–10.

Brown, K. A., Johnson, S. E., Parks, K., et al. (2013). Use of provisioning ecosystem services drives loss of functional traits across land use intensification gradients in tropical forests in Madagascar. *Biological Conservation*, 161, 118–27.

Cardoso, I. M., Guijt, I., Franco, F. S., Carvalho, A. F. & Neto, P. S. F. (2001). Continual learning for agroforestry system design: university, NGO and farmer partnership in Minas Gerais, Brazil. *Agricultural Systems*, 69, 235–57.

da Fonseca, G. A. B. (2003). Conservation science and NGOs. *Conservation Biology*, 17, 345–7.

Duchelle, A. E., Biedenweg, K., Lucas, C., et al. (2009). Graduate students and knowledge exchange with local stakeholders: possibilities and preparation. *Biotropica*, 41, 578–85.

Duffy, R. (2006). Non-governmental organisations and governance states: the impact of transnational environmental management networks in Madagascar. *Environmental Politics*, 15, 731–49.

Eshun, G. & Tonto, J. N. P. (2014). Community-based ecotourism: its socio-economic impacts at Boabeng-Fiema Monkey Sanctuary, Ghana. *Bulletin of Geography: Socio-Economic Series*, 26, 67–81.

ESRI (2016). *ArcGIS Desktop*. Redlands, CA: Environmental Systems Research Institute.

Frasier, C. L., Rakotonarina, J.-N., Razanajatovo, L. G., et al. (2015). Expanding knowledge on life history traits and infant development in greater bamboo lemurs (*Prolemur simus*): contributions from Kianjavato, Madagascar. *Primate Conservation*, 29, 75–86.

Garnett, S. T., Crowley, G. M., Hunter-Xenie, H., et al. (2009). Transformative knowledge transfer through empowering and paying community researchers. *Biotropica*, 41, 571–7.

Gezon, L. L. (2000). The changing face of NGOs: structure and communitas in conservation and development in Madagascar. *Urban Anthropology and Studies of Cultural Systems and World Economic Development*, 29, 181–215.

Githiru, M. & Lens, L. (2007). Application of fragmentation research to conservation planning for multiple stakeholders: an example from the Taita Hills, southeast Kenya. *Biological Conservation*, 134, 271–8.

Goodman, S. M. & Ganzhorn, J. U. (2004). Biogeography of lemurs in the humid forests of Madagascar: the role of elevational distribution and rivers. *Journal of Biogeography*, 31, 47–55.

Google Inc. (2009). Google Earth. 5.1.3509.4636 edn.: Google Inc. and Digital Globe.

Guthrie, N. K., Holmes, S. M., Gordon, A. D., et al. (2017). A lack of cathemeral activity in *Varecia variegata* in Kianjavato, Madagascar. *American Journal of Physical Anthropology*, 162(S64), 205–6.

Hannah, L., Rakotosamimanana, B., Ganzhorn, J., et al. (1998). Participatory planning, scientific priorities, and landscape conservation in Madagascar. *Environmental Conservation*, 25, 30–6.

Harper, G., Steininger, M. K., Tucker, C. J., Juhn, D. & Hawkins, F. (2007). Fifty years of deforestation and forest fragmentation in Madagascar. *Environmental Conservation*, 34, 325–33.

Holmes, S. M. (2012). Habitat use and population genetics of the black-and-white ruffed lemur (*Varecia variegata*) in a fragmented landscape in southeastern Madagascar. MA Thesis, University of Calgary.

Holmes, S. M., Baden, A. L., Brenneman, R. A., et al. (2013). Patch size and isolation influence genetic patterns in black-and-white ruffed lemur (*Varecia variegata*) populations. *Conservation Genetics*, 14, 615–24.

Holmes, S. M., Yaney-Keller, A. M., Rafidimanana, D. V., et al. (2015). Lemur population surveys in the Kianjavato region. *Lemur News*, 19, 9–11.

Holmes, S. M., Gordon, A. D., Louis, E. E. J. & Johnson, S. E. (2016). Fission–fusion dynamics in black-and-white ruffed lemurs may facilitate both feeding strategies and communal care of infants in a spatially and temporally variable environment. *Behavioral Ecology and Sociobiology*, 70(11), 1949–60.

Irwin, M. T., Johnson, S. E. & Wright, P. C. (2005). The state of lemur conservation in south-eastern Madagascar: population and habitat assessments for diurnal and cathemeral lemurs using surveys, satellite imagery and GIS. *Oryx*, **39**, 204–18.

Johnson, S. E., Puyravaud, J.-P., Ratelolahy, F. J., et al. (2004). Biodiversity and anthropogenic disturbance at Ranomafana National Park, Madagascar. Society for Conservation Biology (SCB) Annual Meeting, 2004.

Johnson, S. E., Wright, P., Keitt, T. H., et al. (2005). Predictors of local variation in lemur abundance at Ranomafana National Park, Madagascar. *American Journal of Physical Anthropology*, **40**, 122.

Johnson, S. E., Gordon, A. D., Raichlen, D. A., et al. (2011). Search strategies in frugivorous lemurs in southeastern Madagascar: are lévy walks used? *American Journal of Primatology*, **73**(s1), 57.

Kainer, K. A., DiGiano, M. L., Duchelle, A. E., et al. (2009). Partnering for greater success: local stakeholders and research in tropical biology and conservation. *Biotropica*, **41**, 555–62.

Lovejoy, T. E. (2009). Responsibilities of 21st-century scientists. *Biotropica*, **41**, 531.

Manjaribe, C., Frasier, C. L., Rakouth, B. & Louis, E. E. J. (2013). Ecological restoration and reforestation of fragmented forests in Kianjavato, Madagascar. *International Journal of Ecology*, **2013**, 1–12.

McAlpine, C. A., Ryan, J. G., Seabrook, L., et al. (2010). More than CO_2: a broader paradigm for managing climate change and variability to avoid ecosystem collapse. *Current Opinion in Environmental Sustainability*, **2**, 334–46.

Meijaard, E. & Sheil, D. (2007). Is wildlife research useful for wildlife conservation in the tropics? A review for Borneo with global implications. *Biodiversity and Conservation*, **16**, 3053–65.

Rudel, T. K. (2001). Sequestering carbon in tropical forests: experiments, policy implications, and climatic change. *Society & Natural Resources*, **14**, 525–31.

Schindler, S., Curado, N., Nikolov, S. C., et al. (2011). From research to implementation: nature conservation in the Eastern Rhodopes mountains (Greece and Bulgaria), European Green Belt. *Journal for Nature Conservation*, **19**, 193–201.

Schwitzer, C., Mittermeier, R. A., Davies, N., et al. (eds) (2013). *Lemurs of Madagascar: A Strategy for Their Conservation 2013–2016*, Bristol: IUCN SSC Primate Specialist Group, Bristol Conservation and Science Foundation, Conservation International.

Seagle, C. (2012). Inverting the impacts: mining, conservation and sustainability claims near the Rio Tinto/QMM ilmenite mine in Southeast Madagascar. *Journal of Peasant Studies*, **39**, 447–77.

Shanley, P. & López, C. (2009). Out of the loop: why research rarely reaches policy makers and the public and what can be done. *Biotropica*, **41**, 535–44.

Smith, R. J., Verissimo, D., Leader-Williams, N., Cowling, R. M. & Knight, A. T. (2009). Let the locals lead. *Nature*, **462**, 280–1.

Sterling, E. J., Betley, E., Sigouin, A., et al. (2017). Assessing the evidence for stakeholder engagement in biodiversity conservation. *Biological Conservation*, **209**, 159–71.

Strier, K. B. & Boubli, J. P. (2006). A history of long-term research and conservation of northern muriquis (*Brachyteles hypoxanthus*) at the Estação Biológica de Caratinga/RPPN-FMA. *Primate Conservation*, **20**, 53–63.

Sunderland, T., Sunderland-Groves, J., Shanley, P. & Campbell, B. (2009). Bridging the gap: how can information access and exchange between conservation biologists and field practitioners be improved for better conservation outcomes? *Biotropica*, **41**, 549–54.

Vasey, N. (2005). New developments in the behavioral ecology and conservation of ruffed lemurs (*Varecia*). *American Journal of Primatology*, **66**, 1–6.

White, F. J., Overdorff, D. J., Balko, E. A. & Wright, P. C. (1995). Distribution of ruffed lemurs (*Varecia-variegata*) in Ranomafana National-Park, Madagascar. *Folia Primatologica*, **64**, 124–31.

Wright, P. C. & Andriamihaja, B. A. (2002). Making a rain forest national park work in Madagascar: Ranomafana National Park and its long-term research commitment. In Terborgh, J., van Schaik, C., Rao, M. & Davenport, L. (eds) *Making Parks Work: Strategies for Preserving Tropical Nature*. Washington, DC: Island Press, pp. 112–36.

10 Proboscis Monkey Conservation

Beyond the Science

Stanislav Lhota, John C. M. Sha, Henry Bernard and Ikki Matsuda

10.1 Personal Narrative

I (SL) arrived in Indonesian Borneo in 2005 with the burning ambition to study the ecology and behaviour of one of the most elusive and least-studied primate species, the white-fronted langur (*Presbytis frontata*). I spent a year attempting to track and habituate these monkeys in Sungai Wain Protection Forest (SWPF), Balikpapan Bay (see Figure 10.1). It was perhaps the best year of my life.

Not long after, a proposal to build a provincial road along the boundaries of SWPF started gaining momentum (Gokkon, 2017). I volunteered to collect data for the environmental impact assessment (EIA), which showed the detrimental impact of the proposed road. Despite the proposal of alternative options, the project proceeded. The protection of the land was to be handled by the private sector, which was accelerating the ongoing large-scale destruction of the Balikpapan Bay ecosystem. This was my first bitter experience with the realities of environmental politics.

I soon came to the realisation that the white-fronted langurs never stood a fighting chance of swaying public opinion towards their conservation as they were simply too 'ordinary'. As a proponent for their protection, my opinion had little chance of being aired in public or in the media, and much less chance of reaching the ears of high-level decision-makers. This prompted me to make a strategic decision to abandon the uncompleted research and turn my attention to the proboscis monkey (*Nasalis larvatus*). These large and unique primates attracted immense public attention whenever conservation issues were raised and I saw how the concept of 'charismatic' or flagship species could be put into conservation practice.

By 2007, I had started a new project to study the proboscis monkeys in Balikpapan Bay in the hope of attracting more public attention to this highly threatened area. This work was not easy, as all researchers who have worked in the harsh field conditions of mangrove swamps would appreciate. Slow progress was made on foot on the soft muddy ground. Countless irritants like swarming mosquitoes and sandflies were barely tolerable, but the main threat was the risk of attack by estuarine crocodiles.

Yet, it was not these problems that led me to eventually scale-down much of my research work and focus more on conservation issues. Ironically, there is only so much one can do to conserve the animals one studies by only studying them. The often-romanticised image of a researcher spending much of his/her life in the forests, living with and protecting the animals, to put it bluntly, belongs only in the realm of fairytales. Real-world conservation is as much, if not more so, about campaigning, lobbying and negotiations rather than following monkeys around swamps. Conservation is anthropocentric – people and politicians decide much of the fate of all wildlife and wild habitats on this planet.

On the brighter side, my time working on proboscis monkeys in the field turned out to be an important primer for my current work. It gave me the opportunity to meet many like-minded people, most of whom closely share my interests and the desire to help conserve the animals they study. Most notably, I met my co-authors for this chapter, Ikki Matsuda, John Sha and Henry Bernard.

Ikki had been studying proboscis monkeys in Kinabatangan (see Figure 10.1), Sabah, Malaysia since 2005 and made pioneering contributions to the species' research by conducting full-day continuous observations on foot in riverine forests. His studies revealed important information about their feeding and ranging behaviours, as well as novel findings about their digestive strategy of rumination, the first documented among primate species.

John conducted a state-wide survey of proboscis monkeys in Sabah, Malaysia in 2004, the most comprehensive population survey for the species. His study mapped out all major proboscis monkey population centres as well as isolated populations throughout Sabah, which revealed highly fragmented populations, some of which were severely encroached on by human activities. It was during this time that John met Ikki in the field, which ushered in a decade of collaborations on both field and captive proboscis monkey research.

Henry is the most senior scientist in our group and is a pioneer of proboscis monkey research in Sabah, most notably at his long-term study site in Klias Peninsula (see Figure 10.1). Henry was John's supervisor for his 2004 study and has been an important counterpart and collaborator for numerous researchers throughout the years, including Ikki. He had also worked with the Sabah Wildlife Department (SWD) before embarking on his academic career and is well-steeped in the inner workings of conservation and protection area management in Sabah. In 2006, he spearheaded an important initiative to formulate a 'Proboscis Monkey Protection Plan' in Klias Peninsula, which led to the creation of a new conservation area to connect fragmented proboscis monkey populations.

Although my career has by now taken a different trajectory and the research focus of my collaborators has also extended beyond the proboscis monkey, we remain committed to the long-term conservation of this fascinating species that was so instrumental in sparking our interest in science and conservation. It is my hope that this chapter will take this impetus to another level and motivate more budding scientists to join our cause.

10.2   Introduction

Proboscis monkeys (*Nasalis larvatus*) are endemic to the island of Borneo (Figure 10.1). They are classified as endangered according to the IUCN Red List of Threatened Species (IUCN, 2008), and listed under CITES Appendix I. They are restricted mainly to habitats along waterways, generally travelling up to 800 m inland to forage, and returning to their sleeping sites along riverbanks each evening (Matsuda et al., 2011a). Such riverine refuging behaviour is a hallmark on which most early research on the species was based. As swampy habitats make continuous observation on foot very difficult, research was conducted using boats during the hours that the monkeys were found at their sleeping sites (Bennett & Sebastian, 1988; Bismark, 2010; Murai et al., 2007; Yeager, 1989). This limited a more comprehensive understanding of the ecology and behaviour of the species. Early in the twenty-first century, some researchers (e.g. R. Boonratana and I. Matsuda) began following monkeys on foot in riverine forests, and these efforts revealed novel findings about their feeding and ranging behaviours in inland forests (Matsuda et al., 2009a; 2009b). Such an approach became significant considering that more recent studies using GPS-based tracking revealed that proboscis monkeys can also travel more than 1 km inland to sleep without returning to riverbanks (Stark et al., 2017a; 2017b).

Many proboscis monkey populations were formerly 'naturally protected' by the fact that they live in swampy habitats, which are generally less threatened by human development compared to dry-land forests due to their relative inaccessibility (Nowak, 2012). However, in recent decades modern technology has made it increasingly easy to ameliorate these habitats and reclaim swampland by filling it with compressed soil, so swamps quickly became a cheap source of land available for human exploitation, including industry and human settlements (Lhota et al., 2018).

Indeed, the habitat specificity of proboscis monkeys to swamp habitats, which initially contributed to their protection, is now tightening the noose on their long-term survival. Many populations are now found scattered in small patches of suitable habitats (Sha et al., 2008). Additionally, some populations that have been isolated from water are also emerging, such as on limestone hills in South Kalimantan, in urbanised landscapes near Samarinda Botanical Garden (Figure 10.1; Kebun Raya UNMUL Samarinda) or the central hills of the urbanised Tarakan island (Figure 10.1; Soendjoto, personal communication; Lhota, personal observation).

There has never been a time more urgent than now to carefully consider the long-term future of the proboscis monkey, which in our opinion is highly dependent on how sound conservation measures can be formulated by policy makers and successfully implemented at the local scale. In this chapter, we briefly review the historical progress of proboscis monkey research and examine the most important conservation actions needed for the species in the context of relevant scientific findings.

10.3   The Science of Proboscis Monkey Conservation

Early proboscis monkey research was mainly based on short-term studies from boats focused on the basic understanding of their social organisation and habitat utilisation (Bismark, 1981; Jeffrey, 1979; Kawabe & Mano, 1972; Kren, 1964; Macdonald, 1982; Salter et al., 1985). In the late 1980s, longer-term studies pioneered by Carey P. Yeager, Elizabeth L. Bennett and Ramesh Boonratana were conducted (e.g. Bennett & Sebastian, 1988; Boonratana, 2000; Yeager, 1989; 1991). These works helped to elevate the proboscis monkey from an interesting but little-understood 'weird big-nose' monkey

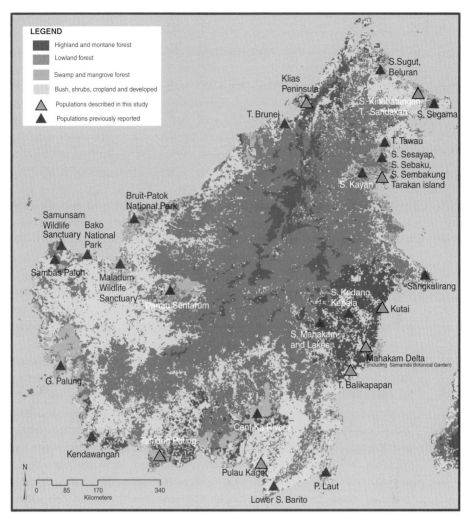

Figure 10.1 Geographical locations of major populations with priority areas for proboscis monkeys in Borneo. Data on populations are partly from Bennett and Gombek (1993), Meijaard and Nijman (2000a) and Sha et al. (2008).

into a flagship species across its range. Local authorities and the general public became increasingly attracted to proboscis monkeys after learning about their unique appearance from the media (i.e. many of the early photographs were taken by researchers, and documentaries were produced at their research sites) or after being able to see the monkeys directly. In fact, research and ecotourism developed simultaneously in most proboscis monkey field sites, including Tangung Puting, Lower Kinabatangana and, later on, Balikpapan Bay (Figure 10.1). These early studies found that, contrary to earlier assumptions that proboscis monkeys mostly ate mangrove-specific leaves, high levels of fruits and/or seeds were consumed in response to local conditions, which in turn influenced their ranging patterns. These authors also described the proboscis monkeys' varied social systems, which can consist of multi-level associations between adjacent monkey groups. By the 2000s, the attention raised for these unique monkeys had gradually attracted more researchers devoting their academic pursuits to the further understanding of the species, with studies still predominantly focused on their socioecology (e.g. Feilen & Marshall, 2014; Matsuda et al., 2010; Murai et al., 2007; Roper et al., 2014; Thiry et al., 2016), but extending to genetic analyses (e.g. Munshi-South & Bernard, 2011; Salgado-Lynn, 2010), and other novel topics about their digestive capabilities and the sexual selection of enlarged noses (e.g. Koda et al., 2018; Matsuda et al., 2011b; 2015). Researchers also began considering conservation issues and the impacts of human activities like tourism (Leasor & Macgregor, 2014) and other landscape changes (Stark et al., 2012; 2017a).

While the progress of scientific inquiry will continue to help increase research knowledge and general public appreciation for the conservation of proboscis monkeys, research that directly considers their conservation is still limited. What we currently know about the overall population status of the species across its range is still based largely on 'guesstimates' from some 2–3 decades ago. The state-wide survey of proboscis monkeys in Sabah, East Malaysia, conducted by Sha et al. (2008), aimed to address this deficiency, after researchers realised that such basic information was lacking in the first proboscis monkey population habitat viability analysis (PHVA) conducted in Bogor in 2004 (Manansang et al., 2005).

Owing to the difficulties in obtaining up-to-date baseline population data on the species, researchers have concentrated on smaller areas to conduct relevant population viability analysis (PVA). Stark and colleagues (2012) assessed three proboscis monkey populations and predicted that the Malaysian population (Kinabatangan) would remain fairly stable, while the two Indonesian populations (Balikpapan Bay and Danau Sentarum National Park) would decrease by more than half within 50 years, with one population in Danau Sentarum National Park predicted to be effectively extinct within 30 years. In related studies, based on population trends over ten years (2004–14) in Lower Kinabatangan, it was found that proboscis monkey population sizes remained relatively stable but that an observed decrease in group sizes and increase in population density was likely related to forest fragmentation (Matsuda et al., 2018b). The latest population survey in Balikpapan Bay in 2017 similarly did not show the population decline predicted by Stark and colleagues' (2012) model (Scott et al., unpublished data). However, Sha and Matsuda (2016) suggested a possibility of delayed effects of habitat loss akin to 'ecological bubbles', which is expected to result in initial high population densities before the population eventually crashes (e.g. 'extinction debt'; Cowlishaw, 1999).

10.4   Beyond the Science

10.4.1   Protected Areas Management

Proboscis monkeys are known to occur in 16 protected areas throughout Borneo (IUCN, 2008). Despite this, major populations still remain outside protected areas.

This situation was described by Bennett (1991) for Malaysia and had improved after the gazettement of two additional reserves: the Lower Kinabatangan Wildlife Sanctuary, and Bukau-Api-api Conservation Area in the Klias Peninsula, which together with the Padas Damit Forest Reserve form the stronghold of the proboscis populations in western Sabah (Bernard & Zulhazman, 2006). Yet less than half of the total Sabah population lived in protected areas in 2006 (Sha et al., 2008). The situation in Indonesia likewise remains relatively unchanged since it was described by Meijaard and Nijman (2000a) and Manansang et al. (2005). For example, less than 2 per cent of the 1400-strong proboscis monkey population of Balikpapan Bay live within the protected boundaries of SWPF.

The main reason why many proboscis monkey populations remain unprotected is that protected areas are generally established in areas of low economic value due to their remoteness and steep terrain. In contrast, suitable proboscis monkey habitats tend to be lowland forests along large rivers and coasts, which are areas of high economic value. In fact, there is a large overlap between proboscis monkey habitats and human habitation, and this situation is exacerbated today with the advent of modern technologies that allow increasingly cost-effective reclamation of swamp habitats (Lhota et al., 2018).

Outside of protected areas, local spatial plans may still include the protection of greenbelts along rivers and coasts and a significant proportion of proboscis monkey habitats could be secured this way. In Malaysia, for example, agricultural companies are required to maintain riparian reserves of 5–50 m from each riverbank, based on federal law (Government of Malaysia, National Land Code No. 56 of 1965), while reserve width requirements are dictated by the size of the river and administrative region, ranging from 20 to 30 m. Similarly, in Indonesia, protected belts are required along riverbanks, lake shores and coastlines (Keputusan Presiden No. 32/1990 Tentang Pengelolaan Kawasan Lindung; Peraturan Menteri Pekerjaan Umum No. 63/1993 Tentang Garis Sempadan Sungai, Daerah Manfaat Sungai, Daerah Penguasaan Sungai dan Bekas Sungai). In addition, Indonesian legislation protects all mangrove forests, even outside protected areas (Muzani, 2014). These overarching national laws and regulations are, however, often not respected at the regional level, as a large degree of autonomy is allowed under Indonesian spatial planning.

Due to the insufficient extent of protected areas, some NGOs have resorted to purchases of land certificates to exert control over the protection of the land. However, land prices are high in the proboscis monkeys' habitat. For example, it costs approximately $13 932/ha in the Lower Kinabatangan Area (Matsuda et al., 2018b). Furthermore, suitable land parcels need to be identified and purchased while prices are still affordable, as they can escalate at an exponential rate. In Balikpapan Bay, the price of land has increased about ten times since the 1990s, after the proposal to build a provincial road along the coast (Lhota, unpublished data). In addition, land purchases are complicated by other factors like pre-release or priority deals between government officials and land speculators or multiple claims for a single piece of land.

10.4.2   Viability of Isolated Populations

Although proboscis monkeys may be highly resilient to forest degradation and thrive even in secondary forests (Matsuda et al., 2018a), they need sufficient space and food resources to maintain viable populations. Owing to the species' preference for areas that are intensively used by humans, many populations have become densely concentrated in small forest patches. Casual observers may consider such high densities of monkeys as a sign of a healthy population, but this is often not the case. This problem applies to most protected tourist parks. For example, the Mangrove Center and Margo Mulyo in Balikpapan Bay are less than 2 km^2 in total size, including the surrounding unprotected mangroves, yet they support a little over 100 individuals. This may seem like a high density, but it is important to note that these monkeys have already become isolated from the major population in Balikpapan Bay, meaning they may not be viable.

Small protected strips of coastal and riverine habitat may provide some connectivity to larger forest patches, but on their own they do not necessarily provide enough food resources for proboscis monkeys as the immediately adjacent land is often allocated to intensive development. For example, *Rhizophora apiculata* dominated mangroves along riverbanks close to the estuaries are very poor in terms of proboscis monkey food resources. In Balikpapan Bay, proboscis monkeys living in this forest type must forage in surrounding dry-land secondary forests in order to obtain sufficient food. Studies in Sarawak and Padas Damit Forest Reserve in Sabah, where mangrove and other forest habitats are contiguous with one another, showed proboscis monkey movement in and out of mangrove forest at different times of the year, indicating seasonal changes in habitat preferences (Bernard et al., 2018; Salter et al., 1985). Likewise, proboscis monkeys inhabiting riverine forests may forage inland for up to 1 km (perpendicular distance) from the river banks into dry-land forests (Matsuda et al., 2009b; Stark et al., 2017b). If these surrounding forests are lost to development, the monkeys may not survive within the limited protected mangrove belts.

An example of the fate of an isolated proboscis monkey population was recorded at Pulau Kaget (Figure 10.1; Meijaard & Nijman, 2000b), where the population collapsed to a fraction of its original size within three years and was preceded by mass mortality of *Sonneratia cassaeolaris* trees. Today we can observe a similar phenomenon in the Somber River in Balikpapan City, where the population density is increasing but as a result the food resources are dwindling, largely due to mass mortality of the major proboscis monkey food plant, *Sonneratia alba*. The overcrowded proboscis monkeys feed on this species' shoots, not allowing enough time for foliage to regenerate.

10.4.3   Enforcing Protection

Even where forest habitats are accorded protected status, enforcement issues often impede effective conservation. Many national parks where proboscis monkeys live are badly degraded and encroached upon by various human activities, e.g. Kutai National Park and Tanjung Puting National Park (Meijaard & Nijman, 2000a). Encroachment on protected forests often occurs in stages, making it difficult to detect at first. For example, corporations often employ the 'salami tactic' (Stark & Flaherty, 2017), which consists of slicing an area by tiny bits until there is nothing left. This could include closing a river, building a road, building an additional port, bulking station or additional warehouse in the protected area, one at a time. Meanwhile, the concession can change owners, the company can change names, and there is often a long succession of different managers, investors and subcontractors. By the time significant geographic change has been detected, it is futile to trace those responsible.

Besides preventing habitat destruction, enforcement is also needed to mitigate hunting pressure. Hunting is not a major threat for the proboscis monkey populations occurring within predominantly Muslim coastal areas, as local people do not hunt primates (Sha et al., 2008). However, in some areas of inner Borneo, such as Danum Sentarum, hunting by local Christian Dayaks, migrants or plantation workers represents a serious threat, especially in the island's interior, such as Danum Sentarum (Stark et al., 2012). Due to their habit of sleeping along river banks, the proboscis monkeys are easy to hunt (Meijaard & Nijman, 2000a). Proboscis monkey numbers dropped by 50 per cent in one hunted area in Sarawak in only five years (Bennett & Gombek, 1993).

To assist with enforcement activities, NGOs and community-level programmes have been established. In Balikpapan Bay, regular environmental monitoring has been conducted since 2008. A small team of local fishermen surveys most of the area monthly, collecting data on all legal and illegal human activities that threaten the natural ecosystem. During ten years of operation, they have gradually developed an extensive network of local informants (fishermen, but even employees of corporations responsible for the major environmental damage). Due to this extensive network, most threats are detected early, sometimes before any damage happens. In Sabah, there is a special provision under the Sabah Wildlife Conservation Enactment (1997, No. 6) for appointments of Honorary Wildlife Wardens, which have been made since 2001. More than 300 persons, including men and women representing the private sectors, government agencies, NGOs and community leaders that are occasionally in close proximity to proboscis monkey habitats have been appointed. Statewide in Sabah these individuals can assist in carrying out some of the provisions of the enactment, including anti-wildlife poaching and wildlife habitat conservation. This effort has been successful to some extent in assisting the SWD in monitoring poaching activities and other crimes against wildlife.

10.4.4   Habitat Restoration

Proboscis monkey habitat that has been destroyed by human activities and/or forest fires can be rehabilitated once the land is afforded proper protection. Mangrove forests in particular are one of the most resilient habitats in Borneo, where natural regeneration can occur given enough time. Regeneration is more difficult for non-mangrove forests, such as freshwater riverine forests, which are more complex and richer in species composition, and often contain rare tree species or species with limited dispersal potential (Matsuda et al., 2018a). Many oil palm plantations are located on unsuitable land: 1400 ha of oil palm plantations in the Lower Kinabatangan Area are of limited productivity and could be rehabilitated (Matsuda et al., 2018b); however, restoration of non-mangrove forests is hampered by economic and sociopolitical factors, such as the costs of replanting and the price of the land that would have to be purchased.

Reforestation programmes have become increasingly popular in Indonesia and Malaysia. The northern part of the Klias peat swamp, which was badly burned by fire in 1997/8, has undergone a forest restoration project (over ten years) conducted by the Sabah Forestry Department, which has allowed it to recover to some extent. However, reforestation can also be abused through greenwashing activities by decision-makers and corporations. Sound science should be applied to ensure reforestation effectiveness, and erroneous practices should be discouraged. For example, planting mangrove species (most often *Rhizophora mucronata*, which are easy to grow in a nursery) at unsuitable sites, such as along open sandy beaches with strong waves or on coastal mudflats in deep-water tidal lines.

10.4.5 Mixed-Use Habitats Management

There is some evidence that proboscis monkeys can adapt to altered habitats, such as tree plantations. Large populations of proboscis monkeys have been reported in South Kalimantan rubber plantations (Soendjoto et al., 2005). These are not industrialised monocrop rubber plantations, but smallholder-owned plantations composed of rubber trees of different ages that are not intensively maintained. Proboscis monkeys can feed on rubber shoots as well as wild species like *Syzigium* spp.

Such an approach can theoretically be extended to other agroforestry systems that may contain fruit trees such as jackfruits, durians, rose apples, cotton fruits, etc., mixed with patches of natural secondary forest. An example of this environment-friendly agriculture system is currently being developed in the Sungai Hitam area (Atmoko, 2002), which contains a population of more than 140 proboscis monkeys. The riverbank is lined with a thin strip of mangroves, behind which there is a highly degraded shrubland and open secondary forest. The shrubland is now being replanted with a mixture of trees, including rubber and fruit trees. Such strategies must, however, consider the cost-effectiveness of small-yield agriculture and opportunity cost for other land use types, which can be improved with the promotion of organic or conservation-friendly products and ecotourism.

Oil palm plantations are the single largest cause of deforestation in Borneo (Buttler, 2013). Therefore, the possibility of conserving proboscis monkeys in palm oil plantations should be explored, as exemplified by the well-known but also rather controversial example of Labuk Bay (Sabah, Malaysia), a major ecotourism destination managed by the owner of the surrounding oil palm plantation (Tangah, 2012).

Other cases of proboscis monkey conservation in riparian zones within plantations include some multinational oil palm corporations (Wilmar International, 2013). The Zoological Society of London has supported this approach for conserving high-conservation-value species and habitats within oil palm landscapes (Persey et al., 2011). It is, however, not known if proboscis monkeys can survive in the linear forest habitat surrounded by oil palm plantations if there is not enough habitat connectivity.

10.4.6 *Ex-Situ* Conservation

As wild proboscis monkey habitats continue to decline unabated, *ex-situ* conservation can help safeguard the species by maintaining viable populations in captivity as assurance colonies. However, maintenance of the species outside their natural habitats is fraught with problems. Owing to their specialised diets, captive management and breeding has achieved limited success (Matsuda et al., 2018), although it is possible with careful husbandry practices (Agoramoorthy et al., 2004; Sha et al., 2013). There are currently very few populations of proboscis monkeys in captivity outside of its natural range, e.g. at the Wildlife Reserves Singapore (Sha et al., 2013), Yokohama Zoo, Japan (2009–present; Inoue et al., 2016) and Chimelong Zoo, China (since 2017). In general, it appears that zoos located in humid tropical climates are more successful in maintaining this species, while attempts to keep and breed proboscis monkeys in a temperate region of Europe and North America have so far failed and cannot be recommended.

Wherever proboscis monkeys have been successfully maintained and propagated in captivity, other issues will arise, such as dealing with excess animals, especially males (Sha et al., 2013). Difficulties with acquiring new bloodlines for captive collections limit their potential and increase inbreeding. Although zoos within the natural distribution range of the species like Lok Kawi Wildlife Park in Sabah are breeding proboscis monkeys successfully, it is difficult to export these animals outside their range countries.

Given the lack of space for cooperation among institutions, captive breeding can pose additional problems, rather than solving any of the existing issues. Zoos can, however, contribute to *in-situ* conservation by means of awareness raising, education, and fundraising. Many conservation programmes are also being supported by zoos like the Usti and Labem Zoo, Singapore Zoo, San Diego Zoo, the European Association of Zoos and Aquaria (EAZA), and the Dutch Association of Zoos.

10.4.7 Collaborations with the Private Sector

There have been examples of successful collaborations between conservationists and the private sector. For example, Sime Darby was one of the influential stakeholders lobbying to halt the proposal to build a bridge across the Kinabatangan River, an environmental case that eventually turned out to be successful (Vanar, 2017). Such corporations are increasingly obligated to manage conservation areas within plantation concessions (Leowinata, 2016) as mandated by the Indonesian legislation as well as by RSPO (Roundtable on Sustainable Palm Oil) Principles and Criteria (RSPO, 2013). Environmental impact assessments (EIAs) are also now mandatory for any project in Indonesia that requires a business permit from the government (Peraturan Pemerintah No. 27/1999 Tentang Analisis Mengenai Dampak Lingkungan Hidup), and this provides opportunities for dialogue between developers and conservationists to minimise development impact. Unfortunately, many if not most of these processes are still open to abuse through exploiting loopholes in the system, including corporate greenwashing and engaging some NGOs to provide positively biased EIA assessments.

10.4.8   Ecotourism

The proboscis monkey is a highly attractive ecotourism commodity that, with the exception of a few zoos, can only be found in the wild in Borneo. Ecotourism can be used as a tool to protect wild proboscis monkeys, with the best examples probably seen at the Kinabatangan River, although there is still much room for improving the conservation value of these activities (Leasor & Macgregor, 2014). Such tourism sites need to be soundly managed as proboscis monkey populations in improperly designed tourist reserves can become overcrowded and face starvation and social stress. The establishment of better-managed ecotourism sites should be encouraged, but careful consideration has to be given to prevent a saturation of such sites, which would dilute the tourist flow and the conservation impact of such activities.

10.5   Conclusions and Future Directions

Recent developments in scientific technology, such as next-generation sequencing (NGS), Global Positioning System (GPS) monitoring and unmanned aerial vehicle (UAV) techniques have given rise to numerous novel findings contributing to the progress of proboscis monkey research (Hale et al., 2018; Stark et al., 2017a; 2017b). Improved statistical modelling on population trends and population viability assessments will also assist in the development of species management plans based on sound science. The challenge, however, lies in whether these efforts could be successfully translated into conservation actions on the ground, where the political will of governments throughout proboscis monkey range countries will be integral to successful implementation. This is a difficult problem to surmount as actions beneficial to the conservation of wildlife and their habitats are often contrary to the goals of economic development.

The political situation is different across the proboscis monkey's range countries. In Sabah, suitable habitats for proboscis monkeys have already been lost or fragmented on a large scale. Given that wildlife-based tourism has become of increasing importance to the state's economy in recent years, the Sabahan government is now prioritising the protection of what is still left of the important habitats for proboscis monkeys, as well as restoration of degraded habitats, including the establishment of forest corridors to connect isolated habitat patches. This approach forms the integrated conservation strategy for the Sabah Proboscis Monkey Action Plan, which is being drafted by the SWD and Danau Girang Field Centre in collaboration with other institutions and experts. Critical to the successful progress of such initiatives is the active participation of wildlife management agencies like the SWD and strong support from the state government, working closely with NGOs and academics towards a common goal of conserving the species while benefiting the political agenda of the state authorities.

On the other hand, the situation is rather different in Indonesia, where extensive areas of proboscis monkey habitat still remain, but are increasingly threatened by changes in spatial planning which, if implemented, will cause unprecedented and rampant development of forest habitats at the expense of wildlife. Therefore, the current conservation approach is often rather antagonistic, with public campaigning against the government's plan being one of the main approaches. In 2012, several groups of Nature Enthusiasts (Pecinta Alam) around Balikpapan Bay formed a platform called Forum Peduli Teluk Balikpapan (FPTB), which focused on a 'hard' frontal campaign utilising demonstrations and other public events to create public pressure for more conservation efforts. However, a 'soft' campaign approach is simultaneously being applied, which focuses on highlighting the beauty and biodiversity values of Balikpapan Bay and promoting Balikpapan Bay as an ecotourism destination (Pusat Pengendalian Pembangunan Ekoregion Kalimantan Kementerian Lingkungan Hidup dan Kehutanan 2016). Such a diversified campaign approach has allowed us to make the first steps towards legal action, including police reports, legal environmental disputation or juridical review of provincial spatial plans. At the time of writing, Balikpapan Bay is being proposed as the new provincial marine protected area (Kawasan Konservasi Laut Daerah).

To ensure the long-term survival of proboscis monkeys, a multipronged approach is needed according to the context and political situation within different proboscis monkey range countries, where mechanisms beyond scientific inquiry should be employed to augment actions that can tilt the balance towards the conservation of this unique species.

Acknowledgements

Proboscis monkey research and conservation in Balikpapan Bay, Klias and Kinabatangan has been supported by Wildlife Reserves Singapore Conservation Fund, European Association of Zoos and Aquaria, South-East Asia Conservation Fund, Conservation Fund of the Dutch Zoos, Primate Conservation Inc., Primatological Society of Great Britain, Czech Coalition for Biodiversity Conservation, Sabah Wildlife Department, Sabah Forestry Department, Sabah Biodiversity Centre, JSPS KAKENHI, the National Geographic Society, Pro Natura Foundation Japan, Ministry of Higher Education Malaysia (MoHE), Hibi Science Foundation and Inamori Foundation.

References

Agoramoorthy, G., Alagappasamy, C. & Hsu, M. J. (2004). Can proboscis monkeys be successfully maintained in captivity? A case of swings and roundabouts. *Zoo Biology*, 23(6), 533–44.

Atmoko, T. (2002). Conservation of proboscis monkey and their isolated habitat in Kuala Samboja. In *East Kalimantan International Conference of Indonesia Forestry Researchers (INAFOR)*. Bogor: Forestry Research and Development Agency Indonesia, pp. 446–53.

Bennett, E. L. (1991). Diurnal primates. In Kiew, R. (ed.) *The State of Nature Conservation in Malaysia*. Kuala Lumpur: Malayan Nature Society, pp. 170–2.

Bennett, E. L. & Gombek, F. (1993). *Proboscis Monkeys of Borneo*. Kota Kinabalu: Natural History Publications.

Bennett, E. L. & Sebastian, A. C. (1988). Social organization and ecology of proboscis monkeys (*Nasalis larvatus*) in mixed coastal forest in Sarawak. *International Journal of Primatology*, 9(3), 233–55.

Bernard, H. & Zulhazman, H. (2006). Population size and distribution of the proboscis monkey (*Nasalis larvatus*) in the Klias Peninsula, Sabah, Malaysia. *Malayan Nature Journal*, 59(2), 1531–63.

Bernard, H., Matsuda, I., Hanya, G., et al. (2018). Feeding ecology of the proboscis monkey in Sabah, Malaysia, with special reference to plant species-poor forests. In Barnett, A. A., Matsuda, I. & Nowak, K. (eds) *Primates in Flooded Habitats: Ecology and Conservation*. Cambridge: Cambridge University Press.

Bismark, M. (1981). Preliminary survey of the proboscis monkey at Tanjung Putting Reserve, Kalimantan. *Tigerpaper*, 8, 26.

Bismark, M. (2010). Proboscis monkey (*Nasalis larvatus*): bio-ecology and conservation. In Gursky, S. & Supriatna, J. (eds) *Indonesian Primates*. New York: Springer, pp. 217–33.

Boonratana, R. (2000). Ranging behavior of proboscis monkeys (*Nasalis larvatus*) in the lower Kinabatangan, Northern Borneo. *International Journal of Primatology*, 21(3), 497–518.

Buttler, R. (2013). Palm oil now biggest cause of deforestation in Indonesia. *Mongabay*, 3 September.

Cowlishaw, G. (1999). Predicting the pattern of decline of African primate diversity: an extinction debt from historical deforestation. *Conservation Biology*, 13(5), 1183–93.

Feilen, K. L. & Marshall, A. J. (2014). Sleeping site selection by proboscis monkeys (*Nasalis larvatus*) in West Kalimantan, Indonesia. *American Journal of Primatology*, 76(12), 1127–39.

Gokkon, B. (2017). 'Ecological disaster': controversial bridge puts East Kalimantan's green commitment to the test. *Mongabay*, 30 August.

Hale, V. L., Tan, C. L., Niu, K., et al. (2018). Diet versus phylogeny: a comparison of gut microbiota in captive colobine monkey species. *Microbial Ecology*, 75(2), 515–27.

Inoue, E., Ogata, M., Seino, S. & Matsuda, I. (2016). Sex identification and efficient microsatellite genotyping using fecal DNA in proboscis monkeys (*Nasalis larvatus*). *Mammal Study*, 41(3), 141–8.

IUCN. (2008). *IUCN Red List of Threatened Species*. Gland: International Union for Conservation of Nature and Natural Resources (IUCN), Species Survival Commission (SSC).

Jeffrey, S. M. (1979). The proboscis monkey: some preliminary observations. *Tigerpaper*, 6, 5–6.

Kawabe, M. & Mano, T. (1972). Ecology and behavior of the wild proboscis monkey, *Nasalis larvatus* (Wurmb), in Sabah, Malaysia. *Primates*, 13(2), 213–27.

Koda, H., Tuuga, A., Goossens, B., et al. (2018). Nasalization by Nasalis larvatus: larger noses audiovisually advertise conspecifics in proboscis monkeys. *Science Advances*, 4(2). DOI: 10.1126/sciadv.aaq0250.

Kren, J. A. (1964). Observations on the habits of the proboscis monkey, *Nasalis larvatus* (Wurmb.), made in the Brunei Bay area, Borneo. *Zoologica*, 49, 183–92.

Leasor, H. C. & Macgregor, O. J. (2014). Proboscis monkey tourism: can we make it 'ecotourism'? In Russon, A. E. & Wallis, J. (eds) *Primate Tourism: A Tool for Conservation?* Cambridge: Cambridge University Press, pp. 56–75.

Leowinata, D. (2016). Borneo conservationists and top oil palm firm work to help orangutans. *Mongabay*, 9 August.

Lhota, S., Scott, K. S. S. & Sha, J. C. M. (2018). Primates in flooded forests of Borneo: opportunities and challenges for ecotourism as a conservation strategy. In Barnett, A. A., Matsuda, I. & Nowak, K. (eds) *Primates in Flooded Habitats: Ecology and Conservation*. Cambridge: Cambridge University Press.

Macdonald, D. W. (1982). Notes on the size and composition of groups of proboscis monkey, *Nasalis larvatus*. *Folia Primatologica*, **37**(1–2), 95–98.

Manansang, J., Traylor-Holzer, K., Reed, D. & Leus, K. (2005). Indonesian proboscis monkey population and habitat viability assessment: final report.

Matsuda, I., Tuuga, A. & Higashi, S. (2009a). The feeding ecology and activity budget of proboscis monkeys. *American Journal of Primatology*, **71**(6), 478–92.

Matsuda, I., Tuuga, A. & Higashi, S. (2009b). Ranging behavior of proboscis monkeys in a riverine forest with special reference to ranging in inland forest. *International Journal of Primatology*, **30**(2), 313–25.

Matsuda, I., Kubo, T., Tuuga, A. & Higashi, S. (2010). A Bayesian analysis of the temporal change of local density of proboscis monkeys: implications for environmental effects on a multilevel society. *American Journal of Physical Anthropology*, **142**(2), 235–45.

Matsuda, I., Tuuga, A. & Bernard, H. (2011a). Riverine refuging by proboscis monkeys (*Nasalis larvatus*) and sympatric primates: implications for adaptive benefits of the riverine habitat. *Mammalian Biology*, **76**(2), 165–71.

Matsuda, I., Murai, T., Clauss, M., et al. (2011b). Regurgitation and remastication in the foregut-fermenting proboscis monkey (*Nasalis larvatus*). *Biology Letters*, **7**(5), 786–9.

Matsuda, I., Sha, J. C., Ortmann, S., et al. (2015). Excretion patterns of solute and different-sized particle passage markers in foregut-fermenting proboscis monkey (*Nasalis larvatus*) do not indicate an adaptation for rumination. *Physiology & Behavior*, **149**, 45–52.

Matsuda, I., Bernard, H., Tuuga, A., et al. (2018). Fecal nutrients suggest diets of higher fiber levels in free-ranging than in captive proboscis monkeys (*Nasalis larvatus*). *Frontiers in Veterinary Science*, **4**. DOI: 10.3389/fvets.2017.00246.

Matsuda, I., Nakabayashi, M., Otani, Y., et al. (2018a). Comparison of plant diversity and phenology of riverine and mangrove forests with those of the dryland forest in Sabah, Borneo, Malaysia. In Barnett, A. A., Matsuda, I. & Nowak, K. (eds) *Primates in Flooded Habitats: Ecology and Conservation*. Cambridge: Cambridge University Press.

Matsuda, I., Abram, N. K., Stark, D. J., et al. (2018b). Population dynamics of proboscis monkeys (*Nasalis larvatus*) over space and time, in the Lower Kinabatangan, Sabah, Borneo, Malaysia. *Oryx*.

Meijaard, E. & Nijman, V. (2000a). Distribution and conservation of the proboscis monkey (*Nasalis larvatus*) in Kalimantan, Indonesia. *Biological Conservation*, **92**(1), 15–24.

Meijaard, E. & Nijman, V. (2000b). The local extinction of the proboscis monkey *Nasalis larvatus* in Pulau Kaget Nature Reserve, Indonesia. *Oryx*, **34**(1), 66–70.

Munshi-South, J. & Bernard, H. (2011). Genetic diversity and distinctiveness of the proboscis monkeys (*Nasalis larvatus*) of the Klias Peninsula, Sabah, Malaysia. *Journal of Heredity*, **102**(3), 342–6.

Murai, T., Mohamed, M., Bernard, H., et al. (2007). Female transfer between one-male groups of proboscis monkey (*Nasalis larvatus*). *Primates*, **48**(2), 117–21.

Muzani (2014). Mangrove management in Indonesia from laws on coastal and small islands. *Developing Country Studies*, **4**(25), 79–83.

Nowak, K. (2012). Mangrove and peat swamp forests: refuge habitats for primates and felids. *Folia Primatologica*, **83**, 361–76.

Persey, S., Imanuddin & Sadikin, L. (2011). *A Practical Handbook for Conserving High Conservation Value Species and Habitats Within Oil Palm Landscapes*. London: Zoological Society of London.

Roper, K. M., Scheumann, M., Wiechert, A. B., et al. (2014). Vocal acoustics in the endangered proboscis monkey (*Nasalis larvatus*). *American Journal of Primatology*, **76**(2), 192–201.

RSPO. (2013). Principals and criteria for the production of sustainable palm oil 2013.

Salgado-Lynn, M. (2010). *Primate Viability in a Fragmented Landscape: Genetic Diversity and Parasite Burden of Long-Tailed Macaques and Proboscis Monkeys in the Lower Kinabatangan Floodplain, Sabah, Malaysia*. Cardiff: Cardiff University.

Salter, R. E., MacKenzie, N. A., Nightingale, N., Aken, K. M. & Chai, P. K. P. (1985). Habitat use, ranging behaviour, and food habits of the proboscis monkey, *Nasalis larvatus* (van Wurmb), in Sarawak. *Primates*, **26**(4), 436–51.

Sha, J. C. M. & Matsuda, I. (2016). Protecting the proboscis. *Asian Geographic*, **116**, 34–9.

Sha, J. C. M., Bernard, H. & Nathan, S. (2008). Status and conservation of proboscis monkeys (*Nasalis larvatus*) in Sabah, east Malaysia. *Primate Conservation*, **23**(1), 107–20.

Sha, J. C., Alagappasamy, S., Chandran, S., Cho, K. M. & Guha, B. (2013). Establishment of a captive all-male group of proboscis monkey (*Nasalis larvatus*) at the Singapore Zoo. *Zoo Biology*, **32**(3), 281–90.

Soendjoto, M. A., Alikodra, H. S., Bismark, M. & Setijanto, H. (2005). Vegetasi tepi-baruh pada habitat bekantan (*Nasalis larvatus*) di hutan karet kabupaten Tabalong, Kalimantan Selatan. *Biodiversitas*, **6**(1), 40–4.

Stark, D. J., Nijman, V., Lhota, S., Robins, J. G. & Goossens, B. (2012). Modeling population viability of local proboscis monkey *Nasalis larvatus* populations: conservation implications. *Endangered Species Research*, **16**(1), 31–43.

Stark, D. J., Vaughan, I. P., Evans, L. J., et al. (2017a). Combining drones and satellite tracking as an effective tool for informing policy change in riparian habitats: a proboscis monkey case study. *Remote Sensing in Ecology and Conservation*. DOI: 10.1002/rse2.51.

Stark, D. J., Vaughan, I. P., Ramirez Saldivar, D. A., Nathan, S. K. & Goossens, B. (2017b). Evaluating methods for estimating home ranges using GPS collars: a comparison using proboscis monkeys (*Nasalis larvatus*). *PLoS ONE*, **12**(3), e0174891.

Stark, P. B. & Flaherty, J. (2017). *The Only Negotiating Guide You'll Ever Need, Revised and Updated: 101 Ways to Win Every Time in Any Situation*. New York: Crown Business.

Tangah, J. (2012). *The Ecology and Behaviour of Proboscis Monkey (Nasalis Larvatus) in Mangrove Habitat of Labuk Bay, Sabah*. Kota Kinabalu: Universiti Malaysia Sabah.

Thiry, V., Stark, D. J., Goossens, B., et al. (2016). Use and selection of sleeping sites by proboscis monkeys, *Nasalis larvatus*, along the Kinabatangan River, Sabah, Malaysia. *Folia Primatologica*, **87**(3), 180–96.

Vanar, M. (2017). Sabah scraps Sukau bridge project. *The Star Online*, 20 April.

Wilmar International (2013). No Peat. No Deforestation. No Exploitation Policy.

Yeager, C. P. (1989). Feeding ecology of the proboscis monkey (*Nasalis larvatus*). *International Journal of Primatology*, **10**(6), 497–530.

Yeager, C. P. (1991). Proboscis monkey (*Nasalis larvatus*) social organization: intergroup patterns of association. *American Journal of Primatology*, **23**(2), 73–86.

Part III

Climate Change in the Anthropocene

11 The Effects of Humans on the Primate Nutritional Landscape

A Review

Jessica M. Rothman and Margaret A. H. Bryer

11.1 Personal Narrative

I (JMR) declared my desire to attend Cornell University and improve animal health to my 'Careers' class when I was 11 years old. I was probably interested in animal biology because our elderly family cat developed diabetes and needed insulin injections along with frequent visits to the veterinarian. Trying to understand the balance of insulin and sugar intake needed for my beloved cat's health was fascinating to me and through this experience I realised that I wanted to improve the lives of animals in some way. I was born and raised in New York City, and I was drawn to wildlife through my visits to the Bronx Zoo. After spending a summer as an intern at the zoo studying captive gorillas as a junior undergraduate student at Cornell, I read a campus newspaper detailing graduate student John Berry's research on potential medicinal plant use by gorillas in the wild. I was enthralled by the idea of animals using their own rainforest medicines. I later met John personally and he generously not only allowed me to assist him with his laboratory research, but obtained funds for me to travel with him to Bwindi forest in Uganda. While climbing the steep hills to track the mountain gorillas in Uganda, I was perplexed that we knew very little about gorilla nutrition – a critical puzzle piece in the ecology and behaviour of these endangered apes. How could we protect them if we didn't even know how they obtained energy, protein and minerals! This summer trip in 1997 propelled me to return to Bwindi the following year to complete a nutritional analysis of the gorilla diet and to apply for graduate programmes in animal nutrition.

As a Cornell graduate student I focused on the nutritional ecology and parasite dynamics of these gorillas and applied my findings to conservation by working closely with the Uganda Wildlife Authority (UWA), the agency responsible for managing all wildlife in Uganda. My research focused mostly on the generation of baseline data for this highly endangered ape, and I integrated my results into park management plans in relation to movement, ecology and habitat use. For example, UWA now knows about the foods that are important to protect in the gorilla habitat, and some of the nutritional drivers for movement patterns.

After finishing my PhD, I was a postdoctoral fellow under the mentorship of Dr Colin Chapman, whose breadth of ecological and conservation experience offered new dimensions to my nutritional ecology research. While continuing work in Bwindi I also initiated research in Kibale National Park, focusing on diets and nutrition of forest monkeys. I became a faculty member at Hunter College in 2008 and was lucky to build an excellent team of students and postdoctoral scholars to tackle questions of nutritional ecology, not only in Uganda but through collaborative work with other primatologists across the globe. My co-author, Margaret Bryer, is currently a PhD candidate and part of this team. Through my longstanding research I was able to develop a Memorandum of Understanding with UWA, whereby our group's research fees fund the Master's tuitions of Ugandan park wardens focusing on nutrition- and conservation-related projects that have direct implications for park management, such as the impacts of crop raiding, exotic species and fragmentation on primate nutrition. Some of the findings from our research are discussed here. Unfortunately, as humans have a greater and greater impact on the globe, we will be hard-pressed to understand species' nutritional flexibility and adaptability to a changing world.

11.2   Introduction

Adequate nutrition is necessary for survival and reproduction of individual non-human primates, influencing the growth of populations. Human activities have altered the acquisition of food by primates, often causing a shift in dietary decisions that impact nutrition and ultimately demography. Here we discuss some of the ways that humans have affected primate nutrition through habitat fragmentation, introduction of exotic foods, the use of pesticides and toxins, provisioning, crop raiding and climate change. We hope this review will stimulate further nutritional research in these areas.

11.3   How Does Fragmentation Affect Primate Nutrition?

One of the most noticeable pressures that humans exert on primate populations is through the destruction of their habitats, including encroachment by communities surrounding primate habitats, logging within primate habitats or outright destruction to convert land to agricultural or urban areas. Though it is difficult to understand and predict the characteristics that allow some primates to survive and thrive better than others in fragmented landscapes (Onderdonk & Chapman, 2000), it is well documented that fragmentation of primate habitat causes a reduction in food availability due to the reduction in patch size available to primates (Arroyo-Rodriguez & Dias, 2010; Baranga et al., 2014; Boyle & Smith, 2010; Chaves et al., 2012; Mbora & Meikle, 2004; Worman & Chapman, 2006). Aside from an overall reduction in the amount of food available to primates, few generalisations about the effects of fragmentation can be made. In some fragments, primates have fewer food species to choose from compared to continuous forests, resulting in a decline in dietary diversity (Irwin, 2008), while in other areas dietary diversity in fragments increases because similar numbers of food species are available, but there are fewer of each type, forcing dietary switching (Chaves et al., 2012). Although it has not yet been studied explicitly, this forced dietary switching may result in a lower-quality diet, in addition to a reduction in the total mass of food consumed overall. Further, activity budgets are affected in fragments as primates generally travel less and rest more (Arroyo-Rodriguez & Dias, 2010; Wong & Sicotte, 2007). This reduction in energy expenditure lessens the amount of food that primates need (Campera et al., 2014). However, when forest fragments are large and degraded, primates could have larger ranges as a mechanism to search for food, and increased energy expenditure might be observed.

A well-studied example of the interactive effects of food availability, disease and stress is at our study site in Kibale National Park, Uganda. It was suggested by Colin Chapman and colleagues that red colobus monkeys in the fragmented areas surrounding the forest are affected by this reduction in food availability, which causes an interaction with immune response. Red colobus are then susceptible to more parasite infections. Together, synergies among food availability, parasite infection and immunity influence population change (Chapman et al., 2006). The authors used cortisol as a measure of nutritional stress, demonstrating that nutritional stress in this population may result from habitat fragmentation.

It is often difficult to tease apart the roles of food quantity and quality. In an earlier study in the fragments surrounding Kibale, Chapman and colleagues (2002) demonstrated that the protein–fibre ratio of the mature leaves in forest fragments predicted the abundance of red colobus and black-and-white colobus monkeys, accounting for 87 per cent of their variance in abundance (Chapman et al., 2004a). This model strongly suggested that the quality of foods, specifically the protein–fibre ratio, has an impact on monkey abundance. However, subsequent research did not show the same result (Gogarten et al., 2012; Johnson et al., 2017). The number of infants per female and group size of red colobus could not be predicted by this ratio (Gogarten et al., 2012). Additionally, regenerating forests had trees with higher protein–fibre ratios, but there was no correspondence with demographic change. While this study found no support for energy being a limiting factor for colobines, the ratio of protein to non-protein energy was the strongest predictor of patch occupancy for black-and-white colobus monkeys (Johnson et al., 2017), suggesting that we need to dig deeper to understand how food quality affects population abundance.

The effect of food reduction in fragments on actual nutrient acquisition by primates is less known, in part because very few studies investigate the nutritional compositions of the diets of primates in fragments. There are challenges to these investigations because primates in fragments tend to be more fearful of humans and habituation is not possible. The studies by Colin Chapman and colleagues have revealed some of the complexities of nutritional explanations for population declines. From studies of a variety of species, it is clear that the balance of nutrients, rather than a single nutrient, is important for animal foraging decisions (Raubenheimer et al., 2009). Like other animals, primates may regulate specific nutrients while consuming others in excess when faced with fluctuations in food availability (Felton et al., 2009a; 2009b; Rothman et al., 2011). A series of experiments by Irwin and colleagues tested hypotheses about nutrient balancing in sifakas (*Propithecus diadema*) living in fragmented and continuous forest. In intact forest these sifakas usually experience a 'lean' season in which they eat less and have a lower caloric intake, followed by a more productive season during which frugivory and energy intake increase. The sifakas in the disturbed habitats always experience this lean season, yet maintain the balance of protein to non-protein energy in their diets (Irwin et al., 2014; 2015). As primates are increasingly faced with fragmentation, it will be essential to understand which nutritional strategy they might use to adapt, based on their physiological, phylogenetic and environmental constraints.

11.4   Do Primates Eat Exotically Introduced Plants?

Exotic plants are those that are found outside their usual geographic area and were introduced by humans intentionally or accidentally into otherwise indigenous landscapes that contain endemic and non-endemic flora, termed native plants. Some exotic species spread rapidly, to the detriment of other plants and the overall environment, and are therefore considered invasive. Many primates face the choice of whether to consume exotic species or not, which may change due to the timing of exotic plant introduction, spatiotemporal variation in availability and/or nutritional content of exotic versus native foods.

Several researchers note that their study species have adapted and incorporated exotic species into their diets, including lemurs (*Eulemur fulvus*) that feed on exotic loquats (*Eriobotrya japonica*) (Figure 11.1; personal observation). Howler monkeys (*Alouatta caraya*) in Brazil consume fruits from introduced orange trees (*Citris sinensis*) as a major portion of their diets; the oranges featured in up to 26 per cent of the feeding records in some months of a one-year study (Bicca-Marques & Calegaro-Marques, 1994). Many lemurs frequently feed on introduced strawberry guava (*Psidium cattleyanum*), which is invasive (Harcourt, 1987; Tan, 1999; Yamashita, 1996), and even the specialised bamboo lemurs occasionally eat *Melaleuca* flowers, an invasive swamp plant (Eppley et al., 2015). In fact, Tecot (2007) reports that guava fruits (both ripe and unripe) were surprisingly the *only* food eaten in one month of her year-long study on red-bellied lemurs (*Eulemur rubriventer*), suggesting that it is a very important and nutritionally balanced resource.

While it is clear that primates rely on exotic plants in some areas as a food source, little is known about the actual nutrients provided by exotic foods compared to those that are indigenous in primate habitats. Presumably, since primates sometimes choose these exotic foods over indigenous species, they are higher in energy and/or protein than indigenous species, or perhaps they provide a specific important vitamin or mineral. For example, the introduced guava that many species of lemurs eat is not only high in sugar and antioxidants, but is also packed with vitamin C; it contains about four times the amount present in citrus fruit (Biegelmeyer et al., 2011).

In a matrix habitat of residential gardens and commercial plantations in the Cape province of South Africa, samango monkeys (*Cecopithecus albogularis labiatus*) consume large quantities of the seeds of the invasive black wattle (*Acacia mearnsii*) and acorns of two oak species (*Quercus* spp.) (Wimberger et al., 2017). These exotic species comprise over 50 per cent of their annual diet, particularly when indigenous

Figure 11.1 Red-fronted lemur (*Eulemur fulvus*) in Andasibe National Park, Madagascar foraging for unripe loquat fruit (*Eriobotrya japonica*), which was originally from China and is exotic to Madagascar.
Photo Credit: David Raubenheimer.

foods are not available. The consumption of both seeds and acorns is curious because the seeds and other parts of black wattle are extremely high in phenolic compounds, particularly condensed tannins, which bind protein and have detrimental health effects (Sherry, 1971). Though they are higher in fat than most primate foods, acorns are also high in hydrolysable tannins, which may be toxic in high quantities (Kirkpatrick & Pekins, 2002). Both of these exotic species should seemingly be avoided by these cercopithecine monkeys, though long retention times and other specialised gut physiology may enable these monkeys to cope with secondary compounds (Lambert, 2002a; 2002b).

An interesting case occurs in Uganda at our field sites. *Eucalyptus* spp. are native Australian trees that were introduced to Uganda in the late eighteenth century. In some areas of Bwindi Impenetrable National Park, *Eucalyptus* was planted as a boundary marker, and outside the park *Eucalyptus* is planted on community land. Similarly, *Eucalyptus* stands are found on the boundary of Kibale National Park because the community has chosen to plant them there. Interestingly, the bark of *Eucalyptus* is a favourite food of both mountain gorillas in Bwindi (Figure 11.2), and two species of colobus monkeys in Kibale. Harris and Chapman (2007) note that the ranging patterns of black-and-white colobus (*Colobus guereza*) were dictated by the distribution of

Figure 11.2 Mountain gorilla (*Gorilla beringei*) in Bwindi Impenetrable National Park, Uganda eating the bark of *Eucalyptus* spp.
Photo credit: Jane Rothman.

Eucalyptus. At both sites, primates are generally sodium deficient and only get sodium from a few sources such as patchily distributed decaying bark (Rothman et al., 2006c), or sodium-rich water plants in swampy areas (Oates, 1974). Surprisingly, the bark of *Eucalyptus* is high in sodium, similar to decaying wood sources (Rode et al., 2003), and much higher in sodium than plants found in the primates' natural diets (Cancelliere et al., 2014; Rode et al., 2003; Rothman et al., 2006c). The consumption of *Eucalyptus* by primates has implications for management. Mountain gorillas frequently come to the edge of the park to feed on *Eucalyptus*, but park management (like other agencies across the globe) is removing exotics from the park since they are by definition not part of the natural ecosystem. The removal of the *Eucalyptus* changes gorilla movement patterns, which presents a conundrum for management: the gorillas' attraction to *Eucalyptus* close to the forest edge enables tourists to view the gorillas more easily, yet the *Eucalyptus* is an exotic species that arguably should be removed. This example demonstrates the complexity of seemingly straightforward management decisions. The removal of an arguably invasive exotic could be detrimental to income from tourism, which is crucial to Ugandan conservation efforts.

11.5   What are the Nutritional Reasons for Primate Crop Feeding Behaviour?

Primates are known to consume human-cultivated crops when they are in close proximity to them, eliciting competition between humans and primates for food. 'Crop raiding' has been documented on all continents where primates exist, and though it occurs with respect to all degrees of dietary specialisation (Hill, 2017), it is more frequent among generalist primates such as baboons, vervets and macaques than among specialist frugivorous primates, such as chimpanzees, red-tailed monkeys and capuchins. Strict folivores such as colobus monkeys and langurs rarely feed on crop foods (but see Dela, 2011).

Potential benefits of consuming crops include: (1) a higher density of food in crop land than in natural habitat; and (2) an increase in the nutritional quality of crop foods compared to forest foods. In Kibale, baboons and forest monkeys consume crop foods when forest food availability is low (Naughton-Treves et al., 1998), but this does not seem to be the case for mountain gorillas in Bwindi. Seiler and Robbins (2015) found that Bwindi gorillas exploited crop foods opportunistically, with no relationship to food shortages within park boundaries. Though there were no food shortages *per se*, the density of crop foods was much higher than forest foods, making it easier for gorillas to access the foods, reducing energy expenditure (Seiler & Robbins, 2016). Human foods are usually bigger and denser than forest foods – consider, for example, a single pineapple compared to a single forest fruit. Regardless of nutritional composition, when they are in season, the availability of crop foods is usually higher than forest foods.

In general, cultivated foods tend to have a higher energy content due to fat and sugar compared to wild foods (Milton, 1999), but few studies have actually examined the nutrients in both the crop and wild foods that primates are consuming. Sugars and other non-structural carbohydrates are higher in the cultivated fruits that chimpanzees eat in Bulindi, Uganda than in forest fruits (McLennan & Ganzhorn, 2017). Cultivated fruits also have lower amounts of fibre and tannins. Similarly, the energy content of cacao is higher than forest foods eaten by Tonkean macaques (*Macaca tonkeana*) (Riley et al., 2013). Riley and colleagues (2013) suggest that both the quality and the availability of cacao compared to the natural diet drives crop feed behavior. It has been suggested that Bwindi mountain gorillas might consume banana pith for its high water content, and perhaps for its high concentration of non-structural carbohydrates compared to natural foods (Rothman et al., 2006a; 2006b).

11.6   Are Primates Exposed to Pesticides and Pollutants Through Their Diet?

Pesticides are used frequently on crop and tea plantations surrounding primate habitats, but we know little about their effects, if any, on primates. Pesticides are important to protect crops against disease and insect herbivores, but pesticides may also have endocrine-disrupting chemicals that affect a wide variety of the physiological functions of vertebrates relating to the endocrine, immune and reproductive systems (Colborn et al., 1993). Pesticides can also cause brain defects and various types of cancer (Mostafalou & Abdollahi, 2013). There are just a handful of studies that investigate whether primates are being exposed to pesticides, and most focus on organochlorine pesticides, which includes the infamous DDT and its derivatives, which is unfortunately still being used in some primate-habitat countries (Krief et al., 2017; Rainwater et al., 2009).

In an assessment of the organochlorine pesticides and metals in ring-tailed lemurs (*Lemur catta*) in the Beza Mahafaly Special Reserve in Madagascar, 14 pesticides and 13 metals were detected in blood and hair, and the lemurs were probably exposed through their leafy diets. Organochlorine pesticides are banned in Uganda but are apparently still in the soils, and potentially harmful levels have been documented in the areas around primate habitats, particularly in the areas surrounding endangered mountain gorillas and chimpanzees (Ssebugere et al., 2010). Preliminary research suggests that several pesticide residues are present in the foods consumed by mountain gorillas (Chemonges Amusa, personal communication). Krief et al. (2014) suggest that wild chimpanzees at the Sebatoli site in Kibale are affected by pesticides. Villages around the parks use eight different pesticides, and they can be detected in the sediments and soils along the borders of the forest. Some of these pesticides are thyroid disruptors, which is suggested to be the cause of observed facial dysplasia, though this has not yet been explicitly tested (Krief et al., 2017).

Little is known about the other environmental pollutants that primates might be exposed to through their diets. Captive rhesus macaques were exposed to several harmful heavy metals such as lead, mercury and arsenic, presumably through contaminated food and water, but they did not reach levels that are of clinical significance (Lee et al., 2012). Howler monkeys (*Alouatta pigra*) may have been exposed to lead through an anthropogenic flooding event (Serio-Silva et al., 2015) as lead was detected in hair at higher levels than in plants and soils.

We have minimal knowledge of how pesticides and other pollutants affect primate nutrition, but use of multiple pesticides in agriculture adjacent to continuous and fragmented habitat areas has wide-ranging and complex implications for primate nutritional landscapes. Through rapid transport through air, water and soil, spray pesticides likely have direct effects on plants eaten by primates. Cascading indirect effects on plants and primates may also occur: pesticides can kill key insect pollinators and cause a decline in beneficial microorganisms in soil, thereby influencing plant nutrient uptake and growth in primate habitats (Aktar et al., 2009; Sarnaik et al., 2006). As primates increasingly are forced to share space with humans, exposure to environmental pollutants and pesticides is inevitable. It will be important to establish baseline levels of these contaminants in relation to any clinical symptoms so that changes can be easily detected and addressed as soon as possible. In addition, it is important for primate researchers to learn more about the chemicals present in the ecosystems they study and to try to mitigate primate exposure.

11.7   How Does Provisioning by Tourists Affect Primate Nutrition?

For the purposes of this chapter, we define two types of tourist provisioning, typically by tourists, tourist agencies and possibly researchers. *Direct provisioning* occurs when visitors wish to attract primates for close viewing and interaction with animals in the wild; *indirect provisioning* occurs when humans enter the landscape of primates and inadvertently provide food through disposing of trash improperly, or when foods are available because they are not protected by a barrier (Figure 11.3). Direct provisioning is pervasive across several primate-viewing sites, particularly in Asia, where different species of macaques (*Macaca* spp.) are fed by tourists, tour operators or residents (Fuentes et al., 2008; Mallapur, 2013; Marechal et al., 2016; O'Leary & Fa, 1993), though it occurs in most primate-habitat countries (McKinney, 2011; Saj et al., 1999).

Perhaps the most notable examples of direct provisioning are in areas of South and Southeast Asia, where temples and their associated forests provide protection for various macaques that might otherwise inhabit small towns or cities. These temples attract large numbers of tourists who not only visit temples for their historical and religious significance, but also to view and feed the macaques (Stephenson et al., 2002). The macaques are provisioned by staff that work at these sites, frequently with carrots, sweet potatoes and rice, but also with high-fat and -carbohydrate foods such as cookies, potato chips, bread and biscuits (Hambali et al., 2012; Pragatheesh, 2011). The results of a 50-year study on free-ranging Japanese macaques (*Macaca fuscata*) that have been provisioned with sweet potatoes, wheat and soybeans in addition to natural foods demonstrated that provisioning has an impact on demography. After provisioning was reduced, the body mass of females decreased, birth percentages decreased, age at first reproduction increased and the population growth rate declined substantially (Kurita et al., 2008). In the Middle

Figure 11.3 Olive baboons (*Papio anubis*) trying to enter a researcher's kitchen in Kibale National Park, Uganda.
Photo credit: Jessica Rothman.

Atlas mountains of Morocco, 60 per cent of the diet of Barbary macaques was provisioned foods in some months (Marechal et al., 2016). While there are no quantitative assessments of the nutritional gains from these feedings, it is clear that increases in the amounts of energy and decreased activity patterns of the macaques impact their nutrition.

Perhaps the most extensive studies on the effects of indirect provisioning (garbage eating) on primates were conducted by Jeanne Altmann, Robert Sapolsky and colleagues. Over several years, the diets, growth rates, activity budgets and movement patterns of 2–6 groups of baboons were studied in Amboseli, Kenya. Two of these baboon groups at different sites were 'lodge' groups that mainly consumed human foods thrown away in the garbage dumps of tourist lodges, and rarely ate natural foods. The other groups ate diets typical of baboons, which included almost entirely vegetation such as grass blades, tubers, shrubs and corms (Altmann & Muruthi, 1988). Although the authors describe that both groups actually ate a surprisingly similar number of calories per day, the wild-foraging groups were much more active as they travelled about 60 per cent more than the lodge groups (Altmann & Muruthi, 1988; Altmann et al., 1993). Lodge baboons were larger in body mass, grew at faster rates and reached sexual maturity earlier than the wild-foraging groups (Altmann & Alberts, 2005). Lodge baboons were also fatter than the wild-foraging groups; individuals in lodge groups had about 23 per cent body fat, while wild-feeding individuals had 1.9 per cent (Altmann et al., 1993). The lodge baboons demonstrated clinical manifestations of obesity, heart disease and metabolic syndrome seen in humans. They had 2–3 times the serum insulin levels and increased total cholesterol compared to wild foraging groups (Kemnitz et al., 2002). Baboons in a lodge group had higher leptin (a protein secreted by fat cells) to body mass ratios compared to baboons that did not have access to garbage (Banks et al., 2003). Surprisingly, in these groups the energy and fat content of wild diets was deemed similar to that in the diet of lodge groups (Muruthi et al., 1991), though more sophisticated nutritional analyses did not seem to be available at the time to account for some of the potential discrepancies in digestibility of fats, proteins and energy (Altmann et al., 1987). Taken together, these studies on yellow baboons provide strong evidence that provisioning can have negative health consequences if food is eaten in excess, and baboons experience clinical symptoms of overeating similar to obese humans.

11.8   Are the Diets and Nutrition of Primates Affected by Climate Change?

Climate change is the shift in the earth's weather patterns as a result of human-induced or natural phenomena and is projected to have a large effect on all aspects of biodiversity (IPCC, 2002; Parmesan, 2006; Parmesan & Yohe, 2003). Climate change is already shifting the suitable ranges of animal and plant communities, with implications for the feeding ecology of primates. Three effects of climate change that affect the feeding and nutrition of primates are: (1) a change in the phenology of primate foods; (2) a change in the distribution of primate food plants; and (3) a change in the nutritional composition of the same trees.

One of the few long-term studies of phenology is from Kibale, where Tom Struhsaker conducted pioneering work in the 1970s and 1980s, and Colin Chapman continued this research starting in 1990. Chapman conducted his studies on phenology in the same manner as Struhsaker, thus extending the records of phenology from 1970 to the present. In 2002, Chapman and colleagues demonstrated that there was a high amount of temporal variability in the fruiting of trees, and he attributes this to climate change because rainfall and fruit production were related, and rainfall changed dramatically during the study (Chapman et al., 2004b). Changing phenology is especially important for primates that reproduce seasonally, such as many Malagasy lemurs. Lactation and fruiting peaks coincide, thus any change in fruiting peaks can have an effect on the life-history and reproduction of many seasonally breeding lemurs (Dunham et al., 2011; Wright, 2007). Infant survival is also related to rainfall (King et al., 2005).

While the change in reproductive cycling of fruits and leaves surely will have an effect on primate diet and dietary switching, it is also imperative that we consider that specialist primates could experience unique challenges meeting their nutritional needs. Grazing geladas (*Theropithecus gelada*) eat a diet almost solely composed of grasses (Dunbar, 1998; Fashing et al., 2014). They avoid areas that have non-grass vegetation, and because their diets are probably tannin-free, they do not have any adaptations to deal with tannins in leafy diets (Mau et al., 2009). Dunbar (1998) demonstrates, through a modelling approach, that the gelada habitat will be greatly reduced with climate change. If there is a 7°C rise in ambient mean temperature, the montane grassland habitat of geladas in Ethiopia will be greatly reduced, and the geographical range will become limited. Since geladas mainly survive on grass and are never seen in forest, they are unlikely to survive if climate change restricts their range (Dunbar, 1998). This is likely true for other primates that live in habitats that have a very small range; in a meta-analysis, rarity (small geographic range and low local density) in primates was related to dietary and habitat specialisation, suggesting that the most specialist primates are the most vulnerable to habitat shifts (Harcourt et al., 2002).

In addition to the more obvious changes such as the ones described above, it is also essential to understand the unexpected or more subtle cascading effects of climate change. One of these effects may be alterations in the nutritional quality of tree leaves and grasses – the food source at the base of most terrestrial food chains. Through mostly experimental studies, it has been demonstrated that elevated temperature, rainfall and CO_2 reduces protein and increases fibre, and increases plant defensive compounds, all of which could have a severe impact on animal nutrition (Rothman et al., 2015). In the 1970s the leaves eaten by red colobus monkeys were collected in Kibale National Park by Tom Struhsaker and analysed for their nutritional composition. We reanalysed the mature leaves from this same tree community and found a 10 per cent increase in fibre over 30 years. The protein–fibre ratio of young leaves declined as well over a 15-year period. Though the protein–fibre model has flaws as described above, it predicts a 31 per cent decline in colobine populations if these declines are generalisable to the rest of the forest (Rothman et al., 2015). Luckily these population declines have not been documented through recent censuses; group sizes of colobines are increasing (Gogarten et al., 2015), and group densities are stable (Chapman et al., 2010), suggesting that colobines in Kibale are not yet affected by these nutritional declines. It will be increasingly important to understand how primates are able to adapt to climate change, which is difficult to predict (Moser & Ekstrom, 2010).

11.9   Summary and Conclusions

While compiling this review, we were surprised that there were only a few studies addressing the effects of humans on primate nutrition. Many studies have reported dietary differences, but few report actual nutritional composition of foods and diets. In addition, baseline data on the nutritional ecology of healthy primates living in relatively intact habitat are needed as a point of reference for anthropogenic disturbance. We need to understand species' nutritional flexibility in a number of habitats, given the intraspecific variability in primate ecology and behaviour (Strier, 2009). It is clear that we need long-term research to continue, and that these long-term studies must monitor both availability and nutritional quality of foods, as these measures will give insight into primate health. We suggest that researchers measure not only food availability over time, but nutrient availability as well where resources are available. There are also many exciting avenues for research that will help us understand human impacts on primate nutrition. For example, despite the known effects of sun exposure, wind and temperature on the physiology of trees, we do not know how tree quality varies in relation to distance to the forest edge (Ganzhorn, 1992). We also need to understand how pollinators of primate foods are potentially affected by pesticide use, and how toxic chemicals ingested by primates might interact or reduce the digestion of nutrients. We know little about how fragmentation affects the nutritional quality of plants, and how nutrition may change in herbaceous vegetation as well as tree leaves and fruits. It is also critical that we move from examining single nutrients in isolation and measure nutrient balance. Studies in primatology have also focused on protein, and while protein can be a limiting nutrient for primates, it is also imperative that energy estimates are included in nutritional ecology studies.

Through our studies, we note that working closely with government agencies, conservation organisations and other in-country partners can provide fruitful results that will help in primate conservation (Rothman et al., 2014). Since nutrition is a key to primate survival, understanding the drivers of feeding behaviours and the consequences of nutritional shortfalls is essential. We have worked closely with park wardens to generate research that is relevant to management plans, and we have also tried to communicate our science effectively through public relations within Uganda (Gessa & Rothman, 2018). We hope that future studies on nutritional ecology will shed light on primate adaptability and survival in the Anthropocene.

Acknowledgements

We are grateful to Alison Behie, Julie Teichroeb and Nicholas Malone for inviting us to contribute to this book. We thank Annika Felton and Wendy Erb for their helpful comments on the manuscript. We are grateful to the National Science Foundation for supporting our work and we thank the Uganda Wildlife Authority and the Uganda National Council for Science and Technology for permission to work in Uganda.

References

Aktar, W., Sengupta, D. & Chowdhury, A. (2009). Impact of pesticides use in agriculture: their benefits and hazards. *Interdisciplinary Toxicology*, 2(1), 1–12.

Altmann, J. & Alberts, S. C. (2005). Growth rates in a wild primate population: ecological influences and maternal effects. *Behavioral Ecology and Sociobiology*, 57(5),490–501.

Altmann, J. & Muruthi, P. (1988). Differences in daily life between semiprovisioned and wild-feeding baboons. *American Journal of Primatology*, 15, 213–21.

Altmann, S. A., Post, D. G. & Klein, D. F. (1987). Nutrients and toxins of plants in Amboseli, Kenya. *African Journal of Ecology*, 25(4), 279–93.

Altmann, J., Schoeller, D., Altmann, S. A., Muruthi, P. & Sapolsky, R. M. (1993). Body size and fatness of free-living baboons reflect food availability and activity levels. *American Journal of Primatology*, 30(2), 149–61.

Arroyo-Rodriguez, V. & Dias, P. A. D. (2010). Effects of habitat fragmentation and disturbance on howler monkeys: a review. *American Journal of Primatology*, 72, 1–6.

Banks, W. A., Altmann, J., Sapolsky, R. M., Phillips-Conroy, J. E. & Morley, J. E. (2003). Serum leptin levels as a marker for a syndrome x-like condition in wild baboons. *Journal of Clinical Endocrinology and Metabolism*, 88, 1234–40.

Baranga, D., Chapman, C. A., Mucunguzi, P. & Reyna-Hurtado, R. (2014). Fragments and food: red-tailed monkey abundance in privately owned forest fragments of Central Uganda. In Marsh, L. & Chapman, C. A. (eds) *Primates in Fragments: Complexity and Resilience*. New York: Springer Science Business, pp. 213–25.

Bicca-Marques, J. C. & Calegaro-Marques, C. (1994). Exotic plant species can serve as staple food sources for wild howler populations. *Folia Primatologica*, 63, 209–11.

Biegelmeyer, R., Mello Andrade, J. M., Aboy, A. L., et al. (2011). Comparative analysis of the chemical composition and antioxidant activity of red (*Psidium cattleianum*) and yellow (*Psidium cattleianum* var. lucidum) strawberry guava fruit. *Food Chemistry*, 76, C991–C996.

Boyle, S. A. & Smith, A. T. (2010). Can landscape and species characteristics predict primate presence in forest fragments in the Brazilian Amazon? *Biological Conservation*, 143, 1134–43.

Campera, M., Serra, V., Balestri, M., et al. (2014). Effects of habitat quality and seasonality on ranging patterns of collared brown lemur (*Eulemur collaris*) in littoral forest fragments. *International Journal of Primatology*, 35, 957–75.

Cancelliere, E. C., DeAngelis, N., Nkurunungi, J. B., Raubenheimer, D. & Rothman, J. M. (2014). Minerals in the foods eaten by mountain gorillas (*Gorilla beringei*). *PLoS One*, 9(11), e112117.

Chapman, C. A., Chapman, L. J., Bjorndal, K. A. & Onderdonk, D. A. (2002). Application of protein-to-fiber ratios to predict colobine abundance on different spatial scales. *International Journal of Primatology*, 23(2), 283–310.

Chapman, C. A., Chapman, L. J., Naughton-Treves, L., Lawes, M. J. & McDowell, L. R. (2004a). Predicting folivorous primate abundance: validation of a nutritional model. *American Journal of Primatology*, 62(2), 55–69.

Chapman, C. A., Chapman, L. J., Struhsaker, T. T., et al. (2004b). A long-term evaluation of fruit phenology: importance of climate change. *Journal of Tropical Ecology*, 21, 1–14.

Chapman, C. A., Wasserman, M. D., Gillespie, T. R., et al. (2006). Do nutrition, parasitism, and stress have synergistic effects on red colobus populations living in forest fragments? *American Journal of Physical Anthropology*, **131**, 525–34.

Chapman, C. A., Struhsaker, T. T., Skorupa, J., Snaith, T. V. & Rothman, J. M. (2010). Understanding long-term primate community dynamics: implications for forest change. *Ecological Applications*, **20**, 179–91.

Chaves, O. M., Stoner, K. E. & Arroyo-Rodriguez, V. (2012). Differences in diet between spider monkey groups living in forest fragments and continuous forest in Mexico. *Biotropica*, **44**, 105–33.

Colborn, T., vom Saal, F. S. & Soto, A. M. (1993). Developmental effects of endocrine-disrupting chemicals in wildlife and humans. *Environmental Health Perspectives*, **101**, 378–84.

Dela, J. D. S. (2011). Western purple-faced langurs (*Semnopithecus vetulus nestor*) feed on ripe and ripening fruits in human-modified environments in Sri Lanka. *International Journal of Primatology*, **33**(1), 40–72.

Dunbar, R. I. M. (1998). Impact of global warming on the distribution and survival of the gelada baboon: a modeling approach. *Global Change Biology*, **4**, 293–304.

Dunham, A., Erhart, E. M. & Wright, P. C. (2011). Global climate cycles and cyclones: consequences for rainfall patterns and lemur reproduction in southeastern Madagascar. *Global Change Biology*, **17**, 219–27.

Eppley, T. M., Donati, G., Ramanamanjato, J. B., et al. (2015). The use of an invasive species habitat by a small folivorous primate: implications for lemur conservation in Madagascar. *PLoS One*, **10**, e0140981.

Fashing, P. J., Nguyen, N., Venkataraman, V. V. & Kerby, JT. (2014). Gelada feeding ecology in an intact ecosystem at Guassa, Ethiopia: variability over time and implications for theropith and hominin dietary evolution. *American Journal of Physical Anthropology*, **155**, 1–16.

Felton, A. M., Felton, A., Lindenmayer, D. B. & Foley, W. J. (2009a). Nutritional goals of wild primates. *Functional Ecology*, **23**, 70–8.

Felton, A. M., Felton, A., Raubenheimer, D., et al. (2009b). Protein content of diets dictates the daily energy intake of a free-ranging primate. *Behavioral Ecology*, **20**(4), 685–90.

Fuentes, A., Kalchik, S., Gettler, L., et al. (2008). Characterizing human–macaque interactions in Singapore. *American Journal of Primatology*, **70**, 879–83.

Ganzhorn, J. U. (1992). Leaf chemistry and the biomass of folivorous primates in tropical forests: tests of a hypothesis. *Oecologia*, **91**, 540–7.

Gessa, S. J. & Rothman, J. M. (2018). The role of public relations in primate conservation: examples from Uganda. In preparation.

Gogarten, J. F., Guzman, M., Chapman, C. A., et al. (2012). What is the predictive power of the colobine protein-to-fiber model and its conservation value? *Tropical Conservation Science*, **5**, 381–93.

Gogarten, J. F., Jacob, A. L., Ghai, R. R., et al. (2015). Group size dynamics over 15+ years in an African forest primate community. *Biotropica*, **47**, 101–12.

Hambali, K., Ismail, A., Zulkifli, S. Z. & Amir, A. (2012). Human–macaque conflict and pest behaviors of long-tailed macaques (*Macaca fascicularis*) in Kuala Selangor Nature Park. *Tropical Natural History*, **12**, 189–205.

Harcourt, A. H., Coppeto, S. A. & Parks, S. A. (2002). Rarity, specialization and extinction in primates. *Journal of Biogeography*, **29**, 445–56.

Harcourt, C. (1987). Brief trap/retrap study of the brown mouse lemur (*Microcebus rufus*). *Folia Primatologica*, **49**, 209–11.

Harris, T. R. & Chapman, C. A. (2007). Variation in diet and ranging of black and white colobus monkeys in Kibale National Park, Uganda. *Primates*, **48**, 208–21.

Hill, C. M. (2017). Primate crop feeding behavior, crop protection, and conservation. *International Journal of Primatology*, **2**, 385–400.

IPCC. (2002). *Climate Change and Biodiversity*. IPCC Technical Paper V. Geneva: IPCC.

Irwin, M. T. (2008). Feeding ecology of *Propithecus diadema* in forest fragments and continuous forest. *International Journal of Primatology*, **29**, 95–115.

Irwin, M. T., Raharison, J. L., Raubenheimer, D., Chapman, C. A. & Rothman, J. M. (2014). Nutritional correlates of the 'lean season': effects of seasonality and frugivory on the nutritional ecology of diademed sifakas. *American Journal of Physical Anthropology*, **153**, 78–91.

Irwin, M. T., Raharison, J. L., Raubenheimer, D. R., Chapman, C. A. & Rothman, J. M. (2015). The nutritional geometry of resource scarcity: effects of lean seasons and habitat disturbance on nutrient intakes and balancing in wild sifakas. *PLoS One*, **10**(6), e0128046.

Johnson, C. A., Raubenheimer, D., Chapman, C. A., et al. (2017). Macronutrient balancing affects patch departure by guerezas (*Colobus guereza*). *American Journal of Primatology*, **79**, e22495.

Kemnitz, J. W., Sapolsky, R. M., Muruthi, P., Mott, G. E. & Stefanick, M. L. (2002). Effects of food availability on serum insulin and lipid concentrations in free-ranging baboons. *American Journal of Primatology*, **57**, 13–19.

King, S. J., Arrigo-Nelson, S., Pochron, S. T., et al. (2005). Dental senescence in a long-lived primate links infant survival to rainfall. *Proceedings of the National Academy of Sciences*, **102**, 16579–83.

Kirkpatrick, R. L. & Pekins, P. J. (2002). Nutritional value of acorns for wildlife. In McShea W. J. & Healy, W. M. (eds) *Oak Forest Ecosystems: Ecology and Management for Wildlife*. Baltimore, MD: Johns Hopkins University Press, pp. 173–81.

Krief, S., Cibot, M., Bortolamiol, S., et al. (2014). Wild chimpanzees on the edge: nocturnal activites in croplands. *PLoS One*, **9**, e109925.

Krief, S., Berny, P., Gumisiriza,F., et al. (2017). Agricultural expansion as risk to endangered wildlife: pesticide exposure in wild chimpanzees and baboons displaying facial dysplasia. *Science of the Total Environment*, **598**, 647–56.

Kurita, H., Sugiyama, Y., Ohsawa, H., Hamada, Y. & Watanabe, T. (2008). Changes in demographic parameters of *Macaca fuscata* at Takasakiyama in relation to decrease in provisioned foods. *International Journal of Primatology*, **29**, 1189–202.

Lambert, J. E. (2002a). Digestive retention times in forest guenons (*Cercopithecus* spp.) with reference to chimpanzee (*Pan troglodytes*). *International Journal of Primatology*, **23**, 1169–85.

Lambert, J. E. (2002b). Resource switching in guenons: a community analysis of dietary flexibility. In Glenn, M. & Cords, M. (eds) *The Guenons: Diversity and Adaptation in African Monkeys*. New York: Kluwer Academic Press, pp. 303–17.

Lee, J., Jung, W. Y., Lee, G., et al. (2012). Heavy metal concentrations in hair of newly imported China-origin rhesus macaques (*Macaca mulatta*). *Laboratory Animal Research*, **28**, 151–4.

Mallapur, A. (2013). Macaque tourism: implications for their management and conservation. In Radhakrishna, S. (ed.) *The Macaque Connection: Cooperation and Conflict Between Humans and Macaques*, London: Springer Science and Businees Media, pp. 93–105.

Marechal, L., Semple, S., Majolo, B. & MacLarnon, A. (2016). Assessing the effects of tourist provisioning on the health of wild Barbary macaques in Morocco. *PLoS One*, **11**, e0155920.

Mau, M., Sudekum, K. H., Johann, A., Sliwa, A. & Kaiser, T. M. (2009). Saliva of the graminivorous *Theropithecus gelada* lacks proline-rich proteins and tannin-binding capacity. *American Journal of Primatology*, **71**, 663–9.

Mbora, D. N. M. & Meikle, D. B. (2004). Forest fragmentation and the distribution, abundance and conservation of the Tana river red colobus. *Biological Conservation*, **2004**, 67–77.

McKinney, T. (2011). The effects of provisioning and crop raiding on the diet and foraging activities of human-commensal white-faced capuchins (*Cebus capucinus*). *American Journal of Primatology*, **73**, 439–48.

McLennan, M. R. & Ganzhorn, J. U. (2017). Nutritional characteristics of wild and cultivated foods for chimpanzees (*Pan troglodytes*) in agricultural landscapes. *International Journal of Primatology*, **38**, 122–50.

Milton, K. (1999). Nutritional characteristics of wild primate foods: do the diets of our closest living relatives have lessons for us? *Nutrition*, 15, 488–98.

Moser, S. C. & Ekstrom, J. A. (2010). A framework to diagnose barriers to climate change. *Proceedings of the National Academy of Sciences*, 107, 22026–31.

Mostafalou, S. & Abdollahi, M. (2013). Pesticides and human chronic diseases: evidences, mechanisms, and perspectives. *Toxicology and Applied Pharmacology*, 268, 157–77.

Muruthi, P., Altmann, J. & Altmann, S. (1991). Resource base, parity, and reproductive condition affect females' feeding time and nutrient intake within and between groups of baboon populations. *Oecologia*, 87, 467–72.

Naughton-Treves, L., Treves, A., Chapman, C. & Wrangham, R. (1998). Temporal patterns of crop-raiding by primates: linking food availability in croplands and adjacent forest. *Journal of Applied Ecology*, 35, 596–606.

O'Leary, H. O. & Fa, J. E. (1993). Effects of tourists on Barbary macaques at Gibraltar. *Folia Primatologica*, 61, 77–91.

Oates, J. F. (1974). *The Ecology and Behaviour of the Black-and-White Colobus Monkey (Colobus guereza Ruppell) in East Africa.* London: University of London.

Onderdonk, D. A. & Chapman, C. A. (2000). Coping with forest fragmentation: the primates of Kibale National Park, Uganda. *International Journal of Primatology*, 21, 587–611.

Parmesan, C. (2006). Ecological and evolutionary responses to recent climate change. *Annual Review in Ecology and Evolutionary Systematics*, 37, 637–9.

Parmesan, C. & Yohe, G. A. (2003). A globally coherent fingerprint of climate change impacts across natural systems. *Nature*, 421, 37–42.

Pragatheesh, A. (2011). Effect of human feeding on the road mortality of rhesus macaques on National Highway 7 routed along Pench Tiger Reserve, India. *Journal of Threatened Taxa*, 3, 1656–62.

Rainwater, T. R., Sauther, M. L., Rainwater, K. A. E., et al. (2009). Assessment of organochlorine pesticides and metals in ring-tailed lemurs (*Lemur catta*) at Beza Mahafaly Special Reserve, Madagascar. *American Journal of Primatology*, 71, 998–1010.

Raubenheimer, D., Simpson, S. J. & Mayntz, D. (2009). Nutrition, ecology and nutritional ecology: toward an integrated framework. *Functional Ecology*, 23, 4–16.

Riley, E. P., Tolbert, B. & Farida, W. R. (2013). Nutritional content explains the attractiveness of cacao to crop raiding Tonkean macaques. *Current Zoology*, 59, 160–9.

Rode, K. D., Chapman, C. A., Chapman, L. J. & McDowell, L. R. (2003). Mineral resource availability and consumption by colobus in Kibale National Park, Uganda. *International Journal of Primatology*, 24, 541–73.

Rothman, J. M., Dierenfeld, E. S., Molina, D. O., et al. (2006a). Nutritional chemistry of foods eaten by gorillas in Bwindi Impenetrable National Park, Uganda. *American Journal of Primatology*, 68, 675–91.

Rothman, J. M., Pell, A. N., Nkurunungi, J. B., et al. (2006b). Nutritional aspects of the diet of wild gorillas: how do Bwindi gorillas compare? In Newton-Fisher, N. E., Notman, H., Paterson, J. D. & Reynolds, V. (eds) *Primates of Western Uganda.* New York: Kluwer Academic, pp.153–69.

Rothman, J. M., Van Soest, P. J. & Pell, A. N. (2006c). Decaying wood is a sodium source for mountain gorillas. *Biology Letters*, 2, 321–4.

Rothman, J. M., Raubenheimer, D. & Chapman, C. A. (2011). Nutritional geometry: gorillas prioritize non-protein energy while consuming surplus protein. *Biology Letters*, 7, 847–9.

Rothman, J. M., Makombo, J., Tumwesigye, C., Rwetsiba, A. & Chapman, C. A. (2014). Integrating research into primate conservation: insights from Uganda. *American Journal of Physical Anthropology*, 153, 225.

Rothman, J. M., Chapman, C. A., Struhsaker, T. T., et al. (2015). Long-term declines in nutritional quality of tropical leaves. *Ecology*, 96, 873–8.

Saj, T., Sicotte, P. & Paterson, J. D. (1999). Influence of human food consumption on the behaviour of vervets. *International Journal of Primatology*, 70, 977–94.

Sarnaik, S. S., Kanekar, P. P., Raut, V. M., et al. (2006). Effect of application of different pesticides to soybean on the soil microflora. *Journal of Environmental Biology*, **37**(2), 423–6.

Seiler, N. & Robbins, M. M. (2015). Behavioural flexibility by mountain gorillas when ranging on community land and feeding on crops. *Folia Primatologica*, **86**, 356–357.

Seiler, N. & Robbins, M. M. (2016). Factors influencing ranging on community land and crop raiding by mountain gorillas. *Animal Conservation*, **19**, 176–88.

Serio-Silva, J. C., Olguin, E. J., Garcia-Feria, L., Tapia-Fierro, K. & Chapman, C. A. (2015). Cascading impacts of anthropogenically driven habitat loss: deforestation, flooding, and possible lead poisoning in howler monkeys (*Alouatta pigra*). *Primates*, **56**, 29–35.

Sherry, S. P. (1971). *The Black Wattle (Acacia mernsii De Wild)*. Pietermaritzburg: University of Natal Press.

Ssebugere, P., Wasswa, J., Mbabazi, J., et al. (2010). Organochlorine pesticides in soils from south-western Uganda. *Chemosphere*, **78**, 1250–5.

Stephenson, R. A., Kurashina, H., Iverson, T. J. & Chiang, L. N. (2002). Visitors' perceptions of cultural improprieties in Bali, Indonesia. *Journal of National Parks*, **12**, 156–69.

Strier, K. B. (2009). Seeding the forest through the seeds: mechanisms of primate behavioral diversity from individuals to populations and beyond. *Current Anthropology*, **50**, 213–28.

Tan, C. L. (1999). Group composition, home range size, and diet of three sympatric bamboo lemur species (genus *Hapalemur*) in Ranomafana National Park, Madagascar. *International Journal of Primatology*, **20**, 547–66.

Tecot, S. R. (2007). Seasonality and predictability: the hormonal and behavioral responses of the red-bellied lemur, *Eulemur rubriventer*, in southeastern Madagascar. PhD dissertation, University of Texas at Austin.

Wimberger, K., Nowak, K. & Hill, R. A. (2017). Reliance on exotic plants by two groups of threatened samango monkeys, *Cercopithecus albogularis labiatus,* at their southern range limit. *International Journal of Primatology*, **38**, 151–71.

Wong, S. N. P. & Sicotte, P. (2007). Activity budget and ranging patterns of *Colobus vellerosus* in forest fragments in Central Ghana. *Folia Primatologica*, **78**, 245–54.

Worman, C. O. & Chapman, C. A. (2006). Densities of two frugivorous primates with respect to forest and fragment tree species composition and fruit availability. *International Journal of Primatology*, **27**, 203–25.

Wright, P. C. (2007). Considering climate change effects in lemur ecology and conservation. In Gould, L. & Sauther, M. L. (eds) *Lemurs: Ecology and Adapatation*. New York: Springer Science and Business Media, pp. 385–401.

Yamashita, N. (1996). Seasonality and site specificity of mechanical dietary patterns in two Malagasy lemur families (Lemuridae and Indriidae). *International Journal of Primatology*, **17**(3), 355–87.

12 Using Vegetation Phenology and Long-Term Demographic Data to Assess the Impact of Cyclone Fanele on a Lemur Population in Madagascar

Rebecca Lewis and Anne Axel

12.1 Personal Narrative

I (RL) knew I wanted to be a primatologist from the time I was eight years old. While it is cliché for my generation, watching nature shows and reading *National Geographic* magazines with images of Jane Goodall, Dian Fossey and Birutė Galdikas studying apes in the wild was inspirational. The similarities between ape and human behaviour fascinated me. I studied biological anthropology and anatomy at Duke University for my undergraduate education, including a senior honour's thesis on female dominance in free-ranging red-fronted lemurs (*Eulemur rufifrons*) at the Duke Lemur Center. After graduation, I volunteered collecting data on the behavioural ecology of two sympatric species of lemurs (diademed sifaka (*Propithecus diadema*) and indri (*Indri indri*)) in the montane rainforest of Mantadia National Park, Madagascar, and on captive pigtail (*Macaca nemestrina*) and rhesus macaques (*Macaca mulatta*) in Louisiana. These experiences solidified my desire to study primates in their natural habitats. I returned to Duke University for my PhD to study bonobos (*Pan paniscus*) and the evolution of intersexual power. However, the Democratic Republic of Congo was in turmoil in the late 1990s, so amid concerns over safety I had to shift my research focus away from wild bonobos. Indeed, it is not uncommon for factors such as political unrest, disease outbreaks, natural/anthropogenic disasters and logistical realities to influence conservation and field research. I ultimately studied cooperation, conflict and power in intersexual relationships in Verreaux's sifaka (*Propithecus verreauxi*) in the Kirindy Forest of Madagascar. While the species and the locations changed, I always focused on the social behaviour of primates.

Sometimes I describe myself as a primate psychologist rather than a primate ecologist because the social relationships interest me most. Everything else – ecology, morphology, physiology, genetics, health – are all topics that I study so that I can better understand the function of social behaviour. After my PhD, I had planned to switch my research focus to an anthropoid and questions about how primates negotiate their social relationships. My research on sifaka, however, led me to ask more questions about why they behave the way that they do. Sifaka, it turns out, are a great study subject for someone interested in challenging existing behavioural theory because they often do not fit expectations.

I explored several possibilities for setting up a new field site to study sifaka (*Propithecus deckeni*, *P. coronatus* or *P. coquereli*) in northwestern Madagascar, but was disappointed to find mostly small, highly disturbed forest fragments and that the sifaka were heavily hunted – not great conditions for long-term behavioural research. When I learned about a relatively new protected area that encompasses the transition among three ecosystems (dry deciduous forest on the west, spiny desert on the south and coastal mangroves) and that includes habitat for Verreaux's sifaka, ring-tailed lemurs (*Lemur catta*) and red-fronted lemurs (*Eulemur rufifrons*), I decided that this location would be a great opportunity for me to study sifaka social behaviour.

In 2006 I set up a new field site and began developing the Ankoatsifaka Research Station in the Kirindy Mitea National Park (KMNP) with the anticipation of studying the social relationships of sifaka. The first years involved cutting trails, habituating animals, identifying individuals, collecting genetic samples, establishing the baseline ecology and training assistants to help collect detailed behavioural data. While sifaka exhibit complex social behaviour, a social interaction does not occur very often, and thus extensive data are required before any statistical analysis can be conducted. Just when I was thinking that I had enough social data to begin answering my questions about social relationships, Cyclone Fanele hit Ankoatsifaka in 2009, causing extensive damage. I was in the unusual position of having data before and after the cyclone, and thus set my behavioural research aside to focus on questions about cyclone ecology. Understanding how endangered animals respond to natural and anthropogenic disturbances, both their short-term and long-term resiliency, is an important part of any wildlife management plan. Consequently, my work shifted from simply practising conservation while studying lemur behaviour to explicitly studying conservation.

In 2013 I was again feeling like I could finally get back to my passion of primate social relationships, when a forest fire nearly burned down the research station. In the same year, I was lucky enough to meet landscape ecologist Dr Anne Axel, and we began a collaboration to study the cyclone and fire ecology of KMNP. With a PhD in wildlife ecology, Anne works primarily in the dry forests of Madagascar, where she uses multiple sensor technologies, such as satellite remote sensing, acoustic recordings, GPS and climate sensors, to understand the impacts of humans on the structure and biodiversity of forests. She is currently engaged in a multi-year study of the interactions of livestock and lemurs at Beza Mahafaly Special Reserve, where she tracks livestock movements and documents grazing impacts on forests, lemurs and soundscapes. Combining our strengths in landscape and behavioural ecology, and by leveraging phenological and demographic methods, together we explore how sifaka respond to changes in their environment.

12.2   Introduction

Natural disturbances, such as tropical cyclones, can have devastating direct consequences for arboreal primates, but indirect effects of these disturbances often contribute to higher mortality in wild populations (Lugo, 2008; Wunderle et al., 1992) because they can modify the ecological space available. Changes to forest structure

(Lugo, 2008) due to snapped and uprooted trees (Lewis & Bannar-Martin, 2012; Pavelka et al., 2003) and to tree communities (Chazdon et al., 2007) due to canopy thinning (Baret et al., 2008) constrain how animals use their habitats. For example, cyclones can relocate significant portions of biomass (e.g. foliage, branches) from the canopy to the forest floor (Lugo, 2008), resulting in decreased food availability and increased terrestriality. This increased terrestriality and decreased foliage cover can leave primates more vulnerable to predation and decrease survival. Tropical cyclones, thus, can impact both directly and indirectly the viability of wild primate populations.

Models of global warming in the Anthropocene project increased intensity of tropical cyclones (Knutson et al., 2010; Sobel et al., 2016). The high wind velocity of these strong storms means that substantial modification of forest structure and complete defoliation are expected to occur more frequently. Rainfall changes associated with tropical cyclones are also projected to increase (Knutson et al., 2010; Scoccimarro et al., 2017). Thus, primates in cyclone-affected areas will increasingly have to cope with these environmental modifications. Importantly, global climate models suggest that cyclone intensity, rather than frequency, is expected to increase, though predicted ranges of intensity vary substantially by region (Knutson et al., 2010; Sobel et al., 2016; Sugi et al., 2017). Moreover, animals in different niches experience different consequences of post-disturbance habitat changes, and thus, vary in their resiliency to tropical cyclones. Conservation strategies must therefore take into account the local effects of these global climate changes and species-specific responses.

Cyclone Fanele made landfall on 21 January 2009 on the western coast of Madagascar, and passed directly over KMNP. It had sustained winds of 185 kmh and gusts up to 260 kmh (Réunion MétéoFrance), making it a Category 3 storm (Saffir–Simpson Hurricane Scale). The cyclone caused substantial damage to the Ankoatsifaka forest: more than 95 per cent of trees experienced some sort of damage, tree mortality was 9 per cent, and stem density and basal area were reduced by approximately 10 per cent (Lewis & Bannar-Martin, 2012).

Despite experiencing substantial damage to their habitat after Cyclone Fanele (Lewis & Bannar-Martin, 2012), the Verreaux's sifaka population in KMNP was not found to suffer major, immediate consequences. Body mass, subcutaneous body fat and reproductive output did not decline during the dry season just several months after the cyclone (Lewis & Rakotondranaivo, 2011). Thus, sifaka, like other lemurs (Wright, 1999) and other medium-sized folivores (Wilson et al., 2008), may be resilient to the immediate effects of cyclonic activity (Lewis & Rakotondranaivo, 2011). Long-term data on Milne-Edward's sifaka (*P. edwardsi*) inhabiting the montane rainforests, however, show reduced fecundity and survival when cyclones occur during gestation (Dunham et al., 2011). Hence, cyclones may have consequences for Verreaux's sifaka that are only apparent after a longer period of time.

Cyclones are argued to have had a significant impact on Madagascar's biodiversity. Nevertheless, few authors have empirically investigated this hypothesis. Our goal was to examine the effects of Cyclone Fanele on a wild population of lemurs in the KMNP of western Madagascar. We used long-term demographic data for Verreaux's sifaka in KMNP and a measure of green vegetation to determine the consequences of changes in food availability on sifaka reproduction. In particular, we examined the effects of habitat perturbations on births and infant survival. Because KMNP is a highly seasonal forest and Verreaux's sifaka reproduction is greatly constrained by this seasonality (Lewis & Kappeler, 2005), we also explored the impact of the timing of habitat perturbations on births and infant survival. We then used these results to predict when demographic effects due to a cyclone are expected. Finally, we test the hypothesis that Cyclone Fanele had a negative impact on the sifaka in KMNP.

12.3   Methods

12.3.1   Study Area

At approximately 150 000 ha, KMNP used to include some of the largest contiguous dry, deciduous forests in Madagascar (Whitehurst et al., 2009). However, as is happening throughout the island, the forest is disappearing at an alarming rate. Large trees are chopped down to build the boats (seaworthy canoes and larger schooners) that are an integral part of the life and economy of the people living on the western side of the park. The livelihoods of the people living inland are based on cattle and agriculture, such as peanuts and maize (Vieilledent et al., 2018). Fire is also an important tool for these ventures (Kull, 2012) because it effectively clears existing forest vegetation, promoting the growth of new grass shoots for cattle-grazing or providing nutrients in the form of ash for cultivated plants, such as maize. Thus, the major and imminent threats to the biodiversity of the park are agriculture and fire (Vieilledent et al., 2018), as well as selective logging. The resulting impacts of these activities, in combination with the destruction caused by Cyclone Fanele (Lewis & Bannar-Martin, 2012), have been especially devastating.

The Ankoatsifaka Research Station is located within KMNP at 20°47′17 S, 44°10′08 E. The dry forest is comprised of a high density of small trees, as well as large emergent trees such as *Adansonia* spp., *Commiphora* spp. and *Hazomalania* spp. (Lewis & Bannar-Martin, 2012; Lewis, unpublished data). The mean annual precipitation is approximately 850 mm, with the majority of rain falling in January and February. Temperature ranges from 7°C in August to 40°C in November, with a mean annual temperature of 24°C (Rasambainarivo et al., 2014). A 1 km^2 grid system has been cut into the forest with trails every 25 m.

12.3.2   Study Subjects: Sifaka

Verreaux's sifaka are medium-sized (~3 kg) arboreal primates inhabiting the dry and spiny forests of western and southwestern Madagascar (Lewis & Kappeler, 2005). They live in small, cohesive social groups of 2–16 individuals (Sussman et al., 2012) with 1–3 adults of each sex in variable sex ratios (Lewis & van Schaik, 2007). While both sexes disperse from their natal groups, dispersal is male-biased (Richard et al., 1993) and males disperse approximately every 3–4 years (Leimberger & Lewis, 2017).

Both males and females reach adulthood at five years of age (Lewis & van Schaik, 2007; Richard et al., 2002) and females give birth every one or two years throughout their lives and can live 25 years or more (Richard et al., 2002).

As folivores living in deciduous forests, sifaka reproduction is dictated by their highly seasonal environment (Lewis & Kappeler, 2005). Although each individual female is in oestrus for only 0.5–96 hours per year (Brockman & Whitten, 1996), conception occurs within a six-week period sometime during the January to March mating season, which happens during the wet season. Singletons are all born almost entirely within a two-month period in the dry season (July–August), and mid/late lactation is timed with increasing food availability in November and December (Lewis & Kappeler, 2005). Weaning is a surprisingly long process that begins in January and can continue into March. Thus, often, subsequent offspring are conceived before current offspring are fully weaned. Additionally, successful reproduction is dependent on females recovering the 10–20 per cent of their body mass lost during the dry season and during mid/late lactation (Lewis & Kappeler, 2005), the phase of reproduction when primates experience the greatest energetic demands (van Schaik & van Noordwijk, 1985).

The Sifaka Research Project maintains a long-term dataset of the Verreaux's sifaka at Ankoatsifaka. Since 2006, researchers have been collecting behavioural and morphological data on individuals from 5–9 focal social groups. All individuals ≥ 1 year of age have been marked with unique collars and tags for consistent identification, and one individual per group is fitted with a radio collar to facilitate location in the trail system. The research team captures a portion of the population annually during a five-week period each June or July (dry season) to collect morphometric, genetic and health data, as well as to maintain the sifaka identification system. The team also conducts a monthly census of all animals in the 1 km^2 grid system.

12.3.3 Plot-Level Changes in Forest Structure

We used detailed data collected in March 2015 on individual tree damage at Ankoatsifaka to determine post-cyclone changes in forest structure. Following the methods outlined by Pavelka and Behie (2005), and repeating a study conducted after Cyclone Fanele in July–August 2009 (Lewis & Bannar-Martin, 2012), all trees ≥ 5 cm diameter at breast height (DBH) in nine 25×25 m equidistant quadrats were assessed for damage. Additionally, height and DBH were recorded.

12.3.4 Vegetation Data

In order to estimate food resources available to the sifaka, we used an index of green vegetation calculated from satellite imagery. The enhanced vegetation index (EVI) correlates with gross primary production (Rahman et al., 2005; Xiao et al., 2004), which is the sum total of solar energy fixed by plants through photosynthesis. In this study, EVI represents the temporal and spatial variability of canopy leaf material and any understorey green vegetation visible to the satellite from treefall gaps.

To characterise the phenology, or seasonal changes, of the forest, we created a monthly time series of EVI for the Ankoatsifaka Research Station forest for a period of 13 years. EVI data were downloaded as MODIS Terra (MOD13Q1) and Aqua (MYD13Q1) 16-day, 250-metre products. For each year of the 2003–15 study period, 46 images (3–4 images/month) were downloaded from NASA's Land Processes Distributed Active Archive Centre, reprojected to UTM Zone 38S, and then clipped to the boundary of the 1 km^2 Ankoatsifaka trail grid system, represented by a group of 36 250-metre pixels arranged in a 6 × 6 georeferenced matrix.

Next, maximum value composite (MVC) images were computed by recording the highest EVI value for each pixel from the set of observations obtained for each month (Holben, 1986). The result is not a 'snapshot' in time of a single month, but rather the maximum value recorded in each of the 36 pixels in each month (Figure 12.1). We computed seasonal and yearly summary statistics from monthly mean EVIs (6 or 12 months × 12 years). We examined 'temporal' variability of green vegetation within the season by using the coefficient of variation (CV) of seasonal EVI, which represents the CV of mean monthly EVIs. EVI data were processed and analysed in R (R Core Team, 2014).

Rainfall is the primary driver of green vegetation at KMNP, with an approximately four-week lag in vegetation response to rainfall. Almost all rain falls here between November and March, yet >80 per cent of the rain falls within only two months (January and February). Rainfall amounts frequently are used as a proxy for vegetation availability, so seasons are frequently designated as either wet or dry. Because we quantified green vegetation, however, we divided the calendar year into two six-month phenological periods, representing green-up (December to May), when trees are flush with green leaves; and senescence (June to November), when leaves undergo senescence/shedding, nutrients in the leaves often decline (Chapman et al., 2003) and the forest appears more yellow than green. While the majority of the rain falls in the green season, this period does not correspond with the actual rainy season.

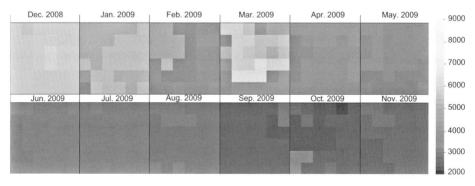

Figure 12.1 Maximum value composite EVI images for Ankoatsifaka Research Station forest over the period December 2008 to November 2009 (multiply by scale factor of 0.001 for actual EVI). Cyclone Fanele passed over the forest on 21 January 2009.

We calculated yearly EVI values from December to November, a 12-month period that begins with the start of the green season. We also delimited a 12-month period based on sifaka life-history (infant year) that begins in the yellow season (sifaka birth and lactation) and ends in the green season (sifaka weaning and early independence). The infant year can also be viewed from the mother's perspective, with the yellow season corresponding to birth/lactation of one infant and the green season corresponding to the period of stacked investment (lactation/weaning of the current infant *and* conception/gestation of the next infant).

Phenological variables included: seasonal and yearly mean EVI; seasonal and yearly CV of EVI; and mean and CV of infant year. To explore the potential lag in demographic effects, all variables were modelled at time lags pre-dating critical demographic events by 0–3 years before birth (for births) or before first birthday (for infant survival) (Table 12.1).

Table 12.1 Generalised linear models used to examine the effects of the variation in green vegetation on sifaka demography

Demographic measure	Phenological variables	Reproductive events corresponding to the time periods modelled
Births	Green season mean and CV	Conception/gestation
	Green season mean and CV	1 and 2 years before conception/gestation
	Yellow season mean and CV	Season prior to conception
	Yellow season mean and CV	2 and 3 years prior to birth
	Infant year mean and CV	Season prior to conception + conception/gestation
	Infant year mean and CV	1 year before season prior to conception +1 year before conception/gestation
	Infant year mean and CV	2 years before season prior to conception +1 year before conception/gestation
	Year mean and CV	Year ending season prior to conception
	Year mean and CV	1 year before year ending season prior to conception
	Year mean and CV	2 years before year ending season prior to conception
Infant survival	Green season mean and CV	Late lactation/weaning
	Green season mean and CV	Conception/gestation
	Green season mean and CV	1 year before conception/gestation
	Yellow season mean and CV	Birth/lactation
	Yellow season mean and CV	1 and 2 years before birth
	Infant year mean and CV	Birth/lactation + lactation/weaning
	Infant year mean and CV	Season prior to conception + conception/gestation
	Infant year mean and CV	1 year before season prior to conception + 1 year before conception/gestation
	Year mean and CV	Late lactation/weaning + first birthday (independence)
	Year mean and CV	Conception/gestation + birth/lactation
	Year mean and CV	1 year before conception/gestation + 1 year before birth

12.3.5 Demographic Models

We examined whether EVI phenological measures lagged at 0–3 years predicted the proportion of females giving birth in a year and the proportion of infants surviving to age one year using logistic regression. First, we calculated variance inflation factors (VIFs) in a stepwise approach to remove correlated explanatory variables. The proportions of births/survivals in each year were then modelled using a stepwise generalised linear model with a binomial distribution and log link function. We used AIC to identify the most parsimonious model from the set of models considered.

12.4 Results

12.4.1 Changes in Vegetation Over Time

Immediately after the cyclone, a third of the trees ≥ 5 cm DBH were severely damaged: trunks were snapped, uprooted and heavily leaning, and branches experienced major damage (Lewis & Bannar-Martin, 2012). In 2015, six years after the cyclone, stem density was reduced by 48 per cent (2420 $\pm$ 1039 stems/ha in 2009 to 1056 $\pm$ 245 stems/ha), nearly a four-fold decrease after the Lewis and Bannar-Martin (2012) study. Despite this substantial loss, the proportion of trees in the various strata was not altered significantly, suggesting that associated mortality of understorey trees occurred when large trees were felled by wind (26 per cent of trees were understorey, 64 per cent canopy and 10 per cent emergent; chi-squared test $\chi^2 = 0.634$, df = 2, ns). The reduction in post-cyclone stem density observed in 2015 was not associated with a concomitant decline in green vegetation (EVI), although a marked difference in EVI occurred following the cyclone (Figure 12.2a).

Vegetation in the green season represents the majority of primary production fixed in the year. Green season vegetation was far more variable than yellow season vegetation and trends in the two seasons' vegetation did not follow the same pattern (Figure 12.2a). The green season with the lowest gain in green vegetation occurred not in the season of the cyclone (green season 2009) but rather in the following year (2010), a year that also coincidentally received significantly less rainfall than in all other years in the study period, making it hard to disentangle the influences of cyclone and drought.

Trends in the temporal variation in green vegetation (CV of EVI) varied widely by year and season (Figure 12.2b). Temporal variability of the yellow season of the cyclone year (2009) was relatively high, but temporal variability of that green season was exceptionally low. A decline in green vegetation in February 2009 (presumably due to loss of canopy trees) was followed by a massive flushing of leaves (Figure 12.1) in response to high precipitation (Garbulsky & Paruelo, 2004) and perhaps to a sudden pulse of nutrients in the form of leaf litter deposition (Lodge et al., 1994).

12.4.2 Demography

Fifteen females (94 per cent of reproductive-age females) gave birth to 52 infants between 2008 and 2015. Thirty (58 per cent) infants born between 2008 and 2014 survived at least one year. The mean ($\pm$SD) proportion of females giving birth in any

(a)

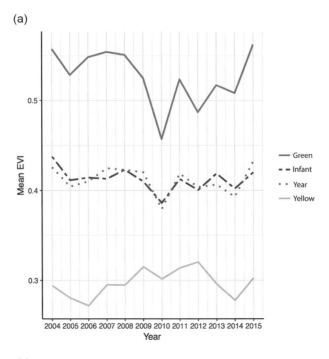

(b)

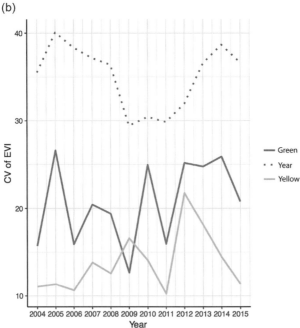

Figure 12.2 Trends in green vegetation at Kirindy Mitea National Park: (a) mean EVI for the green season (December to May), yellow season (June to November), entire year (December to November) and infant year (June to May); and (b) temporal variability of green vegetation for the green season, yellow season and entire year.

given year was 0.80 ± 0.07 and the mean proportion of infants surviving to one year was 0.59 ± 0.21. Infant births and survival did not decline immediately following the cyclone in January 2009 (Figure 12.3). Instead, a steep decline in births occurred in 2013, and infant survival was lowest in 2011 and 2013.

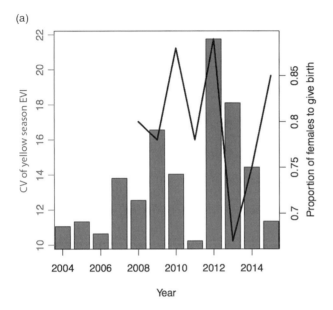

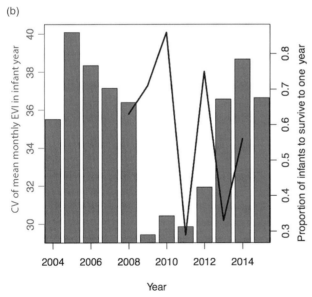

Figure 12.3 Observed green vegetation and demography measures: (a) temporal variation in yellow season vegetation (bars) and proportion of females giving birth (line); (b) temporal variation in mean EVI in the infant year (June to May) (bars) and infant survival (line); (c) mean EVI in the phenological year (December to November) (bars) and infant survival (lines).

(c)

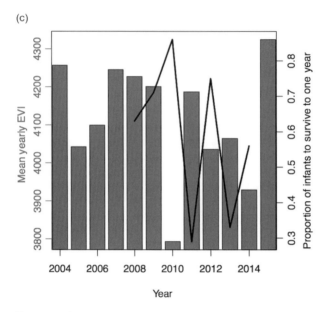

Figure 12.3 Cont.

We next examined which environmental factors were the best predictors of these demographic patterns. Interestingly, most measures of EVI did not significantly predict the proportion of females giving birth, perhaps because the proportion of green vegetation did not vary substantially over the course of the study (Figure 12.2a). In the following we present only the best-fit models based on AIC values.

12.4.3 Vegetation and Births

The best-fit model indicates that high variability in the availability of vegetation during the yellow season one year before birth is associated with decreased reproductive output. The proportion of females giving birth was negatively correlated with the temporal variability of yellow season vegetation (CV of EVI) just prior to conception and one year before birth (Figure 12.4). Temporal variability of vegetation in the yellow season just prior to conception was a significant predictor of the odds of a female producing an offspring (log-odds = − 0.0903 ± 0.033, odds ratio = 0.913, Wald statistic = −2.696, p = 0.035). For every 1 per cent increase in CV of EVI in the yellow season just prior to conception, the odds of a female giving birth one year later decreased by 8.638.

12.4.4 Vegetation and Infant Survival

The only two significant models indicate that infant survival was dependent on the sustained availability of adequate, consistent vegetation over a 12-month period including the season of gestation and the year just prior to gestation. The results from the two models overlap during the yellow season prior to conception, suggesting this

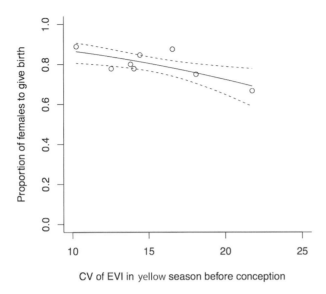

Figure 12.4 Predicted relationship from a binomial logistic regression between temporal variability of green vegetation in the yellow season before conception with 95 per cent confidence limits. Circles indicate observed proportion of females to give birth.

time is critically important for sifaka reproduction. Together these models indicate that: (1) sifaka did not necessarily respond to measures of green vegetation at the seasonal level – rather, they appear to have responded to an annual phenological cycle; and (2) an infant's survival was largely determined prior to its birth by the mother's ability to secure resources in the months leading up to the infant's conception and into the period of gestation.

Mean EVI in the infant year (June to May) beginning in the yellow season just prior to an infant's conception and extending into the season of the infant's conception and gestation was a significant predictor of the odds of an offspring surviving to age one year (log-odds = 0.007 $\pm$ 0.003, odds ratio = 1.007, Wald statistic = 2.465, p = 0.014) (Figure 12.5a). For every 1 per cent increase in mean EVI in an infant year that ends with the infant's gestation, the odds of an infant surviving to age one year increased by 0.675.

Temporal variability of vegetation (CV of EVI) in the year December to November prior to the infant's birth season (July to September) was a significant predictor of the odds of an offspring surviving to age one year (log-odds = 0.197 $\pm$ 0.082, odds ratio = 1.218, Wald statistic = 2.396, p = 0.016) (Figure 12.5b). For every 1 per cent increase in CV of EVI over the year prior to birth, the odds of an infant surviving to age one year increased by 1.219.

12.4.5 Cyclone Effects

We expected to find the demographic effects of the January 2009 cyclone in (1) the proportion of births in 2010 and (2) infant survival in 2010 and 2011 (Figure 12.6). The

(a)

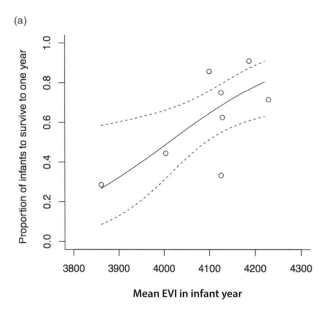

(b)

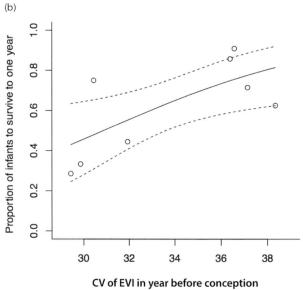

Figure 12.5 Predicted relationship from a binomial logistic regression between (a) green vegetation in infant year beginning in the yellow season just prior to conception with 95 per cent confidence limits; and (b) temporal variability of green vegetation in the year prior to birth with 95 per cent confidence limits. Circles indicate observed proportion of infants to survive to one year.

temporal variability of yellow season vegetation (CV of EVI) in 2009 was higher than average, but contrary to predictions the proportion of females giving birth in 2010 was not low. However, the temporal variability of vegetation across 2009 was low and, as predicted, infant survival in 2011 was exceptionally low. The amount of green

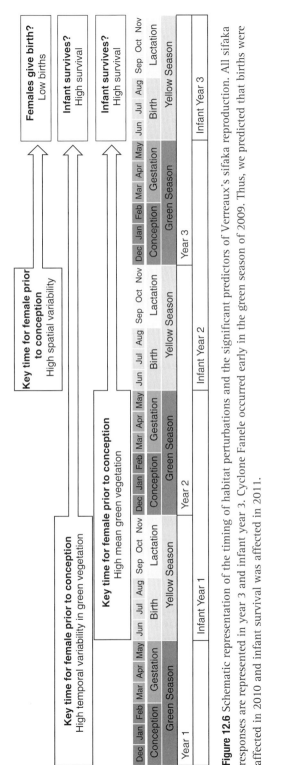

Figure 12.6 Schematic representation of the timing of habitat perturbations and the significant predictors of Verreaux's sifaka reproduction. All sifaka responses are represented in year 3 and infant year 3. Cyclone Fanele occurred early in the green season of 2009. Thus, we predicted that births were affected in 2010 and infant survival was affected in 2011.

vegetation (mean EVI) for the infant year June 2008 to May 2009 was above average, and as predicted, infant survival in 2010 was also high.

The loss in green vegetation associated with dramatic stem reduction during the cyclone did not seem to materialise until the green season of 2010 (Figure 12.2a). Assuming a greater cyclonic effect on vegetation one year post-cyclone, we expected to find the demographic effects of the cyclone in births in 2011 and infant survival of 2011 and 2012. The temporal variability of vegetation in the yellow season in 2010 was medium/high and, as expected, the proportion of females giving birth in 2011 was average. The temporal variability of vegetation in 2010 was low, while the infant survival in 2012 was above average, contrary to prediction.

12.5   Discussion

Long-term conservation strategies have to take into account the effects of climate change on primates and their ecosystems. Madagascar provides an excellent opportunity to study the potential influences of climate change on primates because it has an unusually stochastic climate that has played an important role in shaping the evolution of distinctive characteristics of the island's fauna (e.g. hibernating primates, heterothermic mammals; Dewar & Richard, 2007; Wright, 1999). Cyclones are a major driver of this variability (Jury et al., 1995), but the actual response of Malagasy flora and fauna to cyclones has rarely been studied (Waeber et al., 2015). In this collaborative research, we examined the relationship between changes in the demography of Verreaux's sifaka and changes in the availability of their food resources due to a cyclone. We found that the vegetation biomass at KMNP did not exhibit a multi-year decline, despite a drastic reduction in tree density after Cyclone Fanele. Increased sunlight exposure in the understorey following a disturbance can increase the density of pioneer species (Behie & Pavelka, 2012). Because Verreaux's sifaka are highly folivorous (Lewis & Kappeler, 2005; Norscia et al., 2006), they may have been able to take advantage of much of the new growth in the understorey of large tree fall gaps following major stem loss. Furthermore, the fact that female sifaka often give birth annually despite having an otherwise exceptionally slow life-history (Richard et al., 2002) may help explain why sifaka populations are relatively resilient to cyclones.

Reproduction in sifaka is tightly linked to environmental fluctuations (*P. verreauxi*: Lawler et al., 2009; Lewis & Kappeler, 2005; *P. edwardsi*: Dunham et al., 2011) and we found signatures of these fluctuations in Verreaux's sifaka demography. Most notably, the availability of green vegetation determined both births and infant survival by acting on the mother – no time period after the birth significantly predicted infant survival, and even the season of conception and gestation did not predict births. In fact, all effects had a time lag, with all demographic consequences experienced at least one year after major fluctuations in vegetation. Thus, whether an infant is born and survives is mostly determined before it is even conceived.

Indeed, folivory may help buffer lemurs from severe fluctuations and may be an adaptation to frequent cyclones (cf. Reed & Bidner, 2004). While defoliation immediately following a cyclone can be particularly devastating to folivores, this negative effect may be balanced later by an increase in food supply due to an increase in leaf production (Lewis & Rakotondranaivo, 2011) as trees shift from reproduction (fruit) to leaf production (Vandermeer et al., 1998). Indeed, tropical storms tend to have greater negative effects on frugivorous species (Pavelka et al., 2003; Ramírez-Barajas et al., 2012; Wunderle et al., 1992). Primate leaf consumption often increases following a tropical storm. Hence, the prevalence of folivorous primates in Madagascar may be associated with the frequent tropical storms and cyclones (Reed & Bidner, 2004).

12.5.1 Patterns of Reproduction

Our results build upon the findings of Lewis and Kappeler (2005) from nearby Kirindy Forest. Female Verreaux's sifaka can only successfully reproduce if they have sufficient resources to recover from the fluctuating food availability in a highly seasonal forest. This recovery is especially difficult because they must deal with the costs of lactation during a harsh dry/yellow season (when vegetation quantity and quality is at its lowest) and their overlapping reproductive phases during the lush wet/green season. Female sifaka give birth during the period of low food availability in order to have sufficient resources available for them as the costs of lactation increase and as they attempt to regain sufficient body fat to resume cycling (Lewis & Kappeler, 2005; Figure 12.6). Then they must conceive and begin gestating while simultaneously still nursing the previous year's infant. Our study suggests that variability when the vegetation is senescing negatively impacts a female's ability to be in sufficient reproductive condition the following mating season (odds decrease by 8.638 with increasing variability; Figure 12.4). When the year prior to an infant's birth was especially green, infant survival increased. In other words, high, sustained levels of green vegetation result in increased lemur reproduction, at least in terms of infant survival.

In fact, the entire year prior to an infant's conception significantly predicted infant survival. Hence, one might predict that female sifaka give birth every other year in order to have sufficient internal resources to invest in their offspring. Interestingly, however, sifaka do *not* show a pattern of giving birth every other year (Richard et al., 2002; Lewis, unpublished data), nor do they show a pattern of greater infant survival after inter-birth intervals of greater than one year (Lewis, unpublished data). Instead, females often give birth each year, suggesting that they may use a 'bet hedging' life-history strategy (Richard et al., 2002) to take advantage of the especially green years. Additionally, sifaka infant survival was significantly dependent on how much food was available for the mother during the yellow season. Low variation in food availability the year prior to an infant's conception had negative consequences for survival (Figure 12.6). While this result may seem counterintuitive, in dry forests like KMNP, low temporal variation in monthly vegetation over the course of a year most likely occurs when the rainy season is not very wet. The low rainfall levels then result in lacklustre vegetation gain during the green season. Thus, higher temporal variability in green vegetation likely signifies that (1) a year's rainfall was spread more evenly throughout the year, and (2) longer-lasting and higher-quality vegetation was available as food through the yellow season, allowing the female to be in better condition prior to the infant's conception.

12.5.2 Impact of Cyclones on Sifaka Reproduction

Cyclone Fanele resulted in substantial immediate damage to the KMNP forest in 2009 (Lewis & Bannar-Martin, 2012). Nevertheless, the folivorous sifaka did not seem to suffer much from the immediate consequences of a cyclone. Infants survived the cyclone. Female body condition did not decline (Lewis & Rakotondranaivo, 2011) and they were just as likely to give birth several months after the cyclone (Lewis & Rakotondranaivo, 2011). However, our results show that Verreaux's sifaka did experience the negative consequences of a cyclone after a short time lag (Figures 12.3 and 12.6).

12.5.3 Long-Term Implications

The total cyclonic effects on the forest influencing the sifaka may not be immediately detectable, however. Forest recovery is a long process (Lugo, 2008). Indeed, KMNP tree density was substantially lower six years post-cyclone than eight months post-cyclone, perhaps because tree mortality continued and understorey tree growth had not yet reached our minimum measurement of tree girth. Indeed, a marked extreme in vegetation (as measured by EVI) associated with the predicted demographic response occurred: high yellow season temporal variability in vegetation in 2012 and few births in 2013 (Figure 12.3a). The steep decline in births in 2013 and the low infant survival in 2011 and 2013 may have been associated with the post-cyclone changes in food availability. Nevertheless, ascertaining whether these extremes were lagged vegetation effects of the cyclone is difficult because (1) this tropical dry forest exhibits a fair amount of normal environmental variation, and (2) the accompanying yearly forest plot data are not currently available for analysis. More data on long-term phenology of the forest are required to disentangle these two hypotheses.

In sum, cyclones are thought to have had a substantial impact on the biodiversity of Madagascar, but empirical tests of this assertion are rare because the necessary data are not easily acquired. Taking advantage of a long-term lemur dataset and using an interdisciplinary approach, we showed that the immediate response of Malagasy primates to cyclones may not always follow expectations. The 'bet hedging' life-history strategy of sifaka may allow them to take advantage of the years when food is plentiful. Moreover, our results are consistent with the hypothesis that folivory may be one adaptation to high cyclonic activity and may explain why folivory is unusually prevalent in Malagasy primate communities (Reed & Bidner, 2004).

Our research has important implications for long-term conservation strategies. Most importantly, a single strategy to address the effects of natural disturbances on wild primate populations will not be effective. In addition, taking into account local expectations for changes in rainfall and cyclonic activity, wildlife management plans must address each species' needs and responses individually. Moreover, demographic responses to tropical cyclones may not be immediate. Long-term data, such as the data collected by the Sifaka Research Project, are required to assess the demographic consequences of climate change, especially for primates because of their long and slow life-histories. Our research also demonstrates, however, that multiple decades of demographic and phenology data are necessary to isolate the effects of cyclones from other climatic events.

12.6   Future Directions

Conservation is by its nature an interdisciplinary endeavour. Attempts to understand the effects of climate change on wild primate populations require scientists from many different fields to work together. Our nascent interdisciplinary collaboration has been fruitful and has helped us to realise many new kinds of questions that can be addressed through continued collaboration. Our initial work presented in this chapter shows that a relatively basic phenological analysis of a highly seasonal environment, such as KMNP, promises to reveal insights into the demography of folivores and how primates respond to disturbances. Land surface phenology has tools that are useful to primatologists because they enable researchers to remotely identify green-up and senescence periods of individual years. Furthermore, using landscape ecology tools and the long-term lemur and forest data, we may depict spatial variability of green vegetation within home ranges of each sifaka group at monthly intervals. As the Sifaka Research Project dataset grows, we can examine maternal home-range effects to see if particular females or particular microhabitats influence infant survival. We will also look at other demographic variables, including group size and fecundity.

Within a few years after Cyclone Fanele, KMNP experienced multiple forest fires that caused extensive damage throughout much of the park. These fires were unusually destructive because of the large amount of dry, dead wood present after the cyclone. We plan to expand our research in the future to include the forest fires, and we will investigate the hypothesis that fires in years following cyclone damage result in far greater forest loss. The work in this chapter is just a first step in our long-term collaborative project. By combining the different theoretical and methodological toolkits of our disciplines, we will continue to explore questions about cyclone ecology in the Anthropocene. This type of interdisciplinary work is an important part of efforts to conserve the endangered Verreaux's sifaka and other primates inhabiting cyclone-prone habitats. Moreover, our collaboration, which began out of an unexpected need to study how primates cope with natural and anthropogenic disasters, ultimately has informed the original goal of the Sifaka Research Project: understanding the behaviour of Verreaux's sifaka and primates in general.

Acknowledgements

The authors would like to acknowledge Madagascar National Parks, MICET, Ankoat-sifaka Staff and Research team, CAFF/CORE, the University of Antananarivo Department of Animal Biology; Chris Kirk and Jayme Waldron for discussion; and Alison Behie, Julie Teichroeb and Nicholas Malone for inviting us to participate in this symposium and volume. This research was funded by the University of Texas at Austin, Primate Conservation, Inc., and private donors.

References

Baret, S., Cournac, L., Thébaud, C., Edwards, P. & Strasberg, D. (2008). Effects of canopy gap size on recruitment and invasion of the non-indigenous *Rubus alceifolius* in lowland tropical rain forest on Réunion. *Journal of Tropical Ecology*, **24**, 1–9.

Behie, A. M. & Pavelka, M. S. M. (2012). Food selection in the black howler monkey following habitat disturbance: implications for the importance of mature leaves. *Journal of Tropical Ecology*, **28**(2), 153–60.

Brockman, D. K. & Whitten, P. L. (1996). Reproduction in free-ranging *Propithecus verreauxi*: estrus and the relationship between multiple partner matings and fertilization. *American Journal of Physical Anthroplogy*, **100**, 57–69.

Chapman, C. A., Chapman, L. J., Rode, K. D., Hauck, E. M. & McDowell, L. R. (2003). Variation in the nutritional value of primate foods: among trees, time periods, and areas. *International Journal of Primatology*, **24**, 317–33.

Chazdon, R. L., Letcher, S. G., van Breugel, M., et al. (2007). Rates of change in tree communities of secondary Neotropical forests following major disturbances. *Philosophical Transactions of the Royal Society B: Biological Sciences*, **362**, 273–89.

Dewar, R. E. & Richard, A. F. (2007). Evolution in the hypervariable environment of Madagascar. *PNAS*, **104**(34), 13723–7.

Dunham, A. E., Erhart, E. M. & Wright, P. C. (2011). Global climate cycles and cyclones: consequences for rainfall patterns and lemur reproduction in southeastern Madagascar. *Global Change Biology*, **17**(1), 219–27.

Garbulsky, M. F. & Paruelo, J. M. (2004). Remote sensing of protected areas to derive baseline vegetation functioning characteristics. *Journal of Vegetation Science*, **15**, 711–20.

Holben, B. N. (1986). Characteristics of maximum-value composite images from temporal AVHRR data. *International Journal of Remote Sensing*, **7**(11), 1417–34.

Jury, M. R., Parker, B. A., Raholijao, N. & Nassor, A. (1995). Variability of summer rainfall over Madagascar: climatic determinants at interannual scales. *International Journal of Climatology*, **15**, 1323–32.

Knutson, T. R., McBride, J. L., Chan, J., et al. (2010). Tropical cyclones and climate change. *Nature Geoscience*, **3**(3), 157–63.

Kull, C. A. (2012). Fire and people in tropical island grassland landscapes: Fiji and Madagascar. *The Journal of Pacific Studies*, **32**, 127–35.

Lawler, R. R., Caswell, H., Richard, A. F., et al. (2009). Demography of Verreaux's sifaka in a stochastic rainfall environment. *Oecologia*, **161**(3), 491–504.

Leimberger, K. G. & Lewis, R. J. (2017). Patterns of male dispersal in Verreaux's sifaka (*Propithecus verreauxi*) at Kirindy Mitea National Park. *American Journal of Primatology*. doi: 10.1002/ajp.22455.

Lewis, R. J. & Bannar-Martin, K. H. (2012). The impact of Cyclone Fanele on a tropical dry forest in Madagascar. *Biotropica*, **44**(2), 135–40.

Lewis, R. J. & Kappeler, P. M. (2005). Seasonality, body condition, and timing of reproduction in *Propithecus verreauxi verreauxi* in the Kirindy Forest. *American Journal of Primatology*, **67**(3), 347–64.

Lewis, R. J. & Rakotondranaivo, F. (2011). The impact of Cyclone Fanele on sifaka body condition and reproduction in the tropical dry forest of western Madagascar. *Journal of Tropical Ecology*, **27**(4), 429–32.

Lewis, R. J. & van Schaik, C. P. (2007). Bimorphism in male Verreaux's sifaka in the Kirindy Forest of Madagascar. *International Journal of Primatology*, **28**(1), 159–82.

Lodge, D. J., McDowell, W. H. & McSwiney, C. P. (1994). The importance of nutrient pulses in tropical forests. *Trends in Ecology & Evolution*, **9**(10), 384–7.

Lugo, A. E. (2008). Visible and invisible effects of hurricanes on forest ecosystems: an international review. *Austral Ecology*, **33**(4), 368–98.

Norscia, I., Carrai, V. & Borgognini-Tarli, S. M. (2006). Influence of dry season and food quality and quantity on behavior and feeding strategy of *Propithecus verreauxi* in Kirindy, Madagascar. *International Journal of Primatology*, **27**(4), 1001–22.

Pavelka, M. S. M. & Behie, A. M. (2005). The short-term effects of a hurricane on the diet and activity of black howlers (*Alouatta pigra*) in southern Belize. *Biotropica*, **37**(1), 102–8.

Pavelka, M. S. M., Brusselers, O. T., Nowak, D. & Behie, A. M. (2003). Population reduction and social disorganization in *Alouatta pigra* following a hurricane. *International Journal of Primatology*, **24**(5), 1037–55.

R Core Team (2014). *R: A Language and Environment for Statistical Computing*. Vienna: R Foundation for Statistical Computing. Available at: www.r-project.org.

Rahman, A. F., Sims, D. A., Cordova, V. D. & El-Masri, B. Z. (2005). Potential of MODIS EVI and surface temperature for directly estimating per-pixel ecosystem C fluxes. *Geophysical Research Letters*, **32**(19), 1–4.

Ramírez-Barajas, P. J., Islebe, G. & Calmé, S. (2012). Impact of Hurricane Dean (2007) on game species of the Selva Maya, Mexico. *Biotropica*, **44**(3), 402–11.

Rasambainarivo, F. T., Junge, R. E. & Lewis, R. J. (2014). Biomedical evaluation of Verreaux's sifaka (*Propithecus verreauxi*) from Kirindy Mitea National Park in Madagascar. *Journal of Zoo and Wildlife Medicine*, **45**(2), 247–55.

Reed, K. E. & Bidner, L. R. (2004). Primate communities: past, present, and possible future. *Yearbook of Physical Anthropology*, **47**, 2–39.

Richard, A. F., Rakotomanga, P. & Schwartz, M. (1993). Dispersal by *Propithecus verreauxi* at Beza-Mahafaly, Madagascar: 1984–1991. *American Journal of Primatology*, **30**, 1–20.

Richard, A. F., Dewar, R. E., Schwartz, M. & Ratsirarson, J. (2002). Life in the slow lane? Demography and life histories of male and female sifaka (*Propithecus verreauxi verreauxi*). *Journal of Zoology*, **256**(4), 421–36.

Scoccimarro, E., Gualdi, S., Navarra, A., et al. (2017). Tropical cyclone rainfall changes in a warmer climate. In Collins, J. & Walsh, K. (eds) *Hurricanes and Climate Change*, vol. 3. Cham: Springer, pp. 243–55.

Sobel, A. H., Camargo, S. J., Hall, T. M., et al. (2016). Human influence on tropical cyclone intensity. *Science*, **353**(6296), 242–6.

Sugi, M., Murakami, H. & Yoshida, K. (2017). Projection of future changes in the frequency of intense tropical cyclones. *Climate Dynamics*, **49**, 619–32.

Sussman, R. W., Richard, A. F., Ratsirarson, J., et al. (2012). Beza Mahafaly Special Reserve: long-term research on lemurs in southwestern Madagascar. In Kappeler, P. M. & Watts, D. P. (eds) *Long-Term Field Studies of Primates*. Berlin: Springer, pp. 45–66.

van Schaik, C. P. & van Noordwijk, M. A. (1985). Interannual variability in fruit abundance and the reproductive seasonality in Sumatran long-tailed macaques (*Macaca fascicularis*). *Journal of Zoology*, **206**, 533–49.

Vandermeer, J., Brenner, A. & Granzow-de la Cerda, I. (1998). Growth rates of tree height six years after hurricane damage at four localities in eastern Nicaragua. *Biotropica*, **30**(4), 502–9.

Vieilledent, G., Grinand, C., Rakotomalala, F. A., et al. (2018). Combining global tree cover loss data with historical national forest-cover maps to look at six decades of deforestation and forest fragmentation in Madagascar. *Biological Conservation*, **22**, 189–97.

Waeber, P. O., Wilmé, L., Ramamonjisoa, B., et al. (2015). Dry forests in Madagascar: neglected and under pressure. *International Forestry Review*, **17**(S2), 127–48.

Whitehurst, A. S., Sexton, J. O. & Dollar, L. (2009). Land cover change in western Madagascar's dry deciduous forests: a comparison of forest changes in and around Kirindy Mite National Park. *Oryx*, **43**(2), 275–83.

Wilson, R. F., Goosem, M. W. & Wilson, G. W. (2008). Resilience of arboreal folivores to habitat damage by a severe tropical cyclone. *Austral Ecology*, **33**(4), 573–9.

Wright, P. C. (1999). Lemur traits and Madagascar ecology: coping with an island environment. *Yearbook of Physical Anthropology*, **42**, 31–72.

Wunderle, J. M. J., Lodge, D. J. & Waide, R. B. (1992). Short-term effects of Hurricane Gilbert on terrestrial bird populations on Jamaica. *The Auk*, **109**(1), 148–66.

Xiao, X., Hollinger, D., Aber, J., et al. (2004). Satellite-based modeling of gross primary production in an evergreen needleleaf forest. *Remote Sensing of Environment*, **89**(4), 519–34.

13 Alas the Storm Has Come Again!

The Impact of Frequent Natural Disasters on Primate Conservation

Alison M. Behie, Mary S. M. Pavelka, Kayla Hartwell, Jane Champion and Hugh Notman

13.1 Personal Narrative

Like many students who enjoy high school science, I (AMB) entered university with aspirations of becoming a biologist. In my second year, after one too many organic chemistry courses, I enrolled in a primate behaviour course as an elective, and I was hooked. Primatology allowed me to explore the very questions that had always interested me – questions about why animals behave the way they do and how this relates to human behaviour. While finishing my degree, I increasingly focused on these questions and the explanatory theories that they generated. Writings by Wrangham, van Schaik, Sterck, Sussman and Hrdy captivated me and subsequently guided my initial Master's project working in Mary Pavelka's lab at the University of Calgary, exploring how females impact male social relationships among black howler monkeys (*Alouatta pigra*).

Then, as I was about to head to the field, a hurricane hit the howler monkey site where I was meant to conduct my study, and in an instant my research focus changed to studying the impacts of the hurricane on the animals. While this seemed like a dramatic shift at the time, it did not take me too far from my initial goals of exploring the influences of environmental and social factors on animal behaviour. What this hurricane and my subsequent project did do was brutally demonstrate to me how quickly a healthy, viable population could become vulnerable to potential extinction. As I watched the number of howlers steadily drop and new infants consistently die, I was driven to further explore environmental disasters and the dangers they pose for primates, especially primates living in already-disturbed habitats. The more I carried on with my research, the more I became aware of the multitude of other sites that were being exposed to similar disasters and that were experiencing similar population declines. It was then that I started to identify as a disaster ecologist instead of a behavioural ecologist.

From this new perspective, I was able to consider how many types of disturbances present primates with similar challenges and risks to survival. I then started to wonder how the processes I had studied so carefully following the hurricane may also occur after logging or hunting, and what impact these might have on all non-human primates. This has driven me to ask new questions about how animals respond to a variety of disasters and how this leads to long-term behavioural adaptations across species. I am currently pursuing these questions through my long-term work in Central America, but also by initiating new programmes of study on species in Cambodia and Vietnam that are exposed to logging and hunting pressures.

As I reflect on the above, it seems that without my knowing it, conservation became my unconscious target and my career goal. So, while I still study the underlying causes of behavioural adaptation, which is what drew me to the field over a decade ago, I now accomplish this by exploring how animals are coping in the face of climate change and human encroachment. My identity is no longer grounded in strict behavioural ecology, but rather I see myself as someone who is obliged to focus my research more towards trying to uncover underlying explanations for differential responses to disturbance. Understanding these can help us to better formulate conservation policies in the future, thus ensuring primate survival. I have also felt compelled to work on training the next generation of primatologists to adopt a similar sensibility and perspective, where they also focus on how understanding species biology and adaptation can be used to create more effective conservation management of primate species. This has extended into primate-habitat range countries, where I have worked with local Master's students and research assistants to increase their skillsets, putting them in a better position to make long-lasting changes in conservation practice and policy.

13.2   Introduction

Large-scale, stochastic events such as hurricanes can cause severe damage to forested areas, significantly impacting food availability for animals within those areas. These 'natural disasters' have been a regular feature in the evolutionary history of species whose geographic range overlaps with their occurrence, particularly in Neotropical regions such as Central America (Ford, 2006). The effects that these disturbances have on local populations of animal species, however, are little understood, as such occurrences are unpredictable and infrequent, and pre- and post-comparative data are often lacking. Because the effects of storms tend to be localised relative to the geographic range of most mammals, it is unlikely that they have widespread effects on entire species, although storms have been implicated as a possible force in shaping the social evolution of at least one primate species (black howler monkey; Behie et al., 2015). However, given the increased habitat fragmentation experienced by many species, as well as the potential for increases in both the frequency and intensity of hurricanes as a result of climate change (Midgley et al., 2002; Saunders & Lea, 2008), the impacts of localised storms may increasingly affect overall species viability.

How primate populations that live in tropical, broad-leaf forest habitats respond to severe storms is likely to vary depending on the extent of habitat damage and on species-specific intrinsic factors, such as dietary specialisation, social group cohesion and home-range/territory size (Behie & Pavelka, 2005; LaFleur & Gould, 2009;

Schaffner et al., 2012; Wright, 1999; 2006). For example, as damaged fruit trees typically abandon reproductive functions (i.e. fruit and flower production) in favour of new leaf production (Barone, 1998; Vandermeer et al., 1998), frugivorous species may be disproportionately affected relative to folivores or dietary generalists. This has led to the assumption that species' dietary flexibility is key to enabling local populations to survive major habitat disturbances, as the ability to exploit whatever foods might be available is likely critical to coping with the shortage of preferred foods. Johns and Skorupa (1987) found that 44 per cent of the variation in the likelihood of a population surviving a major habitat disturbance was explained by the body size and diet of the species, and that large frugivores were particularly vulnerable when fruit and flower availability was limited. It could be that the requirements of specialised frugivory, including a relatively large territory, predict-able access to high-quality food resources and the presence of intact, arboreal travel routes combine to make frugivorous species particularly susceptible to any alter-ations in habitat over the long term (Di Fiore & Suarez, 2007; Ramos-Fernández & Ayala-Orozco, 2003). Frugivorous species are therefore of particular interest to researchers studying the effects of habitat disturbance as their viability following a disturbance might be an important indicator of the degree to which local conditions have been altered (Johns & Skorupa, 1987; Van Roosmalen, 1980).

While dietary flexibility clearly has an effect on population viability in a disturbed environment, social organisation and grouping flexibility are also important factors. The ability to adjust group size might offset some of the costs of increased feeding competition in a resource-poor environment. This may be of particular importance for frugivores who rely on patchily distributed food resources (Asensio et al., 2008). In fact, many highly frugivorous species, such as chimpanzees (*Pan troglodytes*), bonobos (*Pan paniscus*) and spider monkeys (*Ateles* spp.), are characterised by high fission–fusion dynamics, in which individual members of a group split (fission) and merge (fusion) into subgroups of varying size, composition and space in response to changes in environmental conditions (Aureli et al., 2008). In contrast, most folivorous species, such as howler monkeys, are hypothesised to live in stable and cohesive social groups that exhibit little short-term variation in size or cohesion because they are less constrained by feeding competition and the uncertainties of an ephemeral and patchy food resource. This situation presents the possibility that the social flexibility associated with high levels of fission–fusion dynamics might be a source of resilience in the face of habitat change, at least in the short term, by mitigating the increased competition over reduced resources (Malone et al., 2012; Schaffner et al., 2012).

Taken together, both dietary and social grouping flexibility might represent two alternative and possibly complementary strategies for coping with periods of resource scarcity, and either condition could offer some defence against sudden changes to a species habitat. What is uncertain is whether one strategy is more effective than the other, or whether species might be able to exploit both strategies in response to sudden and severe habitat alteration, and what this may mean for species vulnerabilities.

The Central American country of Belize is located in the North Atlantic Hurricane Basin and since 1852 it has been in the direct path of 72 storms, 22 of which were hurricanes (NOAA, 2016). Belize is also home to two species of primates: the black howler monkey and the black-handed, or Yucatan spider monkey (*Ateles geoffroyi yucatanensis*). These two species display divergent feeding ecologies and social organisations. Yucatan spider monkeys are specialised frugivores and live in large, fluid communities characterised by high fission–fusion dynamics. Black howler monkeys, on the other hand, live in small, cohesive social groups and exhibit a relatively higher degree of dietary flexibility, consuming a greater proportion of leaves over sustained periods when fruit is not available. Given the increased tolerance for folivory in howler relative to spider monkeys, it might be expected that the short- and long-term effects of nutritional stress that follow storm-affected populations would impact spider monkeys disproportionally more than they would howlers. However, it is also possible that the social flexibility of spider monkeys mitigates the effects of intermittent fruit shortages, and that they might combine this strategy with a tolerance for increased folivory in the short term.

This study compares the behavioural responses of both primate species to two separate hurricane events in Belize: (1) Hurricane Iris and (2) Hurricane Richard. Hurricane Iris impacted black howler monkeys at Monkey River (MR) in 2001 and Hurricane Richard impacted Yucatan spider monkeys in Runaway Creek Nature Reserve (RCNR) in 2010. Specifically, we explore species-specific changes to activity, diet and social grouping patterns in relation to the post-hurricane patterns of mortality. Because this study represents a post-hoc comparison of two different species at different sites impacted by different events at different times, robust analyses of comparable data were not always possible. However, our objective here is to report *how* a population of each of the two primate species with disparate socioecologies responded behaviourally to sudden habitat change in their respective areas, and not to compare them directly with each other. We hope this approach will help to inform further empirical studies that investigate how species might respond to increased anthropogenic and climate-induced disturbances, and what minimum ecological requirements might be necessary to ensure their sustained viability.

13.3　Methods

13.3.1　Study Sites and Hurricanes

The MR study site is part of the larger 9600 ha MR watershed forest fragment in Southern Belize (Figure 13.1). Hurricane Iris was a Category 4 storm that made landfall in this region of Belize on 8 October 2001. It carried sustained winds of 233 kmh, with gusts up to 282 kmh. Hurricane Iris resulted in substantial damage to the entire MR forest fragment. A damage assessment immediately following the hurricane found that trees were 100 per cent defoliated (Pavelka et al., 2003; Figure 13.2). Most howler food trees at MR suffered a 35 per cent mortality rate, and species identified as important fruit sources suffered a 52 per cent mortality rate.

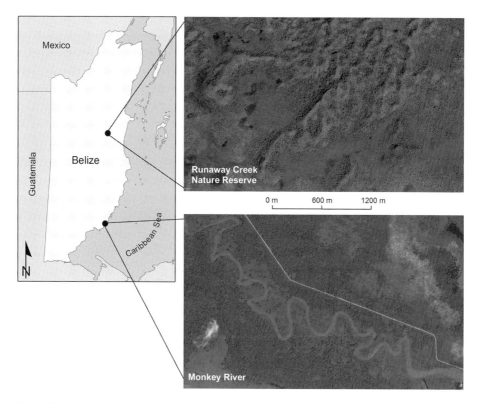

Figure 13.1 Location of two research sites in Belize. Runaway Creek Nature Reserve study site, home to a population of Yucatan spider monkeys (*Ateles geofroyii yucatanensis*) (Image © 2016 Digiglobe, © 2016 Google Earth) and Monkey River study site, home to a population of black howler monkeys (*Alouatta pigra*) (Image © 2016 CNES / Astrium, 2016 Google Earth).

Additionally, no fruit was produced in the first 18 months after the storm and any trees that did produce flowers in the first year subsequently died (Pavelka & Behie, 2005). Before the storm we concentrated our data collection efforts on the monkey groups living within a 52 ha area of forest. After the storm, and in response to declining numbers of monkeys, the boundaries of the research site were expanded to an area of 86 ha.

Runaway Creek Nature Reserve is a 2469 ha private reserve in central Belize (Figure 13.1). The forest landscape is dominated by limestone karst hills, some over 100 m high with an average slope of 15–50°, with some vertical cliff faces. The reserve is part of a larger continuous forested area of approximately 5800 ha and the Central Belize Biological Corridor, connecting the Manatee Forest Reserve to the Rio Bravo. On 25 October 2010, Hurricane Richard made landfall in Central Belize and travelled inland before dissipating a few hours later (Kimberlaine, 2011). As a Category 2 storm, Richard contained wind gusts of up to 125 kmh. Located approximately 45 km from the coast, RCNR was directly in the storm's path, although damage was patchy; windward slopes and ridgetops were severely damaged, while

(a)

(b)

(c)

(d)

Figure 13.2 Hurricane damage at two primate research sites in Belize. (a) Pre-hurricane and (b) post-hurricane forest in Monkey River, Belize, which is home to a population of black howler monkeys (*Alouatta pigra*). (c) Pre-hurricane and (d) post-hurricane forest in Runaway Creek Nature Reserve, Belize, which is home to a population of Yucatan spider monkeys (*Ateles geoffroyi yucatanensis*).
Photo credit (c) and (d): K. S. Hartwell.

leeward slopes and valleys remained relatively intact (Figure 13.2). There was also a forest fire in the area in 2011.

13.3.2 Study Populations

Before Hurricane Iris, eight groups of black howler monkeys (totalling 53 monkeys) were monitored weekly and were known to have been stable in size, composition and home range for two years. However, more detailed behavioural and dietary data were collected on only four of these groups ($n = 30$ individuals). Similarly, data were collected on four groups after the hurricane, but, due to significant changes to the population following the storm, they were not the same groups as before the hurricane (although they may have contained some of the same individuals; $n = 25$–28 individuals).

There are at least two communities of Yucatan spider monkeys in RCNR, although only one of these was under continued observation from 2008 to 2015. This group varied in size from 31 to 37 individuals over the course of the eight-year study in a home range of approximately 134 ha (Champion, 2013). Group composition varied as a result of births, disappearances, immigrations, emigrations and naturally occurring deaths. Individuals were identified by differences in pelage colour, facial markings and/or skin pigmentation of the anogential region.

13.3.3 Data Collection

Mortality Patterns

Hurricane-caused mortality patterns were derived from changes in population density at both sites. At MR this was determined through true counts of the black howler monkey groups within the study site, which was previously found to be representative of the population density of the larger watershed forest fragment (Pavelka et al., 2007). A similar method was used at RCNR following Hurricane Richard; immediately after the storm, researchers surveyed the site over the course of several weeks and were eventually able to identify and count the Yucatan spider monkeys.

Activity and Diet

At MR, pre-hurricane focal animal data were collected from January through April 2001 on 30 individuals living in the four study groups. All state and event behaviours were recorded using ten-minute focal animal samples, and if the subject was feeding, both the plant part (leaf buds, new leaves, mature leaves, leaves of unknown age, fruit and flowers) and plant species (when known) were recorded. Groups were located by walking the trail and road system until monkeys were spotted, and occasionally groups could be located by vocalisations. When a group was encountered, the time, location, weather, group size, group spread and group activity were recorded. The sex of each individual was determined based on the conspicuous external genitalia, and age classes (adult, subadult, juvenile and infant) were based on size. Additionally, records of the size and composition of all the groups in the study area were maintained for both the pre- and post-hurricane populations. Post-hurricane focal animal data were collected from January 2002 through June 2007 using the same protocol as in the pre-hurricane study. Focal data were not collected in the first two and a half months following Hurricane Iris because access to the site was restricted by fallen trees and deadfall (Pavelka et al., 2003).

At RCNR, pre-hurricane data were collected from February 2008, although for consistency with the MR data, only pre-hurricane data from the year prior to Hurricane Richard were used in this analysis (October 2009 to October 2010). The data collection protocol was standardised from the beginning of the study, so pre- and post-hurricane data are directly comparable. Five days per week, members of the research team conducted full- or part-day follows on spider monkey subgroups. Daily follows began either at dawn when the monkeys were still at their sleeping sites or at midday, and continued until dusk when the monkeys bed down for the night. Using 30-minute scan samples, researchers recorded the time, location, sub-group size and composition, group spread, identity of recognisable individuals (age/sex class for those who could not be identified) and the activity of each individual. If an individual was feeding, researchers recorded the plant part and species, and when engaged in a social behaviour they recorded the identity of the other participant. For the purposes of this study, social behaviour was defined as: grooming (received or directed), social play, copulations and aggressive interactions.

Social Groupings

At MR, group counts were recorded whenever groups were encountered. This occurred at least monthly before and after the hurricane, although groups were generally encountered on a weekly basis. Only one group count was available from the pre-hurricane rainy season. As the spider monkeys at RCNR live in groups characterised by high fission–fusion dynamics, a subgroup was defined using a chain rule (Ramos-Fernández, 2005), in which all individuals that associated together while maintaining a distance no greater than 50 m from another monkey were included in the subgroup. A subgroup fission was recorded when an individual moved further than 50 m from another and a fusion was recorded when an individual moved within 50 m of another subgroup member for at least two consecutive scans (Hartwell et al., 2014).

13.3.4 Data Analysis

Activity and Diet

To investigate how diet and activity budgets changed relative to pre-hurricane patterns, we performed repeated measure ANOVA that compared diet and activity in the pre-hurricane dry season (dry season 2001 in MR and dry season 2010 in RCNR) to the first post-hurricane dry season (2002 in MR and 2012 in RCNR – due to a forest fire in the area in 2011). In addition, we compared the first three complete annual cycles of activity budgets (2002–2004 in MR and 2011–2013 in RCNR) to determine how behaviour changed in the longer term, and to account for changes that may have occurred in the rainy seasons that could not be compared to the pre-hurricane dry season data that were available. We again used repeated measures ANOVA with a post-hoc Fisher's least significant difference test for these comparisons. Due to the nature of the diet data, we used non-parametric Kruskal–Wallace analyses of variance tests for both the pre- and post-hurricane dry season comparisons and the annual cycles following the hurricane.

Social Grouping Variables

Due to the stable and cohesive nature of black howler monkey social groups, size was the only grouping variable that we compared pre- and post-hurricane and this was only compared descriptively. For the Yucatan spider monkey data, we compared fission and fusion rates and subgroup characteristics, including subgroup size and spread, using independent t-tests with daily averages of subgrouping variables as the unit of analysis. Independent t-tests were used because pre- and post-hurricane samples did not always include the same individuals, and some group members were not observed for extended periods of time. Sample size is thus not consistent across the statistical analyses due to highly fluid subgroups and changes in the overall group composition over the study period. In cases where sample sizes were not equal, we used Levene's tests to confirm homogeneity of variances.

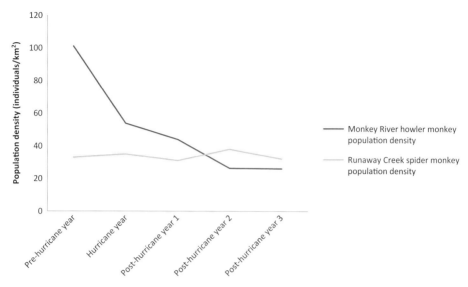

Figure 13.3 Pre- and post-hurricane population densities (individuals/km^2) for the black howler monkey (*Alouatta pigra*) population at Monkey River and the Yucatan spider monkey population (*Ateles geofroyi yucatanensis*) at Runaway Creek Nature Reserve.

13.4   Results

13.4.1   Mortality Patterns

The black howler monkeys at MR experienced an immediate loss of 42 per cent of their population (in terms of overall numbers) in the first six weeks following the hurricane. This was followed by continued population decline that culminated in a loss of 78 per cent of the pre-hurricane population by 2004, three years after Hurricane Iris (Pavelka et al., 2007). At this point the population had declined so dramatically that we feared and predicted a local extinction. However, three years post-hurricane proved to be the low point before the population stabilised and began to increase (Behie & Pavelka, 2015; Figure 13.3). A population assessment immediately following Hurricane Richard at RCNR showed that all individuals were accounted for, and no deaths were associated with the event within the first eight weeks of the assessment. Given the frugivorous nature of the Yucatan spider monkey diet and the fact that many fruit trees at RCNR were damaged, felled, or ceased fruit production, we expected spider monkey mortality to increase in the months following the storm. However, this was not the case, and in fact numbers increased slightly due to births in the second year after the storm (Figure 13.3).

13.4.2   Activity and Diet

When comparing the pre-hurricane and post-hurricane dry season activity budgets, we found that the black howler monkeys spent significantly more time inactive ($t = -2.752$; $p = 0.0094$) and less time engaged in social behaviours ($t = -5.876$; $p = 0.0001$) and feeding ($t = -2.700$; $p = 0.0107$) after the hurricane relative to before (Figure 13.4).

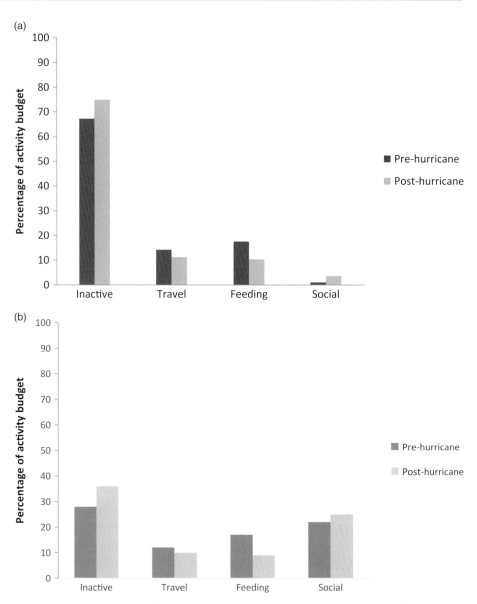

Figure 13.4 Activity budgets of howler monkeys (*Alouatta pigra*) in Monkey River (a) and spider monkeys (*Ateles geofroyi yucatanensis*) in Runaway Creek Nature Reserve (b) in the dry season before and immediately following major hurricanes in Belize.

Similarly, Yucatan spider monkeys spent less time feeding ($t = -2.348$; $p = 0.027$) and more time inactive ($t = -3.894$; $p = 0.00074$), but there was no change in time spent travelling or in time spent engaged in social activities (Figure 13.4).

With respect to diet, black howler monkeys consumed significantly less fruit ($H = 21.65$; $p = 0.001$) and significantly more new leaves ($H = 29.05$; $p = 0.0001$) in the first dry season following Hurricane Iris (Figure 13.5). In contrast, Yucatan spider monkeys showed no significant difference in their consumption of specific plant parts in the first dry season following the storm, although there were trends towards the increased ingestion of leaves and a decrease in ripe-fruit consumption (Figure 13.5). It should be noted that in the wet season immediately following the storm at RCNR (June to December 2011), the spider monkeys ate significantly more leaves and significantly less ripe fruit (Champion, 2013), but we were unable to include these data in this comparison due to the absence of comparable wet season data for MR.

When assessing activity budgets in the first three years following each hurricane, we found that in the post-hurricane environment, black howler monkeys did not show any interannual changes in activity (Figure 13.6). Yucatan spider monkeys, however, spent

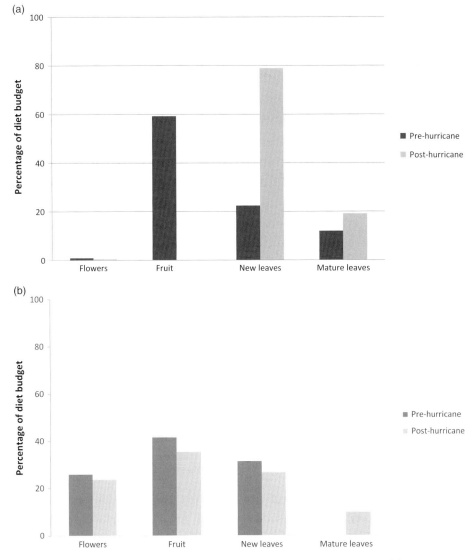

Figure 13.5 Diet budgets of howler monkeys (*Alouatta pigra*) in Monkey River (a) and spider monkeys (*Ateles geofroyi yucatanensis*) in Runaway Creek Nature Reserve (b) in the dry season before and following major hurricanes in Belize (2002 at MR; 2012 at RCNR).

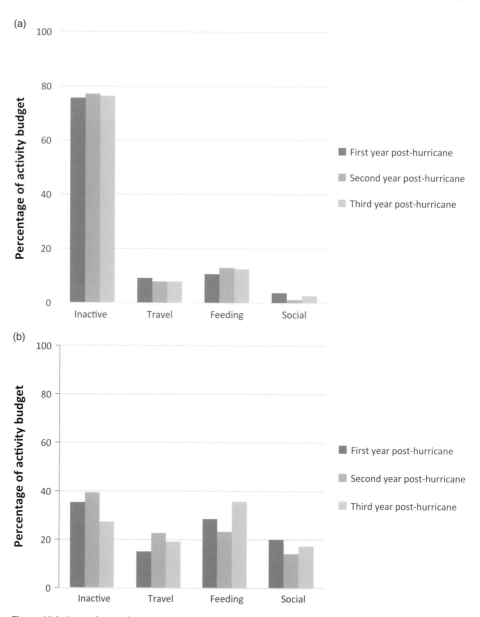

Figure 13.6 Annual post-hurricane activity budgets of howler monkeys (*Alouatta pigra*) in Monkey River (a) and spider monkeys (*Ateles geofroyi yucatanensis*) in Runaway Creek Nature Reserve (b) in the first three years following major hurricanes in Belize.

significantly more time feeding ($t = -2.017$; $p = 0.0355$) and less time inactive ($t = -2.797$; $p = 0.0068$) in the third year following the hurricane compared to the first two years (Figure 13.6), indicating their behaviour was becoming more similar to pre-hurricane patterns. With respect to annual dietary budgets post-hurricane, black howler monkeys consumed significantly more fruit in each subsequent post-hurricane year with an increase from 0 per cent in year one to 10 per cent in year two and 25 per cent in year three, post-hurricane. The consumption of new

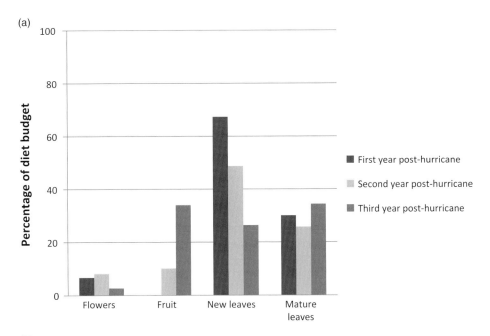

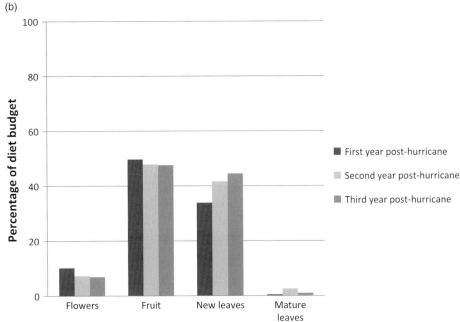

Figure 13.7 Annual post-hurricane diet budgets of howler monkeys (*Alouatta pigra*) in Monkey River (a) and spider monkeys (*Ateles geofroyi yucatanensis*) in Runaway Creek Nature Reserve (b) in the first three years following major hurricanes in Belize.

leaves showed the reverse pattern, becoming less common with more time since the hurricane (64 per cent in year one; 34 per cent in year two; and 26 per cent in year three; Figure 13.7). The consumption of flowers and mature leaves did not show large differences over time. Yucatan spider monkeys showed no variation in their diet from the beginning to the end of the three-year post-hurricane period assessed here (2011–2013; Figure 13.7).

13.4.3 Social Grouping

Black howler monkey mean group size was smaller post-hurricane, averaging 6.32 in both seasons before the hurricane, and falling to 5.67 in the dry season following the storm (June 2002) and to 4.83 by the end of the first post-hurricane rainy season (November 2002). Mean subgroup size for the Yucatan spider monkeys was significantly smaller after the hurricane ($t = 5.639$; $p < 0.0005$), dropping from 5.8 individuals to 3.5 individuals. They were also more spatially cohesive ($t = -2.902$; $p = 0.005$) in the post-hurricane rainy season when compared with the pre-hurricane rainy season, although there were significantly fewer fissions and fusions per hour during this same period ($t = 3.483$; $p = 0.001$). In the dry season, different patterns were seen, with an increase in the rate of fission and fusion events post-hurricane ($t = -4.117$; $p < 0.0005$) and no change to subgroup size or cohesion when compared to pre-hurricane values.

13.5   Discussion

Both anthropogenic and naturally occurring climatic disturbances have a long history of affecting primate habitats, and there is currently growing acknowledgement that both types of environmental modifications will likely increase in the future (IPCC, 2014). Thus, understanding how a species' socioecology constrains their range of behavioural responses to altered environmental conditions has become even more pertinent. We were presented with a unique opportunity to explore how differences in feeding ecology and social organisation might determine resilience to hurricanes in two species of the Atelidae family (black howler monkeys and Yucatan spider monkeys) when two separate hurricanes hit two separate research sites for which pre-hurricane data existed.

The results from this study not only shed light on the behavioural adaptations that might provide a species with increased chances of survival following severe environmental change, but also highlight the need to rethink factors of overall species vulnerability. With the majority of primate species now facing some degree of habitat disturbance we may be – just now – witnessing the full range of, and limits to, their behavioural flexibility. Because so many populations are only recently being pushed to those limits, it is likely that researchers have not fully appreciated what animals are able to tolerate in order to survive a severe habitat disturbance.

The results of previous studies concerning habitat alteration (ring-tailed lemur (*Lemur catta*; LaFleur & Gould, 2009; Ratsimbazafy et al., 2002), ruffed lemurs (*Varecia v. editorium*; Ratsimbazafy, 2006) and lion-tailed macaques (*Macaca silenus*; Menon & Poirer, 1996)) suggest that dietary flexibility is a key determinant of survival following a major habitat disturbance, which may partly explain why ripe-fruit specialists are often regarded as especially sensitive to forest degradation (Johns & Skorupa, 1987). In line with this assumption, we expected the highly frugivorous Yucatan spider monkeys in our study to experience increased mortality

Table 13.1 Infant mortality rates for howler monkeys (*Alouatta pigra*) at Monkey River following Hurricane Iris (2001) and Spider Monkeys (*Ateles geofroyi yucatanensis*) following Hurricane Richard (2010)

	Monkey River howler monkeys (%)	Runaway Creek Nature Reserve spider monkeys (%)
Pre-hurricane year	0	33
Hurricane year	100	0
Post-hurricane year 1	100	0
Post-hurricane year 2	87	14
Post-hurricane year 3	75	25

in response to Hurricane Richard relative to the more generalist and folivorous black howler monkeys at Monkey River following Hurricane Iris. Our results, however, show the opposite scenario: black howler monkeys suffered an immediate population loss of 42 per cent (Pavelka et al., 2003), with continued declines for an additional 18 months (Pavelka et al., 2007), whereas the Yucatan spider monkeys suffered no losses that could be directly attributed to the hurricane as population numbers in subsequent years were well within the normal ranges of fluctuation, given the effects of emigration, births and naturally occurring deaths (see Figure 13.3).

To our knowledge, there were no infants born in the MR howler monkey study groups in the first year after Hurricane Iris, and all infants born ($n = 8$) in the second year died. Only in year three post-hurricane did we observe any infant survival (Behie & Pavelka, 2015; Table 13.1). In the Yucatan spider monkeys at RCNR, however, where we feared the worst after Hurricane Richard, none of the five infants in the community (all born in 2009) died as an immediate result of the storm. In fact, there were no immediate mortalities, infant or otherwise, until July 2011, when one male infant born in early 2009 disappeared and is presumed to have died. In direct contrast to the howler monkeys, three spider monkey infants were born in the three months following Hurricane Richard, two of which were still present in the group in 2013.

We found that both species exhibited altered activity budgets in the direct aftermath of each hurricane, in particular by increasing time spent resting and decreasing time spent feeding. In addition, black howler monkeys also decreased time engaged in social behaviour. This pattern likely reflects a shift towards energy-conserving behaviours in response to forest damage and an accompanying change in food supply. Over the three years after the hurricane, black howler monkeys added more fruit to their diet over time, but their post-hurricane activity budgets remained unchanged, with more inactivity and less feeding relative to before the hurricane. This may be an adaptation to living in a stochastic environment where energy-conserving behaviours are advantageous for maintaining energy stores in periods of prolonged food shortage (Behie et al., 2015; Wright, 1999). In contrast, the Yucatan spider monkeys increased feeding time with each post-hurricane year, so that by year three post-hurricane, activity budgets were not significantly different from before the storm. This may reflect tighter energy constraints on frugivorous species (such as spider monkeys) as both species live in similar environments characterised by high degrees of climate stochasticity.

In our study, both species showed similar dietary flexibility, although this was more pronounced in the black howler monkeys, who relied on a completely leafy diet for the first 18 months after the storm in the absence of available fruit or flowers (Behie & Pavelka, 2015). While our results showed no statistically significant dietary changes in the Yucatan spider monkeys in the first dry season after the storm compared to the dry season before, we did find a trend towards less fruit (both ripe and unripe) consumption and more leaf consumption in the diet – a relationship that was significant in the rainy season after Hurricane Richard when unripe fruit was also consumed more often than ripe fruit (Champion, 2013). This increased consumption of unripe fruit and leaves by the spider monkeys in the first year following the storm suggests a greater degree of dietary flexibility than has previously been appreciated, and is also consistent with data from another spider monkey population following Hurricane Emily in Mexico, where animals also ingested more leaves and less fruit (Schaffner et al., 2012).

It is important to note that no standardised, quantitative assessment of forest damage was conducted after either storm that would allow for direct comparisons between sites. However, the severity of storms did differ, as did the local conditions at each site. MR, where the Category 4 Hurricane Iris made landfall, is topographically flat and lies directly on the Belizean coast, whereas RCNR – where the weaker Category 2 Hurricane Richard hit – is characterised by a more varied topography and is further inland from the coast. One of us (MP) personally witnessed the immediate aftermath of both storms at each site, and it was clear that MR sustained more wide-scale damage than did RCNR. This may account for the relatively higher mortality of howlers at MR, as there were likely monkeys lost *during* the actual storm. However, in the months and years following each storm, the rate of recovery seems to have been much slower for howler monkeys than it was for spider monkeys, despite the fact that the folivorous howlers were not as constrained by potential food shortages, as leaves were plentiful soon after Hurricane Iris.

One possibility that we propose here is that the labile social organisation of spider monkeys that enables them to easily fission into subgroups of varying sizes and composition may have mitigated the costs of increased competition for the few high-quality resources that were available following Hurricane Richard. We found that in the first rainy season following the storm, spider monkey subgroups were smaller in size and more spatially cohesive, with fewer fission and fusion events. The latter finding may relate to the destruction of commonly used arboreal travel routes that occurred during the storm, which may have constrained motivation to fission and travel extensively in unfamiliar terrain. Following two hurricanes in the Yucatan peninsula, Schaffner et al. (2012) also found spider monkeys' highly fluid social system allowed for the group to adapt to the forest damage without any loss of the benefits of sociality.

Black howler monkeys live in small, cohesive social groups that show very high degrees of behavioural synchrony (Pavelka, 2011). Perhaps paradoxically, this type of tight knit social grouping may make any changes in group composition such as those experienced after Iris even more stressful. This pattern has been observed in humans, where stronger social ties are associated with limited overall social network sizes, which can then lead to greater individual isolation (Granovetter, 1973). Weaker social ties, however, such as those seen in the fluid fission–fusion social organisation of spider monkeys, create greater degrees of overlap between the social networks of group members, resulting in individuals having more social ties and being less isolated when social patterns change.

13.6   Future Directions

Our results demonstrate that species vulnerability to severe, short-term habitat disturbance is not necessarily predicted by degree of dietary specialisation alone, but that social factors, such as the degree of fission–fusion dynamics and the ability to adjust subgroup size, might also provide some benefit for coping with shifting ecological conditions. In addition, data from our study sites suggest that specialised frugivores might, at least in the short term, have the ability to decrease their ripe-fruit intake and to supplement their diet with leaves for sustained periods of time without suffering from severe (i.e. mortality-causing) nutritional stress.

It is likely that many of the traditional dietary categories in which species have habitually been placed are based on behavioural observations in relatively undisturbed habitats, where preferred foods are more commonly available. Future studies would benefit from a reevaluation of traditional dietary classifications and our associated expectations of how animals should interact with their environment and respond to disturbance. Moreover, we would benefit from taking a more comparative approach that incorporates long-term datasets from across study sites that have undergone habitat events and which are characterised by a variety of ecological conditions.

Similarly, future studies should consider both dietary and social flexibility and how the two may interact to increase resilience in primate species. While it is recognised that social organisation in primates is complex and shows variation in how fluid animals are in their social patterns (Aureli et al., 2008), this should also be compared across study sites to elucidate how this sort of flexibility may be underpinned by environmental conditions. These sorts of comparative studies will require long-term collaborations between researchers. We would thus urge the new generation of primatologists to enter the discipline with a collaborative mindset and the understanding that to help species survive, we will need datasets that are bigger than one person or team can possibly collect. Studies such as this will allow us to understand the full range of behavioural flexibility that exists among primates. This is certainly the approach we are taking with our own students, where we encourage the sharing of ideas and the incorporation of cross-disciplinary advice into student research projects. This involves teaching students about the value of all stakeholders engaged in primate conservation from academic researchers, to zoo and NGO staff, to government officials. This hopefully instils in them the idea that we are stronger working together than on our own.

It is our hope that this chapter will generate discussion and interest in readers about how we can start to source empirical data that can be used to best make predictions about species' vulnerability in response to severe climatic events. This may involve challenging the theories that we are so often taught in the classroom as many of them may not hold true for animals in severely disturbed habitats. In doing this, we would encourage the new generation of primatologists to think outside the box about how traditional theories relate to our current situation. This will enable us to better mitigate the disproportionate impacts of such events on the species-specific needs of vulnerable and affected populations.

Acknowledgements

We thank the Belize government for granting us permission to conduct this research and the Life and Environmental Science Animal Care Committee for its annual review and approval of our research protocols. Thanks to Dr Gil and Lillian Boese for permission to work in the Runaway Creek Nature Reserve, Birds Without Borders for their assistance with fieldwork, and to Kayley Evans for pre-hurricane data collection. The Monkey River Research Project could not have been done without the assistance of a number of local guides and research assistants who aided in the collection of data and monitoring of the monkey population. Funding was provided by the National Science and Engineering Research Council of Canada (NSERC), National Geographic, the American Society of Primatologists, Conservation International, the International Primatological Society, Sigma XI and the University of Calgary.

References

Asensio, N., Korstjens, A. H., Schaffner, C. M. & Aureli, F. (2008). Intragroup aggression, fission–fusion dynamics and feeding competition in spider monkeys. *Behaviour*, 145, 983–1001.

Aureli, F., Schaffner, C. M., Boesch, C., et al. (2008). Fission–fusion dynamics: new research frameworks. *Current Anthropology*, 49, 627–54.

Barone, J. A. (1998). Effects of light availability and rainfall on leaf production in a moist tropical forest in central Panama. *Journal of Tropical Ecology*, 14, 309–21.

Behie, A. M. & Pavelka, M. S. M. (2005). The short-term effect of Hurricane Iris on the diet and activity budget of black howlers (*Alouatta pigra*) in Monkey River, Belize. *Folia Primatologica*, 76, 1–9.

Behie, A. M. & Pavelka, M. S. M. (2015). Fruit as a key factor in howler monkey population density: conservation implications. In Kowalewski, M., Garber, P. A., Cortes-Ortiz, L., Urbani, B. & Youlatos, D. (eds) *Howler Monkeys: Behaviour, Ecology and Conservation*. New York: Springer, pp. 357–81.

Behie, A. M., Wyman, T. M., Steffens, T. S. & Pavelka, M. S. M. (2015). Hurricanes and coast lines: the role of natural disasters in the evolution of *Alouatta pigra*. In Behie, A. M. & Oxenham, M. F. (eds) *Taxonomic Tapestries: The Threads of Behavioural, Evolutionary and Conservation Research*. Canberra: ANUpress, pp. 75–91.

Champion, J. (2013). The effects of a hurricane and fire on the feeding ecology, ranging behaviour, activity budget, and social patterns of spider monkeys (*Ateles geoffroyi*) in Central Belize. Master's Thesis, University of Calgary.

Di Fiore, A. & Suarez, S. A. (2007). Route-based travel and shared routes in sympatric spider and woolly monkeys: cognitive and evolutionary implications. *Animal Cognition*, **10**, 317–29.

Ford, S. M. (2006). The biogeographic history of Mesoamerican primates. In Estrada, A., Garber, P. A., Pavelka, M. S. M. & Luecke, L. (eds) *New Perspectives in the Study of Mesoamerican Primates: Distribution, Ecology, Behaviour, and Conservation.* New York: Springer, pp. 81–120.

Granovetter, M. S. (1973). The strength of weak ties. *American Journal of Sociology*, **78**, 1360–80.

Hartwell, K. S., Notman, H., Bonenfant, C. & Pavelka, M. S. M. (2014). Assessing the occurrence of sexual segregation in spider monkeys (*Ateles geoffroyi yucatanensis*), its mechanisms and function. *International Journal of Primatology*, **35**, 425–44.

IPCC (Intergovernmental Panel on Climate Change). (2014). *Synthesis Report.* Geneva: IPCC. Available at: www.ipcc.ch/pdf/assessment-report/ar5/syr/SYR_AR5_FINAL_full_wcover.pdf

Johns, A. D. & Skorupa, J. P. (1987). Responses in rain-forest primates to habitat disturbance: a review. *International Journal of Primatology*, **8**, 157–91.

Kimberlaine, T. B. (2011). Tropical Cyclone Report: Hurricane Richard. National Hurricane Center. Available at: www.nhc.noaa.gov/data/tcr/AL192010_Richard.pdf.

LaFleur, M. & Gould, L. (2009). Feeding outside the forest: the importance of crop raiding and an invasive weed in the diet of gallery forest ring-tailed lemurs (*Lemur catta*) following a cyclone at the Beza Mahafaly Special Reserve, Madagascar. *Folia Primatologica*, **80**, 233–46.

Malone, N., Fuentes, A. & White, F. J. (2012). Variation in the social systems of extant hominoids: comparative insight into the social behaviour of early hominins. *International Journal of Primatology*, **33**, 1251–77.

Menon, S. & Poirer, F. E. (1996). Lion-tailed macaques (*Macaca silenus*) in a disturbed forest fragment: activity patterns and time budget. *International Journal of Primatology*, **17**, 969–85.

Midgley, G. F., Hannah, L., Millar, D., Rutherford, M. C. & Powrie, L. W. (2002). Assessing the vulnerability of species richness to anthropogenic climate change in a biodiversity hot spot. *Global Ecology and Biogeography*, **11**, 445–51.

NOAA (National Oceanic and Atmospheric Administration) (2016). Historical hurricane tracks. Available at: https://coast.noaa.gov/hurricanes (accessed 20 December 2016).

Pavelka, M. S. M. (2011). Mechanisms of cohesion in black howler monkeys. In Sussman, R. W. & Cloninger, C. R. (eds) *Origins of Cooperation and Altruism.* New York: Springer, pp. 167–78.

Pavelka, M. S. M. & Behie, A. M. (2005). The effect of Hurricane Iris on the food supply of black howlers (*Alouatta pigra*) in southern Belize. *Biotropica*, **37**, 102–8.

Pavelka, M. S. M., Brusselers, O. T., Nowak, D. & Behie, A. M. (2003). Population reduction and social disorganization in *Alouatta pigra* following a hurricane. *International Journal of Primatology*, **24**, 1037–55.

Pavelka, M. S. M., McGoogan, K. C. & Steffens, T. S. (2007). Population size and characteristics of *Alouatta pigra* before and after a major hurricane. *International Journal of Primatology*, **28**, 919–29.

Ramos-Fernández, G. (2005). Vocal communication in a fission–fusion society: do spider monkeys stay in touch with close associates? *International Journal of Primatology*, **26**, 1077–92.

Ramos-Fernández, G. & Ayala-Orozco, B. (2003). Population size and habitat use of spider monkeys at Punta Laguna, Mexico. In Marsh, L. K. (ed.) *Primates in Fragments: Ecology and Conservation.* New York: Kluwer Academic/Plenum Publishers, pp. 191–209.

Ratsimbazafy, J. H. (2006). Diet composition, foraging and feeding behaviour in relation to habitat disturbance: implications for the adaptability of ruffed lemurs (*Varecia v. editorium*) in Manombo forest, Madagascar. In Gould, L. & Sauther, M. L. (eds) *Lemurs: Ecology and Adaptation.* New York: Springer, pp. 403–22.

Ratsimbazafy, J. H., Ramarosandratana, H. V. & Zaonarivelo, R. J. (2002). How do black-and-white ruffed lemurs survive in a highly disturbed habitat? *Lemur News*, **7**, 7–10.

Saunders, M. A. & Lea, A. S. (2008). Large contribution of sea surface warming to recent increase in Atlantic hurricane activity. *Nature*, **451**, 557–60.

Schaffner, C. M., Rebecchini, L., Ramos-Fernández, G., Vick, L. G. & Aureli, F. (2012). Spider monkeys (*Ateles geoffroyi yucatenensis*) cope with the negative consequences of hurricanes through changes in diet, activity budget, and fission–fusion dynamics. *International Journal of Primatology*, 33, 922–36.

Vandermeer, J., Brenner, A. & Cerda, I. G. (1998). Growth rates of tree height six years after hurricane damage at four localities in eastern Nicaragua. *Biotropica*, 30, 502–9.

Van Roosmalen, M. G. M. (1980). Habitat preferences, diet, feeding strategy and social organisation of the black spider monkey (*Ateles paniscus paniscus* Linnaeus 1758) in Surinam. Doctoral dissertation, Landbouwhogeschool te Wageningen.

Wright, P. C. (1999). Lemur traits and Madagascar ecology: coping with an island environment. *American Journal of Physical Anthropology*, 110, 31–72.

Wright, P. C. (2006). Considering climate change effects in lemur ecology and conservation. In Gould, L. & Sauther, M. L. (eds) *Lemurs: Ecology and Adaptation*. New York: Springer, pp. 385–401.

14 The Effect of Climate Change on the Distribution of the Genera *Colobus* and *Cercopithecus*

Amanda H. Korstjens

14.1 Personal Narrative

I always wanted to do something with animals, so I selected the biology degree that included animal behaviour in Utrecht, the Netherlands. During my studies, I was torn between choosing a subject with more job potential, i.e. medically directed biology, and my interest in understanding how biology underpins behaviour. During my year in Indonesia for an MPhil-equivalent project on Thomas langurs with Romy Steenbeek, Liesbeth Sterck and Jan van Hooff I was committed to working in tropical forests. My subsequent PhD research involved a comparison of the socioecology of three sympatric colobines in Taï National Park, Côte d'Ivoire. I now worked for both Utrecht University's Jan van Hooff and my first supervisor Ronald Noë at the Seewiesen Max Planck Institute, Germany. There are huge cultural differences between Indonesia and Côte d'Ivoire, but for me the first shock was the difference in height and density of the forests. I remember asking when the forest would begin and being told that I was right in the middle of it.

The amazing thing about this and many other African forests is the sheer abundance of primates compared to Asian forests, as long as poaching is not rife. I spent over two years in Taï, studying the differences in social organisation of Taï's three sympatric colobines in relation to ecological differences (Korstjens, 2001; Korstjens & Noë, 2004; Korstjens & Schippers, 2003; Korstjens et al., 2002; 2005; 2007). This alerted me to the fragile future of these forests and their inhabitants. Primates are practically absent and the forests are eerily quiet in areas that receive no protection from poaching. The presence of researchers tends to greatly improve the chances of a forest and its inhabitants remaining relatively untouched. Ronald Noë would also support the local teachers and schools (using donations from his friends and family mostly) in the villages near Taï. As the site manager, I often implemented these activities and saw how important this work was for the local community and for the reputation of our research projects in the local community. Hiring local assistants and support workers/builders also played an important role in how the local community saw the researchers and the forest. After completing my PhD, struggling to find a permanent job or funding, Filippo Aureli (one of Jan van Hooff's many previous PhD students) and Colleen Schaffner took me on as an assistant for their project in Santa Rosa, Costa Rica. I was unprepared for the heat and lack of canopy cover in Santa Rosa's semi-deciduous dry forest, but I loved working with spider monkeys. I also had the pleasure of visiting the other side of Costa Rica to teach a one-month field course in primate ecology at El Zota for DANTA, where rain falls every day (even in the dry season) due to being on the windward side of Costa Rica's central mountain range. The high cloud forests and wildlife everywhere in Costa Rica are simply amazing.

My next career opportunity started with a job interview over the telephone, while I was seated in my dirty forest attire, watching deer and woodpeckers in Santa Rosa. The postdoctoral project with Robin Dunbar from the University of Liverpool was desk-based but learning more about modelling primate responses to climate change and working with Robin as part of the Lucy to Language project (Dunbar et al., 2014) was amazing. I also co-supervised the postdoc project of Norberto Asensio with Filippo to continue my involvement with spider monkey research (Asensio, et al., 2008; 2009).

Overall, my research career was shaped by the opportunities I encountered and a will to work hard. However, a career in primatology is not easy. What has made it all worthwhile to me is my love for tropical forests, the place where I really feel at home. Additionally, it is rewarding to meet such great people. Over the years, conservation has become more and more important and no primatologist can work in the tropics without spending a large proportion of their time trying to support the conservation of these beautiful forests. For me, this has taken the shape of investigating how macro- and micro-level habitat change affect forest structure and the survival of the primates living in these forests. Presently, most of my time is spent teaching others about primate behaviour, ecology and conservation and desk-based modelling work. I started a new research programme, 'LEAP: Landscape Ecology and Primatology', together with Ross Hill, Serge Wich and Matt Nowak. LEAP aims to develop new ways to improve our understanding of primate responses to environmental change and develop better mitigation strategies to ensure the survival of tropical forests and their inhabitants. LEAP has allowed me to return to the Indonesian forests I love.

14.2   Introduction

Although habitat loss and hunting tend to be the most urgent threats to primates, climate change also influences primate survival and can increase the susceptibility (or vulnerability) of primates to other threats (Korstjens & Hillyer, 2016; Schloss et al., 2012). Climate change is a complicated, multifaceted threat to primates because the climate is not changing uniformly across the globe (IPCC, 2014). The changes will affect different species in different ways depending on their intrinsic biological traits, as well as the nature of the climate change in their area (Korstjens & Hillyer, 2016). Primates are thought to be particularly sensitive to climate change and human disturbance compared to other mammals due to several primate-typical biological traits such as: relatively slow life-histories and slow regeneration times, social group living, restricted geographical ranges, restricted individual travel distances, short dispersal distances, and a tendency for sex-biased dispersal (Korstjens & Hillyer, 2016). In particular, species with a more specialised diet and those restricted to arboreal substrates are expected to have more limited flexibility to adapt to changes than species adapted to a generalised diet and those that regularly travel terrestrially (Estrada et al., 2016; Korstjens & Hillyer, 2016). In comparison to most mammals (e.g. ungulates or carnivores), primates are often dietary generalists. Most primate species consume fruit, vegetative plant matter (i.e. leaves, pith, herbs, etc.), flowers and animal matter as their staple. Species differ mostly in the relative contribution of each of these food items in their diet and many species respond flexibly to changes in food availability (Nowak & Lee, 2013). In some human-modified habitats, flexible species may benefit from feeding on crops and living in urbanised landscapes (Estrada et al., 2012; Maibeche et al., 2015). Primates are also predicted to be vulnerable to climate change because their habitats are particularly exposed to large changes in climate (Graham et al., 2016), and many primates live in fragments (Behie & Pavelka, 2013). Here I compare the effects that climate change is likely to have on the spread of species within the genera *Cercopithecus* and *Colobus*.

The main approaches for determining how climate change will affect species distributions are: (1) species distribution/ecological niche models; (2) correlative models incorporating biological traits; and (3) mechanistic models (Wisz et al., 2013; Kamilar & Beaudrot, 2017; Kamilar & Tecot, 2016). Species distribution models (SDMs) identify the main environmental (usually climatic and sometimes also geological or vegetation-related) correlates of a species' current distribution patterns. Species distribution models are also referred to as ecological niche models because they essentially identify the environmental values that explain the ecological or climatic niche of a species. Using the observed correlations between environmental values and presence/absence of a species, you can estimate a 'suitability' value for a site or area. The suitability value is a continuous value that shows how suitable the area is for the study species. A suitability value below 0 typically means that a species is unlikely to survive at the location (the site is unsuitable) and values above 0 mean that the environmental conditions at the site would be suitable for a species' survival. The suitability value can then be calculated for any site, based on a site's current conditions or future conditions to predict how a change in those variables will affect future distributions (Elith & Leathwick, 2009; Lehman & Fleagle, 2006).

The second modelling approach investigates the interactions between biological traits and environmental variables by including trait variables alongside environmental variables in correlative SDMs to predict/explain species' distribution patterns (Beaudrot & Marshall, 2011; Beaudrot et al., 2013; Fleagle & Reed, 1996; Kamilar & Muldoon, 2010).

The third, and most bottom-up approach, is where the mechanisms and processes behind species–environment relationships are used to predict species' responses to change (sometimes using individual-based models). One of the earliest studies to use the third approach to look at mechanisms behind the relationship between climate and primate distributions is the time-budget modelling work led by Robin Dunbar (Dunbar 1992; 1993; 1998; Dunbar & Dunbar, 1988; Iwamoto & Dunbar, 1983). He showed how gelada baboons, *Theropithecus gelada*, are driven to higher altitudes if temperatures increase, and used this approach to understand the demise of the genus *Theropithecus*, which once roamed widely across Africa. Since then, time-budget models have been used to understand how time constraints can explain species distribution patterns (Bettridge & Dunbar, 2012; Bettridge et al., 2010; Carne et al., 2012; Dunbar et al., 2009; González-Zamora et al., 2011; Korstjens & Dunbar, 2007; Korstjens et al., 2006; 2010; Lehmann et al., 2007; 2008a; 2008b; 2010; Teichroeb et al., 2003; Willems & Hill, 2009; Williamson & Dunbar, 1999). To choose the most appropriate modelling approach for a study it is important to consider the limitations and strengths of each approach. To develop an SDM or SDM incorporating trait variables and to test the success of any mechanistic model, reliable species occurrence data (i.e. presence/absence or a geographical range map) are required.

In view of predicting future distribution patterns of a species, it is also important to understand the difference between a species' realised niche (N_R) as opposed to its fundamental niche (N_F) (Hutchinson, 1978). The N_F is the niche that a species could occupy if there were no dispersal limitations and competitive interactions; it includes all areas where a species would be able to have a positive population growth rate. The N_R is shaped by competitive interactions with other species and dispersal limitations, which lead to it being smaller than the N_F of a species. Soberón and Arroyo-Peña (2017) and Guisan et al. (2014) provide recent reviews of these ecological concepts. SDMs, like the one presented here, establish which areas contain environments that are suitable for a species to live in based on where the species is currently established, i.e. the species' N_R. To be able to define a species' N_F, we require detailed knowledge and understanding of the physiological processes that limit a species' survival, something that is seldom available.

In this chapter I develop an SDM for the genera *Cercopithecus* and *Colobus*. Previously I have developed time-budget models for these genera (Korstjens & Dunbar 2007; Korstjens et al., 2018). *Cercopithecus* and *Colobus* belong to the Cercopithecidae family, but each represents an alternative sub-family: *Colobus* represents the Colobinae (colobines) that have specialist digestive adaptations for leaf consumption and detoxification of secondary plant compounds; *Cercopithecus* represents the Cercopithecinae (cercopithecines), which have relatively simple digestive systems. These genera have comparable social and dispersal systems: most *Colobus* and *Cercopithecus* spp. live in one-male multi-female groups with male-biased dispersal (Kingdon & Groves, 2013a). Some *Colobus* spp. aggregate in larger groups (Fashing et al., 2007), but generally those groups still seem organised around the one-male multi-female social group. Home-range sizes vary among *Colobus* and *Cercopithecus* species, but are within the same order of magnitude.

The most obvious ecological difference between *Colobus* and *Cercopithecus* spp. is related to their dietary adaptations. *Cercopithecus* is relatively omnivorous, with a focus on fruit and insects (Chapman et al., 2002). Some species, in particular *Cercopithecus mitis*, also consume large quantities of leaves (Bruorton et al., 1991). Long retention and fermentation times in cercopithecines allow them to digest low-quality foods. Colobines have specialised digestive systems (with a multi-chambered stomach) designed to support leaf eating, but this limits their exploitation of high-quality, sugar-rich ripe fruits (because high consumption of sugary foods will over-stimulate their gut bacteria) (Lambert, 1998). Colobines are able to consume high-quality (fat-rich) seeds (including nuts) that may be toxic to other species (Chivers, 1994; Korstjens et al., 2007), but they also consume a lot of unripe fruit (unripe fruits contain less sugar than ripe fruits) and flowers (or flower buds) when available (Fashing, 2005; Korstjens & Dunbar, 2007). In Kibale, Uganda, cercopithecines are more likely to switch between diets in response to food availability than are colobines, which may be a reflection of greater digestive flexibility of cercopithecines compared to colobines (Lambert, 2002).

Climate change is expected to influence the quality of food sources for primates in a variety of ways (Korstjens & Hillyer, 2016). Increased warming and reduced rainfall will lead to lower digestibility and lower quality of leaves (i.e. lower protein–fibre ratios), and higher concentrations of plant secondary compounds in leaves (Rothman et al., 2014; Zvereva & Kozlov, 2006). Increased CO_2 levels may lead to increased fruit production if plants are not suffering too much climatic stress from drought or intensive rains (Clark et al., 2013). Changes in fruit production as a result of climate change have been observed in Kibale, Uganda and Taï, Ivory Coast (Chapman et al., 2005; Polansky & Boesch, 2013). Currently, there is no model to predict how the food sources of primates will respond to climate change across Africa due to the flexibility in most primates' diets.

Another reason for comparing these genera is that both are relatively dependent on forested or reasonably well-wooded areas in a comparable way; indeed, they are often found in sympatric associations. *Cercopithecus* (specifically *Cercopithecus mitis/albogularis*), however, are more widely distributed across southern Africa and appear to cope better with relatively open woodlands than do *Colobus* (Kingdon & Groves 2013a; 2013b; Figure 14.1). With an overall increase in temperatures and

(a)

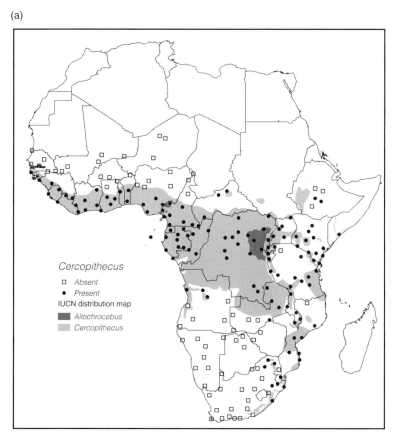

Figure 14.1 Distribution of the genera (a) *Cercopithecus* and (b) *Colobus* following current IUCN distribution map data (IUCN, 2017) and location of the sample sites where the genera are present or absent. Dark grey area in (a) represents the distribution of *Allochrocebus* (overlapping with that of *Cercopithecus* species).

(b)

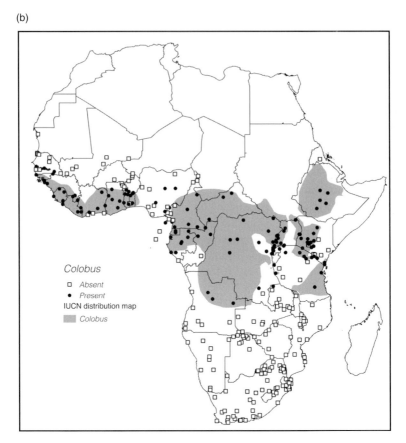

Figure 14.1 Cont.

decrease in rainfall in large parts of Africa (but some increase in rainfall in the east), open woodlands could become more prevalent across southern and western Africa. I predict that both species will suffer from the predicted increased temperatures and decreased precipitation in southern and western Africa, leading to a retraction of their geographical ranges. I predict that *Cercopithecus* may lose less of its current range than *Colobus* because *Cercopithecus* is more capable of using open woodlands. Therefore, a comparison between these two genera will help us investigate whether genera that only mildly differ in their habitat requirements will have similar distributions under future climate change scenarios.

Another aspect that requires consideration is the potential for a pole-ward shift of suitable climates away from the equator (Chen et al., 2011; Iverson & McKenzie, 2013) as opposed to my prediction that the central African regions will remain suitable and the outer regions less suitable. Pole-ward range shifts for primates are unlikely, however, because the north of sub-Saharan Africa is unlikely to expand in forest or even savannah area, but there may be some emerging biomes in the south-east (Sato & Ise, 2012).

14.3   Methodology and Methods

14.3.1   Species Distribution Data

Presence and absence of cercopithecids (i.e. Old World monkeys) across sub-Saharan Africa was determined for 327 sites. The United Nations Environmental Programme (UNEP) World Conservation Monitoring Centre (WCMC) database on protected areas (accessed between 2003 and 2006) and the African Protected Areas Assessment Tool, APAAT (Hartley et al., 2007), accessed in 2013–14, were used as a basis for locating potential sites. The WCMC and APAAT data are now part of the Digital Observatory for Protected areas (DOPA; http://dopa.jrc.ec.europa.eu/node/4). Subsequently, search engines (e.g. Google, Google Scholar) were used to locate reports and scientific publications about primate presence at those locations using the site's name to verify or complete the data available in the WCMC and APAAT database. If this search produced country- or region-wide primate surveys that included further locations, those were also included in the dataset. Locations of sites were then projected onto a map of Africa to identify gaps in distribution information and an intensive search on the internet was conducted to fill those gaps, using the keywords: country name with census, primates, mammals, *Cercopithecus*, *Colobus*, or monkey.

Most information on species' presence/absence represents information from recent years, but I deliberately included reports of presence from 1970 to 2000 as well because many local extinctions are the result of anthropogenic pressures and not climatic differences. The data used here for 'current' climate cover observed data of the period 1960–90. The dataset used includes only those sites that had complete information on the presence and absence of both *Cercopithecus* and *Colobus*, and contains 327 sites across sub-Saharan Africa; at these: 121 sites had both genera; 71 had *Cercopithecus* but no *Colobus*; 20 had *Colobus* but no *Cercopithecus*; and 115 had neither genus (Figure 14.1). A common alternative practice to using actual presence/absence data is to use species range map data (Figure 14.1) to generate random presence sites (located anywhere within the range) and absence sites (located anywhere outside the range) (Gouveia et al., 2014); however, these tend to overestimate presence (Hurlbert & Jetz, 2007) and niche breadth. Therefore, although a smaller overall area is covered using site-specific presence/absence data, it is likely to be more accurate than using range maps alone.

High-resolution climate data (30 arcsecond intervals, ~1 km resolution) were compiled from WorldClim's global climate database version 1.4 following Hijmans and Elith (2016) to instruct data analyses. The climate variables used were: T_{ann}, mean annual temperature; $T_{dayrange}$, mean difference between the minimum and maximum temperatures for each day (temperature diurnal range: mean of monthly (maximum temp – minimum temp)); T_{moSD}, temperature seasonality (standard deviation of mean monthly temperatures $\times$ 100); $T_{minCold}$, minimum temperature of the coldest month; P_{ann}, mean annual precipitation; P_{moCV}, precipitation seasonality (coefficient of variation of mean monthly rainfall); P_{Wet}, precipitation of the wettest quarter; and P_{Dry}, precipitation of the driest quarter. These climate variables were selected because they have been shown to play an important part in primate distribution patterns (Dunbar et al., 2009). In addition, if two climate variables correlated strongly with each other ($r > 0.04$), only one was included. For each site, latitude/longitude values were used to extract a single data point for each climate measure in R version 3.1.1 (R Core Team, 2016) using the RStudio version 0.99.903 for Macintosh interface.

Generalised linear models (GLMs) with logistic link function (GLM logit link; family: binomial) were run to identify which climate variables most strongly predicted current distribution patterns of each of the genera (Hijmans & Elith, 2016). The resulting equation of the best-fit model (based on AICc values and extracted from the global model using the dredge function in R's MuMIn package; Bartoń, 2016) was then used to calculate the estimated current and future distribution of suitable habitat of each genus. After running the dredge function, I used the top model with the lowest AICc value. AIC stands for Aikake's information criterion (e.g. Burnham & Anderson, 2002). AIC is a number that is used to compare how well models fit the variation observed in the data, while taking into account the complexity of the model (the GLM in this case). A more complex model (i.e. with more variables included) will have to have a better fit to the data than a model with fewer variables to achieve the same low AIC value. When you have a relatively small sample, the AICc is more appropriate than the AIC because it penalises more for greater complexity. When using model selection and reporting AICc values, it is important to note that the AIC values are only comparable between models based on the same number of cases from the same dataset (i.e. you cannot compare two models with AIC if model 1 uses a variable that has more missing values than the variables included in model 2).

To test how well a GLM (i.e. your multivariate equation) fits the species distribution data, you can split your dataset into a training and a test dataset. You develop the model using only the data from the training dataset and then test how well your model performs by using the model equation on your test dataset (for easy-to-follow instructions, see Hijmans and Elith (2016)). Because here I am interested in modelling future climate, I used the model equations produced using the full dataset from the start. The model produces a continuous 'suitability' value for each location in your dataset. The model is considered a good predictor of the ability of a genus to survive at a site if the suitability value is significantly larger at sites where the genus is present compared to those where it is absent. The suitability value thus functions as an indicator of the quality of the location for that species. In addition, I determined the accuracy of the model equation in predicting presence or absence in a binary way by using Cohen's kappa (using SPSS 22.0; Cohen, 1968; Liu et al., 2011) and reporting the percentage of cases for which the model correctly predicts a species to be present or absent. Cohen's kappa uses the percentage of correct predictions but corrects for sampling discrepancy between sites with and without your species. The area under the receiver operator curve (AUROC, abbreviated to AUC usually) is another indicator of how well the model outcomes fit observed presence/absence (using R; following Hijmans & Elith, 2016).

For future climate conditions I used the WorldClim 1.4 downscale (CMIP5) data (www.worldclim.org/CMIP5v1). CMIP5 stands for Coupled Model Intercomparison Project Phase 5. CMIP5 provides a multi-model context for estimating the future climatic conditions across the world. The WorldClim website provides a whole set of models of what the climate is predicted to look like in 2050 and 2070. I decided to select the HadGEM2 family's ES model (Collins et al., 2008). HadGEM2 is developed by the UK MET office (Collins et al., 2008). The choice for this particular model is based on a multi-model comparison done by Brands et al. (2013) that supported this model as the best for Africa and Europe. Choosing the model family and model itself is, however, not the end of the selection process. There is a further choice between four representative concentration pathways (RCPs). These four pathways represent scenarios that would result from four greenhouse gas concentration trajectories as adopted by the IPCC for its *Fifth Assessment Report* (AR5) in 2014 (Moss et al., 2008). Here I present the results of an average of the RCP2.6 (best case) and RCP8.5 (worst case) scenarios because these represent the two extremes of potential future conditions. The four RCPs (RCP2.6, RCP4.5, RCP6 and RCP8.5) are named after a possible range of radiative forcing values in the year 2100 relative to pre-industrial values (+2.6, +4.5, +6.0 and +8.5 W/m^2, respectively).

The map of modelled current and future suitable habitats for each genus was created by multiplying the relevant climate layers with the relevant values in the equations obtained from the GLM. This was done using the raster-calculate function in QGIS (QGIS Development Team, 2016). I prefer using this method, over the much-used alternative of using the 'predict' function in R because the QGIS raster-calculate functionality is extremely fast and easy to use despite combining several large raster files. Similarly, the difference between current and future suitability was calculated by deducting the current raster from the future raster.

14.3.2 Comparing Current to Future Suitable Habitat

The suitability values (i.e. the value that emerged from the GLM equation) of sites where a genus was absent were compared to suitability values at sites where it was present using Mann–Whitney *U* tests. Spearman rank correlations were used to test whether the suitability value correlated with the number of species present for the *Cercopithecus* genus. This test was not possible for *Colobus* because most sites only had one species of *Colobus*. Matched pairs Wilcoxon signed ranks tests were used to compare suitability values of individual sites for future and current conditions. These current-versus-future comparison tests were done in SPSS 22.0.

The maps (created in QGIS 2.6) of current and future suitable habitats reflect the predicted areas suitable for *Colobus* and *Cercopithecus* spp. (Figure 14.2) according

(a)

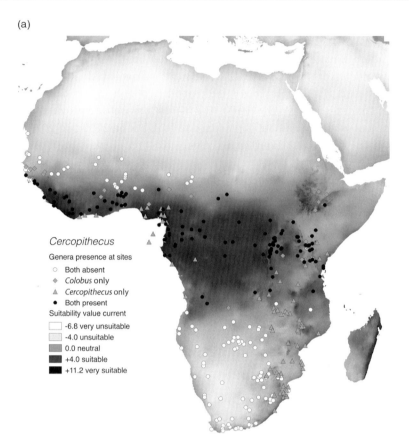

Cercopithecus

Genera presence at sites
○ Both absent
◆ *Colobus* only
▲ *Cercopithecus* only
● Both present
Suitability value current
☐ -6.8 very unsuitable
☐ -4.0 unsuitable
☐ 0.0 neutral
■ +4.0 suitable
■ +11.2 very suitable

Figure 14.2 Current suitability values for (a) *Cercopithecus* and (b) *Colobus* across Africa with current presence/absence at sites plotted for each genus.

to our GLM and are not exact replicas of the observed species distribution maps (Figure 14.1). Because I compare current situations to future situations, I compare these modelled distributions for both situations rather than using the real distribution maps for current conditions and the modelled maps for future distributions.

14.4   Results

14.4.1   Current Climate Analyses and Model Accuracy Test

The strongest models for habitat suitability for the two genera showed that most of the climate variables were significant contributors to the models (Table 14.1). As required of a good model, the suitability values per genus were significantly greater for sites where the respective genus is present compared to where it is absent (*Colobus*: $N_{absent} = 192$, $N_{present} = 135$, $Z = -13.87$; *Cercopithecus* $N_{absent} = 141$, $N_{present} = 186$, $Z = -13.10$; $p < 0.001$; Figure 14.3). Furthermore, the suitability

(b)

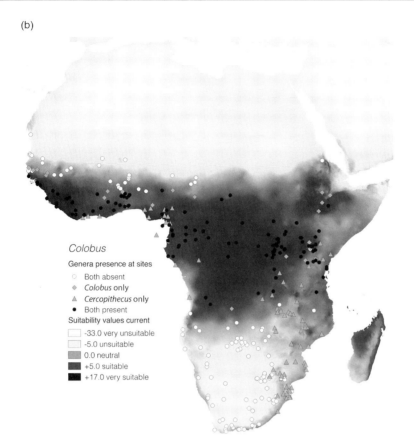

Figure 14.2 Cont.

value correlated strongly and positively with the number of *Cercopithecus* species present at sites (excluding sites where no species were present; $N = 186$, Spearman's rho $= 0.74$, $p < 0.001$; including the absent sites only made the relationship stronger). There was some overlap in suitability values for absence and presence sites, but overall the most informative cut-off value for suitability was 0 for both genera (Figure 14.3). Note that taking a cut-off value of 0 after a binary logistic regression analysis is not always the best option (Liu et al., 2011). For example, a researcher may choose a lower cut-off value when a few false 'presence' predictions are considered better than excluding any potentially suitable sites. In this study, the minimum suitability values for sites where the genus is currently present are –2.27 for *Colobus* and –1.92 for *Cercopithecus* (Figure 14.3). I chose the cut-off value of 0 as it had the most equal balance between correct and false predictions for both presence and absence sites. Model predictions fitted well with observed presence/absence ($AUC_{Col} = 0.95$, $kappa_{Col} = 0.73$; $AUC_{Cerc} = 0.87$, $kappa_{Cerc} = 0.64$) and distribution patterns (Figure 14.2).

Table 14.1 Outcomes of the best-fit generalised binomial linear model (with logistic link function) for (a) *Colobus* and (b) *Cercopithecus*

(a)

	β	SE	Z	p
Intercept	4.962	1.980	2.506	0.012
T_{ann}	0.068	0.018	3.686	<0.001
T_{moSD}	−0.005	0.00063	−7.155	<0.001
$T_{minCold}$	−0.061	0.017	−3.616	<0.001
P_{ann}	−0.003	0.001	−2.295	0.022
P_{moCV}	−0.060	0.017	−3.552	<0.001
P_{Wet}	0.006	0.003	2.309	0.021

Resulting equation: Suitability value$_{Colobus}$ = 4.962 + (0.068 × T_{ann}) − (0.005 × T_{moSD}) − (0.061 × $T_{minCold}$) − (0.003 × P_{ann}) − (0.060 × P_{moCV}) + (0.006 × P_{Wet}).

(b)

	β	SE	Z	p
Intercept	2.825	1.330	2.125	0.034
$T_{dayrange}$	−0.029	0.008	−3.44	<0.001
T_{moSD}	−0.001	0.0002	−2.827	0.005
P_{ann}	0.006	0.001	3.943	<0.001
P_{Wet}	−0.006	0.002	−2.704	0.007
P_{Dry}	−0.008	0.005	−1.502	0.133

Resulting equation: Suitability value$_{Cercopithecus}$ = 2.82 − (0.029 × $T_{dayrange}$) − (0.00058 × T_{moSD}) + (0.0058 × P_{ann}) − (0.0058 × P_{Wet}) − (0.0082 × P_{Dry}).
T_{ann} = mean annual temperature; $T_{dayrange}$ = temperature diurnal range; T_{moSD} = temperature seasonality; $T_{minCold}$ = minimum temperature of the coldest month; P_{ann} = mean annual precipitation; P_{moCV} = precipitation seasonality; P_{Wet} = precipitation of the wettest quarter; and P_{Dry} = precipitation of the driest quarter.

14.4.2   Future Climate Analyses

The suitability values in 2050 and 2070 were significantly more likely to be below those for current conditions for *Cercopithecus* at sites where they are currently present or absent (Table 14.2). For *Colobus*, suitability values of future sites were only more likely to be consistently lower for the sites where they are currently present (Table 14.2). To evaluate how many suitable sites were lost or gained, I only considered the subsample of African sites at which current presence or absence of a site was correctly identified by the model (i.e. a value of 0 or above for presence sites and <0 for absence sites). Most sites that currently have suitable habitat remained suitable and unsuitable sites remained unsuitable in the future for both genera, but *Colobus* lost more sites than *Cercopithecus* (Table 14.3).

(a)

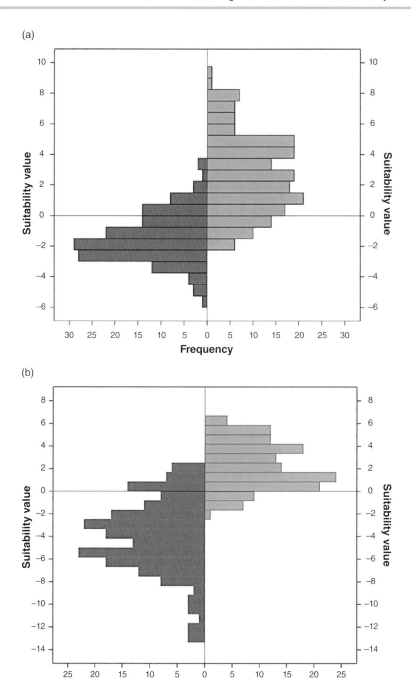

(b)

Figure 14.3 Histograms of the suitability values for (a) *Cercopithecus* and (b) *Colobus* under current climatic conditions at the sites where they are absent (left-hand side) or present (right-hand side).

Table 14.2 Comparison of the suitability values for the African sites where the genera are currently present or absent for 2050 and 2070 predictions, showing the test results of Wilcoxon signed ranks matched pairs test

| | Cercopithecus | | | | Colobus | | | |
| | 2050 | | 2070 | | 2050 | | 2070 | |
	Absent	Present	Absent	Present	Absent	Present	Absent	Present
$N_{Reduced}$	82	125	86	121	98	76	103	76
$N_{Increased}$	59	61	55	65	94	59	89	59
Z	−2.44	−5.13	−3.51	−4.48	−0.67	−2.59	−1.50	−3.48
p	0.015	<0.001	<0.001	<0.001	0.502	0.010	0.134	0.001

$N_{Reduced}$ and $N_{Increased}$ are the number of cases for which the suitability value decreased and increased respectively. In all cases where $p < 0.05$, the mean rank for the future sites is larger than mean rank for the current sites (i.e. mean rank of $N_{Reduced}$ > mean rank of $N_{Increased}$). This means that in all but two cases, the suitability of sites decreased from current to 2070 conditions.

Table 14.3 Comparison between climatic scenarios showing how many currently suitable sites became unsuitable (N_{lost}) and how many unsuitable sites became suitable (N_{gained}), using only those sites for which the suitability value for current conditions correctly identified it as a site with ($N_{present} = 156$ for *Cercopithecus* and 118 for *Colobus*) or without the genus ($N_{absent} = 113$ for *Cercopithecus* and 165 for *Colobus*)

| | | Cercopithecus | | Colobus | |
Currently	Future	2050	2070	2050	2070
Present	Lost N_{lost}	4 (2.6%)	8 (5.1%)	12 (10.2%)	18 (15.3%)
	Remain suitable	152 (97.4%)	148 (94.9%)	106 (89.8%)	100 (84.7%)
Absent	Gained N_{gained}	4 (3.5%)	4 (3.5%)	3 (1.8%)	3 (1.8%)
	Remain unsuitable	109 (96.5%)	109 (96.5%)	162 (98.2%)	162 (98.2%)

Percentages are calculated as: percentage of sites lost = $\%N_{lost}$ = $100\% \times (N_{lost}/N_{present})$; percentage sites gained = $\%N_{gained}$ = $100\% \times (N_{gained}/N_{absent})$; percentage remain suitable = $100\% \times (N_{suitable}/N_{present})$; percentage remain unsuitable = $100\% \times (N_{unsuitable}/N_{absent})$, with $N_{present}$ and N_{absent} relating to the number of cases where the genus is currently present and absent respectively.

For both genera, future suitability values were highest in the central regions of Africa (2070 conditions are shown in Figure 14.4; 2050 conditions looked very similar). Despite the fact that there were more sites at which suitability values decreased than increased for the genus *Cercopithecus*, this is not true across Africa, and in some regions the suitability values increased (darker regions in Figure 14.5a) and in many places the suitability values remained above 0.0 in currently suitable

(a)

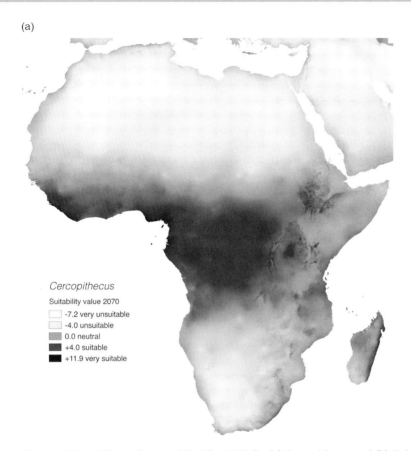

Cercopithecus

Suitability value 2070

☐ -7.2 very unsuitable
▨ -4.0 unsuitable
▨ 0.0 neutral
▨ +4.0 suitable
■ +11.9 very suitable

Figure 14.4 Suitability values modelled for 2070 for (a) *Cercopithecus* and (b) *Colobus*.

regions. For *Colobus*, on the other hand, suitability values decreased throughout Africa (Figure 14.5b). The model predictions suggest that both genera lose a large part of suitable habitats in Western Africa (around Senegal and around Ivory Coast, where the climate is getting hotter and drier) and also the edges of mid-Eastern Africa by 2070. Both genera were predicted to maintain a reasonably large area of suitable climate in central Africa, but the area was predicted to become more fragmented (Figure 14.4).

14.5   Discussion

In this study I explore the influence of predicted climate change on *Cercopithecus* and *Colobus* as two monkey genera with different dietary adaptations but similar biome preferences (woodland and forest) (Kingdon & Groves 2013a; 2013b). As predicted, most of Africa becomes less suitable for *Colobus*, which is not found in some of the hotter environments where *Cercopithecus* occurs. For *Cercopithecus*, on the other hand, there are large areas that become more suitable as well as areas that become less suitable. Although *Cercopithecus* is currently distributed farther southwards than

(b)

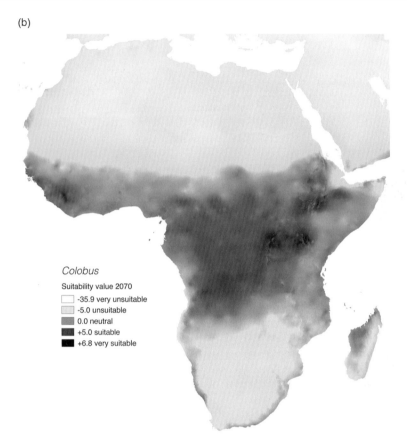

Figure 14.4 Cont.

Colobus, the overall current climate niche for *Colobus* actually covers a larger area towards the east and north than that for *Cercopithecus*. For the future predictions, however, very few areas become more suitable for *Colobus* and their overall distributional range shrinks and becomes smaller than the predicted future distribution of *Cercopithecus*. Thus, only a small change in suitability may lead to the disappearance of *Colobus*, whereas most of the sites where *Cercopithecus* occurs now become less suitable for them but still remain within the range of environments they can cope with. These results show how two genera that generally seem to have similar habitat requirements can have a very different response to climate change.

The results support an earlier analysis of how increased temperatures affect minimum required (enforced) resting time for primates (Korstjens et al., 2010). That analysis showed a clear difference between species depending on the amount of leaves they generally consumed: folivorous species would need to rest more and have less time for foraging than frugivorous species when temperatures increase. Furthermore, a related analysis using a time-budget model (a mechanistic modelling approach) showed that increased temperatures and temperature variation were associated with reduced consumption of leaves in *Cercopithecus* (Korstjens et al., 2018)

(a)

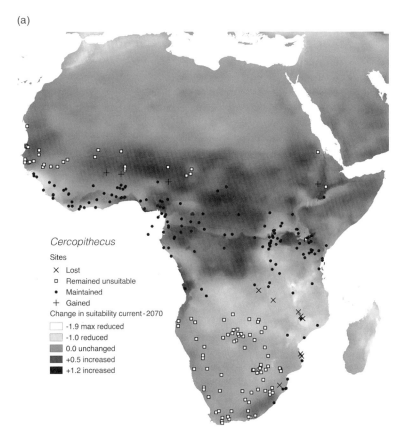

Figure 14.5 Absolute change in suitability values between current and 2070 values (= suitability$_{current}$ – suitability$_{2070}$) and the sites that were lost, gained, remained unsuitable or remained suitable for (a) *Cercopithecus* and (b) *Colobus*.

and *Colobus* (Korstjens & Dunbar, 2007). This is most likely related to the increased concentration of fibres and secondary compounds in leaves in dryer, hotter environments, thereby making them less palatable (Rothman et al., 2014; Zvereva & Kozlov, 2006). Thus, both genera may survive by relying more on fruits and less on leaves in response to climate change, but *Colobus* are constrained in their ability to do so due to their specialised digestive system.

I also considered whether there was evidence of a habitat shift away from the equator (Chen et al., 2011; Iverson & McKenzie, 2013). As climate conditions become unsuitable in some areas, they may become more suitable in other areas, and the overall climatic shift tends to be up-slope and away from the equator. Such a shift in suitable habitat can help species survive in newly colonised locations as long as they can keep up with climate change (Estrada et al., 2016; Schloss et al., 2012). Primates are thought to be among the slowest animals to take advantage of possible habitat shifts, i.e. they have limited dispersal ability, because they have slow life-histories, restricted geographical and social ranges and are dependent on social groupings (Schloss et al., 2012). Dispersal limitations among primate species differ along a

(b)

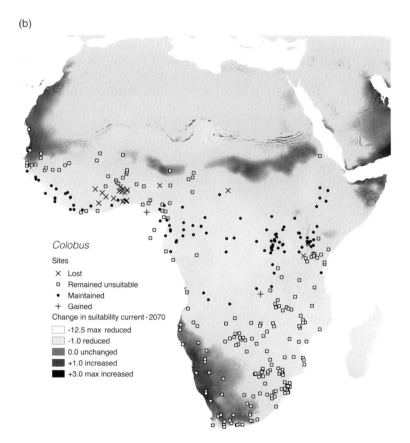

Figure 14.5 Cont.

latitudinal gradient, with species assemblages that live near the equator being more limited than those occurring further away from the equator (Beaudrot et al., 2014). This is probably related to greater flexibility in species that live in environments with a greater variation in climatic conditions. Beaudrot et al. (2014) specifically mention *Cercopithecus* and *Colobus* as examples of arboreal dispersal-limited species that are mostly found near the equator. Nonetheless, even if they did not have such biological constraints, it appears that there are no emerging new habitats for *Colobus* or *Cercopithecus*. My study, in combination with the study by Sato and Ise (2012) on future biome shifts in sub-Saharan Africa, suggests that these animals will struggle to find new habitats in a changing African landscape.

In the *Cercopithecus* model, some northern regions improve, but do not improve enough to become suitable for the species. Some coastal regions in the southern, northern and western parts of the continent may become more suitable if the primates are able to reach these regions and human land use does not preclude primates from occupying the suitable areas. The analyses show that *Colobus* and *Cercopithecus* lose a large part of their suitable habitats under future climatic conditions in Africa. Despite this loss, however, large stretches of suitable habitats will remain in central Africa that deserve protection to safeguard primate biodiversity in Africa.

Finally, the species distribution modelling (i.e. ecological niche modelling) approach used here has been shown to work well for animals in sub-Saharan Africa for a general exploration of species' responses to climate change (Garcia et al., 2016). Still, the SDM approach assumes: (1) that species do not adapt to new conditions (i.e. that $N_R = N_F$); (2) that newly emerging suitable environments (niches) are readily accessible to the species; and (3) that the environment does not provide temporary refuges (e.g. microhabitats with more suitable conditions, such as caves) from climatic conditions. Unlike the first assumption, species may have wider ecological niches than are identifiable by their current distributions and may adapt behaviourally to fast-changing environments (see Korstjens & Hillyer, 2016). The second assumption is probably not applicable for primates because they will often not be able to disperse fast enough to take advantage of newly emerging habitats in the same way that, for example, birds or butterflies do, and such habitats may not be accessible due to anthropogenic habitat modifications. The third assumption is only recently getting more attention as we start to appreciate the importance of microclimates, i.e. small areas within a species' habitat that provide noticeably different climatic conditions (Bramer et al., 2018). The use of caves to avoid the heat by chimpanzees in savannahs is a clear example of how animals take advantage of micro-climatic conditions (Preutz, 2007).

Despite these weaknesses of SDMs, they are relatively easy to achieve and do not require the detailed knowledge of both study species and environments that the other two modelling approaches (i.e. SDMs incorporating biological traits and mechanistic models) require. Therefore, SDMs are often still the most appropriate and least resource-intensive way to determine the likely response of a species to environmental changes, as long as people interpret the results with an understanding of the assumptions of SDMs.

14.6   Future Directions/Conclusion

Based on my research activities, I conclude that primates are flexible animals and some species are adapting well to anthropogenic environments, while others are likely to become extinct. Therefore, I think the future generation of primatologists needs to remain optimistic that mitigation of climate change can be achieved for many species, but with a sense of realistic appreciation of the limitations of conservation ideals.

Following the example of the people who taught me, I like to stress the importance of hypotheses testing. Understanding the assumptions and limitations of a study or research approach is important. For example, the results of the above analyses must be interpreted with an understanding of the three assumptions of the SDM approach. Primates are likely to be able to adapt behaviourally by changing group size or using microclimate refuges smartly. In addition, ensuring that large forest reserves are protected can mitigate climate change, because rainforests are essential in sequestering carbon and influence global climatic conditions. Full support and cooperation of local people is essential for any conservation programme, and local conservation heroes, like Rudi Putra (Indonesia) and Inza Kone (Côte d'Ivoire), are needed to ensure continuation of conservation work.

In the end, I strongly believe that nature is resilient and although I doubt the future primate community will look the same as it does now, it will still be fascinating and beautiful.

Acknowledgements

Special thanks go to Prof. Jan van Hooff and Prof. Robin Dunbar who are truly amazing and inspiring scientists that I have had the pleasure to work with closely. I also greatly benefited in my career through conversations with and support from all members of the Taï Monkey Project (especially Klaus Zuberbühler, Ronald Noë, Scott McGraw, Johannes Rehfisch and Redouan Bshary), and other inspiring scientists I regularly meet. I thank all the primatologists who over the years have been amazingly generous with data-sharing and support, and have been open to collaborations. I thank Phillipa Gillingham for support with species distribution modelling and climate scenario selection, John Stewart for proofreading, and Julia Lehmann, Marusha Dekleva and Helen Slater for their contributions to establishing the dataset of primate distributions. The work presented is part of the LEAP: Landscape Ecology And Primatology programme (www.go-leap.wixsite.com/home).

References

Asensio, N., Korstjens, A. H., Schaffner, C. M. & Aureli, F. (2008). Intragroup aggression, fission–fusion dynamics and feeding competition in spider monkeys. *Behaviour*, 145(7), 983–1001.

Asensio, N., Korstjens, A. H. & Aureli, F. (2009). Fissioning minimizes ranging costs in spider monkeys: a multiple-level approach. *Behavioral Ecology and Sociobiology*, 63(5), 649–59.

Bartoń, K. (2016). MuMIn: multi-model inference. R package version 1.15.6.

Beaudrot, L. H. & Marshall, A. J. (2011). Primate communities are structured more by dispersal limitation than by niches. *Journal of Animal Ecology*, 80(2), 332–41.

Beaudrot, L. H., Struebig, M. J., Meijaard, E., et al. (2013). Co-occurrence patterns of Bornean vertebrates suggest competitive exclusion is strongest among distantly related species. *Oecologia*, 173(3), 1053–62.

Beaudrot, L. H., Kamilar, J. M., Marshall, A. J. & Reed, K. E. (2014). African primate assemblages exhibit a latitudinal gradient in dispersal limitation. *International Journal of Primatology*, 35(6), 1088–104.

Behie, A. M. & Pavelka, M. S. (2013). Interacting roles of diet, cortisol levels, and parasites in determining population density of Belizean howler monkeys in a hurricane damaged forest fragment. In Marsh, L. K. & Chapman, C. A. (eds) *Primates in Fragments: Complexity and Resilience*. New York: Springer, pp. 459–74.

Bettridge, C. M. & Dunbar, R. I. M. (2012). Modeling the biogeography of fossil baboons. *International Journal of Primatology*, 33(6), 1278–308.

Bettridge, C. M., Lehmann, J. & Dunbar, R. I. M. (2010). Trade-offs between time, predation risk and life history, and their implications for biogeography: a systems modelling approach with a primate case study. *Ecological Modelling*, 221, 777–90.

Bramer, I. Anderson, B., Bennie, J., et al. (2018). Advances in monitoring and modelling climate at ecologically relevant scales. *Advances in Ecological Sciences*, **48**, 101–61.

Brands, S., Herrera, S., Fernández, J. & Gutiérrez, J. M. (2013). How well do CMIP5 Earth System Models simulate present climate conditions in Europe and Africa? *Climate Dynamics*, **41**(3–4), 803–17.

Bruorton, M. R., Davis, C. L. & Perrin, M. R. (1991). Gut microflora of vervet and samango monkeys in relation to diet. *Applied and Environmental Microbiology*, **57**(2), 573–8.

Burnham, K. P. & Anderson, D. R. (2002) *Model Selection and Multimodel Inference: A Practical Information-Theoretic Approach*, 2nd edn. New York: Springer.

Carne, C., Semple, S. & Lehmann, J. (2012). The effects of climate change on orangutans: a time budget model. In Druyan, L. M. (ed.) *Climate Models*, Rijeka: InTech, pp. 313–36.

Chapman, C. A., Chapman, L. J., Cords, M., et al. (2002). Variation in the diets of *Cercopithecus* species: differences within forests, among forests, and across species. In Glenn, M. E. & Cords, M. (eds) *The Guenons: Diversity and Adaptation in African Monkeys*. New York: Kluwer Academic, pp. 325–50.

Chapman, C. A., Chapman, L. J., Struhsaker, T. T., et al. (2005). A long-term evaluation of fruiting phenology: importance of climate change. *Journal of Tropical Ecology*, **21**(1), 31–45.

Chen, I.-C., Hill, J. K., Ohlemüller, R., Roy, D. B. & Thomas, C. D. (2011). Rapid range shifts of species associated with high levels of climate warming. *Science*, **333**(6045), 1024–6.

Chivers, D. J. (1994). Functional anatomy of the gastrointestinal tract. In Davies, A. G. & Oates, J. F. (eds) *Colobine Monkeys*. Cambridge: Cambridge University Press, pp. 205–27.

Clark, D. A., Clark, D. B. & Oberbauer, S. F. (2013). Field-quantified responses of tropical rainforest aboveground productivity to increasing CO_2 and climatic stress, 1997–2009. *Journal of Geophysical Research: Biogeosciences*, **118**(2), 783–94.

Cohen, J. (1968). Weighted kappa: nominal scale agreement with provision for scaled disagreement or partial credit. *Psychological Bulletin*, **70**(4), 213–20.

Collins, W. J., Bellouin, N., Doutriaux-Boucher, M., et al. (2008). *Evaluation of HadGEM2 Model*. Exeter: Meteorological Office Hadley Centre.

Dunbar, R. I. M. (1992). Time: a hidden constraint on the behavioural ecology of baboons. *Behavioral Ecology and Sociobiology*, **31**(1), 35–49.

Dunbar, R. I. M. (1993). Socioecology of the extinct theropiths: a modelling approach. In Jablonski, N. G. (ed.) *Theropithecus: The Rise and Fall of a Primate Genus*. Cambridge: Cambridge University Press, pp. 465–86.

Dunbar, R. I. M. (1998). Impact of global warming on the distribution and survival of the gelada baboon: a modelling approach. *Global Change Biology*, **4**(3), 293–304.

Dunbar, R. I. M. & Dunbar, P. (1988). Maternal time budgets of gelada baboons. *Animal Behaviour*, **36**, 970–80.

Dunbar, R. I. M., Korstjens, A. H. & Lehmann, J. (2009). Time as an ecological constraint. *Biological Reviews*, **84**(3), 413–29.

Dunbar, R. I. M., Gamble, C. & Gowlett, J. A. J. (2014). *Lucy to Language: The Benchmark Papers*. Oxford: Oxford University Press.

Elith, J. & Leathwick, J. R. (2009). Species distribution models: ecological explanation and prediction across space and time. *Annual Review of Ecology Evolution and Systematics*, **40**, 677–97.

Estrada, A., Raboy, B. E. & Oliveira, L. C. (2012). Agroecosystems and primate conservation in the tropics: a review. *American Journal of Primatology*, **74**(8), 696–711.

Estrada, A., Morales-Castilla, I., Caplat, P. & Early, R. (2016). Usefulness of species traits in predicting range shifts. *Trends in Ecology & Evolution*, **31**(3), 190–203.

Fashing, P. J. (2005). African colobine monkeys: patterns of between-group interaction. In Campbell, C. J., Fuentes, A. F., MacKinnon, K. C., Panger, M. & Bearder, S. (eds) *Primates in Perspective*. Oxford: Oxford University Press, pp. 201–24.

Fashing, P. J., Mulindahabi, F., Gakima, J. B., et al. (2007). Activity and ranging patterns of *Colobus angolensis ruwenzorii* in Nyungwe forest, Rwanda: possible costs of large group size. *International Journal of Primatology*, **28**(3), 529–50.

Fleagle, J. G. & Reed, K. E. (1996). Comparing primate communities: a multivariate approach. *Journal of Human Evolution*, 30(6), 489–510.

Garcia, R. A., Cabeza, M., Altwegg, R. & Araújo, M. B. (2016). Do projections from bioclimatic envelope models and climate change metrics match?. *Global Ecology and Biogeography*, 25(1), 65–74.

González-Zamora, A., Arroyo-Rodríguez, V., Chaves, O. M., et al. (2011). Influence of climatic variables, forest type, and condition on activity patterns of Geoffroyi's spider monkeys throughout Mesoamerica. *American Journal of Primatology*, 73(12), 1189–98.

Gouveia, S. F., Villalobos, F., Dobrovolski, R., Beltrão-Mendes, R. & Ferrari, S. F. (2014). Forest structure drives global diversity of primates. *Journal of Animal Ecology*, 83, 1523–30.

Graham, T. L., Matthews, H. D. & Turner, S. E. (2016). A global-scale evaluation of primate exposure and vulnerability to climate change. *International Journal of Primatology*, 37(2), 158–74.

Guisan, A., Petitpierre, B., Broennimann, O., Daehler, C. & Kueffer, C. (2014). Unifying niche shift studies: insights from biological invasions. *Trends in Ecology & Evolution*, 29(5), 260–9.

Hartley, A. J., Nelson, A. & Mayaux, P. (2007). *The Assessment of African Protected Areas: A Characterisation of Biodiversity Value, Ecosystems and Threats, to Inform the Effective Allocation of Conservation Funding.* Luxembourg: Office for Official Publications of the European Communities.

Hijmans, R. J. & Elith, J. (2016). *Species Distribution Modeling with R.* n.p.: R CRAN Project.

Hurlbert, A. H. & Jetz, W. (2007). Species richness, hotspots and the scale dependence of range maps in ecology and conservation. *PNAS*, 104(33), 13384–9.

Hutchinson, G. E. (1978). *An Introduction to Population Ecology.* New Haven, CT: Yale University Press.

IPCC (2014). *Climate Change 2014: Impacts, Adaptation, and Vulnerability. Summaries, Frequently Asked Questions, and Cross-Chapter Boxes. A Contribution of Working Group II to the Fifth Assessment Report of the Intergovernmental Panel on Climate Change.* Geneva: World Meteorological Organization.

IUCN (2017). *The IUCN Red List of Threatened Species.* Version 2017-3. Available at: www.iucnredlist.org (accessed 19 September 2017).

Iverson, L. R. & McKenzie, D. (2013). Tree-species range shifts in a changing climate: detecting, modeling, assisting. *Landscape Ecology*, 28(5), 879–89.

Iwamoto, T. & Dunbar, R. I. M. (1983). Thermoregulation, habitat quality and the behavioural ecology of Gelada baboons. *Journal of Animal Ecology*, 52(2), 357–66.

Kamilar, J. M. & Beaudrot, L. H. (2017). Quantitative methods for primate biogeography and macroecology. In Shaffer, C. A., Dolins, F., Hickey, J. R., Nibbelink, N. P. & Porter, L. M. (eds) *GPS and GIS for Primatologists: A Practical Guide to Spatial Analysis.* New York: Cambridge University Press.

Kamilar, J. M. & Muldoon, K. M. (2010). The climatic niche diversity of Malagasy primates: a phylogenetic perspective. *PLoS One*, 5(6), e11073.

Kamilar, J. M. & Tecot, S. R. (2016). Anthropogenic and climatic effects on the distribution of *Eulemur* species: an ecological niche modeling approach. *International Journal of Primatology*, 37(1), 47–68.

Kingdon, J. & Groves, C. P. (2013a). Genus *Colobus* black-and-white colobus monkeys. In Butynski, T. M., Kingdon, J. & Kalina, J. (eds) *Mammals of Africa: Volume II Primates.* London: Bloomsbury Publishing, pp. 95–6.

Kingdon, J. & Groves, C. P. (2013b). Tribe cercopithecini. In Butynski, T. M., Kingdon, J. & Kalina, J. (eds) *Mammals of Africa: Volume II Primates.* London: Bloomsbury, pp. 245–7.

Korstjens, A. H. (2001). The mob, the secret sorority, and the phantoms: an analysis of the socio-ecological strategies of the three colobines of Taï. PhD Thesis, Utrecht University.

Korstjens, A. H. & Dunbar, R. I. M. (2007). Time constraints limit group sizes and distribution in red and black-and-white colobus monkeys. *International Journal of Primatology*, 28(3), 551–75.

Korstjens, A. H. & Hillyer, A. P. (2016). Primates and climate change: a review of current knowledge. In Wich, S. A. & Marshall, A. J. (eds) *An Introduction to Primate Conservation*. Oxford: Oxford University Press, pp. 175–92.

Korstjens, A. H. & Noë, R. (2004). Mating system of an exceptional primate, the olive colobus (*Procolobus verus*). *American Journal of Primatology*, **62**(4), 261–73.

Korstjens, A. H. & Schippers, E. P. (2003). Dispersal patterns among olive colobus in Taï National Park. *International Journal of Primatology*, **24**(3), 515–40.

Korstjens, A., Sterck, E. H. M. & Noë, R. (2002). How adaptive or phylogenetically inert is primate social behaviour? A test with two sympatric colobines. *Behaviour*, **139**(2), 203–25.

Korstjens, A. H., Nijssen, E. C. & Noë, R. (2005). Inter-group relationships in western black-and-white colobus, *Colobus polykomos polykomos*. *International Journal of Primatology*, **26**(6), 1267–89.

Korstjens, A. H., Lugo Verhoeckx, I. & Dunbar, R. I. M. (2006). Time as a constraint on group size in spider monkeys. *Behavioral Ecology and Sociobiology*, **60**(5), 683–94.

Korstjens, A. H., Bergmann, K., Deffernez, C., et al. (2007). How small-scale differences in food competition lead to different social systems in three closely related sympatric colobines. In McGraw, S., Zuberbuhler, K. & Noë, R. (eds) *The Monkeys of the Taï Forest, Ivory Coast: An African Primate Community*. Cambridge: Cambridge University Press, pp. 72–108.

Korstjens, A. H., Lehmann, J. & Dunbar, R. I. M. (2010). Resting time as an ecological constraint on primate biogeography. *Animal Behaviour*, **79**(2), 361–74.

Korstjens, A. H., Lehmann, J. & Dunbar, R. I. M. (2018). Time constraints do not limit group size in arboreal guenons but do explain community size and distribution patterns. *International Journal of Primatology*. https://doi.org/10.1007/s10764-018-0048-4

Lambert, J. E. (1998). Primate frugivory in Kibale National Park, Uganda, and its implications for human use of forest resources. *African Journal of Ecology*, **36**(3), 234–40.

Lambert, J. E. (2002). Resource switching and species coexistence in guenons: a community analysis of dietary flexibility. In Glenn, M. E. & Cords, M. (eds) *The Guenons: Diversity and Adaptation in African Monkeys*. New York: Springer, pp. 309–23.

Lehman, S. M. & Fleagle, J. G. (2006). Biogeography and primates: a review. In *Primate Biogeography: Progress and Prospects*, Boston, MA: Springer, pp. 1–58.

Lehmann, J., Korstjens, A. H. & Dunbar, R. I. M. (2007). Fission–fusion social systems as a strategy for coping with ecological constraints: a primate case. *Evolutionary Ecology*, **21**(5), 613–34.

Lehmann, J., Korstjens, A. H. & Dunbar, R. I. M. (2008a). Time and distribution: a model of ape biogeography. *Ethology Ecology & Evolution*, **20**(4), 337–59.

Lehmann, J., Korstjens, A. H. & Dunbar, R. I. M. (2008b). Time management in great apes: implications for gorilla biogeography. *Evolutionary Ecology Research*, **10**(4), 517–36.

Lehmann, J., Korstjens, A. H. & Dunbar, R. I. M. (2010). Apes in a changing world: the effects of global warming on the behaviour and distribution of African apes. *Journal of Biogeography*, **37**(12), 2217–31.

Liu, C., White, M. & Newell, G. (2011). Measuring and comparing the accuracy of species distribution models with presence–absence data. *Ecography*, **34**(2), 232–43.

Maibeche, Y., Moali, A., Yahi, N. & Menard, N. (2015). Is diet flexibility an adaptive life trait for relictual and peri-urban populations of the endangered primate *Macaca sylvanus*? *PLoS One*, **10**(2), e0118596.

Moss, R., Babiker, M., Brinkman, S., et al. (2008). Towards new scenarios for analysis of emissions, climate change, impacts and response strategies. IPCC Expert Meeting Report.

Nowak, K. & Lee, P. C. (2013). 'Specialist' primates can be flexible in response to habitat alteration. In Marsh, K. L. & Chapman, A. C. (eds) *Primates in Fragments: Complexity and Resilience*. New York: Springer, pp. 199–211.

Polansky, L. & Boesch, C. (2013). Long-term changes in fruit phenology in a West African lowland tropical rain forest are not explained by rainfall. *Biotropica*, **45**(4), 434–40.

Pruetz, J. D. (2007). Evidence of cave use by savanna chimpanzees (*Pan troglodytes verus*) at Fongoli, Senegal: implications for thermoregulatory behavior. *Primates*, 48, 316.

QGIS Development Team (2016). QGIS Geographic Information System. Available at: www.qgis.org.

R Core Team (2016). *R: A Language and Environment for Statistical Computing*. Vienna: R Foundation for Statistical Computing.

Rothman, J. M., Chapman, C. A., Struhsaker, T. T., et al. (2014). Long-term declines in nutritional quality of tropical leaves. *Ecology*, 96(3), 873–8.

Sato, H. & Ise, T. (2012). Effect of plant dynamic processes on African vegetation responses to climate change: analysis using the spatially explicit individual-based dynamic global vegetation model (SEIB-DGVM). *Journal of Geophysical Research*, 117(G3), G03017.

Schloss, C. A., Nuñez, T. A. & Lawler, J. J. (2012). Dispersal will limit ability of mammals to track climate change in the western hemisphere. *Proceedings of the National Academy of Sciences*, 109 (22), 8606–11.

Soberón J. & Arroyo-Peña, B. (2017) Are fundamental niches larger than the realized? Testing a 50-year-old prediction by Hutchinson. *PLoS One* 12(4): e0175138.

Teichroeb, J. A., Saj, T. L., Paterson, J. D. & Sicotte, P. (2003). Effect of group size on activity budgets of *Colobus vellerosus* in Ghana. *International Journal of Primatology*, 24(4), 743–58.

Willems, E. P. & Hill, R. A. (2009). A critical assessment of two species distribution models: a case study of the vervet monkey (*Cercopithecus aethiops*). *Journal of Biogeography*, 36(12), 2300–12.

Williamson, D. K. & Dunbar, R. (1999). Energetics, time budgets and group size. In Lee, P. (ed.) *Primate Socioecology*. Cambridge: Cambridge University Press, pp. 321–38.

Wisz, M. S., Pottier, J., Kissling, W. D., et al. (2013). The role of biotic interactions in shaping distributions and realised assemblages of species: implications for species distribution modelling. *Biological Reviews*, 88(1), 15–30.

Zvereva, E. L. & Kozlov, M. V. (2006). Consequences of simultaneous elevation of carbon dioxide and temperature for plant–herbivore interactions: a metaanalysis. *Global Change Biology*, 12(1), 27–41.

15 Research(ers) and Conservation(ists) in the Anthropocene

Nicholas Malone, Julie A. Teichroeb and Alison M. Behie

15.1 Introduction

In August 2016, at an early stage in the development of this book, we convened a symposium at the joint meeting of the American Society of Primatologists and International Primatological Society in Chicago, USA. In light of the emerging primate extinction crisis, eight expert presenters, representing their respective research teams, were asked to address such questions as: how have your field sites, and correspondingly your research methods, changed? Are we still able to include evolutionary analyses in our primarily conservation-driven projects? And how can career trajectories in primatology align with the oft-competing interests of research and conservation activities? The presentations, and the lively discussion that followed, made apparent the extent to which researchers have refocused their investigations to better align with conservation imperatives. Those productive conservation and research insights form the core of the present volume and have been enhanced by additional contributions by an array of early-career and senior researchers/conservationists.

A unique feature of our book is the inclusion of personal narratives by the authors. These narratives, in combination with the research findings, demonstrate robust interconnections among people at every step in the research process. Mentors, assistants, collaborators, participants and local actors are part and parcel of primate research and conservation. And undoubtedly this is true, to varying degrees, for the entire extent of primate research and conservation activities the world over. Additionally, extra-local human interconnections (e.g. human-induced climate change; agroforestry economies of various scale) pervade our field sites. As the contributions to this volume attest, research and conservation are inextricably intertwined. As such, we should be sceptical of any isolated primate research findings or conservation prescriptions that fail to engage or acknowledge this inseparability. These points have been made elsewhere within the larger primatological and ecological literature (Ellis, 2015; Fuentes & Baynes-Rock, 2017), and align particularly well with the now mature field of ethnoprimatology (Dore et al., 2017; Fuentes, 2012; Fuentes & Wolfe, 2002; Malone et al., 2014).

15.2 Summary

15.2.1 Review of Part I: The Human–Non-human Primate Interface

This section started out with the title 'Hunting in the Anthropocene', but it quickly became apparent that the contributions had much more depth than just documenting animal loss due to hunting. Primate populations are decreasing due to a host of anthropogenic factors causing both direct and indirect mortality. The chapters in this section deal more with managing and monitoring populations that are already small, trying to stop and predict habitat changes that may be detrimental to the remaining animals, as well as finding ways to integrate local communities into conservation efforts and teach children about the interconnectedness of human and animal populations (Chapters 2–4). The one chapter that focuses on hunting (Chapter 5) shows how, in the right habitat, sustainable hunting of primates as a subsistence strategy is possible with local monitoring and buy-in for conservation. Together, these chapters accurately paint the complex picture of how human and non-human primates interact across four different landscapes on three different continents and demonstrate the positive results to both humans and animals from careful conservation strategies.

15.2.2 Review of Part II: Habitat Alteration in the Anthropocene

This section was originally entitled 'Habitat loss in the Anthropocene' but as contributions started coming in we realised that it wasn't only about the loss of habitat, which conjures up images of massive expanses of land being converted to unsuitable habitat, but was more about how primate habitats are being altered by humans and how primates are adapting, or not, to those alterations. The days of studying primates in pristine habitat are gone, and even forests that are remote and have low human population density are becoming altered by activities like selective logging. This is the case in Veun Sai-Siem Pang National Park, which is a 55 000 ha forested area where many primates are thought to live at high population densities, despite its bordering the 320 000 ha Virachey National Park. Chapter 6 starts this section by describing the impact of even small-scale illegal logging on the immediate behaviour of animals in this vast habitat. Such studies, which document how animals are responding to the activity of logging itself, through reactions to chainsaws, are some of the first to document how primates are adapting in these initial stages of disturbance. Following from this, Chapter 7 describes how a primate population (Angolan colobus monkeys) responds in the immediate aftermath of logging – in this case the logging had ceased and the impact could be assessed. Chapter 8 focuses our thoughts on the long-term impact of habitat alteration and the potential impact it may have on ecosystem dynamics, particularly through host–parasite relationships. Thus, while these chapters take us on a journey through the stages of impacts, one of the most interesting and relevant themes to come out of this section was the importance of collaboration and community involvement in successfully combating the impacts of habitat alteration. Chapters 9 and 10 both highlight the importance of forest regeneration as a strategy to restore lost or changed habitat for primates. Chapter 9 also gives a hopeful and successful example of the Madagascar Biodiversity Partnership and their involvement with local people. Similarly, Chapter 7 recounts how local people worked together to protest and stop both legal and illegal timber extraction in Uganda to protect the habitat of the Angolan colobus, and Chapter 10 takes us beyond the science to explore how local spatial plans are being used to protect proboscis monkey habitat. This gives us hope and provides further evidence for our important role in the training and empowering of local people to engage in the protection of land and ecosystems so that both primates and humans can thrive.

15.2.3 Review of Part III: Climate Change in the Anthropocene

With the advent of the Anthropocene, and especially in the wake of the 'Great Acceleration' (the post-1950, exponential growth in human population and consumption levels), alterations of the planet's land, oceanic and atmospheric systems interact in complex ways to impact biodiversity (Steffen et al., 2007; 2015). A changing climate produces significant challenges to primates and the researchers who study them. Chapter 11 reviews the effects of human activity with respect to the primate nutritional landscape. In light of agricultural intensification, habitat fragmentation, the introduction of pesticides and pollutants and a changing climate, these experts stress the need for ongoing assessment of the quality and distribution of feeding resources – a fundamental component of primate life. In some cases, as detailed in Chapters 12 and 13, natural disasters have intervened stochastically, providing opportunities to study vital recovery processes within ecological communities, and shifting research agendas along the way. Chapter 14 models habitat requirements (in conjunction with biological characteristics) for different primate genera in an effort to predict the presence of suitable habitats within the context of future climate change. Careful attention to the assumptions and limitations of the research is stressed, but these research efforts can refine our conservation priorities and management tactics. As all of the chapters in this section demonstrate, understanding the key factors and thresholds for primate feeding and nutrition is a complicated undertaking, but one that is of paramount importance.

15.3 Setting an Agenda: Beyond the Anthropocene

One ideological point of debate remains among the editors – is it preferable, or indeed even possible, to return to a time when researchers had the luxury in engage in 'pure' behavioural or ecological research? When many of today's established primatologists entered the field a decade or more ago, most were driven by evolutionary questions centred in the field of behavioural ecology. Initial interests may have been born out of questions such as, how do animals decide what to eat or who to interact with, or when and with whom to reproduce? Should we prove successful in stemming the tide of threats, and manage to provide robust protections to viable populations of primate taxa, it may be possible to return to a more purely research-focused primatology. Indeed, some primatologists may perceive their work to have maintained its evolutionary and behaviourally driven attributes, viewing it as their role to arm conservationists with salient datasets. Some might see this as the desired outcome of our present research/conservation hybridity.

Alternatively, the accumulation of ongoing, anthropogenic influences on primate populations (and our heightened awareness of the present condition) has altered the primatological endeavour fundamentally and permanently. In embracing the Anthropocene, we've declared a present where 'nature' is shaped and defined by human activity. Will the future involve an untangling of our entanglements, a selective enhancement or rejection of our management over formerly wild places and species, or indeed an embrace of our multispecies, post-nature relationships and, correspondingly, a shift in what we mean by 'conservation' (Lorimer, 2015). What will our research questions and/or our conservation prescriptions look like as a new generation of primatologists embark on studies within a 'growing array of gray sites' (Braverman, 2014: 54) – where distinctions between captive and wild animals, or natural and managed behavioural contexts, become less discernible? Our research questions, methods and ethics may very well be altered with these shifts (Palmer & Malone, 2018). The future of primatology will likely involve a plethora of approaches as practitioners work amid more or less intensely human-modified ecological systems.

In this book, we have examined these themes from both a practical and personal perspective. The contributions to this volume demonstrate an ability to balance research and conservation agendas. In some cases, we are presented with evidence suggestive of resilience and the flexibility of certain species to withstand anthropogenic alterations. In others we are confronted with the devastating extent to which human activities threaten the very existence of our study taxa. In both instances, the continued engagement of well-trained, well-resourced teams of researchers and conservationists is paramount. Our field sites and research agendas will undoubtedly be different from primatology's past, but our primary motivation endures: to understand the evolutionary trajectories and complex ecologies of the fascinating species within the Order Primates, and to ensure that future generations of curious minds have the opportunity to do the same.

References

Braverman, I. (2014). Conservation without nature: the trouble with in situ versus ex situ conservation. *Geoforum*, 51(Supplement C), 47–57.
Dore, K. M., Riley, E. P. & Fuentes, A. (eds) (2017). *Ethnoprimatology: A Practical Guide to Research at the Human–Nonhuman Primate Interface*. Cambridge: Cambridge University Press.
Ellis, E. C. (2015). Ecology in an anthropogenic biosphere. *Ecological Monographs*, 85(3), 287–331.
Fuentes, A. (2012). Ethnoprimatology and the anthropology of the human–primate interface. *Annual Review of Anthropology*, 41, 101–17.
Fuentes, A. & Baynes-Rock, M. (2017). Anthropogenic landscapes, human action and the process of co-construction with other species: making anthromes in the Anthropocene. *Land*, 6(1), 15.
Fuentes, A. & Wolfe, L. D. (2002). *Primates Face to Face: The Conservation Implications of Human–Nonhuman Primate Interconnections*. Cambridge: Cambridge University Press.
Lorimer, J. (2015). *Wildlife in the Anthropocene: Conservation After Nature*. Minneapolis, MN: University of Minnesota Press.
Malone, N., Wade, A. H., Fuentes, A., et al. (2014). Ethnoprimatology: critical interdisciplinarity and multispecies approaches in anthropology. *Critique of Anthropology*, 38, 8–29.
Palmer, A. & Malone, N. (2018). Extending ethnoprimatology: human–alloprimate relationships in managed settings. *International Journal of Primatology*. DOI: 10.1007/s10764-017-0006-6.
Steffen, W., Crutzen, P. J. & McNeill, J. R. (2007). The Anthropocene: are humans now overwhelming the great forces of nature? *AMBIO: A Journal of the Human Environment*, 36(8), 614–21.
Steffen, W., Broadgate, W., Deutsch, L., Gaffney, O. & Ludwig, C. (2015). The trajectory of the Anthropocene: the great acceleration. *The Anthropocene Review*, 2(1), 81–98.

Index

activity budget
  of colobus, 131, 135
  effect of provisioning, 208
  of howler monkey, 245
  of spider monkey, 245–50
  response to habitat disturbance, 9, 131, 135, 201
  response to natural disaster, 245, 251
  response to temperature increase, 272
Africa
  bushmeat, 7
  deforestation, 122
  habitat suitability and shifting, 270–1
agriculture
  cacao, 205
  cocoa, 53
  conservation and, 187, 190
  deforestation, 8
  inclusion in primate diets, 202
  Madagascar, 168
  nutrition in primate diets, 202, 205
  oil palm, 190
  pesticides, 205
  rubber, 190
Alouatta. See howler monkey
Amazonia. *See also* South America
  bushmeat, 77
  interactions between human and non-human primates, 76
  pet trade in, 78
  primate hunting in, 76–8
  primate population decline, 76
Ankoatsifaka Research Station, 219
anthromes, 5
Anthropocene, 5–6, *See also* anthromes, bushmeat, climate change, conservation, deforestation, extinction, habitat disturbance, hunting, interactions between human and non-human primates,

  logging, natural disaster, primatologists' role and shifting priorities, provisioning, temperature changes, viability
arboreality and species viability, 258
Ateles. See spider monkey
Ateline hunting, 78
Avahi. See lemur

baboon
  crop-raiding by, 205
  provisioning, diet and nutrition, 208
  response to provisioning, 208
Balikpapan Bay
  ecotourism, 193
  environmental monitoring, 189
  land prices, 187
Belize, 240
benefits, economic of primates to locals, 66
biodiversity
  in Cambodia, 102
  conservation, 82
  Ernst Mayr quote, 158
  fragmentation and, 69
  in indigenous reserves, 82
  of parasites, 144, 157
  in Southeast Asia, 102
  threats to, 219
biomass, primate in Neotropics, 77
body mass and size, primate
  effects of provisioning, 207–8
  habitat disturbance and, 123
  parasite species richness and, 154
  population viability and, 239
Borneo and oil palm plantations, 190
Brachyteles. See spider monkey
bushmeat. *See also* hunting
  in Amazonia, 77
  in Congo Basin, xiv, 7
  as an industry, 7

Bwindi Impenetrable National Park, 203

Cagar Alam Leuweung Sancang, 20
  habitat disturbance, 25
Callicebus. See titi monkey
Cambodia
  biodiversity in, 102
  conservation in, 102
  deforestation in, 102
  enforcement of laws, 102
  logging in, 101–2, 110–12
canopy use and logging, 107, 112
captive breeding of proboscis monkey, 191
capuchin
  crop-raiding by, 205
  hunting of, 77, *87*
Cebus. See capuchin
Cercocebus. See mangabey
Cercopithecus. See guenon
Cheirogaleus. See lemur
chimpanzee
  crop-raiding by, 205
  crop-raiding nutrition, 205
  dispersal, 36
  exposure to hunting, 66
  fragmentation and genetic diversity, 69
  habitat loss, xiv
  hunting of, 60, 66, 68
  interactions with humans, 66
  locals' feelings towards, 69
  nesting, 60–1, 68
  pesticide exposure, 206
  population decline, xiv
  population size, 55
  reproduction, 36
  response to habitat disturbance, 70
  threat status and population size, 54
  vulnerability to habitat disturbance, 123
Chiropotes. See saki

Chlorocebus. See vervet monkey
climate change, 208, *See also* temperature changes, deforestation
  disease and, 143
  effects on nutrition and food, 208–9, 261
  extinction risk, 122, 258–9
  gelada habitat, 209
  habitat shifting and suitability, 262, 273
  modelling of, 259, 266
  natural disaster, 218, 238
  phenology and, 209
collaboration with local researchers, 4, 174, 178
  in Africa, xvi
  changing priorities, xvi
  in Madagascar, 177–8
  in Tanzania, 46
  Waiwai, 92–3
colobine. *See also* colobus, langur, proboscis monkey, snub-nosed monkey
  crop-raiding by, 205
  diet, 260
  population decline at Udzungwa Scarp Nature Reserve, 44
  response to habitat disturbance, 103, 111, 123
colobus
  activity budget, 131, 135–6
  diet of, 132–3, 203
  distribution, 124, 261
  extinction, xiv
  gut physiology, 260
  habitat suitability and shifting, 268, 271, 274
  hunting of, 123
  nutrition of, 209
  parasite susceptibility, 201
  population decline at Lake Nabugaboo, 134
  population viability, 210
  protein-to-fibre ratio, 201
  ranging, 203
  response to habitat disturbance, 103, 123, 133, 135, 201
  social groups and dispersal, 124, 131, 260
  threat status, 124

Colobus. See colobus
conservation. *See* ecotourism, education programmes, reforestation and rehabilitated habitat
  as an academic discipline, 3
  agriculture, 190
  biodiversity and indigenous reserves, 82
  buying land, 187
  in Cambodia, 102
  collaboration with private sector, 187, 191
  comparison between sites, 176
  compromise, 173–4
  at conferences, 4
  cultural context, 173
  early policy, 167
  economic development, 172
  environmental education programme, 175
  evidence of efficacy, 174
  ex-situ, 191
  in Indonesia, 193
  keys to success, 175
  logging compatibility with, 113
  in Madagascar, 168
  oil palm agriculture, 190
  proboscis monkey, 191–2
  reforestation, 173
  research–conservation balance, 176
  researcher role, 166–7
  resiliency definition, 28
  role of zoos, 191
  in Sabah, 192
  Sabah Proboscis Monkey Action Plan, 193
  social benefits and goals, 173
  socioeconomic surveys, 175–6
  trust and, 173
Conservation Fusion, 172, 177–8
conservation, challenges to
  baseline data, 175
  communication, 166, 177
  conflicting goals, 93, 173
  enforcement. *See* enforcement, failure and lack of
  many interacting variables, 176
  research focus, 166, 176
crop-raiding, 202, 205

  conflict, 70
  dietary breadth and, 205
  feeding benefits for primates, 205
  food availability and, 205
  by gorilla, 61–2, 205
  Udzungwa Mountains National Park, 34
  by vervet monkey, 121
crops. *See* agriculture
cultural beliefs, 28
  hunting and, 78, 89, 121
  primates, 89, 92
  Waiwai, 89
cyclone. *See* natural disaster

Daubentonia. See lemur
deforestation
  Africa, 122
  agriculture, 8
  Borneo, 190
  Cagar Alam Leuweung Sancang, 7
  Cambodia, 102
  extinction risk and debt, 122
  Ghana, 120
  genetic diversity and, 36
  Java, 19
  Kianjavato, 168
  logging, 8, 122
  Madagascar, 168, 219
  prevention in indigenous reserves, 82
  tropics, 122
  worldwide, xiv, 8
diet. *See also* nutrition, crop-raiding
  baboon, 208
  chimpanzee, 205
  colobus, 132, 203, 260
  crop-raiding and, 205
  gelada, 209
  gorilla, 203, 205
  guenon, 202, 260
  habitat disturbance and, 123, 239
  habitat disturbance and species viability, 239, 250, 258
  howler monkey, 202, 246, 248, 252
  langur, 35
  lemur, 202, 230
  macaque, 205, 208

nutrition and, 201
proboscis monkey, 185
spider monkey, 247, 252
response to habitat disturbance,
    9, 132, 134
response to natural disaster, 239,
    246, 248, 251, 253
response to temperature increase,
    272
sodium, 204
diet, flexibility and breadth
crop-raiding and, 205
digestive flexibility, 260
habitat disturbance, 123, 200
habitat shifting and suitability,
    209
nutrition, 209
dipterocarp logging, 112
disease
African apes, 143
climate change and, 143
effect on primates, 158
extinction risk and, 122
human–non-human primate
    interactions, 143
population decline due to, 143,
    156
reservoir hosts, 143
dispersal
costs and risks, 36, 45
fragmentation and, 36, 44
genetic diversity and, 36, 45
habitat suitability and shifting,
    273
hierarchy and, 45
lemur, 219
mangabey, 41, 44–5
population growth, 36
population viability and, 36
reproduction, 45
distribution, population. See
    population size and survey
distribution, species
colobus, 261
gorilla, 69
guenon, 261
modelling, 259–60

ecologically noble savage, 79
ecotourism
Balikpapan Bay, 193

disadvantages of, 172
proboscis monkey, 185, 190, 192
EDGE of Existence programme, 146
education
community-based, 54
environmental education
    programme, 34, 46–7, 172
elephant, local extinction of, 67
enforcement of logging laws, 101,
    106, 110
enforcement of rules, failure and
    lack of
Cambodia, 101–2, 104–5
Java, 19
proboscis monkey conservation,
    188
ethnoprimatology, 2, 5, 53, 70
Eulemur. See lemur
exotic plants, 202, See agriculture
eucalyptus, 203
extinction. See genetic diversity;
    habitat disturbance; hunting;
    viability, population and
    species
in Africa, 122
colobus, xiv
debt, 122, 186
elephant, 67
parasite host range and, 156
platyrrhine in Amazonia, 76
primate vulnerability to, 53, 143
proboscis monkey, 186
rates, xiv
result of hunting, 78
risk, 122, See also threat status
in South America, 82

feeding. See activity budget
feelings towards primates by locals,
    64–6
chimpanzee, 66, 69
gorilla, 64, 69
fertility. See reproduction, life
    history
fires. See natural disasters
fission–fusion
frugivory and, 239
response to natural disaster, 252
flagship species
gorilla, 70
proboscis monkey, 185

folivory. See also diet
crop-raiding and, 205
resiliency to natural disasters,
    231, 239
response to habitat disturbance,
    103, 135
response to natural disaster, 218
social stability, 239
species viability and habitat
    disturbance, 123
food availability
crop-raiding and, 205
dietary and social flexibility as
    adaptations to, 239
effect on colobus, 201
effect on nutritional regulation,
    201
for proboscis monkeys, 188
habitat disturbance and, 112, 200
immune response and, 201
infant survival and, 134, 231
interactions with parasites and
    immunity, 201
forest conversion, exploitation,
    degradation, and extraction.
    See habitat disturbance,
    deforestation, natural disasters
forest structure and phenology
changes in response to natural
    disaster, 217–18, 223, 230,
    232, 239
frugivory. See also diet
crop-raiding and, 205
habitat disturbance and species
    viability, 123, 231, 239
population growth, 134
response to habitat disturbance,
    103, 135
response to natural disaster, 239
social flexibility, 239

gelada
diet of, 209
habitat shifting and suitability,
    209
modelling distribution and
    climate change, 259
parasite effect in, 159
genetic diversity
chimpanzee, 69
dispersal and, 36, 45

genetic diversity (cont.)
  effect on population growth, 36
  gorilla, 69
  habitat disturbance and, 36, 44,
    69
  infant mortality and, 36
  lemur, 170
  mangabey, 45
  spider monkey, 36
Ghana, deforestation and hunting
    in, 120
gibbon
  distribution, 19
  group size and composition, 23
  illegal trade of, 27
  population size, 19
  ranging, 23
  response to logging, 135
  threat status, 1
  threats to, 28
  vocalisations, 21
Global Mammal Parasite Database,
    144–5
gorilla
  crop-raiding by, 61, 69, 205
  diet of, 203
  distribution, 69
  exposure to hunting, 66
  feelings towards by locals, 69
  as a flagship species, 70
  fragmentation and genetic
    diversity, 69
  hunting of, 62, 66
  interactions with humans, 64
  life-history of, 35
  nesting, 60–1, 64, 68
  pesticide exposure, 206
  population growth, 35
  population size, 52, 55
  ranging, 68, 204
  reproduction, 35
  response to habitat disturbance,
    70
  threat status and population size,
    54
Gorilla. See gorilla
Gorilla Guardian programme, 55,
    64, 66
group density calculation, 128
group size and composition
  colobus, 131

gibbons, 23
lemur, 219
mangabey, 38
group size, structure, flexibility. See
    social grouping
Guaja hunting, 78
guenon
  crop-raiding by, 205
  diet of, 202, 260
  distribution, 261
  gut physiology, 260
  habitat suitability and shifting,
    267–71, 274
  population decline, 44
  social groups and dispersal, 260

habitat disturbance. See also
    agriculture, deforestation,
    habitat suitability and shifting,
    hunting, logging, natural
    forests and behaviour
  behavioural response to, 131,
    201, 259
  biodiversity and, 69
  body size and resiliency to, 123
  Cagar Alam Leuweung Sancang,
    25
  chimpanzee, xiv
  coping strategies, 233, 239
  dietary flexibility and species
    viability, 103, 123, 135, 239,
    250
  dietary response to, 132, 200,
    202
  dispersal and, 36, 44
  folivory and, 123
  food availability and, 200
  frugivory and, 123, 230
  genetic diversity and, 44, 69
  immune response and, 201
  infant recruitment and, 134, 231
  nesting response to, 70
  non-timber forest product
    collection, 25
  pesticides and toxins, 206
  phenotypic plasticity and, 18
  population decline in mangabey,
    44
  proboscis monkey, 184, 192
  ranging response to, 24, 68–9,
    107, 201

response by chimpanzee, 70
response by colobine, 111, 123,
    186, 188, 190, 201
response by gorilla, 70
response by sifaka, 202, 231
sacred sites, 25
social flexibility and, 239
social grouping response, 18
species viability and, 250, 258
habitat loss. See deforestation
habitat quality and population
    viability, 44
habitat suitability and shifting
  Africa, 268–71
  climate change, 209, 262, 273
  colobus, 268–71, 274
  dispersal limitations and, 273
  gelada, 209
  guenon, 267–71, 274
  modelling of, 266, 275
Hapalemur. See lemur
health consequences of
    provisioning, 208
helminths. See parasite
hierarchy effects on dispersal and
    reproduction in mangabey, 45
home range. See ranging
Honorary Wildlife Wardens, 189
Hoolock. See gibbon
howler monkey
  activity budget, 245
  diet of, 202, 240, 246, 248, 252
  group structure, 250, 252
  hunting of, 78, 88
  Hurricane Iris in Belize, 240
  infant survival and natural
    disaster, 251
  natural disasters and evolution,
    238
  parasites and mortality, 158
  response to natural disaster, 245,
    250–1
  social grouping, 239–40
  toxin exposure, 206
human and non-human primate
    interactions
  conflict, 187
  niche construction, 18, 27
human population and hunting
    sustainability, 79–80, 82,
    91, 93

hunting. *See* also hunting, primate
  Amazonia, 78
  by indigenous groups, 83, 88
  by non-indigenous groups, 77
  cultural beliefs and, 66, 90, 92
  ecologically noble savage, 79
  effect on chimpanzee and gorilla
    nesting, 68
  enforcement of rules, 66
  extinction risk and, 122
  Ghana, 120
  logging and, 123, 136
  nearby chimpanzee and gorilla,
    66–7
  pet trade, 7, 78
  self-monitoring programme, 84,
    91
  social group response to, 18
  species viability and, 19
  sustainability, 78–80, 92
  weapon technology and, 79–80,
    82, 86, 88
hunting, primate. *See* also hunting
  Atelines, 77
  biomass, 86
  by indigenous groups, 76–80, 88,
    91–2, *See* also Ka'apor,
    Kayapo, Matis, Matsigenka,
    Shuar, Waimiri-Atorai,
    Waiwai, Waorani
  by Waiwai, 86, 89
  capuchin, 77, 87
  chimpanzee, 60, 68
  colobus, 123
  cultural beliefs and, 78, 89, 92,
    121, 189
  gibbon, 23, 28
  gorilla, 62
  howler monkey, 78, 88
  population decline and
    extinction, 78
  prehistoric, 76
  proboscis monkey, 189
  saki, 77, 86, *87*
  seasonality, 88, 92
  South America, 76–9
  spider monkey, 77, 86, 90
  squirrel monkey, 88
  sustainability, 7, 76, 78–80,
    91–2
  tamarin, 78, *87*

  titi monkey, 78
  woolly monkey, 77
  weapon technology and, 88, 91
hurricane. *See* natural disasters
Hylobates. See gibbon

illegal trade of gibbon, 27
immune response interactions
    with food availability,
    fragmentation and
    parasites, 201
inactivity. *See* activity budget
inbreeding. *See* genetic diversity
indigenous reserves
  biodiversity and, 82
  conservation and, 93
  deforestation in, 82
  Konashen Community Owned
    Conservation Area, 82
  population density in, 82
  South America, 76, 80, 82
Indonesia, conservation in, 19, 187,
    190, 192–3
Indri. See lemur
infant survival, recruitment and
    mortality
  food availability and, 231
  in langur, 112
  in lemur, 230
  in mangabey, 40
  phenology and, 226–31
  rainfall and, 209
  response to logging, 103, 134
  response to natural disaster,
    225–8, 232, 251
infanticide, minimising the risk of
  deceptive sexual swellings, 43
  dispersal, 45
interactions between human and
    non-human primates. *See* also
    feelings towards primates by
    locals, crop-raiding, disease,
    parasites
  Amazonia, 76
  chimpanzee, 66
  conflict, 34, 70, 121
  disease transmission, 143
  gorilla, 64
  niche construction, 53
  parasite transmission, 143
  vervet monkey, 121

inter-birth interval. *See*
    reproduction, life-history

Java, 19
  deforestation in, 19
  primates of, 19
Javan Primates Rehabilitation
    Centre, 28

Ka'apor primate hunting, 77
Kayapó primate hunting, 77
Kianjavato Ahmanson Field Station,
    168
Kianjavato Commune, 168, 173
Kibale National Park
  eucalyptus, 203
  logging in, 136
  protein-to-fibre ratio, 201
Kirindy Mitea National Park, 219
  deforestation, 219
  fires, 233
  rainfall, 221
Konashen Community Owned
    Conservation Area, 82–3
Konashen Ecosystem Health Project,
    93

Lagothrix. See woolly monkey
Lake Nabugabo, 124
langur
  diet of, 35
  dispersal, 36
  infant recruitment and mortality,
    112
  life-history, 35
  reproduction, 35–6
  response to logging, 103,
    111–12, 135
  social group, 104
lemur, 219
  conservation efforts, 174
  Cyclone Fanele, 218
  diet of, 201, 230
  dispersal, 219
  distribution, 170, 219
  genetic diversity in, 170
  group size and
    composition, 219
  infant survival, 231
  nutrient balancing, 201
  pesticide exposure, 206

lemur (cont.)
  reproduction, 220, 223–7,
    230–1
  resiliency to natural disaster, 230
  response to natural disaster, 218,
    232
  Sifaka Research Project, 220
  threat status, 1, 168
Lemur. See lemur
life-history, 35
  bet hedging, 231
  chimpanzee, 36
  collection of data, 36
  effect of natural disasters, 218
  effect of nutrition, 35
  effect of phenology, 209, 226
  effect of provisioning, 35
  gorilla, 35
  langur, 36
  lemur, 220
  spider monkey, 35
local community. *See* education
    programmes, stakeholder
    collaboration
  employment of, 34, 172
  involvement in conservation,
    167–8, 171–3, 189
logging. *See also* habitat
    disturbance
  behavioural response to, 9, 103,
    107, 111, 113, 123, 130–3, 135
  Cambodia, 101–2, 110–12
  canopy use and, 107, 112, 135
  consequences to forest, 110,
    112–13, 122, 129–30, 133–6
  conservation compatibility, 113
  deforestation due to, 8, 122
  dietary flexibility and viability,
    123
  dietary response to, 132–4
  enforcement of laws, 104–6, 110
  folivory and, 123
  hunting and, 123, 136
  infant mortality and, 103
  Madagascar, 168
  Malaysia, 113
  Manwa Forest Reserve, 125
  Nabugabo, 133
  population response to, 112, 123,
    130, 134
  population viability and, 113

ranging response to, 103, 107,
    135
  response by colobine, 103, 123,
    133, 135
  response by gibbon, 135
  selective, 122
  species selected for, 107, 110–12,
    130
  the tropics, 122
  Uganda, 122
  Veun Sai-Siem Pang National
    Park, 106

Macaca. See macaque
macaque
  crop-raiding by, 205
  diet of, 208
  nutrition and provisioning,
    208
  provisioning of, 207–8
  response to logging, 103
  toxin exposure, 206
Madagascar
  climate change modelling, 230
  conservation in, 168, 178
  Cyclone Fanele, 218
  folivory and natural disasters,
    231
  habitat disturbance in, 168,
    219
  primate population decline, 1
Madagascar Biodiversity
    Partnership, 168, 170, 172–3
  reforestation, 174
  sustainability, 178
Malaysia, conservation and
    reforestation in, 187, 190
mangabey
  discovery of new, 37
  dispersal, 41–6
  distribution, 37
  genetic diversity in, 45
  group size and composition,
    38
  hierarchy, 45
  life-history, 36
  population changes, 44
  population survey, 37
  reproduction, 38, 40–5
  threat status, 37
Manwa Forest Reserve, 124

Matis hunting, 78
Matsigenka hunting, 77, 80
Microcebus. See lemur
modelling
  biodemographic, 85
  climate change, habitat suitability
    and species distributions,
    259–60, 266, 275
  conservation, 35
  gelada, 259
  habitat suitability and shifting,
    266, 268–71
  hunting sustainability, 79–80,
    90–2
  settlement spread, 91
  socioecological, 26
  spider monkey local extinction
    risk, 91
  weapon technology, 91
Mone-Oku Forest complex, 54, 67
  human population in, 55
Monkey River, 252, 254
mortality. *See* infant survival,
    recruitment and mortality
mortality from natural disasters,
    217
muriqui. *See* spider monkey

Nabugabo
  forest structure, 129
  logging in, 133
Nasalis. See proboscis monkey
natural disaster
  behavioural response to, 238,
    245–9, 251
  Belize, 240
  climate change and, 238
  conservation and, 233
  Cyclone Fanele, 218
  dietary response to, 246–9, 251,
    253
  dietary specialisation and
    viability following, 231, 239
  effect on forest and phenology,
    217–18, 223, 230, 232,
    239–42
  effect on life-history, 218
  energy conservation and, 251
  grouping response to, 252
  Hurricane Iris, 240
  Hurricane Richard, 240–1

infant survival, recruitment and
    mortality, 225, 230, 232, 251
Madagascar, 230
mortality from, 217
Neotropics, 238
population response to, 245,
    250–1
population viability, 218
reproduction and, 232
response by howler monkey, 238,
    245–6, 250–1
response by lemur, 218, 232
response by spider monkey,
    245–51
social structure and resiliency to,
    252–3
species evolution and, 238
natural forests and behaviour, 3, 19,
    53, 75, 93, 284
Neotropics. *See* South America
nesting
    chimpanzee, 60–1, 68
    gorilla, 60–4, 68
    great apes, 56
    response to hunting, 68
    sites, 56
niche
    construction between human and
        non-human primates, 27
    realised versus fundamental, 260
non-governmental organisations.
        See conservation, stakeholder
        collaboration
North Atlantic Hurricane Basin,
    240
nutrition. *See also* diets
    agriculture and, 205
    climate change and, 208–9, 261
    colobus, 209
    exotic plants and, 202
    food availability and, 201
    habitat disturbance and, 202
    lemur, 201
    life-history and, 35
    pesticides and toxins and, 206
    provisioning and, 35, 208
    quality and balance, 201, 209
    sodium, 204

orangutan
    discovery of new, xiv

threat status, 1
vulnerability to habitat
    disturbance, 123

Pan. See chimpanzee
PanTHERIA database, 146
parasite
    co-infection, 156
    colobus, 201
    distribution, 146
    diversity in, 144, 157–8
    effect on primates, 144, 158
    generalist. *See* primate host range
        and
    Global Mammal Parasite
        Database, 144
    human–non-human primate
        interactions, 143
    interactions with food availability
        and immunity, 201
    primate body mass and, 154
    primate group structure and,
        158
    primate host range and, 144–5,
        149–57
    primate population viability and,
        156
    primate threat status and, 144–5,
        149–56
    specialist. *See* primate host range
        and
pesticides
    effect on primates, 205
    exposure and presence in primate
        foods, 206
    nutritional consequences, 206
    Uganda, 206
phenology
    climate change and, 209
    effect on lemur, 209, 226
    infant survival, recruitment and
        mortality and, 227–30
    life-history and, 209
    natural disaster effect on, 230–1,
        241
    primate reproduction and, 226,
        230–1
philopatry. *See* dispersal
Piliocolobus. See colobus
Pithecia. See saki
Pongo. See orangutan

population change
    Amazonia, 76
    chimpanzee, xiv
    colobine, 10, 44, 134, 186, 188, 210
    dispersal and, 36
    due to disease, 142–3, 156
    due to habitat disturbance, 44,
        102, 112, 122–3, 131, 134, 143
    due to hunting, 78
    due to natural disaster, 245
    due to provisioning, 207
    extinction debt and, 122
    genetic diversity effect on, 36
    gorilla, 35
    guenon, 44
    howler monkey, 245
    interaction of food availability,
        immunity, parasites, 201
    mangabey, 44
    Madagascar, 1
    Neotropics, 1
    parasites, 156
    primates, 1
    Southeast Asia, 102
    spider monkey, 35
    parasites and, 144, 157
population size and survey
    chimpanzee, 55
    gibbon, 22
    gorilla, 55
    importance of, 20
    lemur, 174
    mangabey, 37
    vocalisation methods, 21
postpartum amenorrhoea. *See*
        reproduction
Presbytis. See langur
primatologists' role and shifting
        priorities, 1–2, 4, 47, 166, 183,
        283
proboscis monkey, 183
    conservation, 187–8, 190–2
    diet of, 185
    distribution, 184, 186–7
    early research of, 184–6
    ecotourism and, 185, 190, 192
    ex-situ conservation, 191
    flagship species, 184
    food availability for, 188
    habitat disturbance to, 192
    habitat preference, 183, 187–8

proboscis monkey (cont.)
  hunting of, 189
  media attention, 185
  population and species viability
    of, 184, 186
  population decline, 188
  population density, 188
  protected areas of, 187
  response to habitat disturbance,
    190
  social groups, 186
  threat status, 183
Procolobus. See colobus
Prolemur. See lemur
Propithecus. See lemur
protein-to-fibre ratio
  effect on colobus, 201, 210
  Kibale National Park, 201, 209
  regenerating forests, 201
protists. *See* parasite
provisioning
  behavioural response to, 207–8
  direct and indirect, 206
  health consequences of, 208
  in Asia, 207
  life-history effects, 35
  nutrition and, 35, 208
  of baboon, 208
  of macaque, 207–8

ranging
  colobus, 204
  effect of habitat disturbance, 24
  gibbon, *22*, 24
  gorilla, 68–9, 204
  parasites and, 157
  response to habitat
    disturbance, 68–9, 103,
    130, 201
rank. *See* hierarchy
reforestation and rehabilitated
    habitat
  green-washing, 190
  Indonesia and Malaysia, 190
  proboscis monkey, 189
reproduction. *See also* life-history
  bet-hedging life-history, 231
  chimpanzee, 36
  dispersal and, 45
  effect of natural disaster, 226,
    230, 232

effect of phenology, 209, 226,
    230–1
  effect of provisioning, 207–8
  gorilla, 35
  hierarchy and, 45
  langur, 35–6
  lemur, 220, 223–7, 230–1
  mangabey, 40–3, 45
resilience framework, 28
Rhinopithecus. See snub-nosed
    monkey
Runaway Creek Nature Reserve,
    241, 252
Rungwecebus. See mangabey

Sabah, conservation in, 192
sacred sites, 24, 28
  Sancang forest, 24
Saguinus. See tamarin
Saimiri. See squirrel monkey
saki, hunting of, 77, 86, *87*
Sancang forest, 24
Sapajus. See capuchin
Semnopithecus. See langur
sexual maturity. *See* life-history,
    reproduction
sexual swelling. *See* reproduction
Shuar hunting, 77
sifaka. *See* lemur
Sifaka Research Project, 220
snub-nosed monkey response to
    logging, 103
social grouping
  colobus, 133, 260
  folivorous species, 239
  guenon, 260
  howler monkey, 250
  langur, 104
  spider monkey, 250
  parasite exposure and, 158
  population viability and, 239
  response to habitat
    disturbance, 18
  social flexibility, population
    viability and habitat
    disturbance, 239
sociobiology and socioecology, 2,
    18
sodium in primate diets, 204
South America. *See also* Amazonia
  indigenous reserves in, 76, 80, 82

natural disasters in, 238
  primate population decline, 1
Southeast Asia
  biodiversity in, 102
  primate provisioning in, 207
spider monkey
  activity budget, 245–9
  demography, 35
  diet of, 240, 247, 252
  genetic diversity of, 36
  hunting of, 77, 86,
    88, 90–1
  Hurricane Richard and, 240
  infant survival and natural
    disaster, 251
  ranging, 242
  response to natural
    disaster, 245–51
  social grouping, 240, 242, 250
  social structure and natural
    disaster, 252
  vulnerability to habitat
    disturbance, 123
squirrel monkey, hunting of, 88
stakeholder
  collaboration, 4, 9, 22,
    54, 75–6, 82–3, 91–3,
    166–8, 170–5, 189, 191,
    193, 210
  compromise, 173
  conflict, 34, 66, 93, 167
storms. *See* natural disasters

tamarin, hunting of, 78, *87*
temperature changes
  climate change and, xv
  effect on primate behaviour and
    diet, 272
tenure. *See* dispersal
terrestrialism and species
    viability, 258
Theropithecus. See gelada
threat status
  lemur, 168
  parasites and primate, 144–5,
    149–56
  primates, 1
  proboscis monkey, 183
titi monkey
  hunting of, 78
  response to logging, 103

toxins, exposure and presence
    in primate foods and
    nutritional consequences, 206
Trachypithecus. See langur
traditional medicine, 7
training of locals, 127, 167, 172, 174
transfer. *See* dispersal

Udzungwa Mountains National
    Park, 33, 38
Udzungwa Scarp Forest/Nature
    Reserve, 37, 44
Uganda
  logging in, 122
  pesticides, 206

Varecia. See lemur
vervet monkey
  crop-raiding by, 121, 205

interactions with humans,
    121
Veun Sai-Siem Pang National Park,
    104
  logging in, 106
viability, population and species
    arboreality versus terrestriallism,
      258
    climate change and habitat
      disturbance, 258
    dispersal and, 36
    effect of body size, 239
    effect of diet, 239, 258
    effect of habitat features, 44, 123
    logging and, 113
    gibbon, 26
    natural disaster and, 218, 238,
      253
    parasites and, 156

proboscis monkey, 186, 188
    social structure and, 239, 252

Waimiri-Atorai primate hunting,
    77
Waiwai, 83
  human population, 83
  hunting, 90
  land rights, 75, 82
  primate hunting by, 86, 88–9,
    91–2
  weapons used in hunting, 88
Waorani primate hunting, 77
weapon technology and hunting
    sustainability, 93
Wildlife Conservation Society
    and Mone-Oku Forest
    complex, 55
woolly monkey, hunting of, 77